Secularization and Cultural Criticism

RELIGION AND POSTMODERNISM
A series edited by Mark C. Taylor and Thomas A. Carlson

Recent books in the series:
Slavoj Žižek, Eric L. Santner, and Kenneth Reinhard, *The Neighbor: Three Inquiries in Political Theology* (2005)

Paolo Apolito, *The Internet and the Madonna: Religious Visionary Experience on the Web* (2004)

Kevin Hart, *The Dark Gaze: Maurice Blanchot and the Sacred* (2004)

Mark C. Taylor, *Confidence Games: Money and Markets in a World without Redemption* (2004)

Michael Kessler and Christian Sheppard, editors, *Mystics: Presence and Aporia* (2003)

Secularization and Cultural Criticism

RELIGION, NATION, & MODERNITY

Vincent P. Pecora

The University of Chicago Press   Chicago and London

VINCENT P. PECORA is the Gordon B. Hinckley Professor of British Literature and Culture at the University of Utah. He is the author of two previous books, most recently *Households of the Soul*, and the editor of *Nations and Identities: Classic Readings*.

The University of Chicago Press, Chicago 60637
The University of Chicago Press, Ltd., London
© 2006 by The University of Chicago
All rights reserved. Published 2006
Printed in the United States of America

15 14 13 12 11 10 09 08 07 06   5 4 3 2 1

ISBN-13 (cloth): 978-0-226-65311-2
ISBN-13 (paper): 978-0-226-65312-9
ISBN-10 (cloth): 0-226-65311-0
ISBN-10 (paper): 0-226-65312-9

Library of Congress Cataloging-in-Publication Data

Pecora, Vincent P., 1953–
    Secularization and cultural criticism : religion, nation, and modernity / Vincent P. Pecora.
        p.   cm.
    Includes bibliographical references and index.
    ISBN 0-226-65311-0 (cloth : alk. paper)—ISBN 0-226-65312-9 (pbk : alk. paper)
    1. Secularism.   2. Religion and culture.   I. Title.
    BL2747.8.P43   2006
    200.9'04—dc22
                                        2005035603

♾ The paper used in this publication meets the minimum requirements of the American National Standard for Information Sciences—Permanence of Paper for Printed Library Materials, ANSI Z39.48–1992.

FOR KAREN

Contents

Acknowledgments ix

Introduction 1

1 Secular Criticism and Secularization 25

2 Benjamin, Kracauer, and Redemptive History 67

3 Durkheim's Modernity
 From Theory of Religion to Political Theology 101

4 Arnoldian Ethnology
 Nation Between Religion and Race 131

5 The Modernist Moment
 Virginia Woolf Voyages Out 157

Conclusion
 Humanism and Globalization 195

Bibliography 209

Index 225

Acknowledgments

I have collected a large number of intellectual debts while working on this project. I am especially grateful to Dominick LaCapra and Tom Carlson for their very helpful reading of the manuscript. Many others offered valuable advice on different parts of the book: Susan Buck-Morss, Jim Buzard, Joe Childers, Stuart Culver, Manthia Diawara, Prasenjit Duara, Simon During, Sander Gilman, Eleanor Kaufmann, Uchang Kim, Richard Kroll, Steven Mailloux, Tim Murphy, Nicoletta Pireddu, Dominic Michael Rainsford, Ken Reinhard, Haun Saussy, Doris Sommer, Scott Sprenger, and Ann Van Sant. I must also thank the participants in the seminar I led at the School of Criticism and Theory in 2002. Sharon Cameron provided some much-needed assistance at the very beginning of this project. Alan Thomas has been as sharp an editor as one could ask for. I appreciate the able assistance of Emily Daniell Magruder, Mary Holland, and Allison Adler Kroll with the research, and of Barbara Norton for her expert editorial help. The book has also benefited in numerous ways from my discussions with Jeffrey Alexander, Rogers Brubaker, Patrick Geary, Jim Gelvin, Giles Gunn, Andrew Hewitt, Seth Jameson, Nikki Keddie, Efrain Kristal, Vinay Lal, Hartmut Lehmann, Saree Makdisi, Mark Seltzer, Brian Silverstein, and Eric Sundquist. I am deeply indebted to the wise counsel of Joe Natterson. But my deepest gratitude goes to my wife, Karen McCauley, and my daughters, Olivia and Ava, who patiently endured so much while this book was being written.

The National Endowment for the Humanities generously provided a fellowship to work on this project in 2001–2. UCLA supplied several Faculty

Senate Research Grants. Earlier versions of chapters 2, 3, and 4 were published respectively in *Genre* 35, no. 1 (2002): 55–83; *Studies in the Humanities* 29, no. 1 (2002): 52–69; and *Victorian Studies* 41, no. 3 (1998): 355–79, used by permission of the publisher, Indiana University Press. All appear here in revised and enlarged forms.

Introduction

On n'a jamais fini de se débattre contre Dieu. PROUDHON

Today, in a global environment increasingly unified economically yet fractured by religious contestation, it is not uncommon for those who engage in the study of society and culture to assume two somewhat contradictory things more or less simultaneously: that all religious traditions are inextricably caught up in, even defined by, questions of material and political power; and that religion, whatever a largely secular elite may think, matters a great deal. On the one hand, we feel that the real basis of collective life, both as matter and as representation, lies elsewhere than in religious belief, and it does so more or less universally. On the other hand, we find ourselves routinely invoking deep-seated differences of civilization between, say, Christianity and Islam (including, for historians such as Michel Foucault and anthropologists such as Talal Asad, the somatic perception of pleasure and pain!), differences that at times allow very little room for what John Rawls has called "overlapping" moral consensus. We want to criticize the imperial hubris of the Western, Judeo-Christian tradition, even as we worry about ignoring that tradition's role as a (perhaps *the*) foundation of the secular Enlightenment, that is, the moral-political outlook of a modernity that we would be loath to abandon.

The central argument of this book is that, without some careful consideration of the relationship of cultural criticism to secularization, which is to say, of what might alternately be described as the translation, transformation, "worlding," or simple negation of religious categories and relations, the humanistic scholarly recourse to the putatively neutral language of secular thought in a global age implicates us in an intellectual history that we at other times would like to disavow. This history includes the term "secular" itself. As John Milbank reminds us, "The s*aeculum,* in the medieval era, was not a space, a domain, but a time—the interval between fall and *eschaton* where coercive justice, private property, and impaired natural reason must make shift to cope with the unredeemed effects of sinful humanity" (Milbank, *Theology* 9).

In its more practical sense, "secular" originally defined those members of the clergy who lived "in the world" rather than in monastic seclusion—for example, the secular abbot or canon—and it is this sense of worldliness, produced from within religious tradition, that I believe has been a core if often disavowed component of extrareligious and anticlerical humanist sensibilities in cultural criticism up to the present day. (The idea that the humanist intellectuals of the academies represent a sort of secular clerisy is very old, and long possessed a sort of literal truth in places such as England, where religious orders were required of academics well into the nineteenth century.) What Edward Said has called "secular criticism" may be an important component of any perspective that hopes to overcome the debilitating sectarian strife that is now all too routinely understood as a "clash of civilizations." But in what follows I want to make clear that what we may complacently understand as "secular" about such criticism comes with certain historical and religious strings attached, that these are awfully hard to get rid of, as the example of Jürgen Habermas in my first chapter will show, and that those of us of a liberal-universalist persuasion have difficult problems to address on this score, something Max Weber well understood at the beginning of the twentieth century.

Secular Criticism and Its Others

One problem is that what people mean by "the secular" tends to define itself, in a variety of ways, by reference to a religious worldview from the start, so that the juxtaposition of the two perspectives entails a more complicated and often richer history—even in the contemporary period—than is generally acknowledged by the emphasis on secular*ism*. On some deeper level, for example, Said's notion of secular criticism begins with the distinction made by Giambattista Vico between "gentile" and "Jewish" history.

Both the savage and the philosopher are alien to God's temporal order, to sacred history; for according to Vico, most history is a human and *gentile* affliction, whereas for the Jews there is a life "founded by the true God." Here Vico is at his most profoundly suggestive, and he uses etymological puns to make his point beautifully.... The crucial distinction is between the gentiles who divine or imagine divinity, on the one hand, and the Hebrews whose true God prohibits divination, on the other. To be a gentile is to be denied access to the true God, to have recourse for thought to divination, to live permanently in history, in an order other than God's, to be able genetically to produce that order of history. Vico's concerns are everywhere with this order, the word of history made by men. (Said, *Beginnings* 349–50)

Vico's opposition of sacred (Hebraic) to worldly (gentile) history is, I think, a foundational one for Said, though one should also note that such distinctions, akin to that drawn by early comparative philology between Indo-Germanic and Semitic languages, or between what Matthew Arnold called Hellenism and Hebraism, have had a decidedly troubling role in modern Western culture. Indeed, Said himself would later adopt a far more critical attitude to Renan, whose sense of the inferiority of Semitic to Indo-European language families, directly parallel to Vico's binary sense of history, becomes a primary example of the Orientalist's classificatory will to power (Said, *Orientalism* 140–42). In Said's account of Vico, by contrast, what is "profoundly suggestive" is Vico's idea of a "gentile" relationship to the world, in which any access to God has been permanently foreclosed, thus forcing the gentile nations to turn their attention to *human* history, history they can understand "genetically" precisely because, unlike divine history, it is something they have made from the beginning. What one does with a putatively God-made nature—and hence with natural science—in Vico's scheme is somewhat unclear. It is the problem Spinoza had solved for the Enlightenment in his own way almost a century before Vico by conflating the natural and divine realms, and it is in part Vico's mythic attitude toward the natural world that caused Isaiah Berlin to classify him as part of the counter-Enlightenment. In this sense, for Said's notions of secular criticism, Vico is a herald not of science, but of sociality, not of knowledge of either God *or* nature, but of peoples and the nations they make.

In Said's subsequent work, it is this Viconian idea of gentile history that is more fully elaborated as the basis of "secular criticism," with various borrowings from Enlightenment materialism, Marxian historicism, and most of all a romantic and at times admittedly conservative emphasis on the power of the individual's heroic, creative will. And in this broader configuration, secular criticism becomes "oppositional" not only with regard to the sacred history preserved by scripture, but to all forms of what Marx called "ruling ideas," class related or not, such as Western knowledge of the Orient. Indeed, Said would appear to be closest at points to the libertarian perspective of Marx's left-Hegelian rival Max Stirner, who eventually came (at the cost of Marx's ridicule) to see nearly every human belief, abstraction, ideal, generalization, or system as a form of "sacred" thought that the truly free and unfettered mind must reject. For Said, secular criticism is

> reducible neither to a doctrine nor to a political position on a particular question.... In its suspicion of totalizing concepts, in its discontent with reified objects, in its impatience with guilds, special interests, imperialized fiefdoms, and orthodox habits of mind, criticism is most itself and, if the paradox can be tolerated, most unlike itself at the moment it starts turning into organized dogma. "Ironic" is not a bad word to use along with "oppositional."... Its social goals are noncoercive knowledge produced in the interests of human freedom. (Said, *World* 29)

Secular criticism, one might finally say, is thus a humanism—it aims to promote human freedom through the production of humanly attained knowledge—but one that fulfills itself primarily by constant vigilance not only against received accounts of the sacred, but against all ideas or ideals that might share some of the characteristics of unquestioned sacred truth.

My point in all this is twofold. First, there is something missing when cultural critics today routinely conceive "secular criticism" only in its most superficial and doctrinaire senses as something that defines a "worldly" or "cosmopolitan" approach, one that perhaps too easily imagines itself as concerned purely with the "real" history that human beings have made. There is something missing because embedded in most notions of the secular—including Said's—are quite particular and often significant assumptions about how secularization has occurred. As Said develops the idea of secular criticism, for example, he draws upon a specific version of the religious history of the West, in which we find, among other things, Vico's idea that gentiles and Jews are to be understood more or less as different species ("human" is synonymous with "gentile" in Vico's prose, not with Hebrews); in which the gentile nations and the modern nation-states that are built upon them are thought to come into existence only with the foreclosure of the sacred; and in which the individuated human will, presumably unfettered by allegiance to any collectively maintained or even pseudo-sacred beliefs, becomes the only measure of authentic human existence. In short, what is missing in the formulaic conception—one might even say, with Said, in the "reified object"—that occupies the position of "the secular" in "secular criticism" is the larger, complicated, and often quite contradictory process of secularization. This larger process not only serves to define Western history for the Western intellectual (even for Said, who depends on a rather broader idea of secularization as a form of historical explanation in *Orientalism;* Renan supposedly turns to the intense study of Semitic languages as a replacement for his lost Christian faith), but that itself can be comprehended by very different forms of historical explanation. My second point is that, despite all the libertarian critical energy that seems to permeate Said's idea of secular criticism, when one looks at the larger body of his work it is not difficult to see that a number of master ideas—the sanctity of the heroic individual, the near-sacred pursuit of freedom, the ideal of ironic self-awareness, the collective right of every "people" to self-determination, and so forth—retain their doctrinal, pseudo-sacred character in this thinking, perhaps inevitably. That is, it would be impossible, even with the help of Stirner's egoism, Adorno's negative dialectics, and Derrida's deconstruction, to imagine a mental world *entirely* liberated from dominant conceptions, and many of these conceptions—or so I will argue—cannot be divorced from the complicated exchange, translation, and contest of ideas that have occurred under the name of secularization in the West.

From Weber and Durkheim, to Talcott Parsons, to Peter Berger, to Talal Asad, "secularization" has been defined in a number of ways. For the purposes of this volume, a particular and, I think, usefully reductive opposition of meanings will be my focus. In a recent account of the debate over secularization from Hegel to Hans Blumenberg, the contemporary French philosopher Jean-Claude Monod outlines two dominant ways of characterizing what secularization has come to mean. "In effect, ... if secularization signifies the *retreat of religion* as a dominant sphere and the reconstruction of institutions on a rational basis, it accords well" with two fundamental assumptions about modernity, which Monod adapts from Reinhart Koselleck:

> the belief that the present epoch opens a new perspective without precedent, and the belief according to which men are capable, and more and more capable, of "making" history.

In this sense, secularization becomes one of the "guiding-concepts" of modern times. On the other hand,

> if secularization designates essentially a transfer having consisted of schemes and models elaborated in the field of religion; if religion thus continues to nourish modernity without its knowledge, the theory of secularization constitutes a putting into question of the two fundamental modern beliefs. Modernity would live only as something consisting of a bequest and inheritance, despite the negations and illusions of auto-foundation. Modernity would then not be a new time, founded and conscious of its foundations, but would be only the moment where there is effected a change of plan, a *"worlding" of Christianity*. (Monod 23)

Monod's dualism runs throughout the argument of this book. My goal is less a dissolution of the dualism than a working through of the dilemma we confront in it, a dilemma that is simultaneously conceptual and political, abstractly philosophical and terribly worldly. (Said's two versions of the secular, for example, correspond closely to Monod's dichotomy: Vico's idea of *genetically* "gentile" or "human" history corresponds to Monod's first account, while Renan's substitution of Semitic linguistics for his lost faith corresponds to Monod's second account.) Such a working through begins with the acknowledgement that although the second of Monod's alternatives—secularization as transference, if I may put it that way—makes at times irresistible claims on our *ethical* understanding of cultural history, the first alternative, in which secularization provides a new and viable understanding of human progress, makes an equally powerful claim on our *epistemological* sensibilities. But first, it may be useful to see why the problem of secularization as modernization is worth addressing once again, and why the problem should matter to cultural criticism.

Revising the Secularization Thesis

In general, whenever we yoke the words "religion" and "modernity" together, the term "secularization" tends to appear along with them. The last is an idea that gained a certain sociological centrality in the middle of the twentieth century, in part as an element of liberalizing political trends in Europe and America, but it has more recently entered into new sorts of discussion. Not surprisingly, religion and secularization have once again become objects of intense public debate and analysis with the end of the cold war and the current round of globalization. This debate must in turn be related to prior decades of fundamentalist revival in many parts of the world, often in response to Western power but also within the West itself, and subsequently to a rash of conflicts that would at least appear to have a strong basis in religious sensibilities, from the Balkans to the destruction of the World Trade Center towers in New York on September 11, 2001. By the same token, secularization has come under renewed, often revisionist scrutiny in a wide array of disciplines (see, for example, Asad; Barker, Beckford, and Dobbelaere; Bruce; Chadwick; Crusius; Davie; Ferry; Lehmann; McLeod; Milbank; Monod; Porter and Schama; Prüfer; Stark; van der Veer and Lehmann; Waché; and the essays collected in Berger, *Desecularization*). As Graham Ward has recently observed in his own critique of liberal assumptions about ongoing secularization: "Religion is, once more, haunting the imagination of the West" (Ward, *True* vi). Nevertheless, in the common idiom (whether scholarly or popular), modernization is still generally believed to entail secularization to a very large extent, though this belief is often colored by quite different moral or political valuations depending on one's cultural location in an increasingly unified world economy. Whether one is a scholar or populist, in the academies of old imperial metropolises or on newer postcolonial peripheries, the developmental perspective that has shaped much of the political and philosophical discourse of the West since the Enlightenment has assumed the inexorability of the process by which religious beliefs are subordinated to nominally secular ones, such as a desire for individual self-determination, affiliation with one's occupational identity, and political allegiance to the nation-state. (For the two texts that have had perhaps the greatest impact on current sociological reexaminations of the secularization thesis, see Dobbelaere, and D. Martin; prior to these, for the broadest general history of the concept, see Lübbe. Davie provides a good current bibliography.)

In turn, "modernization" has tended to imply three historical developments: (1) social differentiation, that is, the increasing division of labor, fragmentation of life-worlds, and separation of economic, legal, political, cultural, and religious spheres of action; (2) societalization, that is, the increasing dependence on large-scale administrative institutions, such as the nation-state bureaucracy, capitalist corporations, and mass culture, rather than the local community and the local community's church and customs; and (3) rationalization of religious beliefs, in which the increased distance of a monotheistic god allows for the decreasing use of magic, the increasing invocation of ethics based on utility, the dominance of purposive or instrumental rationality, and hence the more efficient pursuit of worldly aims in science, economics, and politics (see Wallis and Bruce). For the revisionists, however, "an alternative suggestion is increasingly gaining ground: the possibility that secularization is not a universal process, but belongs instead to a relatively short and particular period of European history which still assumed (amongst other things) that whatever characterized Europe's religious life today would characterize everyone else's tomorrow" (Davie 1). It is thus the necessity and universality of the link between secularization and modernization that is at the heart of much recent discussion. In this way, we are once again reminded of how two superficially different scholarly debates necessarily encounter one another, and have done so at least since Max Weber, often with bewildering results: on the one hand, the debate over the meaning of the term "secularization" itself, as captured by Monod's dichotomy, within a largely European history; and, on the other, the debate over the possible global universality of the secularizing process that has occurred—however we end up representing it—in the West, and that has been thought to have enabled something we call economic, social, and political modernity.

It may come as no surprise that the empirical study of religion and secularization in the West is itself a mass of contradictions and opposed perspectives.

These perspectives range from Peter Laslett's dictum that "all our ancestors were literal Christian believers, all of the time" to Callum Brown's view that "there is no 'ideal state' in which religion grasped the total world-view of the people, and which has been dissipating for the history of mankind" (Brown 39; Laslett 74). Though many would still maintain that secularization in the West has been inevitable, however uneven, recent revisionists suggest that the story is far more complicated. For example, Brown points out that the increasing urban concentration of the population, which is normally accompanied by economic differentiation and hence secularization in the standard model, on the contrary correlates quite closely in both Scotland (between 1849 and 1920) and the United States (between 1890 and 1980) with increasing church adherence, perhaps because of the increased availability of places of worship in the cities.

On the whole, however, the subordination of religious to secular values has been described both where there has been a measurable decline in overt church affiliation over the last hundred years, as in Western Europe, and where church attendance in a climate of religious pluralism has been more sustained, as in the United States (see D. Martin for a good comparative empirical approach). The fact that the United States has come to represent both a high degree of modernization and a high degree, relative to other developed countries, of participation in organized religion has long been an anomaly—both Tocqueville and Marx commented on it—that the sociology of religion has tried to explain. One could invoke, for example, the statistics in Kosmin and Lachman, and more recent statistics from the Pew Forum on Religion and Public Life, "Religion and Politics: Contention and Consensus," gathered in the summer of 2003, showing that America is not only the most religious—and overwhelmingly Christian—nation in the developed world, with 81 percent of the nationwide survey saying they are believing Christians and 35 percent saying they believe that the Bible is the literal word of God. There has even been a slow but steady increase in the number of people who claim that religion is "very important" in their lives between 1978, which was something of a low point in America for religious affiliations, and 2003: 52 percent in 1978, 61 percent in 2003.

Nevertheless, in the discussion of religion in the modern Christian West, it is still commonly assumed that the separation of duties to one's religion from duties toward oneself, one's profession, and one's political state became fairly well established as a fundamental part of the rise of bourgeois civil society from the late seventeenth century onward, when the disaggregation of economic, social, cultural, religious, and political life became a more or less permanent feature of the modern nation-state. (For an overview of recent debates about the rise of the nation-state, see Smith, *Nationalism and Modernism;* see also Pecora, *Nations* 1–42.) Because modernization in the West emerged in practical terms through technological development and a higher average standard of living, the empirical observation that secularism increases with per capita income firmly aligned modernization with secularization as well. Recent polls on the importance that individuals around the world assign to religion continue to bear this out, if only in the broadest terms (see statistics gathered by Pew Global Attitudes Project, which I have adapted as table 1). Western Europe is clearly far less religious than are Latin America, Africa, and much of Asia, and the wealthier countries of Asia (such as Japan and South Korea) are less religious than are the poorer ones (such as Indonesia and India), though Eastern Europe, perhaps because of its recent history of communism, seems less religious than one might expect judged by economic predictors—far less, in fact, than the United States. By such measures, America is quite obviously an outlier where the correlation of declining religious attitudes and increasing economic development is concerned, a paradox variously attributed to its deep Puritan heritage, its founding emphasis on religious pluralism, and its status as a nation of immigrants (and of course slaves), where each new wave maintained its religious affiliations as forms of cultural identity and defense, perhaps weakening the lure of a simpler ethnonational form of collective consciousness such as one once found in Germany, for example. The conclusion of empirical sociology faced with such data is that, with few exceptions, secularization is associated with (that is, both an effect of and a stimulus to) economic development and prosperity, and it is this conclusion that forms one of the cruxes of the debate over globalization, especially since so-called development never occurs along egalitarian lines, and religious traditions often become bulwarks, as they have throughout history, against economic exploitation.

Bernard Lewis has notoriously argued that the whole issue of the separation of church and state, and hence the rise of a clear distinction between private religious beliefs and public political duties, is unique to Christianity—"Render therefore unto Caesar the things which are Caesar's; and unto God the things that are God's" are the words of Christ he cites, from Matthew 22:21—while such separation has been largely unknown in other religious traditions, and especially in the Muslim world (see Lewis, *What Went Wrong* 96–97). Whatever we think of Lewis's thesis, we should recognize that it is deeply embedded in Western social theory. Max Weber's sociological focus on the Protestant Reformation—or rationalization—of Roman Catholicism has, despite criticism from the historians, had a long afterlife. One of the most influential elaborations of Weberian sociology of religion in English—Peter

Table 1. Poll of 44 nations and 38,000 people by Pew Global Attitudes Project, December 2002 (http://www.people-press.org/reports)

Question: How important is religion in your life—very important, somewhat important, not too important, or not at all important?

Religion very important

NORTH AMERICA
- United States — 59%
- Canada — 30%

WESTERN EUROPE
- Great Britain — 33%
- Italy — 27%
- Germany — 21%
- France — 11%

EASTERN EUROPE
- Poland — 36%
- Ukraine — 35%
- Slovakia — 29%
- Russia — 14%
- Bulgaria — 13%
- Czech Republic — 11%

CONFLICT AREA
- Pakistan — 91%
- Turkey — 65%
- Uzbekistan — 35%

LATIN AMERICA
- Guatemala — 80%
- Brazil — 77%
- Honduras — 72%
- Peru — 69%
- Bolivia — 66%
- Venezuela — 61%
- Mexico — 57%
- Argentina — 39%

ASIA
- Indonesia — 95%
- India — 92%
- Philippines — 88%
- Bangladesh — 88%
- Korea — 25%
- Vietnam — 24%
- Japan — 12%

AFRICA
- Senegal — 97%
- Nigeria — 92%
- Ivory Coast — 91%
- Mali — 90%
- South Africa — 87%
- Kenya — 85%
- Uganda — 85%
- Ghana — 84%
- Tanzania — 83%
- Angola — 80%

Berger's *Sacred Canopy: Elements of a Sociological Theory of Religion* (1967)—claims that the Judeo-Christian tradition carried the seeds of secularism within it from the beginning (105–25; for a good summary of Berger's contributions, see Dobbelaere 22–26). In Berger's view, the Hebrew Bible's monotheism, positing a God completely outside the world, "demythologized" the space between God and humanity (Berger, *Sacred* 117). Medieval Catholicism, with its miracles, its focus on the mystery of the incarnation, and its neomagical system of sacraments mediating between God and humankind, for a time remythologized the world and allowed a fully transcendent divinity once more to inhabit the earth. The resulting intertwining of secular and religious authority—which began with Constantine, produced a Holy Roman Empire that dominated Europe for centuries, and fueled crusades and persecutions—is thus presented as the de facto rejection of the verse from Matthew. Only with the Reformation did the process of ethical rationalization emerge again, despite numerous attempts (such as Cromwell's, or that of the early American colonies) to produce a Protestant theocracy, and with the Reformation came the "disenchantment of the world" that Weber so compellingly described. The distinction Calvin argued for in the *Institutes of the Christian Religion* (1535) between the two kingdoms—"that the spiritual kingdom of Christ and civil government are things very different and remote from each other" (Calvin 2:633)—was one that had been prefigured in a way by Augustine's binary *civitas* of God and of man and signaled even earlier, perhaps, by the Manichean dualism of the Gnostics. But it may also be persuasively understood as a prime exemplification of what was for Berger the reemergence of ethical rationalization in early modernity, however complicated by Calvin's dictatorial role in a quasi-theocratic Geneva, and his assertion that one of the main functions of civil government was the safeguarding of religious practice. (One might thus conclude that both the strengths and weaknesses of American-style religious pluralism find their roots in Calvin and derivative Presbyterian thought of the Scottish Enlightenment.)

"Religious developments," writes Berger,

> originating in the Biblical tradition may be seen as causal factors in the formation of the modern secularized world. Once formed, however, this world precisely precludes the continuing efficacy of religion as a formative force. We could contend that here lies the great historical irony in the relation between religion and secularization, an irony that can be graphically put by saying that, historically speaking, Christianity has been its own gravedigger. (Berger, *Sacred* 127)

Behind Berger and Weber stands Nietzsche, who went so far as to reduce the European ideal of a scientific will to truth to a consequence of Christian asceticism. Nietzsche juxtaposed this ascetic ideal to the more truly "free" spirits of the eleventh-century Islamic order of Assassins, who abrogated faith both in religion and in truth itself with the watchword "Nothing is true, everything is permitted" (*Genealogy*, essay 3, section 24). Secular modernity is thus for Nietzsche (as for Weber and Berger) primarily the last phase of a Judeo-Christian but especially Protestant ascetic ideal, though for Nietzsche with rather more apocalyptic consequences: "the awe-inspiring *catastrophe* of two thousand years of training in truthfulness that finally forbids itself the *lie involved in belief in God*" (*Genealogy*, essay 3, section 27). Provocatively taking his own cue from the Assassins, but situating himself firmly within a Christian tradition, Nietzsche wants to push this training one step further along, so that Christian asceticism finally begins to undermine "*the meaning of all will to truth*" (*Genealogy*, essay 3, section 27). Nietzsche's larger focus on the blurred traditions of Judaism and Protestant Christianity as self-consuming enterprises, *because* of the peculiar ascetic will to truth embedded in their iconoclasm, has I think been formative for the sociology of religion that followed.

The grand, and many today would say false, idea that Christianity alone carried the seeds of secularism within it certainly did not go uncontested in earlier scholarship, though even here it was often contrasted with Islam. Robert Bellah, for example, who was for some time the dean of American religious sociologists, noted in 1968 that outside a very small philosophically educated elite,

> the enormous influence of Plutarch, Livy, and Cicero on European political thought and action from the sixteenth and seventeenth centuries on was completely missing in Islam. It was the revival of the classical notion of citizenship that played so important a role in early modern European political development. This whole avenue of independent political development was virtually absent in the Islamic world. Thus the political resources of the Islamic tradition in the modern world have been limited to the powerful but necessarily utopian—in advanced traditional societies not to speak of industrial society—image of the fusion of religion and politics in the first decades of Islam (Bellah 154)

Bellah acknowledged that there were indeed periodic and large-scale divergences between religious and political authority in classical Islam too, such as the return to hereditary kingship under the Ummayyads in the seventh- and eighth-century Muslim Empire, and again in eighth-to-eleventh-century Spain, a development that both ibn Khaldun in the fourteenth century and some modern Islamic scholarship has tried to rehabilitate (Bellah 151). But it was the category of Muslim believer rather than state citizen that for him proved to be the most useful device in politically transcending the familial and tribal affiliations of Arab society in the modern period (153). Nevertheless, following Weber, Bellah also argued that many religious traditions, including Judaism, Christianity, Islam, Buddhism, and Confucianism, must paradoxically also be seen as "among the great *secularizing* forces in human history" (see 157). Even Lewis points out that classical Islamic rulers were far more tolerant religiously than their Christian counterparts: medieval Islam knew no Inquisition and suffered no religious wars such as those that afflicted the West in the seventeenth century (Lewis, *What Went Wrong* 114). And as the example of Buddhism in India and China would show, the exchange of religious forms of knowledge was often accompanied by, and indeed may have spurred, the exchange of knowledge in nonreligious realms such as mathematics and astronomy (see Needham). Some recent scholarship in fact emphasizes the existence, within certain limits, of intellectual exchange and religious tolerance between Christian and Islamic communities under medieval Islamic rule (see Fletcher).

At the same time, as Lewis, Berger, Bellah, and many others admit, the rise of secularism has in fact been a relatively slow and uneven story in Christianity. The sort of political tolerance that granted equal civil rights to Catholics and to the range of Protestant sects actually achieved a more or less permanent and widespread legitimacy in the West only in the wake of the American and French Revolutions, and even here it was an uneven process. And the achievement of true religious freedom for Jews within nominally Christian nations, which may be the clearest expression of a meaningful separation of church and state in modernity, was tragically belated. One of the two great formative political events of the twentieth century—German Nazism's attempt to eradicate the Jews—was simultaneously a racial and a *religious* persecution, a fact that has often been lost in the contemporary concentration on the Nazi pseudo-sciences of race, especially in medicine and ethnology. (The other great event, the spread of communism, was equally involved in religious persecution.) We must add to this unevenness the fact that the oldest meaning of the term "secularization" refers to the expropriation of church property by the state, a fact that has had a role in the thinking of some who see secularization in the terms of Monod's second assumption, that is, as the "transfer" of intellectual property from one set of owners to the other (see Blumenberg, *Legitimacy* 13–26). Henry VIII's forced conversion of ecclesiastical buildings and land to lay ownership could thus be said to constitute the material historical root of what we call secularization. In fact, it has been cogently argued that such "top-down" domination or destruction of religious authority by more powerful court, state, and military institutions, as opposed to the internal intellectual discontent and resistance that well up from within, is actually a far more common path to secularization, both old and (as in the case of modern Turkey) new, than scholars usually acknowledge, and that sociologists of religion still pay far too little attention to it (see Keddie; for an earlier gesture in this direction, see Hill 39).

This unevenness of secularization continues well into the contemporary world. In the United States, where the constitution's First Amendment has long upheld the secular nature of the federal government, Christian prayer in state-controlled public schools was not barred until 1962, and still it goes on in some places with the approval of the local community and, implicitly, of the state leadership. And local communities in America are quite capable of getting exercised over art that appears to blaspheme against religious (primarily Christian) beliefs. Governments in Western Europe collect taxes to support churches despite radically diminished church membership. The British government is still officially allied with the Church of England. And in modern Ireland, though the secular state owned what Americans would call the public school system, it was the Catholic Church that actually operated the schools until the early 1960s.

If it is true that the international consensus among social elites in support of separating religious institutions and the secular state has for the most part grown during the last two centuries, it is also true that in many parts of the world, partly in response to secularizing forces perceived to have been imported from the West and partly because of Western manipulation of religious movements during the cold war—including, as Tariq Ali reminds us, "the Muslim Brotherhood against Nasser in Egypt, the Sarekat-i-Islam against Sukarno in Indonesia, the Jamaat-e-Islami against Bhutto in Pakistan and, later, Osama bin Laden and friends against the secular-communist Najibullah" (see Ali 275)—such separation has been severely challenged in recent decades. When we look at relatively new nations formed in the wake of decolonization, we find that religion has been a salient and in many cases irreducible component of national identity, and hence of social and political life (something Clifford Geertz and others have been pointing out since the 1960s; see especially Geertz 170–89). As some have noted more recently, the religious fundamentalism outside Europe that has grown in the last half century and that has been given further impetus by the new wave of globalization in the last two decades has been at least partially matched by the growth of fundamentalism in America during the same period (see Almond, Appleby, and Sivan; Lincoln). Ronald Reagan referred in biblically prophetic terms to the Soviet Union's "evil empire," and George W. Bush invoked scriptural "evildoers" and a "crusade" (though the latter term has long been used in an unthinking way in the West) as valid categories of supposedly secular foreign policy. While there would seem to be little danger of actually establishing an American theocracy, there is now a substantial minority that might welcome it.

I have no wish to downplay the effects of purely economic and technological innovation in the formation of the modern nation-state, as Ernest Gellner and his followers have quite clearly and persuasively elaborated them (see Gellner; for an important revision of Gellner along the lines of material culture, see B. Anderson). But it seems to me that Gellner's modernization did not occur in a religious or, as Anthony Smith in *National Identity* and others have cogently argued, ethnic void, and the shift of religious energies from nominally religious to nonreligious social institutions throughout the nineteenth and twentieth centuries is a central part of what I would call modernity (see, for example, Waché). Both nationalism and communism came to represent effective substitutions for religious affiliation in many parts of the world (see Prüfer; Sironneau); this is an important element of what constitutes the "political theology" of the last century.

But it is also important to acknowledge that, on a global view, and as the revisionists argue, secularization does not form a singular or uniform narrative in which religion succumbs to economics, technology, and individualism as the nation-state arises. Like racial affiliation, religious forms of social solidarity continue to play significant political roles within and among nation-states, whether in exoteric or highly attenuated forms. The major political transformation of the last half century—the collapse of the Soviet Union and its empire in Eastern Europe, and along with it the collapse of Soviet-inspired forms of communism—had deep roots in economic dysfunction. But for many who had lived under Soviet hegemony and endured economic dysfunction for some time, the central political trigger was the rise of Solidarity, the anti-Soviet labor movement, in Poland in the early 1980s, which was, if we believe the testimony of union leaders such as Lech Walesa, directly inspired by the election and visit of the Polish Pope John Paul II. By the same token, the so-called ethnic cleansing that erupted in the wake of Soviet empire's fall, exemplified by the struggle between Bosnian Serbs and Muslims, was often an attempt to eradicate a religiously as well as a politically opposed community. In many areas recently, in Iran and the Balkans, in India and Chechnya, in Sri Lanka, Cyprus, Algeria, Tunisia, the Sudan, and Iraq, religion has played a powerful social role both in determining national aspirations and in resisting the imposition of secular nation-state goals. This has certainly been true in much of the Islamic world and has prompted in some quarters a wholesale revaluation of the way secularism should be understood, both in the Christian West and within Islam (see especially Asad).

Almost all empirical sociologists of religion allow for the persistence of religion in what has been called cultural defense, which might at present fall under the domain of cultural and postcolonial studies in the humanities. That is, the "normal" trend toward secularization tends to be inhibited, so the argument goes, whenever religious affiliations can be mobilized to function in resistance to a group's domination by another group, especially when the dominating group brings either alien religious beliefs or forced secularization with it. This is in many ways a reversal of an older imperial history: Spanish Conquistadors carried the cross and the sword in pillaging the New World; Cromwell's Protestant militias systematically looted and defaced saints' statues in Irish Catholic churches; and Evangelical Christianity played an important role in the spread of the British Empire in the nineteenth century. It is precisely the general, if periodically questioned, presumption among Western political elites of the value and historical inevitability of the secular state that makes it important to recall the numerous examples of how religion has been a dominant, even growing, force shaping social and political resistance to the great empires as well, both for good and ill. When José Martí argued in defense of the "mute Indian masses" against the "false erudition" of the Creole and the "blond nation of the continent" (that is, the United States), he did so "with the rosary as our guide" and "under the standard of the Virgin" (Marti 143). Gandhi's successful anticolonial campaign against the Raj was religious in both rhetoric and methods, and the tumultuous fate of Indian national life ever since, even with its secular state and its separation from an overtly Muslim Pakistan, has been powerfully shaped by Hindu-Muslim communal rivalry that has only worsened since 1995 because of the struggle over Kashmir. The Gandhi-influenced campaign for black civil rights in the United States in the 1960s would have been very different without the power and prestige of the African American churches, whose immense and liberating significance in the lives of once-enslaved black Americans the rather secular W. E. B. Du Bois attributed, in *The Souls of Black Folk*, to "the deep religious feeling of the real Negro heart" (see Du Bois 168).

It may thus be true that the more straightforward or standard narrative of secularization is at this point distinctly frayed at the edges. We may be living through a period of great experimentation in this regard, especially outside Western Europe, where the seemingly antithetical imperatives of nation building and globalization are providing ample opportunities for testing the idea that "modernization"—at a bare minimum in the economic and legal-administrative spheres, but also and more contentiously in the sociocultural (for example, in the treatment of women)—requires secularization to succeed. At the same time, it is clear that a more functional definition of religion, of the kind pioneered by Emile Durkheim, which focuses on the social cohesion religion provides rather on the depth or efficacy of specific beliefs, may allow for a broader and richer understanding of the persistence of religious motifs in nominally secular social life. For later functionalists, modern nonreligious concepts—society, the nation-state, progress—come to be "over-extended," in Hans Blumenberg's term, and hence made to "reoccupy" the ideological positions held by religious answers to previous religious questions, questions for which the modern answers may be quite inadequate (see Blumenberg, *Legitimacy* 65). Here the important issue, as Monod points out, is less the global uniformity of secularization than whether the answers provided by secular thinking to formerly religious questions can be reduced merely to inconsistent and half-hearted versions of the religious tradition itself or, on the contrary, actually represent (as Blumenberg himself argues) a substantive and positive alteration in our approach to the world.

Regardless of one's view of the authentic meaning of secularization, however, it is hard not to acknowledge that the practical link between modernization and secularization remains alive and well, and that the role of "science" as an antidote to "superstition" remains a significant part of what major Western social institutions—from the academies to the courts of law—consider the social good. It is at best a questionable solution that encourages us to embrace either a return to a specific religious code (with the Ten Commandments in the courtroom) or a purely formal and arbitrary sense of "legality," in which we simply abandon the idea that political norms should not be divorced from a search for universally acceptable moral truths. In this sense, the continuing need to account for the powerful social role of secularization does not disappear when the "secularization thesis" is questioned. Rather, the ambiguities entailed by the concept of secularization become perhaps more salient, and more significant, than ever.

Cultural Criticism and Secularization

Cultural criticism, at least in the way I am using the term here, is more or less coeval with a modern and secular sense of culture that we associate with the age of the Western nation-state and large-scale capitalism since the eighteenth century. The social differentiation, societalization, and rationalization invoked above as commonly accepted hallmarks of such a culture entail not only the spiritual and intellectual autonomy of the individual, with all the duties and rights of "free expression" this demands, but, further, that culture comes increasingly to define itself in its opposition to all that is "Official": "Culture is only true when implicitly critical" (Adorno, *Prisms* 22).

Nevertheless, just as the problem of secularization did not disappear with the advent of a more thoroughly rationalized society, it did not vanish from culture and the discourses about it. To the extent that secular modern culture came to define itself as in some sense critical or oppositional in relation to an ever more secular official status quo, the apparent historical logic summed up by Weber's "disenchantment of the world" was bound to have profoundly paradoxical consequences where culture, which so depends on its ability to charm, was concerned.

At least since Matthew Arnold, cultural criticism thus found itself intimately caught up in the question of secularization: its central concern was with those elements of culture that would be most powerfully affected by "modernization," and hence, whether explicitly or not, with the difficulties posed by a secularizing process that threatened to embrace a purely instrumental or technical rationality. Even as enlightened, freethinking culture in the West came to be understood as the negation and replacement of a religious worldview, culture thus struggled to resist the radical secularization that attended modernity. The event of secularization, when looked at closely, is thus nothing if not complex and contradictory where culture and cultural criticism are at issue. (Indeed, some revisionists have made the strong claim—one resting on religious assumptions that, from my perspective, cannot finally be sustained—that the contemporary critical turn toward language is itself a path to a newly viable theology; see Milbank, *The Word Made Strange;* Ward, *Theology and Contemporary Critical Theory.*)

Adorno, forced into American exile by Nazism and war, in 1945 published in the *Kenyon Review* one of the few essays he would write in English: "Theses upon Art and Religion Today" (Adorno, *Notes* 2:292–98). Adorno notoriously recoiled against the treatment he received from American editors, who had little patience for the dialectical twists and reversals in his long, knotty sentences. He decided against including the essay in his collected four-volume *Noten zur Literatur.* Yet this very brief piece, even if comprising a perhaps too easily digested set of statements for his taste, is unmistakably Adorno's.

In seven brief theses Adorno argues that (1) the "lost unity" of art and religion cannot be recovered by contemporary efforts, because such past unity depended less on an artist's autonomous will than on "the whole objective structure of society during certain phases of history"; (2) in any case, this unity is far more problematic than many assume, and autonomous artistic expression had already made its protest against institutionalized religion with the classical Greeks, and even within medieval Catholicism; (3) modern attempts to add a religious content to works of art—for example, Rainer Maria Rilke's poetry, Stravinsky's *Symphonie des psaumes,* and popular "best-seller" religious novels—reduce religion to mere decorative ornament, where "religion is on sale"; (4) it is equally futile to translate older religious forms such as the mystery play (here Bertoldt Brecht may be the target), minus their religious contents, into modern movements such as collective socialism, and attempts to do so result only in the totalitarian repression of individual freedom of expression; (5) autonomous art cannot take up the mantle of lost religion, and any attempt to convey in art religious or philosophical messages of human solidarity, love, and universality will render both art and thought "cultural goods" that are "harmless and impotent"; (6) *nevertheless* (and here we find the dialectical reversal so characteristic of Adorno's work) "every work of art still bears the imprint of its magical origin," an imprint visible now not in specific religious contents but in the expressive traits of art as a category: its "halo of uniqueness, its inherent claim to represent something absolute," a "spell" that the Enlightenment's unerring tendency toward the domination of nature, embodied in the modern artist's ever more instrumental and conscious control of his or her materials, actually keeps alive in the rigorous attempt to eliminate all facile or commonly accepted versions of it; and (7) modern art can be universal, not because it represents the universal as religious or philosophical truth, but only as an example of Leibniz's windowless monads—that is, by becoming "infatuated with its own detached world, its material, its problems, its consistency, its way of expression," so that the obsessive focus on the most "insignificant" and "fugitive" memories of an enclosed world (as we see in Proust) ironically realizes a major religious theme: immortality.

In one sense, Adorno's larger perspective on the temporal transcendence achieved by art is hardly original—*ars longa, vita brevis* was the blunter Latin version of the idea—and the banality of this concluding sentiment when expressed so baldly in English may be one of the reasons Adorno decided against reprinting the essay. And yet there may be something worth examining more closely in Adorno's suggestion that magical thought's resistance to demystification is paradoxically intensified by the Enlightenment's (and the modern artist's) desire to dominate or extirpate whatever is not rational. "The powers of rational construction," Adorno writes in the sixth thesis, "brought to bear upon this irrational element seem to increase its inner resistance rather than to eliminate it, as our irrationalist philosophers want to make us believe," which means primarily that "the only way to save the 'spell' of art is the denial of this spell by art itself." It is an argument built upon a central ambiguity: modern art, and implicitly modern culture as a whole, in *consciously* striving for the complete elimination of the magical and auratic—the religious—as its secular emphasis on technical control demands, is in fact *unconsciously* working to ensure that the "spell" of art is preserved in an even stronger, because more rarified and rigorously achieved, form. The modernist work of art becomes a trial by fire, as it were, a technically severe, purifying cauldron for burning away the vestiges of outmoded religious and metaphysical thinking, so that only the essential, and hence noninstrumental, religious character of the artwork—its immortal, which is also to say universal, "spell"—remains to indict the irrationality of the falsely rationalized society. (For a good overview of the "theological moment" in Adorno, see Connell.)

This argument supplies the metaphysical content, as it were, and for an American audience, of what Adorno had argued at length on more formal grounds in his *Aesthetic Theory:* that the enlightened, autonomous emphasis on technique in modern art paradoxically (or dialectically) provides the only viable form of resistance to the dominating impulses of purely instrumental thought in modern society. "Form is the law of the transfiguration of the existing, counter to which it represents freedom. Form secularizes the theological model of the world as an image made in God's likeness, though not as an act of creation but as the objectification of the human comportment that imitates creation; not *creatio ex nihilo*, but creation out of the created" (*Aesthetic* 143). Writ large, Adorno's perspective suggests that, through a process paralleling Nietzsche's elaboration of the scientific will to truth as simply one more version of the ascetic ideal, secularism itself becomes the paradoxical path to a more profound, because more rational, sense of the religious than had ever existed before (a point that would be argued on broader philosophical terms by Odo Marquard as well; see Blumenberg, *Legitimacy* 56–61). Adorno succinctly captures the paradox of any totalizing process of secularization for cultural criticism: "The theological heritage of art is the secularization of revelation.... The eradication of every trace of revelation from art would, however, degrade it to the undifferentiated repetition of the status quo" (*Aesthetic* 106). The will to secular rationality in modern culture thus preserves the imaginative rudiments of its religious traditions, not merely as a kind of strategic resistance to the irrationality of capitalism's "iron cage" and its demand that everything have a price, that all things be treated equivalently as no more than commodities, but because secularism, in constantly redefining and reenergizing itself by reference to outworn religious traditions, is finally a way of preserving, at a more rarified and rationally persuasive level of awareness, precisely what it seeks to destroy.

Hegel would have referred here to the *Aufhebung*, or the negating-overcoming-preserving, of the tradition, which is primarily the register of the dialectical progress of human consciousness toward absolute knowing, one that cancels out tradition yet leaves nothing, no matter how counterproductive, behind. Heidegger wrote instead of a *Verwindung*, a "distortion," but also, in Gianni Vattimo's words, "a going-beyond that is both an acceptance and a deepening" (see Vattimo 172; see also Heidegger, *Identity and Difference* 36–37, 101), which Vattimo finally, and rather tendentiously, interprets as "secularization" (Vattimo 179). For Heidegger, this *Verwindung* entailed a "step back" behind the history of Western metaphysics and science rather than (as in Hegel) an *Überwindung* or "overcoming" of it. Heidegger wanted to comprehend from the outside, as it were, the entirety of the human relationship to Being, either as metaphysical ground or as transcendent God. In the wake of what he outlined as a Western tradition of knowledge—the "onto-theo-logical constitution of metaphysics" that culminated in the nuclear technology punctuating the end of World War II—Heidegger imagined an "event" (*Ereignis*) or epochal opportunity to rethink, or reappropriate, the larger history linking Western philosophy and religion with the technological domination of nature that so determines modernity.

It is no doubt impossible to say whether Heidegger's sense of a postmodern *Ereignis* actually does mark a significant turning point in Western thought—the "closure of metaphysics" that would be so crucial to Derrida's thinking—because such "epochal thresholds" (to borrow a term from Hans Blumenberg), such as the transition from the Greek to the Christian world or from the medieval to the modern, generally come to appear as such only well after the fact. We would do well, in other words, to be suspicious of Heidegger's hubris as postmodern prophet, especially given the postwar context of his remarks and his earlier political investments in a new German—that is, National Socialist—awakening. Likewise, I see little reason to credit Heidegger's sense that the nature of "Western" languages is at the root of our philosophical-religious-technological condition (a view that goes back at least to Hegel, and that also played so large a role in the emergence of Derrida's deconstructive project; see especially *Grammatology* 3–73). "Our Western languages," Heidegger writes, "are languages of metaphysical thinking, each in its own way. It must remain an open question whether the nature of Western languages is in itself marked with the exclusive brand of metaphysics, and thus marked permanently by onto-theo-logic, or whether these languages offer other possibilities of utterance—and that means at the same time of a telling silence" (Heidegger, *Identity* 73). Nevertheless, in what follows, I want to adapt Vattimo's suggestive—if itself distorting—reading of *Verwindung* as "secularization," which is to say, not as an epochal opportunity that has only recently come to pass in the history of Western thought, but rather as an extended, errant process of recollection, transformation, convalescence and emancipation, a process that is constantly doubling back upon itself.

I thus intend to use—or perhaps creatively misuse—the idea of *Verwindung* as a way of signaling that secularization, especially from a global perspective in which the West's self-understanding is put more broadly into question, might be best understood not merely as the implacable process through which (as in Hegel) reason unfolds, ruses and all, in its pursuit of universal comprehension. Rather, I want to approach secularization as something bound to take a more circuitous, partial, and uneven path, one filled with digressions that periodically call its basic (Weberian) premises into question, and that may provide, both for good and ill, a powerful resistance to any attempt to finish once and for all what Habermas has called the "project" of rationalized modernity. In particular, secularization can be considered simultaneously curative and distorting in the sense that its consequences can be understood to include both an enlightened liberation from dogma and an opening up of certain collective possibilities—redemptive revolution, nationalism, imperialism, racism—that could not have attained their full and often destructive potential otherwise. In the most striking accounts of this more ambiguous process—and for me, Durkheim's reduction of the social and the religious to the same inchoate logic of collective life is chief among them—the secularization through which magic or myth is eliminated by reason may never in fact be complete. This is not simply a function of language or geography but is perhaps something to be acknowledged as the result of an irreducible set of needs in human and group psychology. One might then conclude that the society that produces Enlightenment never fully outgrows its desire for religious sources of coherence, solidarity, and historical purpose, and continually translates, or transposes, them into ever more refined and immanent, but also distorted and distorting, versions of its religious inheritance.

And yet the mere fact that, at least since Feuerbach and certainly since Freud, we so often pose the question of religion in this latter way—that is, with varying degrees of irony, as the effect of a desire or need or wish rather than as a set of substantive beliefs based on the evidence of scripture and nature—already suggests that Monod's first definition, in which secular modernity marks a decisive break with *all* religious traditions, may have more to recommend it than my previous remarks allow. That is, although many accounts of secularization have come from positions of strong religious belief, it would seem that modern modes of overtly nonreligious empirical and scholarly historiography by their nature foreclose, or at least severely limit, the viability of all nonsecular accounts of the rise of secularism. Whether secularization, understood to be a continual refinement-as-convalescing-distortion, actually entails a progress toward universally acceptable moral truths—a secular "international life" that would "universalize religious beliefs," as Durkheim put it (Durkheim, *Elementary* 446)—is a question that must remain open, though I believe that the commitment to such progress may provide the only ethical ground we possess within a nontheological (and nonteleological) intellectual framework. Still, as will be clear in what follows, I find the twisting ambiguities and reversals of the secularizing process—the *Verwindung*—more intriguing than its potential end.

The Shape of This Discussion

This volume is a reflection on the paradoxes and ambivalences of secularization, which is treated as an intractable problem for culture and cultural criticism in the post-Enlightenment West, and which becomes especially important for the early twentieth century. Each chapter is an attempt to trace out secular culture's *Verwindung*, the overcoming but also the distortion and reemergence of received religious concepts and patterns of thought. Moreover, I have attempted to do so without completely abandoning a commitment to culture's materiality. As I hope will be especially evident in the last chapter, my goals here include understanding how secularization involves transformations that occur simultaneously in mind and in matter, in systems of belief as well as in social relations and forms of community. After all, what had been called religious perspectives, once deeply embedded in social rhetoric, institutions, and traditions, may continue to function very well without any overt religious affiliations to justify or ground them.

The book focuses on a cluster of interrelated issues, worked through in large part in reverse historical chronology. Chapter 1 invokes figures as diverse as Edward Said, Gauri Viswanathan, Talal Asad, Ashis Nandy, Jürgen Habermas, Alasdair MacIntyre, and Hans Blumenberg in order to address the vicissitudes, value, and potential impasses of secular cultural criticism in the context of an increasingly global understanding of culture. The discussion underlines and queries the Western intellectual's implicit recourse to a deeper relationship between a secularized Judeo-Christian tradition and Enlightenment notions of truth and progress. Chapter 2 examines the promise as well as the pitfalls of a cultural criticism built around notions of social and historical redemption, further elaborating problems entailed by the notion of progress addressed in the previous discussion. This chapter displays the tension between Walter Benjamin's quasi-religious rejection of the notion of progressive enlightenment, or "bourgeois history," and Siegfried Kracauer's fragmented and incomplete attempt to salvage that notion, or at least reconcile with it, by rethinking Benjamin's eschatological *Stillstand*. Chapter 3 explores the intimate but distorting relationship between the rise of modern social theory and political theology, in which the idea of the religious is both negated and variously rediscovered in the idea of the social. What is at stake here is the possibility that the process of secularization in the West paradoxically may have enabled the making sacred of "society," with decidedly ambiguous consequences. Chapter 4 focuses on the way that Matthew Arnold's approach to the secularization of the religious components of national identity, beginning with his interpretation of St. Paul and Protestant dissent, seems to have entailed the troubling invocation of its racial components. In elaborating his notion of secular Hellenistic Enlightenment versus Hebraistic religious morality, Arnold may have been relying on racial theories more evident in his study of the Celts, theories that would often supplant the religious bases of national identity in the century after him. Finally, chapter 5 examines how the secular modernist novel preserves an image of religious tradition in the representation of a particular social habitus, one that derives from the Evangelical Clapham Sect of Virginia Woolf's great-grandfather and grandfather, persists in the "profane" clan gathered at Bloomsbury, and intersects in crucial ways with Woolf's sense of and resistance to her own bodily experience. In Woolf, a particular kind of household sociality is itself the most intimate sign of secularized religion—a *Verwindung* that simultaneously satirizes and subtly makes a separate peace with an Evangelical tradition central to British culture in the century before her.

The book's brief conclusion addresses the vicissitudes of humanism (and the study of the humanities) in the context of globalization, emphasizing the question whether the increasing interdependence of humanist discourse across disparate cultural traditions will enhance or diminish the persistence of humanism's own secularized religious heritage. More important, by emphasizing the utility of thinking about the process of secularization in terms of Kracauer's multilayered yet still "bundled" temporalities rather than in terms of an ever fully achieved or univocal "secular*ism*," I try to suggest that there may be broader and deeper links than we generally acknowledge between the Western intellectual's struggle with the semantic resonances of religious thought (as in Habermas) and the avowedly oppositional perspectives of various intellectuals (from Dipesh Chakrabarty and Asad to Nandy) struggling with the problem of secularization in the postcolonial world.

1 * Secular Criticism and Secularization

Ideologically speaking, nothing characterizes the Westernness of modern Western thought more profoundly than the acceptance by its elites of what became a fairly naturalized idea of ongoing secularization rooted in the Enlightenment. Any talk of secularism or secularization in the academy is bound to take us back to the Enlightenment, to what is commonly called the scientific revolution of the sixteenth through eighteenth centuries, and to the fitful but seemingly inescapable disenchantment of the world it inaugurated (for rather different approaches to the coherence of the term scientific revolution, see Cohen; Shapin). For the European and American intellectual, secularization is the essential developmental narrative inculcated by university training, the sine qua non enabling that training's truth claims. The usual story goes something like this: Increasingly skeptical and mechanistic forms of knowledge take root (Descartes and Hobbes), with humanism as their foundation and astronomy as their leading edge (Galileo). This "Great Instauration," as Francis Bacon called it, overturned the old physics of Aristotle and put knowledge on a new and firmer footing. One could claim that the entire epistemological reform boiled down to one simple transformation: the reduction of Aristotle's fourfold conception of causality (in *Physics* 2.3), which had once encoded the entelechy of nature, to one kind only—blind efficient, or mechanical, causality (see Aristotle 194b17–195b30).

The new knowledge was still in certain ways indebted to old paradigms. For example, Bacon still hoped to improve human understanding by returning it to some "perfect and original condition" in which the empirical and the rational are once again lawfully married (see Abrams 60). Nevertheless, as the general story of Enlightenment has it, the scientific revolution in turn engendered technological modernization, possessive individualism, a capitalist ethic toward labor and production, social differentiation, and administrative rationalization—all of which added up to a shift from a static, traditional, but also non-Western society to a dynamic, modern, Western one. In this sense, the process of secularization is akin to the structural and evolutionary distinction between prehistoric and proto-historic (post-Neolithic) civilization that Claude Lévi-Strauss once encapsulated in terms of societies being either "cold" (small, homogeneous, resistant to change) or "hot" (drawing upon the energy and desire for change supplied by caste and class division)—though Lévi-Strauss's Marxism led him to believe that the "utopian" society would be a Hegelian synthesis of "cold" and "hot" processes raised to the level of culture (Lévi-Strauss, *Structural Anthropology* 28–30).

What the educated mind sharpens its tools against and then supposedly leaves behind as Enlightenment descends upon it is "religion," however the historical dawn of modern science is understood in its particulars. Recent accounts in this vein have placed Spinoza's early critique of divinely inspired scripture at the heart of a "radical Enlightenment," one in which secularization and egalitarian liberation were closely related (see Israel). Thus, the core of the secularization idea, which takes various forms, is the claim that overt belief and participation in religion are abandoned as Enlightenment science, technological modernization, and the fragmentation of social life into separate and autonomous spheres of endeavor are embraced. Karl Löwith, among others, further noted that it was the West's belated recognition in the eighteenth century of the antiquity, richness, and humanity of the non-Christian civilizations of China, India, and Persia that led figures such as Voltaire to reject the revealed, sacred history of the Christian West—though, it must be admitted, at the price of a certain anti-Semitism (see Löwith 106–7). Today, by contrast, we seem increasingly compelled to acknowledge that traditional religion has not really disappeared in anything like the wholesale way this version of the secularization thesis predicts. For many, the Enlightenment's triumph of reason over nature has become a historically impoverished narrative unless it is seen in relation to the religious heritage with and against which it was dialectically defined. Moreover, there is renewed interest in one account of secularization, which claims that the emotional and psychological energies formerly exercised in religious activity simply migrated elsewhere. Whether we follow Emile Durkheim or Carl Schmitt or Löwith, we could point to nationalism and socialism as the great twentieth-century sublimations of what was once called religion.

Skepticism toward the old grand narrative of progressive enlightenment has been a staple of what is often called postmodernism. Michel Foucault has come to be most closely associated with the antihistoricist, antihumanist questioning of Enlightenment reason, though his skepticism had many precursors. We generally point first to the genealogy practiced by Nietzsche and to the antihumanist philosophy of the late Heidegger (see Heidegger on language, especially *Poetry* 189–210). But one might also invoke the radical rejection of the Enlightenment articulated early on by clearly very different religious thinkers such as Joseph de Maistre and Kierkegaard. When some, perhaps expanding on Isaiah Berlin's perspective, call the story of twentieth-century social thought from Freud to Foucault "the Counter-Enlightenment," they conflate the various and, to many in the humanities, quite different responses to the Enlightenment found in all these figures: Maistre is not Heidegger, and neither of them is Foucault, but they all at times are seen as trying to subvert an easy confidence in the European Enlightenment (see Berlin 1–24). I will stick with Foucault's account for a moment, because what it leaves out has come to be, I think, important once again.

Foucault's Enlightenment

The Enlightenment was for Foucault a product not of "disenchanted" reasoning and observation, but of a sudden shift in the grammar of our thinking, in the mode of representation. Foucault refused to accept the Enlightenment's grand narrative about clearer thinking, distinct ideas, and better evidence replacing superstition and myth and insisted instead on arbitrary transformations in the "regularities" by which knowledge was constituted. He also claimed, in *Madness and Civilization* especially, that the Enlightenment was able to consolidate itself not by defining reason against religious belief, but by defining reason against a new and differently codified other—madness—which reason had to invent, as it were, in order to distinguish itself in the first place (see Foucault, *Histoire*). Foucault's argument on this point was both brilliant and influential, but it had some unfortunate consequences. It helped many Western intellectuals forget, and at a most untimely global moment, several older and perhaps still viable theses: (a) that religion was the primary rival of the new science in the Enlightenment; (b) that, at the same time, the transformation of religious belief and practice was as much an engine of the Enlightenment as its effect, as Max Weber in his *Protestant Ethic* had implied; and perhaps most of all, (c) that religion did not suddenly disappear as a result of the Enlightenment, but continued, in both spirit and practice, to be a shaping force in the creation of the modern world (see Cassirer 134–96).

My point is that, until fairly recently, Foucault's work helped us to dismantle the received and uncritical story of Enlightenment *progress*, which Benjamin once satirized as homogeneous, bourgeois history, but only by obscuring the question of *secularization* (see Benjamin 260–61). Obscured, too, was the way Enlightenment rationality made an enduring separate peace with religion, largely through deism, pantheism, Hegelian history, and the private *moralität* of the disavowed religious conscience—all the compromises (Israel refers to them as the "moderate Enlightenment") that Nietzsche, and to an extent Hume before him, energetically and for the most part ineffectually denounced. We need to recall this dialectical dance of reason and religion in the West, not because we might otherwise be less than vigilant in defending reason against the onslaughts of new religious fervor, but rather because the simpler narrative it complicates is the most deeply rooted and enduring element of what we might call the Western ideology: the belief, as Grace Davie puts it, "that whatever characterized Europe's religious life today would characterize everyone else's tomorrow" (Davie 1). In effect, as students of Foucault, we learned how to rethink the Enlightenment's idea of progress, but not necessarily the story of secularization that accompanied it.

But in other quarters, and especially in the history and sociology of religion, the secularization thesis has received increasing attention in recent decades, and some historians have recently advanced the often unacknowledged role of religious thought in the development of Enlightenment rationality more generally (for good examples, see D. Bell; Jacob). The latter half of the twentieth century witnessed various forms of religious revival, many connected to new forms of postcolonial nationalism, while the end of the cold war turned discussion away from the capitalism-communism polarity toward what we might call the globalism-sectarianism polarity (and what has been called "glocalization"). There is nothing accidental in the fact that what appears from one perspective to be the great age of economic globalization seems from another perspective to be the great age of religious sectarianism. The problem of secularization is thus being confronted anew, this time in what Edward Said would have called contrapuntal terms, with one eye on Europe and America, and the other on the formerly colonized worlds of the Middle East, India, Africa, and Asia. The questions being asked are not necessarily new, and many were asked by Max Weber in his various examinations of religious history, however differently we may answer them today (see, for example, Weber's concluding chapter, "The General Character of Asiatic Religion," in his *Religion of India* 329–43). What, precisely, does secularism entail? Why has secularization taken radically different forms outside a few Western European nations? And most basically: Can we speak of modernization *without* secularization?

Recently such questions have acquired a new urgency, especially in the midst of a so-called war on terrorism. To confront the process of secularization that Foucault neglected, to address the significance of secularization within the idea of progress, means to recast the terms of the discussion.

It may not be possible to provide definitive answers to such questions, and in any case it is not my purpose—and it is certainly beyond my abilities—to provide a new global and historical overview of what secularization has meant. Moreover, I want to argue neither that the West has tragically never been as secular and scientific as is often claimed, nor that the West's commitment to secular reason has, via some destructive dialectic of enlightenment, led it inexorably toward inhuman horrors. Both revisionist views can be, and have been, cogently argued, a point I will take up in chapter 3. Instead, I want to emphasize here that the dialectical narrative of Western enlightenment and religion should not hastily be put aside when those in the West begin to talk about its relationship to non-Western parts of the world. The depth and persistence of the secularization story, its capacity to inflect even the most critically self-aware corners of Western thinking, is the surest sign that recurrent debates surrounding cultural relativism are both inescapable and irresolvable. For such debates are in many ways functions of Western secularization. The historical narrative of the advent of secular rationality in the West is almost never told as if it were reversible, as if the West would one day return, for example, to a medieval religious cosmology. (Yeats and Spengler toyed with such reversibility in the form of cyclical return, and we find it in Vico's proto-romanticism and in Nietzsche, but the notion was in fact one of the first victims of the Enlightenment and has practically no place in university curricula today.) As a result, the question of cultural relativism cannot help but turn endlessly on itself once the narrative of secularization acquires a certain credibility and consensus.

The relativistic historical perspective that allows "us" to see our own approach as embedded in and dependent upon cultural determinants, and thus no more "natural" than the determinants of other cultures, depends in turn upon a certain latitudinarianism, if I may borrow a term from Western religious history. That is, such relativism depends on tolerance that grows out of or fosters a harmonizing rather than an antagonistic stance—as in Lévi-Strauss's utopian synthesis of hot and cold societies—and hence a more universal view of the whole range of possible sectarian differences, as we would find in Diderot's deism. In this way, our ability to be comfortable with relativism oddly depends on, or slides inexorably toward, a thin but broad and pluralistic universalism. But this universalism, this sense that through a less judgmental and more dispassionate gaze one has grasped the most truly general characteristics of human being, human civilization, even "human rights," as the Abbé Sieyès and others obviously thought they had with ideas like the "the rights of man," can be explained away—indeed, I think it often *is* explained away these days—as a fiction embedded in a specific kind of Judeo-Christian humanist culture, that is, the kind that believes in the secularizing narrative that entails a latitudinarian tolerance based on individual rights rather than communal duties, on a putatively dispassionate separation of private from public beliefs, and on a sentimental or "natural" identification with others. (For an account of and response to this sort of critique of the legitimacy of "human rights," see Habermas, *Postnational* 113–29.) Hence, it is just as true to say that universalism depends upon, or slides inexorably back toward, relativism—and so on and so forth. Still, secularization is most often understood, and by definition, as a one-way street, quite despite a very widespread disavowal of the cultural evolutionism that characterized nineteenth-century anthropology. (We might consider Durkheim here, for example, for whom a muted form of the secularization narrative persisted in the historical development he outlined that took us from mechanical to organic solidarity, despite his rejection of evolutionism. It is precisely Durkheim's equivocal evolutionism that persists within Lévi-Strauss's structuralism.) Even in the anomalous United States, where religious observance, as sociologists have long noted, seems to accommodate itself quite well to social modernization, underlying assumptions about the inevitability of secularization remain powerful among the cultural, judicial, and scholarly elite. Once civilization embarks upon it, there would seem to be no turning back.

What this means is that, for the secular Western intellectual, a vital public life driven by religious sentiments, as is the case in America today—by religion that is not simply a private affair of the heart—remains the clearest sign that, as Habermas once concluded, modernity is an "unfinished project" (see Passerin d'Entrèves and Benhabib). Such a phrase is designed to indicate the incomplete historical fulfillment of our rational capabilities. When the public political face of religion does appear, as it does both throughout the Middle East today and, via more muted Protestant forms, in America too, it is generally attributed, especially by a liberal cultural elite, to a defect, as it is by Marx, or at least an unfortunate detour in the normal course of human development. When more essential distinctions about the central role of religion in creating a unified sense of "a whole civilization which grew under the aegis of that religion" are invoked in the West (Lewis, *Islam* 4), the author may seem willing to embrace a model of global politics that finds little room for constructive compromise, let alone unifying consensus (as seen in Samuel Huntington's "clash of civilizations" thesis, itself derived from Lewis's work). Moreover, the only sort of religiousness that is widely acceptable for most of the Western intelligentsia is the intensely private sort of belief associated with the nonevangelical sects of Protestantism. And yet, as numerous anthropologists, sociologists, and cultural pundits have noted in recent years, it is precisely the idea of a public life infused with religious sentiment that can be found in many parts of the globe today, and not only in the underdeveloped world (see, for example, Almond, Appleby, and Sivan). Despite the commitment to secular truth among many intellectuals, America, as the recent Pew Forum polls have shown, remains both profoundly homogeneous when Christianity at large, rather than race or ethnicity, is considered, and very much at ease with the audible and visible presence of Christian sentiment in public life.

In this context, I want to point briefly to several exemplary, and decidedly different, positions on the larger question of secularization. These views have a special relevance, I think, in a world the religious complexity of which has been newly impressed upon a secular academy since the end of the cold war and the dissolution of its opposed stabilizing blocs of political hegemony. The collapse of this bipolar geopolitical world helped to usher in a variety of global religious revivals, especially Islamist, Hindu nationalist, and Christian fundamentalist, and to open a new wave in the religious politics of terrorism and counterterrorism.

Said, Asad, and Discrepant Experience

The first position can be represented by Edward Said, who in countless ways throughout his career championed two basic Enlightenment ideas: that truth is a material production of human, rather than divine, history, and that all political life should be based on the autonomy and dignity of the individual human will. It is thus perhaps obvious that this most important heir to Foucault's dismantling of the Enlightenment's hubris about universal progress was paradoxically yet deeply committed to the secularization that Diderot's Enlightenment required. That is, Said routinely challenged the West's presumption to have achieved a level of moral and political superiority insofar as it remained blind to an oppressive imperialism rationalized as the spread of reason and Christianity. And yet, the problem of the process and meaning of secularization per se—as opposed to the achieved position of a secular criticism that has risen above the religious motives of those it discusses—rarely arises in Said's work. In its broadest and most idealized sense, Said's notion of secular criticism is designed to challenge dogmatism of every stripe. It is aimed not simply at religion, but at all modes of thought that simulate the certainty and unquestioned authority of religious dogma: racism, nationalism, imperialism, indeed any form of system-building—here Swift is his unlikely ally—that seems divorced from personal experience (see Said, *World* 1–30, 72–89). But religious belief remains the template of all such systems, and it is the historical impulse toward secularization that remains the engine of Said's antidogmatism. (For a good appraisal and critique of Said's own rather dogmatic distinction between the religious and the secular, see Gunn 73.)

In a sensitive and subtle comparison of the Orientalism of Renan and Massignon, for example, Said provides portraits of thinkers who emerge as substantially moved by religious sentiments (Said, *World* 268–89). At the same time, he castigates those who would see "Walter Benjamin not as a Marxist but as a crypto-mystic" as examples of a "curious veering toward the religious" that he aligns with a most regressive and "uncritical religiosity," which "expresses an ultimate preference for the secure protection of systems of belief (however peculiar these may be) and not for critical activity or consciousness." The idea that careful critical analysis of religious motivations might be useful in the case of Massignon but not in Benjamin is defended, it seems, because Benjamin was a Left-utopian, like Ernst Bloch, "whose work was an attempt to metamorphize the social enthusiasm of millenarianism into everyday life" (292). Unlike Said's discussion of Massignon, the commentary of those who attempt to investigate religious traditions and motives in Benjamin's work today do so only "as the result of exhaustion, consolation, disappointment" (291).

Said's judgment, in my view, is rather reductive on this point. Were Frank Kermode's *Genesis of Secrecy* and Northrop Frye's *Great Code*, both of which Said invokes as examples of a "curious veering toward the religious," really signs of exhaustion and disappointment? In Frye's case, after all, the "veering" had surely been going on for decades by the time *The Great Code* appeared. Is the "social enthusiasm of millenarianism" embraced by some on the Left somehow beyond critical evaluation, as if it were above rational suspicion? More important, there is for me as well the questionable assumption that matters of religion are not worth investigating in Bloch and Benjamin, precisely because in these latter figures such matters are somehow all made subservient to "everyday life." But this simply begs the question, assuming what an account of secularization would need to address: that "everyday life" in modernity really has nothing to do with religious thinking, even though in Said's view all sorts of other irrational ideological formations, such as racism, play powerful roles in mundane affairs. For me, the subtle disconnection between religious modes of thought and modern "everyday life" is one of the significant characteristics of Said's work. It is all the more significant if we consider that Said was not averse to treating Orientalist prejudice as itself akin to "religious discourse," in that "each serves as an agent of closure, shutting off human investigation, criticism, and effort in deference to the authority of the more-than-human, the supernatural, the other-worldly" (290).

After all, secularization is at the very heart of what Said means by modern Orientalism.

> My thesis is that the essential aspects of modern Orientalist theory and praxis (from which present-day Orientalism derives) can be understood, not as a sudden access of objective knowledge about the Orient, but as a set of structures inherited from the past, secularized, redisposed, and re-formed by such disciplines as philology, which in turn were naturalized, modernized and laicized substitutes for (or versions of) Christian supernaturalism. (Said, *Orientalism* 122)

Here, Said is in fact the heir not of Foucault and his idea of arbitrary historical rupture, but of Meyer Abrams's *Natural Supernaturalism*. On the one hand, the secularizing process was a moral and political liberation, embodied in a wide range of comparative historical projects from Vico to Herder, and given aesthetic form in the transcultural sympathies of Mozart's *Magic Flute* and Goethe's *West-Ostlicher Diwan* (see Said, *Orientalism* 118; Said's introduction to Auerbach xv). In this sense, secularization meant that "notions of human association and of human possibility acquired a very wide general—as opposed to parochial—legitimacy" (Said, *Orientalism* 120). At the same time, the secularization of religious tradition is precisely what enabled the more precise, controlling, and scientific disciplines, including "lexicography, grammar, translation, [and] cultural decoding" (121), which made modern Orientalism—quite unlike the religiously based "precolonial awareness of Dante and D'Herbelot"—"fatally tend towards the systematic accumulation of human beings and territories" (123). Buried within the process of secularization for Said there is a paradox, akin though not identical to what Adorno and Horkheimer had called a "dialectic of enlightenment." On the one hand, secularization enabled the increasing possibility of sympathy with the other through the transcendence of religious parochialism, precisely as the deism of the Enlightenment would suggest, and Said himself is, like Auerbach in this respect, very much an intellectual product of that transformation. On the other, secularization enabled the systematic ability to accumulate both knowledge of and power over the Orient, and it is this corrupting transformation that impedes the fulfillment of the more sympathy-inducing and humane fruits of secularization. In this sense, secularization was simultaneously necessary for achieving broadened human sympathies, and the non-West's worst enemy.

Said's methodological antidote to this paradox of Western secularization is the imperative to read culture contrapuntally, and it is perhaps fair to say that no other gesture has had as profound an effect on the academic practice of cultural criticism in the last half century. At its heart, as Said acknowledges in *Culture and Imperialism,* this is an expansion and decentering of the ruling ideas behind Western comparative literature, which were themselves originally broader applications of the ideas behind comparative philology and Goethe's notion of *Weltliteratur.* Said's idea is to juxtapose what he calls "discrepant experiences"—that is, experiences that may be quite different in terms of history, geography, cultural and religious contexts, and political power, but that nevertheless coexist, interact with, and shape each other because of the framework of Western empire. To read "contrapuntally," then, is to read "with a simultaneous awareness both of the metropolitan history that is narrated and of those other histories against which (and together with which) the dominating discourse acts" (Said, *Culture* 51). In this way, we learn both that cultural identities are not "essentializations," since Greeks require barbarians, Europeans require Africans and Orientals, and so forth, in an ongoing process of dialectical oppositions, but also that part of the appeal of cultural identities is that "they seem and are considered to be essentializations" (52). There are many things one might say about Said's notion of contrapuntal interpretation, but I will restrict myself to a few of the most salient issues.

I want to emphasize the degree to which such a perspective is, as Said notes, primarily an outgrowth of a long European tradition of comparative scholarship that, at least from the time of Herder and William Jones, has insisted upon the study of the diversity of Western and non-Western cultures as central to the educated mind. It was Said's signal achievement to have pushed this scholarship toward an ethical recognition of its role in the domination of colonized peoples and cultures, and toward an epistemological revaluation of its assumptions about the status and superiority of the West. That the colonized world had been changed by imperial practices, no one doubted; but Said's work also encouraged Western scholarship on Western culture to acknowledge to what extent imperialism had created the culture of the West as well (Said, *Culture* 35). Said's perspective is, as he recognizes by pairing it with what he calls "secular interpretation," at heart a latter-day version of perhaps the central achievement of the Enlightenment where "discrepant" cultural experience is concerned—secularization. What I am saying, in perhaps too hurried a fashion, is that Said's sense of the ethical and epistemological virtue of "contrapuntal" reading is the product of a notion of rational tolerance, underwritten by early eighteenth-century English natural religion and the deism of the Encyclopedists, which is itself a consequence of the process of secularization that began as early as the late medieval Catholic humanists and the Protestant Reformation.

As Diderot quite succinctly observed in the vivid terms of "De la suffisance de la religion naturelle," which provides a ground of sorts for both Lévi-Strauss's utopianism and Said's secular contrapuntalism, natural religion "is that which reconciles civilized man and barbarian, Christian, infidel, and heathen, philosopher and people, the learned and the ignorant, the old man and the child, even the wise and the insane"; revealed religion, on the other hand, "estranges father from son, arms man against man, and exposes the learned and wise to the hatred and persecution of the ignorant and fanatic, and from time to time soaks the earth with the blood of all of them" (Diderot 1:63). This is not to say, as Said points out numerous times, that curiosity about the other is somehow a peculiar product of the Western mind (a claim Bernard Lewis once made; see Said, *World* 37). Nor, obviously, is it to imagine that non-Western societies, as Lewis has also implied at times (see the introduction), have failed to generate or accommodate what the Western scholar would call secular thought, in the form either of atheism or of something that might translate the idea of "humanism" (see, for example, Asad, *Formations*, on the "translation" [207] of Western notions of secularism by Egyptian thinkers in the nineteenth century; Sanson on *laïcité islamique* in modern Algeria). But it is to suggest that the belief that the seeming incommensurability of different and apparently unequal cultural traditions can be overcome by a more cosmopolitan and wholly secular understanding of their interrelations begins, at least in Said's work, with those strains of Enlightenment thought that sought to overcome religious sectarianism by weakening the power of revealed religion and diverting its energies into other forms of culture such as art.

That Europe had more success in this regard with the competing confessions of Christianity internal to it than with the competition between Christianity and Islam—or, I would hasten to add, between Christianity and Judaism—is an enduring part of the history of the West. And yet in *Culture and Imperialism*, Said allows little space for the discussion of religion per se and refers to Christianity and Islam primarily as the geopolitical divisions of a world that empire has made. But this also means that the modern, post-Enlightenment idea of "culture" remains for him rather Arnoldian in its parameters. It is largely the culture of *already* cosmopolitan and worldly modern writers and artists, primarily European but also of formerly colonized regions, for whom specific religious heritages remain primarily as survivals. When the question of strong, fundamentalist religious belief in modern non-Western societies does arise, it is seen primarily as the consequence of Western domination and interference, of "a deep-seated anti-Westernism that is a persistent theme of Egyptian, Arab, Islamic, and Third World history," which too often tends to "return to its Meccan roots the better to combat the West" (Said, *Culture* 34). This is a compelling view, but it also raises interesting questions. Are we then to assume that secularization in the modern world is the transcultural norm, one that would flourish indigenously everywhere if given a chance, while religious belief, especially strong religious belief that wants political acknowledgement, is an aberration caused by imperial domination? Or is secularization, in the West and elsewhere, in fact a rather complicated and protracted historical process, as a return to religious roots in many parts of the world would suggest? Indeed, because of the close historical alignment of Christian tradition and the modernization processes that led to social rationalization and nation-state bureaucracies, modern Western imperialism itself would seem to promote simultaneously, and paradoxically, retrenchment in indigenous traditions as cultural defense, conversion to a new faith, and a potentially deracinating secularization.

Gauri Viswanathan's discussions of religious conversion in contrapuntal terms are designed to address this sort of problem. One of the consequences of the introduction of Evangelical missionaries into India, against which British Orientalists had unsuccessfully argued, was the use of education to wean Indians away from dogmatic Hindu belief and toward Christianity. But this process—based, as Macaulay's *Minute* had recommended, on the teaching of English literature—was inseparable in the event from the production of a new and secular civil society on a British model, in which there was "a relocation of cultural value from belief and dogma to language, experience and history" (Viswanathan, *Masks* 117; see also van der Veer and Lehmann 28). In Viswanathan's subsequent account, though missionaries may have regarded the conversion of Hindus to Christianity as also entailing a conversion of native subjectivities to "English concepts of 'nation,' 'community,' 'rights' and 'equality,'" the actual effect could be "associated with a deconstructive activity central to modernity itself" (Viswanathan, *Outside* 76). That is, because of the ambivalence of British colonial law, which treated religion, in secular fashion, more as an administrative category of civil society than as a publicly meaningful system of belief, and was hence willing to consider Hindu converts to Christianity as "legally" Hindu whenever it seemed appropriate (at times to the convert's material benefit), Christian conversion in Viswanathan's view was less about dissolving an individual's native religious affiliations and creating an allegiance to the community of the governing class than it was "designed to induce...a permanent dislocation and exile from a sense of community at large" (88).

In reading the imperial history of religious conversion contrapuntally, Viswanathan instead wants to insist upon a deeper and more authentic significance to the act of religious conversion, not as an effect of mere ideology, but as part of a lived tradition that can be a form of liberating dissent to the deracinating and often intolerant (when linked with nationalism) effects of Western secularization. It is a resistance to the arbitrary authority of the civil state she also finds, albeit in equivocal terms, in John Henry Newman's conversion to the dissenting position of Roman Catholicism in Victorian England. At the least, this puts an interesting new wrinkle in Said's idea of contrapuntal reading as the critical path to a secular and enlightened transcendence of religion and absolutism alike. In its broadest sense, however, and despite Viswanathan's attempt to put some distance between herself and more thoroughgoing critics of the Western-style secular state such as Ashis Nandy, this view ultimately wants to treat religious "belief as a form of knowledge" (Viswanathan, *Outside* 253; see also Nandy, "Politics"), that is, as effective, public truth—precisely what secularism undermines—while rejecting the more absolutist forms that would punish heresy and, as in the case of Salman Rushdie, blasphemy. As Nandy has put it, secularism is viable primarily for the "culturally dispossessed and the politically rootless," and it often paradoxically creates a fundamentalist ideological reaction; for those not thus deracinated, a different path is more compelling: "the opposite of religious and ethnic intolerance is not secularism but religious and ethnic tolerance. Secularism is merely one way of ensuring that tolerance" (Nandy, *Romance* 77).

In broader terms, Nandy has argued that the secular modernity of the West, with its ideology of progress, hardens distinctions between self and other, and between different religious faiths, precisely because the state's need to "manage the public realm" entails not only the separation and relatively autonomous functioning of the different spheres of civil society—the economic, legal, cultural, religious, and so forth—but also the debilitation of religion, which "is an open or potential threat to any modern polity" (Nandy, "Politics" 74). By contrast, he claims, "traditional" Indian "ways of life" did not separate religion from politics, or self from other, and have, "over the centuries, developed internal principles of tolerance and these principles must have a play in contemporary politics" (84). Nandy's perspective is trenchant, as far as it goes. But what it neglects is the degree to which premodern, largely dynastic polities were "political" in a very different sense than are modern ones. It is precisely the need to accommodate a large, more or less equally enfranchised, individuated, and no longer passive citizenry, with their powerful desires and institutions, that over time makes the traditional and more casual accommodation between religion and politics problematic in modernity.

In effect, if political modernity seems to entail secularization, it may be because so much more is at stake for the modern citizen, whose political role is far more active and self-determining, and who as a result sees the political state as an important facilitator of or hindrance to individual and collective happiness. Nandy argues against "India's Westernized intellectuals" and their more rigorous demand for a secular public sphere by calling for a kind of pluralism that derives from Victorian England, where, he claims, secular*ism* first emerged as a doctrine with George Holyoake and religion still overtly permeated political life (Nandy, "Politics" 74). But Victorian England's dominant political regime, which could hardly be called multiconfessional in reality, fostered political pluralism only by virtue of its secularizing tendencies—we need only imagine the nature of Disraeli's political career had he not been as fully assimilated and in fact baptized into Christian society—and the same would likely be true of Nandy's version of a religiously infused but tolerant Indian state, based as it is on Gandhi's understanding of traditional Hinduism. It thus remains unclear how Nandy's preferred idea of a culturally rich and nonsecular religious tolerance, with a dynamic interfaith dialogue, can exist in modern, democratic, self-fashioning societies without some measure of state and administrative secularization.

In its own way, Viswanathan's contrapuntal reading of secular and religious cultures winds up doing something similar: it persuasively emphasizes the role of religions, of various sorts and in fluid relationships to one another, in creating viable public culture and politics, but it implicitly falls back on the notion of a secular pluralistic civil society to undermine all absolutist claims and to guarantee the possibility of critical dissent from the religious hegemony of the majority. "The pressing problem," she not unexpectedly writes, "is how modern secularism can accommodate and absorb the reality of religion and the power of religious conviction experienced by believers, while at the same time protect the rights of those who believe differently" (Viswanathan, *Outside* 173). But what does it finally mean for secularism to "absorb the reality of religion"? On the one hand, this formula seems perfectly congruent with American-style religious pluralism, especially as promoted by George W. Bush, as opposed to the more rigorous republican secularism of the French state. But it also invites an even greater and potentially riskier public role for religious values and meaning in civic life than current American sensibilities, already quite religious, might be willing to allow. On the other hand, it is precisely the secular and pluralistic idea of civil society, even in America, and especially in the law, that finds the reality and public role of religious *knowledge* difficult to accommodate, and that moreover is so often seen by religious sociology as a function of the particular path of secularization itself in the West.

The sense of permanent dislocation or deracination that such secularization may produce has of course often been decried (as Alasdair MacIntyre has done in his work) or celebrated (as Nietzsche has done) as consequences of the Christian tradition, even *within* that tradition. Yet if a political structure—a civil society—that protects "those who believe differently" is really to be sustained in a rigorous way in modernity, then some turn toward privately held religious beliefs, and away from religion as the shared public and political "knowledge" that both Nandy and Viswanathan want us to recognize, may be the inevitable result.

Contrapuntal reading, at least as I understand Said's use of the term, is thus not a method particularly well suited to the fruitful synthesis of secular humanist traditions and still-powerful religious ones. This is precisely where it will hesitate, for the moral vision behind the impulse to contrapuntal thought and secular criticism depends on *some* version of pluralism, on the ultimately compatible nature of a wide array of moral, religious, and cultural affiliations, a pluralism underwritten in the West by the often unsatisfying moral mix of toleration and individual rights preached by secular humanism. It is a mix that for Said made possible a dismantling of Western imperialism's chauvinism by holding it up to the measure of its own Enlightenment promise, though it is just this mix that Stanley Fish has quite trenchantly criticized as underwriting "liberal complacency" (see Fish 45).

It may not be true that *only* the Christian tradition, as both Bernard Lewis on the Right and Jürgen Habermas on the Left have suggested, can produce the secular perspective that allows this sort of tolerance, worldliness, and, as John Rawls puts it, noncomprehensive or "overlapping" political consensus, in which the idea of justice "remains independent of comprehensive religious, philosophical, and moral doctrines" (see Rawls 144). (Rawls's "overlapping consensus" indeed bears a certain vague resemblance to Wittgenstein's claim that "rational" and "religious" discourses should not be considered simply "incommensurable"—the one cognitive, the other not—but rather that such different ways of referring still have "overlapping" similarities; see Putnam 73; Wittgenstein 53–72.) But it surely is true that the process of secularization that takes us from Luther to Diderot is a crucial feature of the modern history of the West, and that Said's ideal of secular criticism is one of its signal manifestations. In this sense, a notion such as secular criticism cannot be employed in any depth without at the same time invoking a parallel set of problems about the process of secularization that produced it, a process that is itself asymmetrical—and not only as a result of imperialism, as we move from one culture to the next—and that is still in many cases at the very heart of what we mean when we talk about "discrepant" cultural experiences. In the end, secular criticism at some level entails talking about the specific processes of secularization that have both enabled it and mark its limitations.

Interestingly, Said may have confronted the problem of Western secularization itself most directly in one of the last things he wrote—his introduction to the fiftieth-anniversary edition of Erich Auerbach's *Mimesis*. To be sure, Said's underlying perspective returns us to the heroic individualism that appears throughout his work. "Thus it all unmistakably comes down to a personal effort," he writes of Auerbach. It is a judgment that refers most immediately to Auerbach's powers of sympathetic cultural synthesis, based on experience rather than interpretive systems; but it just as surely refers back to Auerbach's heroic ability, as a German Jew writing in Islamic Istanbul, to identify imaginatively with the history of Christian European culture. And yet, Said is more explicit here than in earlier work about the degree to which the long and tortuous process of secularization is a (perhaps *the*) central issue for Western culture, one that profoundly shapes Auerbach's subject matter and methods alike. Thus, Auerbach's sympathetic and nonsystematic humanism is itself the final product of the long development of such humanism in the West, one that begins in what Auerbach discerns as the mixture of styles and the imaginative sympathy for the lower social orders in the Gospel of St. Mark (something not found in Petronius or Tacitus), which is in turn rooted in the doctrine of Christ's human incarnation in the humblest of circumstances.

But the full measure of what humanist secularization came to mean for Auerbach—and for Said too, I think—emerges with Dante. "Auerbach's choice of Dante for advancing the radically humanistic thesis carefully works though the great poet's Catholic ontology as a phase transcended by the Christian epic's realism, which is shown to be 'ontogenetic,' that is, 'we are given to see, in the realm of timeless being, the history of man's inner life and unfolding'" (Auerbach xxvi; quotation of Auerbach 202). Dante draws technically from the forceful presentation of the human figure in pre-Christian classical literature. Yet it is precisely the secularization of Christian doctrine as human history in Dante that propels Auerbach's narrative, right up to his account of the kinship between his own methods and the culturally fragmented, yet also more deeply human, techniques of literary modernists such as Proust, Joyce, and Woolf. It would not be too much to say, I think, that Said's account of Auerbach's work elaborates it as the effect of the cultural secularization Auerbach himself did so much to describe, and that this account is implicitly also a description of Said's intimate and agonistic relationship to his own secularized Christian culture.

I want to contrast Said's influential perspective very briefly with an opposed position more sympathetic to the continuing significance of religion, though one equally critical of Western imperialism, found in the work of Talal Asad. An anthropologist, Asad is interested primarily in how the secular and the religious codetermine one another. For him, the secularization thesis, and by implication Said's idea of "secular criticism," are unsustainable, primarily because the body of representations fostered by religion can never in practice be confined to the delimited space accorded them by modern nation-state constitutions, with their clear separation of church and state. "If the secularization thesis no longer carries the conviction it once did, this is because the categories of 'politics' and 'religion' turn out to implicate each other more profoundly than we thought, a discovery that has accompanied our growing understanding of the power of the modern nation-state" (Asad, *Formations* 200). This does not mean that Asad wants to portray modern secular political structures simply as reformulations of religious ones, as had Karl Löwith and Carl Schmitt, but rather that he wants to see multiple traditions of religious beliefs and secular responses in constant relation to one another. "The secular, I argue, is neither continuous with the religious that supposedly preceded it (that is, it is not the latest phase of a sacred origin) nor a simple break from it (that is, it is not the opposite, an essence that excludes the sacred). I take the secular to be a concept that brings together certain behaviors, knowledges, and sensibilities in modern life" (25).

The disruption of any straightforward narrative of secularization also means that religion is inevitably forced into a militantly political role in an effort to maintain itself against the monopolization of power by the secular state. "Islamism's preoccupation with state power," Asad writes, in terms that to some extent recall the critique of Nandy, "is the result not of its commitment to nationalist ideas but of the modern nation-state's enforced claim to constitute legitimate social identities and arenas. No movement that aspires to more than mere belief or inconsequential talk in public can remain indifferent to state power in a secular world" (200). In Asad's larger terms, the consequence of the tolerance toward competing religious traditions displayed by Western civil society is the reduction of religion to "mere belief" and "inconsequential talk." It is similar to what Viswanathan, who follows Asad's lead in many ways, means when she writes that "in a disestablished society where 'truth' is no longer a function of belief but of what is amenable to codification, proof, and administration, the potential of private judgment to act upon a world enveloped and defined by public doctrine is minimized, even marginalized" (Viswanathan, *Outside* 47). For Asad, Islam is properly political, though not a function or champion of nationalism, when it finds itself increasingly contested by the controlling political structures of a secular state apparatus in which only "mere belief" can be tolerated. Like Christian fundamentalism in America, Islam must assume a public, political role if it is to be taken seriously in a civil society defined and regulated by a secular state.

If we accept Asad's reasoning completely, the idea of the universal character of human rights, so central to a secular humanist like Said and, not incidentally, for many others one of the great achievements of post-Holocaust political thought, is defined as no more than a projection of secularized Christian nation-states (for Said on human rights, see Said, *Reflections* 411–30; see also Mailloux 1592–93). That is, particular religious beliefs have supplied substantive norms that are then elaborated, self-interestedly, as "universal." It is most clearly in this sense that modern "secularism" for Asad must be considered an ideology, no less than the religious belief it contests. But this point of view also raises interesting dilemmas. Asad notes that Western intellectuals decry female genital mutilation in Africa (practiced both within and outside Islamic areas) as a violation of human rights, though no one says anything about what Asad calls "the custom of male genital mutilation"—that is, circumcision—in the Judeo-Christian West (Asad, *Formations* 148–49). The outrage in the West over female genital mutilation rests for him primarily on a culturally specific belief, which he traces to Christianity's views about bodily integrity and suffering, that individuals have a right to sexual pleasure as part of their human-rights inheritance, as Martha Nussbaum has argued, invoking Rawls's notion of "overlapping consensus" (see Nussbaum 78). For Asad, the perspective expressed in the Universal Declaration of Human Rights is in fact a secular emanation of Christian culture, and the idea of some cosmopolitan transcendence of specificity is a too-convenient political fiction.

On the one hand, it is easy to sympathize with Asad's view of the shortcomings of the Christian West's application of "human rights"—a view substantially shared by Said. Asad is surely correct to note, for example, that the Muslim Malcolm X's secular framing of racial oppression in the United States as a human-rights violation, one worthy of international intervention, met only with scorn among America's political elite, while Martin Luther King's framing of the issue in terms of prophetic Christian belief could be recognized in an American context of civil rights and eventually gained widespread support. He is also right to call our attention to the need for an "anthropology of secularism," by which he means a critique of the enabling myths, the disavowed violence, and the redemptive, universalizing attitude toward the rest of the world underwriting the idea of secular liberalism. But in the end Asad must implicitly accept some of the most unyielding and reductive accounts of the difference between a secularized West and a religious non-West, despite his claim to keep these boundaries fluid.

In his earlier *Genealogies of Religion,* Asad seems loosely to accept the validity of Lévi-Strauss's opposition between "cold" and "hot" cultures as a way of comparing religiously traditional societies in many parts of the Islamic world, in which change is supposedly never desired, to more secular Western societies that in his view find themselves coercively harnessed to the endless and compulsive pursuit of growth and transformation. Such societies are divergent and opposed; they embody the idea of "discrepant experience" to a perhaps unbridgeable degree. But this means that Asad begins to approach, albeit in a relativistic fashion, the perspective of figures like Huntington and Lewis in the West, and Nandy in India, for whom there really are large-scale, essential differences of civilization separating the Christian West from the nations composing the Islamic world, differences mainly of religious heritage that seem to allow neither overlapping consensus nor, perhaps, codevelopment. Such differences cannot be evaluated from, or superseded by, the supposedly neutral Archimedean position of secular humanism. Whatever one may think of Asad's particular claims—I find his reasoning about female "circumcision" to be simplistic in the extreme, for example—it is clear that comparing religious traditions as forms of strong belief desiring political recognition, rather than mere tolerance, to the secularized ethical and political cultures dominant in Western nation-states does not yield easily to what Said means by "contrapuntal" thought.

Between Asad's civilizational and often polarizing approach to what secularization represents and Said's tendency to characterize this process as something increasingly less significant for the study of global culture from the eighteenth century onward, cultural criticism has so far found little room to maneuver. The most important imperative today may be a perspective that remains discomfited both by Said's heroic secularism and by Asad's equivocating relativism, which tends at times to refuse the philosophical and political possibilities of secular consensus altogether. This would mean embracing secular criticism's potential autonomy and sympathy, wielded by humanists such as Said who were shaped by the West's Enlightenment ideals, while acknowledging Asad's claims about the continuing and globally asymmetric historical interpenetration of religious and secular thought. (In *Provincializing Europe,* Dipesh Chakrabarty attempts to accomplish such a synthesis, albeit with mixed results that I shall address in my conclusion; see Chakrabarty.) The secular can perhaps be thought of simultaneously as a strategically occupied critical standpoint and as the result of uneven cultural developments that are in fact far from—and perhaps can never be—complete, even in highly developed Western nations.

Marcel Gauchet points up what is at stake for cultural criticism if it takes seriously the problem of secularization as a continuing theoretical issue.

> The diametrically opposed standpoints of aloofness and passion, involvement and uninvolvement, hostility and partisanship conspire to deny the historical role of the religious. . . . It is not enough to dispute the validity of the apologists' reconstruction dictated by faith, which tries to salvage the transhistorical perpetuity of *homo religiosus,* by relativizing its historical connections. We must also free ourselves from the atheist's illusion that religion may tell us something about the underlying psychology of the human race or about the workings of the savage mind, but tells us very little about the nature of the social bond and the real driving force behind history. The picture created by this groundless assumption is no less distorted than the first. It may even more effectively conceal what a society structured by religion is, and what religion itself is. (Gauchet 5–6)

I believe that in an increasingly globalized world no religion anywhere can remain permanently untouched by the corrosive yet also liberating forces of secularization that we associate with the term Enlightenment. At the same time, I think religion continues to be too basic and ubiquitous a phenomenon to be relegated to a pre-Enlightenment world, or to the unfortunate effects of political domination, and in this sense widely different varieties and degrees of secularization may be the expected effects of an increasingly global economy and culture.

Habermas's Dilemma

One of the central problems of Western secularization arises in the tension between what we might call the epistemological imperative of secular criticism and the recognition of the morally generative force of religious belief itself. This tension can be neatly illustrated by turning to a few passages from the work of Jürgen Habermas. In the immediate aftermath of the collapse of the Soviet Union and, with it, the cold war, the influential German social philosopher published an essay reflecting upon the future of European integration. The argument of the essay distinguishes between (a) the universalistic potential of political culture, embodied in civil rights and democratic self-determination, in short, the whole range of republican notions of citizenship associated with the French Revolution, and (b) what Habermas calls the "ethical-cultural form of life as a whole," which can be roughly translated by the terser idiom of American social thought as "ethnicity." Habermas's point is that ethnicity cannot be allowed to restrict the universal ideals behind the republican notion of citizenship.

The tension Habermas outlines between the cultural solidarity provided by ethnicity and the political rights of citizens would have been, in 1992, familiar enough to Americans prepared by two decades of debate about multiculturalism, as would his pluralist conclusion that "only within the constitutional framework of a democratic legal system can different ways of life coexist equally. These must, however, overlap within a common political culture, which again implies an impulse to open these ways of life to others" (Habermas, "Citizenship" 17). To Europeans, however, and especially to West Germans suddenly facing both the difficulties caused by a large and mostly Islamic-Turkish guest-worker population and by the burdens imposed by reunification with their impoverished and suspicious East German compatriots, Habermas's critique of cultural chauvinism and his support for liberal immigration policies had significant implications. Moreover, as best demonstrated by the French president Jacques Chirac's calls for legislation banning the wearing of religious symbols in French state schools, including large crosses, yarmulkes, and headscarves on Islamic women, what would pass for pluralism in the European context might yet be a long way from religious pluralism in America.

Habermas's version of pluralism—that is, his belief that a single political culture of republican democracy can accommodate within it "different ways of life," with different "ethical-cultural" foundations—is not detailed enough for us to tell whether it is closer to the French or the American understanding of the term. But it draws directly, if implicitly, on the later work of John Rawls, in that what Habermas hopes for is what Rawls calls an "overlapping consensus" between different ethical-cultural perspectives, each of which would contain what Rawls calls "comprehensive" moral doctrines, and the purely political culture that takes shape formally in the space of the *civitas* alone. Though Habermas surely intends that religion be understood as one of the elements contained in the phrase "ethical-cultural life as a whole," the specific issue of "religion" does not appear at all in his essay. More important, Habermas's account of the historical evolution of the nation-state is distinctly secular in this 1992 essay, as indeed would be most convenient in an explanation of the nation-state's transcultural, or purely political, function at the present time.

In the sixteenth century, kingdoms gave birth to those territorial states—such as England, France, Portugal, Spain, and Sweden—which were later on, in the course of democratization in line with the French example, gradually transformed into *nation states*. This state formation secured the overall conditions under which capitalism was then able to develop worldwide. The nation state provided both the infrastructure for rational administration and the legal frame for free individual and collective action.

> Moreover, and it is this which shall interest us here, the nation state laid the foundations for cultural and ethnic homogeneity on the basis of which it then proved possible to push ahead with the democratization of government since the late eighteenth century, although this was achieved at the cost of excluding ethnic minorities. The nation state and democracy are twins born out of the French Revolution. From a cultural point of view, both have been growing in the shadow of *nationalism*. (Habermas, "Citizenship" 2)

The logic of the passage is subtle and dialectical, but significant: it is the new nation-state, born of old kingdoms and empires, and consolidated by the French Revolution, that both allows at first for the production of a certain ethnic homogeneity via discrimination against minorities, and that in turn subsequently allows for the progress of democratization and cultural pluralism that Habermas argues will be central to the new Europe. That is, the nation-state may have been an instrument of cultural (including, presumably, religious) solidarity and exclusivity, but the link between the two is arbitrary, and in any case would be dismantled by the progress of democracy.

Habermas's secular account of the evolution of democratic governance in the nation-state is congruent with how he has responded elsewhere to ambiguities in Weber's approach to "rational authority," where political domination preserves itself not only by coercion and by appeal to the material, emotional, or ideal interests of the dominated, but also by cultivating belief in the *legitimacy* of its authority. Habermas approaches the question of legitimacy by referring to the evolution of a universal moral consciousness, based on the presupposition

> that the values and norms in accordance with which motives are formed have an immanent relation to truth [*Wahrheitsbezug*]. Viewed ontogenetically, this means that motivational development, in Piaget's sense, is tied to a cognitively relevant development of moral consciousness, the stages of which can be reconstructed logically, that is, by concepts of a systematically ordered sequence of norm systems and behavioral controls. To the highest stage of moral consciousness there corresponds a universal morality, which can be traced back to fundamental norms of rational speech. (Habermas, *Legitimation* 95)

While Habermas is here more interested in the systematic than the empirical superiority of this developmental presupposition, it is as a whole nevertheless the cornerstone of his long opposition to Niklas Luhmann's "systems theory" approach to the legitimacy of social authority.

Luhmann has argued that once law in modern societies is "positivized"— which is to say, once law is respected as legitimate based purely on the procedural legality of its making, "because it is made by responsible decision in accordance with definite rules"—then "arbitrariness becomes an institution" as far as the legitimacy of authority is concerned (quoted in Habermas, *Legitimation* 98; see Luhmann, "Soziologie" 167). Oddly, like Carl Schmitt, though without Schmitt's fear of pure legalism and emphasis on sovereignty as extralegal exception, Luhmann reduces the question of norms and law to that of a decision legitimated by nothing more than other decisions: "The positivization of law means that legitimate legal validity [*Rechtsgeltung*] can be obtained for any given contents, and that this is accomplished through a decision which confers validity upon the law and which can take the validity from it. Positive law is valid by virtue of decisions" (quoted in Habermas, *Legitimation* 98; see also Luhmann, "Positives" 180). While formal rules may reflect a necessarily latent set of norms that stabilize expectations, no further justification can be found for validating those norms beyond the fact of belief in them. In effect, such norms must remain implicit: explicit criticism of them would only be destructive in the end, as is the belief that one *could* subject them to criticism if needed, because all validity claims for deeper norms are "functionally necessary deceptions [*Täuschungen*]. The deception may not, however, be exposed if the belief in legality is not to be shaken" (Habermas, *Legitimation* 99).

One might say that it has been Habermas's lifelong project to refute this line of reasoning, this decisionist theory of social solidarity, norms, and legitimacy that for Schmitt had formed the basis of modern political theology. Habermas's longer answer is that although system integration takes on a life and direction (or entelechy) of its own in highly administered, bureaucratic capitalist states, social integration nevertheless requires the elaboration of a neo-Kantian notion of communicative ethics, in which deeper norms can in fact be validated as true by reference to certain essential components and limits of rational speech, and to the sort of explicit, consensus-driven, and openly criticized norms embodied in bourgeois constitutions (see Habermas, "Citizenship" 8). What is important is that this sort of answer is based on the presumption of a developmental model of universal moral consciousness, even as it rejects as untenable either the return to a tradition of natural law or right (as proposed in the work of the influential conservative philosopher Leo Strauss) or to the pure value-rationality of religious belief. Habermas's secular, pluralistic nation-state, which can presumably accommodate very different "ethical-cultural" ways of life within its borders, would nevertheless seem to be based on a natural, and in the end fairly coherent, evolution of moral consciousness toward universally valid norms.

In a recent interview with Habermas prepared for inclusion in a collection of some of his writings touching on religion, an interview that clearly responds to the resurgence of broader scholarly interest in religious sectarianism in the decade that has elapsed since his essay on "Citizenship and National Identity" was published, his approach toward the rise of the nation-state is rather different. In this conversation, published in 2002, Habermas gives religion an historical centrality it did not possess earlier.

In the West, Christianity not only fulfilled the cognitive initial conditions for modern *structures* of consciousness; it also demanded a range of *motivations* that were the great theme of the economic and ethical research of Max Weber. For the normative self-understanding of modernity, Christianity has functioned as more than just a precursor or a catalyst. Universalistic egalitarianism, from which sprang the ideals of freedom and a collective life in solidarity, the autonomous conduct of life and emancipation, the individual morality of conscience, human rights and democracy, is the direct legacy of the Judaic ethic of justice and the Christian ethic of love. This legacy, substantially unchanged, has been the object of continual critical reappropriation and reinterpretation. Up to this very day there is no alternative to it. And in light of the current challenges of a postnational constellation, we must draw sustenance now, as in the past, from this substance. Everything else is idle postmodern talk. (Habermas, *Religion* 148–49)

It would not be an exaggeration to say that *this* account of religion's role in the formation of Western political culture, which penetrates to the moral and epistemological roots—the "*structures* of consciousness" and the "substance"—of a Judeo-Christian legacy underlying the rise of republican democratic citizenship and its putatively universal claims to legitimacy, opens up rather new sorts of questions. (Habermas's interview, originally in German, was translated for inclusion in this English-language volume only. Though no German text has been published, his terminology here echoes that in previously translated essays.) If, as Habermas claims, the Judaic ethic of justice and the Christian ethic of love really do constitute the indispensable legacy of any secular political culture that would tolerate and contain religious difference, then we face an interesting problem.

The universal potential of this republican *political* culture now appears to derive and draw sustenance from a distinct and actually quite limited *religious* culture. We are suddenly taken back to the Gordian knot Marx tried to cut in his much-debated essay, "On the Jewish Question," which is largely a response to Bruno Bauer's claim that no Christian state—Prussia was the example in question—would be able to sustain the political emancipation of the Jews. Interestingly, despite the salient examples of the French Revolution and the United States' Bill of Rights, both of which granted Jews equal civil rights with Christians, neither Bauer nor Marx had much faith in religious or "ethical-cultural" pluralism, as we understand it in America today. Bauer was convinced that only the complete renunciation of religion by a nation's citizens would allow for true equality of rights (the position adopted, though certainly not without contradiction, by current antipluralist French republicanism), while Marx famously argued that religion, being a defective product of defective social conditions, would in fact disappear of its own accord once one abolished the more basic inequalities of private property that were left intact (as, for example, they had been in the United States) by purely political emancipation. The ambiguity in Habermas about the particular religious foundations of a supposedly universal political culture reminds us that neither the French Revolution and the American Bill of Rights nor Bauer and Marx finally solved the dilemmas posed by pluralism. Indeed, I would suggest that Habermas's position, suspended as it is between a secular, or "enlightened," history of Western political life and a recognition of the religious legacy underwriting that history, is exemplary for Western intellectuals today, who find themselves increasingly caught between the universal claims of secular political ideals and the undeniable, perhaps foundational, and in any case ambiguous role of a particular religious heritage behind those claims.

Habermas has long used phrases like "semantic potentials" and "semantic energies" to describe those fragments of utopian idealism left behind by the Judeo-Christian tradition that he feels must not be forgotten in contemporary secular political life (see, for example, his essay "Walter Benjamin: Consciousness-Raising or Rescuing Critique," discussed in chapter 2). As a summary of his views on religion as a "semantic" resource, he is fond of citing a passage that appears in his *Nachmetaphysiches Denken:* "As long as religious language bears with itself inspiring, indeed, unrelinquishable semantic contents which elude (for the moment?) the expressive power of a philosophical language and still await translation into a discourse that gives reasons for its positions, philosophy, even in its postmetaphysical form, will neither be able to replace nor to repress religion" (Habermas, *Nachmetaphysiches* 60). The passage quoted above from his recent interview perhaps gives us a somewhat broader sense of what he means, and it points as well to the underlying importance of Max Weber's religious sociology.

For Weber, the essential question concerned the historical influence of world religions upon "economic mentalities"—"*structures* of consciousness" and economic "motivations," in Habermas's terms—and, more particularly, the degree to which specific religious ethics fostered or hindered the rationalization of economic life typical of capitalism (see Giddens 169). Weber did not claim that there was any simple correspondence between religious and economic ethics, acknowledging that capitalism was indeed compatible with a range of religious beliefs. He saw history as the complex result of ideological and material resources, and was no more willing to subscribe to a religious determinism than to an economic or Marxian one. The important context for understanding Weber's thinking is history: the question for him is not simply "what is the logical link between religion and economics or politics?" as if one could produce or be sustained by the other, but always, "what, in the event, was the logic of the historical link?" This latter is a question entailing the nonteleological idea that things might always have been otherwise. Indeed, Weber's thesis about Protestantism's role in the rise of capitalism rests squarely on the idea that Protestant reformers, from Luther and Calvin to Zinzendorf and Wesley, were inspired by religious—not ethical—ideals, so that "the cultural consequences of the Reformation [including the ethical, economic, and social alterations that are Weber's main object of study] were to a great extent, perhaps in the particular aspects with which we are dealing predominantly, unforeseen and even unwished for results of the labours of the reformers" (Weber, *Protestant* 48). It is also important to recognize that, at least in the hands of later theorists of secularization such as Berger, Weber's work itself often wound up being more unambiguously accepting of capitalist modernity than his more cynical (or tragic) view of an increasingly bureaucratized Europe would imply. Nevertheless, there are points in the Weberian perspective that for our purposes remain especially problematic.

Given his remarkable later analyses of world religions, for example, Weber's work still implies that there was something specific about the rationalization achieved and stimulated at the time of the Protestant Reformation—and hence by means of an evolving Christian tradition—that made it especially suited to the forms of economic and political development pursued by Europe. Moreover, he appeared to claim—with the rhetorical finesse of the opening line of the author's preface to his *Protestant Ethic*—that such rationalization was universal in its significance: "A product of modern European civilization, studying any problem of universal history, is bound to ask himself to what combination of circumstances the fact should be attributed that in Western civilization, and in Western civilization only, cultural phenomena have appeared which (as we like to think) lie in a line of development having *universal* significance and value" (Weber xxviii). The conditional nature of this sentence is somewhat belied by the assurance with which Weber makes a case for this sentiment in the rest of the preface, but the parenthetical "(as we like to think)" signals that, even for Weber, all such claims in the end remained shaped by the underlying demands of political self-interest. Hence, pinning down specifically what sorts of cultural particulars might possess "*universal* significance" has always been controversial.

The recent attention to religion from a global and comparative perspective has intensified the controversy, since it is precisely the supposedly quite different capacity of other religious traditions, such as Islam, to rationalize and secularize that is often at issue when a "clash of civilizations" is invoked; this has been true for figures such as Lewis and Huntington, as well as Nandy and to some extent Asad. Because for Weber the historical event of religious rationalization, driven by prophetic reforms within Christianity, contributed to the creation of a fully fledged capitalist psychology, however irrational it may have become, and hence enabled the administrative modernity of the Western nation-state, secularization and modernization appeared to be inextricably linked, yielding what has now become a much-disputed "secularization thesis." Although the secularization thesis has taken somewhat different forms in the Anglo-American and European literature, its yoking together of modernization and secularization (and along with them, nationalism), as if one necessarily implied the other, has once again become an issue, if only because secularization and modernization on a global scale may also imply Westernization, even if the process, as it is playing out in India, Indonesia, Egypt or Turkey, seems to be occurring in very different ways. That is, the vaguely Weberian notion that modernity depends upon increasingly rationalized religious belief is for many less compelling at the beginning of the twenty-first century, when such a process is now routinely associated with the global cultural domination of an American and European consciousness, than it was at the dawn of the twentieth.

The contemporary resurgence of interest in the global interaction of religion, economics, and politics forces us to confront these issues anew. In an insightful essay, for example, Austin Harrington surveys this ground from another angle, that of Ernst Troeltsch's concept of Europe, and demonstrates just how far Weber, Troeltsch, earlier figures such as Georg Jellinek, and later followers such as Hans Joas try to emphasize the "contexts of religious value formation" in the creation of modern secular notions of human rights—contexts that go beyond Kantian formalism—without reducing such notions to their religious roots. Harrington's sense that such writers claim "universal validity on behalf of western political principles while at the same time acknowledging the historical specificity of these principles" captures perfectly for me the dilemma of the Western intellectual in the era of an increasingly global world order (Harrington 492).

The difficulties of the Weberian view of religion and secularization leave us with basic problems in understanding the significance of what Habermas calls the legacy of Judaic and Christian ethics for modern secular culture. When Habermas refers to the idea that modernity's "cognitive initial conditions" are to be located in Christianity, and when he traces the "substance" of universal equality, individual conscience and moral autonomy, democracy, and human rights to Judaic and Christian traditions specifically, we have a right to wonder whether he is in fact implying that this ethical "substance" is actually rooted in a natural and essential human condition—that is, in human nature, however broadly conceived, and in ideas of natural law and right regulating that nature. In this construction of Habermas's meaning, which is at least plausible given his embrace of the secular, the Judaic and Christian legacies are significant not because of some "revelation," either scriptural or theosophic, of truth and justice that was vouchsafed to them alone, and which Habermas has explicitly refused, but because they happened to have elaborated historically contingent, yet coherent and compelling, versions of some more innate or natural human truth, which has in some sense enabled secular modernization (as Weber's account has it), but which would be theoretically available to all ethico-religious traditions under the right circumstances.

But to put things in this fashion suggests that Habermas's statements on the unique significance of the Judeo-Christian legacy depend somewhat cryptically on notions of natural right and law that have themselves depended in his work on nothing more than the power of a putatively contingent and deliberative ethics of communication. Habermas elsewhere has distinguished between "classical [or Aristotelian] Natural Law," where "the norms of moral and just action are equally oriented in their content toward the good—and that means the virtuous—life of the citizens," and "the formal law of the modern age," which "is divested of the catalogues of duties in the material order of life, whether of a city or of a social class. Instead, it allows a neutral space of personal choice, in which every citizen, as a private person can egoistically follow goals of maximizing his own needs" (Habermas, *Theory* 84). Hence modern invocations of natural law (seen in both the American and French Revolutions), which eventually require its reduction to positive statutes, "cannot be legitimately preceded by anything but the autonomy of isolated and equal individuals and their insight into the rational interdependence of Natural Law norms" (*Theory* 85). It may be, then, that Habermas's references to the "structures of consciousness" endowed by a Judeo-Christian tradition are necessary supplements to, or replacements for, the decidedly compromised status of classical natural law theory in his work.

For example, it is clear from other remarks Habermas makes in his interview that quite specific elements of the Christian legacy represent for him "an entirely new perspective," one that is central to his sense of a democratic modernity: the idea of an Incarnate God who is both "Creator and Redeemer," through which a "finite spirit acquired a standpoint that utterly transcends the this-worldly" (*Religion* 148); the dialogism of Aquinas (152); and the Judeo-Christian roots of the "capacity for decentering one's own perspectives, self-reflection, and a self-critical distancing from one's own traditions" (154). Moreover, Habermas notes that his doctoral dissertation focused on the Gnostic/Kabbalist idea of God's capacity for self-limitation and withdrawal, or *tsimtsum* (in Jacob Böhme and Isaac Luria, in Schwabian Pietism, and in Schelling and von Baader), and that the Judeo-Christian myth of the fall is what for him opens up the space for the "*intersubjective constitution* of autonomy and the meaning of the *self-binding* of the will's arbitrary freedom to *unconditionally* valid norms" (160–61)—in short, the space that structures his larger ethics of communicative action.

The contradiction Habermas's interviewer, Eduardo Mendieta, finds on this point is from my perspective fairly significant: "in one tendency, religion is liquefied and sublated in discourse ethics and the theory of communicative rationality; in the other, religion is given the function of preserving and even nurturing a particular type of 'semantic' content that remains indispensable for ethics and morality, but also for philosophy in general" (162). Habermas denies the discrepancy by insisting, as he has in previous writings, on a vaguely Hegelian model in which secular philosophy has simply not yet been able to translate all the politically significant religious and presumably still Judeo-Christian concepts into a viable public and universal discourse. But does this process really have the shape of a univocal unfolding (or "translation") that Habermas implies? And if it is merely a "translation," does this mean that the end result is still dependent upon religious "structures of thought"? The question mark included in his recognition that religion possesses "unrelinquishable semantic contents which elude (for the moment?) the expressive power of a philosophical language" would suggest a confidence perhaps less certain than Hegel's.

I want to suggest that Habermas's lack of clarity about the precise meaning and function of the Western religious tradition in his social philosophy is representative of numerous dilemmas facing Western intellectuals generally today. What, ultimately, *is* the ethical basis for universal notions of "human rights," which are now routinely invoked by international courts but, as Asad notes, unequally applied? If they are specifically Judeo-Christian as Asad asserts, and Habermas in his interview at least implies, what should be their function in a global culture? If they belong to an older classical model of the moral substance and virtues, do they then vitiate the liberal idea of a Kantian modernity built on nothing but consensus? To what extent do *bienpensant* global initiatives rooted in Western political thought and its Judeo-Christian heritage, and dominated by Western power even via the United

Nations and nongovernmental organizations, inevitably promulgate both Enlightenment ideals of knowledge and selfhood and Judeo-Christian ethical-political traditions while weakening indigenous ones, as Nandy and Asad might argue? What collective political and military roles should powerful Western governments assume to enforce "human rights" (rather than civil ones) on their immediate borders in places such as Kosovo and Srebrenica? Does some responsibility for violent and not just humanitarian intervention remain the same, increase, or diminish in formerly colonized regions of decidedly different religious-ethical traditions, such as Rwanda, and how would one distinguish a restraint of neocolonial prerogatives from simple racial disregard? If internally generated political struggles generate a crisis of genocidal proportions—for example, in the Sudan, but one could cite many other places—is the military intervention of the nominally Christian Western powers a "humanitarian" duty or a sign of imperial hubris?

Moreover, should not Western nations, to be consistent, put their *own* courts and their adventures abroad under the jurisdiction of international tribunals, in effect recognizing that globally enforced human rights supersede the civil rights granted by particular nation-states as well as their legal and military sovereignty? If the ideas of Europe and, more consequentially, of the European Union are really as "semantically" dependent on the Judaic and Christian legacies as Habermas suggests, is it not at least plausible to oppose the expansion of the European Union to include developed Islamic nations such as Turkey, no matter how modernized (as has Giscard D'Estaing, author of a proposed EU constitution, and others in the French government), or even to oppose the accommodation of large Islamic populations and their distinct traditions in the "Christian" nations of Europe? Is the very idea of the European Union destined to come apart—as a recent referendum of French citizens would imply—in the face of such uncertainties?

Writing from the position that modernity in Europe represents the complete collapse of the rational tradition in morality he traces back to Aristotle, Alasdair MacIntyre has claimed that we have in fact no grounds on which to support the notion of universal human rights at all. For MacIntyre, this collapse begins with Luther's Reformation and with Hobbes (MacIntyre 164). What remains for modernity is only an endless dispute over "too many disparate and rival moral concepts," and "the moral resources of the culture allow us no way of settling the issue between them rationally." Hence, the great liberal ideal, from Kant to Rawls, of a moral and political world built out of consensus is a fiction: "It follows that our society cannot hope to achieve moral consensus" (252). To be rational, morality must be embedded in a living moral tradition that both structures and enables the debates over rival goods, and such traditions could only be maintained by a return to an Aristotelian sense of virtue (223). All this is lacking in the modern notion of universal human rights, now even more commonly evoked, he notes, than the eighteenth-century ideas of natural rights, which were largely no more than negative assertions of freedom from interference: "In the United Nations declaration on human rights of 1949 what has since become the normal UN practice of not giving good reasons for *any* assertion whatsoever is followed with great rigor" (69). In short, "natural or human rights then are fictions—just as is utility—but fictions with highly specific properties" (70). The only rational morality would be one that abjured the modern notion of "rights" altogether and returned to morality narrativized by tradition and supported by Aristotelian virtue.

Habermas has always been skeptical of such views: he is far too committed to the liberal, Kantian dream of a *sensus communis*—that is, of right as the product of self-legislation and the good as the possibility of a discursively built social consensus (however "overlapping," in the Rawlsian sense) underwritten by humanly constructed state constitutions—and far too concerned about the dogmatism that would result were MacIntyre's wish for a return to Aristotelian virtue, defined by substantive notions of excellence or *aretē*, human nature, "the good life," and so forth, actually fulfilled. This is not to say that Rawls and Habermas necessarily agree; indeed, each thinks the other is more metaphysical, or morally "comprehensive," than he ought to be (see Rawls 372–434). It is also not to deny that versions of what Habermas calls "classical Natural Law," of the type at least vaguely congruent with Aristotelian virtue rather than autonomous choice, have survived into the mainstream of modern liberal social philosophy in the work of Locke and the Scottish Enlightenment, in the American founding fathers, and in Matthew Arnold, Emile Durkheim, the Frankfurt School, and more recent figures such as Hans Georg Gadamer and Martha Nussbaum. Like a certain continuing regard for more or less fixed elements of mind in "nativist" accounts of cognition from Kant to Noam Chomsky, modern versions of "natural law," with or without Aristotle's sense of the virtues, have had a long and productive life even after Hobbes—intellectual history is not a punctual, all-or-nothing affair, despite what Foucault may have claimed, and operates on multiple levels (as I show in chapter 2 through Kracauer's work).

But MacIntyre is in general right to emphasize the tremendous weakening of the classical or Aristotelian account in modern social thought, where the sort of consensual and deliberative model that Habermas favors becomes far more central. Adam Smith, for example, includes in his *Theory of the Moral Sentiments* a discussion titled "Of the character of virtue"; but it is immediately clear that Smith's "virtues" take root from those bare, mechanical Hobbesian "appetites, of procuring pleasure and avoiding pain" (Smith 248). We need only recall how "sympathy" works for Smith: unlike spontaneous emotion, sympathy is very much the product of highly socialized individuals, which is itself a natural condition, and depends on a spectator's imaginative projection into the situation of the person being observed. Smith's "amiable and respectable virtues" are finally nothing more than the adjustment of the higher passions of the concerned agent with the cooler gaze of a less interested observer (29). In Aristotle, "virtue" was never so negotiable a commodity.

For Habermas, then, dogmatism would be the effect of what in MacIntyre is the only valid ground for coherent moral thought: Aristotle's sense of entelechy in human nature, a final cause or teleological purpose, which had been called by Aquinas "the cause of causes" (Aquinas 172). It is this Aristotelian scheme, whereby "untutored human nature" becomes "man-as-he-could-be-if-he-realized-his-*telos*" by following historically established moral precepts, a scheme still enshrined in medieval Catholic and even early Protestant theologies, that collapses with secular humanism. The Enlightenment's "scientific and philosophical rejection of Aristotelianism was to eliminate any notion of man-as-he-could-be-if-he-realized-his-*telos*," that is, his entelechy (MacIntyre 54). Modern science had to abandon all such Aristotelian notions in favor of blind mechanical causality, and it was perhaps only to be expected that the modern moral sciences would do so too in favor of purely instrumental, or what MacIntyre calls "managerial," modes of thought. Although many struggled to maintain a sense of human nature, what finally remains once moral discourse is severed from a notion of human *telos* is, as Schiller once put it, no more than the conflict of duties with inclinations (see Schiller 31). Hence, in MacIntyre's version of modernity, "moral judgments are linguistic survivals from the practices of classical theism which have lost the context provided by these practices," a situation that yields only morality as irrational "emotivism" (MacIntyre 60).

But if Habermas, like many other liberal social theorists today, finds any return to an Aristotelian sense of human *telos* and virtue unsustainable in the face of the sheer diversity of desires, goals, and worldviews enabled by modern democratic societies, and (perhaps more important) by the self-fashioning, acquisitive social mobility they often encourage, the vision of moral universals achieved by consensus, such as the idea of human rights, is, as MacIntyre notes, as strong as ever. The question remains, is MacIntyre right to conclude both that consensus is impossible, and that whatever fragmentary notions of morality remain are no more than "linguistic survivals" from a classical theism now dismantled by secularization? Habermas has never abandoned an implicit sense of historical development—his notion of modernity as an "unfinished project" depends on it—and it is this sense of history in the interview cited above that is inseparable from both the Judeo-Christian tradition and its secularization, and quite different from Aristotle's far more stable, and socially immobile, sense of human purpose. As Auerbach puts it:

> The Old Testament...presents universal history: it begins with the beginning of time, with the creation of the world, and will end with the Last Days, the fulfilling of the Covenant, with which the world will come to an end.... Thus while, on the one hand, the reality of the Old Testament presents itself as complete truth with a claim to sole authority, on the other hand that very claim forces it to a constant interpretive change in its own content; for millennia it undergoes an incessant and active development with the life of man in Europe. (*Mimesis* 16)

For Auerbach, and I think for Habermas as well, the Greek worldview offered no such vision of world history, one through which the divine came to be understood as incarnated in the humblest of social orders, which were thereby granted a kind of recognition unknown in Aristotelian virtue.

In short, it is this sense of teleology embedded in temporality, such as Hegel's secularization of what Auerbach calls universal history, that is still encoded in Habermas's belief that the Judeo-Christian "legacy, substantially unchanged, has been the object of continual critical reappropriation and reinterpretation" and that "up to this very day there is no alternative to it." But this also means that how we elaborate the character of this "reappropriation and reinterpretation"—which is to say, secularization—is important, and that if MacIntyre is right, there is in fact no coherent meaning to be derived from it at all. In the next section, the tension between two directly opposed positions on the question of secularization may shed some light on what is at stake in Habermas's claim of "no alternative" to the Judeo-Christian legacy. But the debate will also serve to illustrate both that there are no complete answers to MacIntyre's concerns, and no good way of avoiding the task that MacIntyre insists is impossible.

Löwith, Blumenberg, and Impossible Progress

The first account of secularization is that of Karl Löwith in *Meaning in History* (1949). Writing in the period immediately following World War II, with the horrors of the Holocaust and Stalinism fresh in his mind, Löwith mounts a wholesale critique of the Enlightenment's idea of progress both as scientific and moral achievement, which he associates initially with Voltaire and Condorcet, and then with Comte, Hegel, Marx, and others. Löwith's primary theme is that modern notions of a universal "philosophy of history," following the dissolution of more naive eighteenth-century beliefs in reason and progress, are "entirely dependent on theology of history, in particular on the theological concept of history as a history of fulfillment and salvation" (Löwith 1). In effect, the progress represented in and by the history of Western civilization, which is in the end conceptually encoded by philosophy of history, is no more than a secularized version of Judeo-Christian eschatology. For Löwith, the homelessness of modern thought reveals itself most poignantly as a form of secular theodicy—as a means of justifying the presence of worldly evil and suffering in a scientific age. The Hegelian State and Marxian revolution are but two versions of this secularized eschatology; Christianity was from the start a cult that consecrated a "transcendent faith in future redemption" (30).

But modernity cannot recuperate any such authentic meaning in history without a genuine, which is to say transcendently anchored, theodicy. By contrast, Löwith follows Burckhardt in seeing that modern history, if it is to be truly rational and secular, must refuse both Christian theodicy and its sense of progress toward a utopian harmony. For Löwith, the only truly secular and rational approach to history, divorced from transcendent justification as well as from all expectation of progress toward redemption, would entail a return to classical Stoicism and its acceptance of circular time untouched by moral or political improvement. Instead, he points out, modern intellectuals are often "neither ancient ancients nor ancient Christians, but . . . a more or less inconsistent compound of both traditions" (Löwith 19)—that is, they are both pagan and progressive, and they cannot legitimately be both. For Löwith, only a sober classical Stoicism would dispel the religious ghost haunting secular philosophy of history, a sense of history "as a sheer 'happening' or a *Geschehen* as automatic, autonomous, and inevitable as the happenings in nature" (Riesterer 79). In the face of the profound disappointments that the first half of the twentieth century had brought to the Enlightenment idea of moral progress and social redemption, Löwith concludes that historical reflection can consistently claim to be rational while still articulating some form of continuity only by embracing a classical theory of circular movement, "for only on the basis of a circular, endless movement, without beginning and end, is continuity really demonstrable" (Löwith 207). Otherwise, the modern mind will remain contradictory, hobbled by a sort of split personality that sees "with one eye of faith and one of reason."

Löwith's desire for the radical divorce of a rigorously secular modernity from all traditions of religiously inflected historical progress points toward what Arnold Gehlen once called *post-histoire*, that condition in which the displacement of the certainty of progress from religious, then to scientific, and finally to aesthetic forms of judgment eventually leads to the dissolution of the idea of progress itself in an ever more futile search for aesthetic novelty. It is a condition that prompted the antiprogressive utopianism of Bloch and Benjamin. But it also leads to what Gianni Vattimo called a postmodern *pensiero debole,* or "weak thought," where one must somehow eschew both the "natural linearity" implied by cumulative knowledge and conceptual refinement and the "Spenglerian nostalgia for 'decline'" (Vattimo 107). Löwith insists that the only consistent historical position is a return to the ancient Stoics' acceptance of meaningless and natural cycles of advancement and decay.

The second account of secularization is that of Hans Blumenberg, whose book *The Legitimacy of the Modern Age* (1966) was in many ways a response to Löwith's compelling, but rather pessimistic, arguments. (For Blumenberg's genealogy of the idea of progress itself, see Blumenberg, "Lineage." For an earlier account of the Löwith-Blumenberg debate, see Wallace.) Blumenberg's discussion is both large and dense and involves not only treatments of classical and modern thought, but also, in its final pages, a close reading of Nicholas of Cusa and Giordano Bruno, who between them frame for Blumenberg the initial breakdown of medieval Christianity's Aristotelian (and Platonic) inheritance as represented by Aquinas and the Schoolmen. Blumenberg emphasizes as a positive transformation precisely the moment in medieval Christianity that a French Catholic Straussian such as Pierre Manent laments: the turn away from the Greek notions of the multileveled concept of soul and world, with its separation of the rational and the passionate, the sublunar and supralunar, and away from the Aristotelian fixity of human substance, relation, and achievement that MacIntyre (with certain reservations about Aristotle's acceptance of slavery) wants to recover; the intensification of God as an utterly transcendent being—in this way looking forward to the God of the deists—and at the same time "the advancement both of man and the cosmos toward the qualities of this transcendence" (Blumenberg, *Legitimacy* 484–85), thus anticipating the modern idea of progress; the holding fast to philosophical nominalism, with its acceptance of the idea that human universals are but conventional signs that may not correspond to real universals in the way Aristotle suggested in his deduction of the four kinds of causality, thus overcoming the philosophical realism of the post-Platonic Greeks; and the emphasis on "the world" as a concept possessing "metaphysical dignity" in itself and worthy of philosophical inquiry.

At heart, all these transformations for Blumenberg derive from the theological problem created by an all-powerful God, who may or may not be "rational" in our limited understanding of the term—a point the Gnostics had also explored, though in vain—and whose unfathomable power, later embedded in Luther's emphasis on irrational grace and faith rather than works and in Calvin's equally arbitrary idea of predestination, transforms the world into a place of utter contingency. In Max Weber's account of the Reformation's unintended consequences, for example, this emphasis on worldly arbitrariness and contingency in the event paradoxically leads not to increased asceticism and renunciation of the world as a vale of tears (though the monastic solution never actually disappears), but instead to what Blumenberg calls a modest impulse to self-assertion. It is, I think, not unlike what Weber identifies as "the calling," or vocation, in Luther's thought. Modernity is not simply then one "arbitrary commitment" (*Legitimacy* xxix) among others. Contrary to Löwith, Blumenberg insists that theological expectations built into Christian eschatology could only have been understood as a hindrance from the point of view of progress (31); all revolutionary ideas of a "standstill" in time (Benjamin may be the unmentioned reference here) then emerge as the very opposite of progress (86). Blumenberg thus refers to "secularization *by* eschatology," where the failed expectations of an end-time force instead a turn to an increasingly extended sense of human temporality, rather than (as in Löwith) the secularization *of* eschatology (43–45). It is this changed sense of temporality that separates Aristotle from Descartes: understanding nature and history "is accomplished precisely not by the absolutism of the self-guarantee but rather by the idea of method" (33).

Blumenberg's focus on the "epochal threshold" between Nicolas of Cusa and Giordano Bruno—with Copernicus's cosmological revolution in between—is illustrative of the process. While Nicholas of Cusa had emphasized that "man can be a human God and can be God in a human manner" (*Legitimacy* 592), this "Godlikeness" is still predicated on the "hypostatic union," imprinted on each human being, of God's intervention in human history through Christ's Incarnation. For Giordano Bruno, by contrast, such Godlikeness is evident, but it is to be achieved only as an ideal in the progress of humankind (591). The Incarnation thus becomes something of a historical scandal that must be denied: when Bruno, the heretic mounted on his pyre for execution, turns his face away from the upheld crucifix, with its embodied representation of a human-divine duality, he is at the same time acknowledging "a unity of reality in which everything was indeed self-reproducing, self-manifesting God, and man also was a being who becomes God, a unity, however, in which the universality of the transformation that embraces all realities did not admit the singularity of a God who forces His way into human history" (593; see also 115).

With Bruno, the unbridgeable gap between a transcendent divinity and a godlike humanity reopens, this time irrevocably. For Blumenberg, the crossing of this epochal threshold within medieval Catholicism itself marked the rejection of the Aristotelian cosmos and soul that had been embraced by the Schoolmen, and it is this nascent humanism that prepared the way for the modern idea of progress. But quite contrary to Löwith, Blumenberg argues that understanding the idea of secularization and progress in this essentially Weberian way—that is, as a consequence of transformations within the Christian tradition—does *not* mean that it can simply be reduced to a secularized version of Christian eschatology and theodicy.

Blumenberg's basic argument on this score is that modernity's notion of progress, established most directly by the Enlightenment, is indeed in part the consequence of earlier Christian thought, but it is so primarily as a formal "reoccupation" of earlier and now "vacant" theological "answer positions." The appearance in Löwith of some transfer of religious substance in modernity is a function of mere reasoning by analogy. For Blumenberg, heterogeneous modern ideas are overextended in order to respond to already established epistemic needs—including, perhaps, "a human interest that lies deeper than the mere persistence of the epochal carry-over" (*Legitimacy* 69)—so that modern answers take over the *function* of the earlier theological account. Modern thought is thus not simply a secularized repetition of an earlier *content*, in which philosophical or historical understanding would be nothing more than a watered-down version of the substance of no-longer-acknowledged Christian belief, as found in both Löwith and MacIntyre. Hence, although modern answers to ancient questions may retain an important place in our larger reflections on life and history—we ought not imagine any revolution in thought radical enough to abolish the durable significance of a tradition's questions and should thus acknowledge that no "absolute beginning" for the modern dispensation could ever have occurred in any case (48, 74)—the content of the modern answers is essentially different, based on the modern (one might say "protest-ant" as well as "critical") idea of worldly self-assertion rather than the medieval concept of extraworldly salvation.

It is only through an illicit overextension of the idea of self-assertion, for example, that Schmitt can refer—in his critique of Blumenberg—to modernity's false pretense to "self-foundation" (*Legitimacy* 97). Likewise, Marxian dialectical history may be formally a reoccupation of Christian eschatology, and it has certainly been elaborated at different moments as if it could or should respond to transcendent questions, but it actually requires no divine intervention, depends completely on human action and need, and expects results only in this world, not the next. Modern notions of progress thus involve an immanent—or this-worldly—notion of development that has nothing to do with the "fear and trembling" that characterized the medieval Christian anticipation of the end of time, as Löwith had admitted, and that is reworked by antihistoricists such as Kierkegaard. As John Bury, who in some ways anticipates Blumenberg on this point, argued: "It was not until men felt independent of providence that they could organize a theory of progress" (Bury 22; cited in Löwith 60). Blumenberg thus modifies Hobbes's central idea of self-preservation, which underwrites the dissolution of earlier Scholastic notions of natural law and substance, so that it is less concerned with the brute struggle for survival that governs the passions in Hobbes than with a broader and less egoistically defined orientation toward the future—that is, to predicting and controlling the future in order the better to satisfy a wide array of human interests beyond mere survival (see *Legitimacy* 137ff.).

This orientation toward the future, which is indeed different from anything found in the Greeks but could be described as a formal reoccupation of Christian expectation, thus yields for Blumenberg a sense of historical development, that is, of possible and infinite, though not inevitable or necessary, progress. It arises in the sciences with the overthrow of Aristotelian physics, and even earlier in the arts with the overthrow of Aristotelian ideas of *aretē* and perfection. (Blumenberg's commitment to an idea of infinite but not inevitable progress also bears a certain resemblance to the nineteenth-century neo-Kantianism of the Marburg School—Hermann Cohen, Wilhelm Windelband, Alois Riehl, and Heinrich Rickert—which considered the pursuit of knowledge an infinite task. It is this neo-Kantian attitude that Benjamin would ridicule in the Social Democratic Party of his time, as he does in his "Theses on the Philosophy of History," considered in chapter 2; see Benjamin, *Selected Writings* 4:408, n. 3.)

One of Blumenberg's significant observations for my purposes is that the modern idea of infinite, though not inevitable, progress may actually provide us with the only valid moral heuristic in the secular world of "possessive individualism" that many, both on the left and the right, have decried as inescapably ruled by nothing more than private interests and historical contingency. Progress is thus neither a necessary component of history, nor part of an eschatological vision—again, it is both infinite and nonteleological—but rather the ambiguous foundation of a modern *moralität*, and hence the key to the persistent, if often abused, significance of the idea for modern societies.

The danger of this hyperbolizing of the idea of progress is the necessary disappointment of each individual in the context of history, doing work in his particular situation for a future whose enjoyment he cannot inherit. Nevertheless, the idea of infinite progress also has a safeguarding function for the actual individual and for each actual generation in history. If there were an immanent final goal of history, then those who believe they know it and claim to promote its attainment would be legitimized in using all the others who do not know it and cannot promote it as mere means. Infinite progress does make each present relative to its future, but at the same time it renders every absolute claim untenable. This idea of progress corresponds more than anything else to the only regulative principle that can make history humanly bearable, which is that all dealings must be so constituted that through them people do not become mere means. (*Legitimacy* 35)

If we cannot return, as Strauss, Manent, and MacIntyre propose, to the world of substance, natural law, entelechy, and pursuit of unchanging excellence that we often associate with the life-world and circular history of the Greek Stoics—and Habermas is surely right that there is no reason to believe we can—then Blumenberg's neo-Kantian reflections on the historical world that modern society has half made and half inherited might seem to provide the beginnings of a response.

But it is important to admit that Blumenberg's reformulations of the ideas of secularization and progress in fact also raise all sorts of problems, for Blumenberg's ethics remain as purely formal as those of Kant. As Matthew Arnold would have noted, Blumenberg cannot give a substantive content to the idea of progress he articulates—he cannot finally tell us the purpose of this progress—precisely because at this point in history he fears the consequences of invoking any human entelechy or utopian eschatology more than he admires its potential, and perhaps for good reasons. His ability to recognize in Western modernity a formal echo of, or analogy with, Christian themes while denying any similarity of content may thus be a bit too clever for its own good.

For Blumenberg also implies that as secular humanists we can acknowledge the historically Christian character of Western thought while denying its status as revealed or divine truth, but claim at the same time that there was something special about the Christian tradition that allowed it to transform itself—or rather, reverse itself—into a secular universal project that no other religious tradition has, or could have, achieved.

There are entirely harmless formulations of the secularization theorem, of a type that can hardly be contradicted. One of these plausible turns of phrase is "unthinkable without." The chief thesis then, roughly put, would be that the modern age is unthinkable without Christianity. That is so fundamentally correct that the second part of this book is aimed at demonstrating this fact—with the difference, however, that this thesis gains a definable meaning only through a critique of the foreground appearance—or better: the apparent background presence—of secularization. (*Legitimacy* 30)

Blumenberg's "critique" is based on the idea that only the disappointment of transcendental expectations could have enabled the "natural step" of a projection of possibilities in this world—an aggregate of hopes regulated by methods across generations—as opposed to redemption in the next. There is no identity of meaning, nor a direct historical necessity, in this transition, and yet modernity is still "unthinkable without Christianity." But then in what sense is the thesis "harmless"—which is to say, insignificant? This is the same sort of problem, after all, that haunts Weber, and it is not hard to see how much Blumenberg has influenced Habermas, with the latter's own difficult sense that a still "unfinished" modernity in the West must continue to find "semantic potentials" in the religious tradition that gave birth to it.

In fact, Blumenberg's arguments for the "legitimacy" of modernity cannot respond directly to Löwith's or MacIntyre's underlying complaint that modern thought is confounded by its loss of permanent and transcendent ideas of substantive reason and human nature, because rather than finding natural or materialist substitutes (as some have done by turning to evolutionary psychology, neuropsychology, and perhaps even genetics, and as Habermas had in part done by turning to Piaget), Blumenberg treats the permanent loss of these ideals as the only remaining ethical or political compass. That is, Blumenberg does not defend the idea of progress against critics such as Löwith by returning with Hegel to the attenuated substance of reason unfolded by progressive history. Rather, he treats the idea of contingent, endless, and, strictly speaking, purposeless historical progress as the only available ground, however formal and impoverished, of a secular and human-centered, or neo-Kantian, ethical perspective and of all morally justifiable modern social orders. Blumenberg's claim that modern morality effectively depends on a notion of noneschatological and contingent progress suggests that Habermas's sense of modernity as an "unfinished project," one that has not yet been but ought to be realized in full, requires a slightly different inflection. The only modernity that anyone should want, Blumenberg implies, is one that would remain both historically unnecessary and never complete.

Perhaps more important, it is perfectly obvious that Blumenberg's passing acknowledgement of the "disappointment" bred by faith in an endless collective progress that no particular mortal individual will ever fully enjoy is not a sufficient recognition of the immense suffering caused by blind confidence in progress on a global scale. For it fails almost completely to consider the horrors—gladly highlighted by Löwith, MacIntyre, and Nandy, on the one hand, and by the larger field of postcolonial criticism after Said, on the other—inflicted by those nations bent on universal progress (and these have been until recently Western European for the most part) against peoples whose understanding of civilization and change may have been radically different. As Conrad's Marlow famously noted, European progress seemed to entail "the conquest of the earth, which mostly means the taking it away from those who have a different complexion or slightly flatter noses then ourselves" (Conrad 10). The more recent idea of universal human rights is for some tainted by this problem as well, as Asad points out, since even "progress" in this area has historically generally meant the domination of non-Western and non-Christian peoples by the Christian West. In this sense, progress of the moral no less than the technological sort has often been achieved at a heavy price—a price that led Benjamin to the grandly reductive perspective in which the very idea of progress is itself a barbarism, even *within* the West, though it has generally been the non-Christian peoples, including the Jews, who have paid it. Such considerations make the cultural benefits of modernity appear to be the necessary and unique historical effect of a single religious evolution, at a moment when a new global awareness has made such perspectives more difficult and untenable than ever.

Nevertheless, although Blumenberg's view acknowledges that the modern invocation of some global idea of human progress is inextricably part of the Western Enlightenment, which means that it has been shaped by the universal claims of the Judeo-Christian tradition as well as by an invidious imperial quest for universal hegemony, it also usefully undermines the claim that the formal similarity of such progress to Judeo-Christian notions of redemption and salvation means nothing more than an incoherent reproduction of the content of Judeo-Christian teaching, as Löwith would claim, insofar as any *future* progress is understood as an open-ended and contingent process. From this point of view, the great evils of empire appear to be less a function of some Lyotardian *grand récit* justifying a colonizing belief in progress itself—though this is the sort of claim that a postmodern, academic anti-imperialism has made with great success—than of a self-declared prerogative (defended usually at the point of a gun) to decide unilaterally what would count as progress, especially in the realms of political organization. After all, it is only in the context of a belief that an at least marginally better state of things, both locally and globally speaking, can be had that one would rationally resist such unilateral determinations of the meaning of progress in the first place. What this implies, I think, is that no viable secular modernity, that is, one based solely on those bare Hobbesian imperatives of self-preservation and deliberation, can do without both a notion of progress and a refusal of redemption.

If Löwith and MacIntyre are correct, there is no reason to assume that anything like global human rights, much less universal standards of justice, could be pursued in modernity on grounds other than those of a contradictory political theology, or Luhmannian systems theory, that posits social self-deception as the only true basis of functioning norms. In what could be taken anachronistically as the logical consequence of Luhmann's work, Strauss's political philosophy actually allows for the legitimate production of this social deception on the part of enlightened rulers, who keep the more disturbing truth about truth—the open-ended, even subversive nature of the search for knowledge, as opposed to the illusory but necessary moral opinions of political society—to themselves (see Strauss, *Natural* 141–42; *Political* 229). But if Blumenberg is correct, one must still reckon with the question whether a "legitimate" idea of progressive, secular modernity must continue to draw ethical "sustenance," as Habermas puts it, uniquely from its Judeo-Christian heritage, or can sustain itself by reference to other religious traditions or without reference to any religious traditions at all. (For example, is a putatively godless French Republicanism, putatively based on nothing but its secular Enlightenment perspective, as independent of all religious underwriting as it generally presumes itself to be? Asad would say no, and I would say he was right.)

Moreover, one must then also address the real difficulty that any Habermasian invocation of a single ethical-political legacy with "no alternatives" poses for truly global, cosmopolitan, and pluralistic or overlapping notions of justice. Recovering the precarious deist faith of Diderot may indeed seem impossible, but there may yet be good reasons not to abandon completely, not to forsake reoccupying, the thin but broad consensual universalism embedded in Diderot's vision. It is the larger question that remains the most salient: Can that vision itself be made sufficiently self-conscious of and hence relatively autonomous from its simultaneously Judeo-Christian and imperialist foundations, and articulated with similar tendencies in other ethical-religious traditions, to be serviceable in a global age? It should come as no surprise if many, both within and outside the West, remain more than a little skeptical.

2 * Benjamin, Kracauer, and Redemptive History

The opposition drawn by Jean-Claude Monod between two different ways of accounting for secularization—the dissolution of religious concepts in the face of a new and autonomous secular modernity versus the "worlding" or transfer of religious models that constitutes no more than a redirection of the substance of religious thought—is itself a summary of the argument between Hans Blumenberg and Karl Löwith in the middle of last century. But this distinction can be mapped further onto the tension between the work of two central and earlier figures of modern cultural criticism: Siegfried Kracauer and Walter Benjamin. While Benjamin's very influential reinscription of theology (especially in the form of messianic time, derived from an uneasy blend of Jewish mysticism, or Kabbalah, and nineteenth-century Catholic philosophy of history) as Marxian historical materialism presents us with a rich and complex example of Monod's second account of secularization, Kracauer's final response to his friend Benjamin's quasi-religious historical vision provides an attempt to realize Monod's first option. But in doing so, that is, in taking up Blumenberg's sense of modernity as infinite yet open-ended and not inevitable progress now detached from its religious substance, and hence undoing the messianism at the heart of Benjamin's work, Kracauer also comes close to dissolving altogether the Enlightenment's view of secularization as the uniform advancement of moral understanding and material knowledge. I argue in what follows that the kinship and divergences between Kracauer and Benjamin can tell us much about the relationship between secularization and history in modern cultural criticism, and about the legacy of this relationship for postmodern modes of thought.

Grand Narratives and Present Interests

The Enlightenment idea of history as progressive development, or, what amounts to the same thing in an idealist key, the idea of history as progressive enlightenment, has been a central target of postmodern cultural criticism. Embodied in rather different ways by Condorcet's optimistic materialism, by Hegel's teleology of unfolding *Geist*, and by subsequent traditions of positivism, evolutionism, and socialism, universal history as technical and moral progress has become for many today one of the "grand narratives" that can no longer be sustained. "The grand narrative," in Jean-François Lyotard's well-known obituary of the idea, "has lost its credibility, regardless of what mode of unification it uses, regardless of whether it is a speculative narrative or a narrative of emancipation" (Lyotard 37). These narratives have been further conflated with "bourgeois" or "Whiggish" history, and, most revealingly, with what Walter Benjamin calls "empty" or "homogeneous" time. (Lyotard himself discerned such grand temporalities behind the totalitarianism of Stalin and the "ontological pretensions" of Heidegger's turn to Nazism; see Lyotard 36–37.) Certainly the horrors of two world wars and the genocide of the Holocaust did great damage to the eighteenth century's progressive ideals. Just after World War II, Karl Löwith argued in *Meaning in History* that the modern historian's notion of progress, derived from Voltaire, Condorcet, and Marx, was simply a secularized version of a Judeo-Christian salvation narrative, a notion no longer legitimated by religious faith; it could not be reconciled, even by critical historians such as Arnold Toynbee, to a stoic and putatively more scientific view of the "tragic human comedy" of cyclical triumph and ruin, in which nothing like progress could be found (Löwith v). But Enlightenment history has actually been deeply suspect for certain strains of thought for quite some time.

In Hegel's famous allegory (Hegel, *Phenomenology* 111–19), the bondsman who finds himself chained by (and to) his lord wins, over time, self-consciousness, recognition, and emancipation through work, while the spirit of the lord atrophies. Nietzsche's counter-Enlightenment rejection of historical progress, which had important precursors in Joseph de Maistre's virulent religious diatribes against the social sufficiency of Voltaire's reason and Rousseau's contract, and in Hobbes's emphasis on the social passions, in effect declares Hegel's anecdote nothing more than a fantasy of the slave mentality. One of the important turning points in nineteenth-century historicism,

Nietzsche's logic has had a profound influence on the postmodern rejection of progressive history, whether Western or universal in orientation. Nietzsche does not actually reject the study of history; indeed, he recognizes its necessity, but insists that it be employed in the service of "life and action" (Nietzsche, *Use and Abuse* 3), that is, by "turning the past to the uses of the present" (8). It is the excess of history that is debilitating, that stunts the will to act. Nietzsche's vitalism focuses finally on the power of youth to destroy humanist educational conventions and create a true (that is, organic and "Greek") rather than decorative (or "Roman") culture (72–73)—an idea that would have politically ambiguous repercussions in Germany's early twentieth-century Youth Movement.

Moreover, in placing history in the service of present interests, Nietzsche also emphasizes, first, that the essential lesson of history is discontinuity and arbitrariness, or "the accidental nature of the forms in which [we] see and insist on others seeing" (Nietzsche, *Use and Abuse* 9); and second, that the only rule guiding historical interpretation is thus, as it is throughout Nietzsche's work, the will to power: "*You can explain the past only by what is most powerful in the present*" (40; Nietzsche's italics). In such a sentiment can be found the rudiments of Nietzsche's later notion of genealogy, in which history becomes a succession of arbitrary moral interpretations of enduring practices that are extramoral in origin. But the consequences of such a view include the idea that history is finally no more than a "mediator" between great men calling to one another "across the waste space of time," men who rise above the "wan stream of becoming," in which the dwarfed masses are trapped, and who live "out of time, as contemporaries . . . as the Republic of geniuses. . . . The aim of mankind can lie ultimately only in its highest examples" (59). Nietzsche shatters the Enlightenment ideal of human progress, identified on one side with idealist metaphysics and on the other with the rise of the modern empirical sciences, along with the putative "slave morality" that hopes to control our collective fate along with it. But another kind of extrahistorical and equally mythical continuity arises in its wake, this time driven by the eternal return of the master's will, in which the least of humanity find meaning only in those who triumph over it.

In his final and unfinished work—*History: The Last Things before the Last*—Siegfried Kracauer discerns a secret complicity between universal or progressive history and its putative opposite, the fragmentary "present interest" history of thinkers such as Nietzsche. (Kracauer's manuscript remained unfinished at his death. Paul Oscar Kristeller completed some of the later chapters based on notes, synopses, and published essays intended for the book, but there is sufficient repetition in the text to be reasonably sure of

Kracauer's intentions.) Focusing on Benedetto Croce's dictum that "only an interest in the life of the present can move one to investigate past fact" (quoted in Kracauer, *History* 63) and on R. G. Collingwood's similar emphasis on present-day concerns, Kracauer's criticism is pointed. "Both thinkers," writes Kracauer, "are alert to the necessity for them to justify their emphasis on the present by endowing it with metaphysical significance. This gets them into deep waters, for both of them refute, or pretend to refute, any principle governing the whole of human history and yet cannot help reintroducing it in order to explain the uniqueness of the present moment" (Kracauer, *History* 63). In sum, "Hegel's 'world spirit' pops up behind the bushes" (Kracauer, *History* 64) as soon as the present is conceived in any way as the raison d'être of history, or as the Archimedean point from which what is essential in history can be deduced. In placing history at the service of what is finally an extrahistorical notion of will to power, Nietzsche's transvaluation of progressive history is subject to much the same objection, an objection that Kracauer extends to twentieth-century immanentist and existential philosophy of history, from Dilthey's vitalist *Geisteswissenschaften* to Heidegger's "closure of metaphysics," and that we might extend today to Michel Foucault's notion of genealogy or "effective history" (*Wirkungsgeschichte,* or *wirkliche Historie*), borrowed from Nietzsche and Dilthey (see Foucault, "Nietzsche").

If Kracauer rejects both Enlightenment progress and present-interest history, what does he suggest instead? His difficult and ultimately inconclusive search—one that still occupies us today—for an alternative that rescues from oblivion illuminating moments of the past in service of the present, yet remains in some sort of dialectical relation to ideas of provisional continuity, even progress, is at the center of his book. The empty, homogeneous time of universal history tends toward a complacent reproduction of philosophical (that is, extrahistorical) truths, the ultimate or transcendent truths that Kracauer calls the "last things," but that might also be identified with historical *telos,* the end or goal of history that Alexandre Kojève famously identified with Hegel as sage. In bracketing off the teleological imperative to identify "last things," Kracauer is trying to avoid embracing the complacency of a uniform narrative of progress and the metaphysical assuredness of the present's temporal superiority, as well as the confusion of unconditional *prophecy* with conditional *prediction* that Karl Popper critically attributed to historicism (see Popper). At the same time, he wants to forestall the supposedly antiteleological surrender to the vicissitudes of present interests and will to power, which prove to be equally dependent on a veiled form of "last things."

Instead, Kracauer argues, the writing of history should concentrate on the "last things before the last," that is, on provisional universals that emerge from an apprehension of history, including the present, in all its unsystematic particularity. There are moments when he sounds remarkably close to Nietzsche and Foucault in his rejection of Hegelian totality: "History is also the realm of contingencies, of new beginnings," writes Kracauer. "All regularities discovered in it, or read into it, are of limited range" (*History* 31; see also Foucault, "Nietzsche"). In this regard, Kracauer wants to insist that, whatever individual historians have claimed, the writing of history is by its nature closer to what Richard Rorty calls hermeneutics, or "edifying" philosophy—thinking premised, in Rorty's account, on the resistance to metaphysical totality—than to the universal truth claims of "systematic" philosophy (see Rorty 357–94).

Kracauer's approach likewise has a certain affinity with the countermemory practices of romantic and postmodern revisionism alike. "Proust shares Burckhardt's nostalgia for lost causes" (Kracauer, *History* 79), he writes, and Proust remains symbolic of the openness to a forgotten *promesse de bonheur* in historical events that is a basic tenet of Kracauer's critique of homogeneous progress. This is the sort of progress capable of rationalizing the most horrific developments by invoking Hegel's "ruse of reason," in which the actual is by definition the rational. Still, Kracauer remains far less willing than either Nietzsche or Foucault to relinquish the interpretation of the past completely to the present exigencies (and hidden metaphysics) of authority and power. "Philosophical truths have a double aspect," he writes. "Neither can the timeless be stripped of the vestiges of temporality, nor does the temporal wholly engulf the timeless" (200). Kracauer argues that the myth of continuous progress should not inspire such credulity that, following nineteenth-century historians such as Leopold von Ranke, the present is granted a moral and epistemological superiority able to afford a view of the past "the way it really was."

But to extirpate from historical accounting any claim to continuity or progressive development within certain limited trajectories of accumulated knowledge, and any form of understanding not dominated by current events and the will to power, is to suspend the interpreter's "now" in a hermetic cloud of significance that is just as mythical as Ranke's historicism. In his suspicion of the Nietzschean reaction against progressive history, Kracauer comes close to and cites Hans Blumenberg's early essays criticizing Löwith and others after 1945. Summing up his views in *The Legitimacy of the Modern Age* (first German edition, which Kracauer seems not to have known, published in 1966), Blumenberg rejects Löwith's reduction of all progressive history to a secularization of religious eschatology and observes on the contrary that the expectation of theological redemption from outside the world could only have appeared "as a hindrance to the attitudes and activities that can secure for man the realization of his possibilities and the satisfaction of his needs" (*Legitimacy* 31). Behind Kracauer's critique of "last things" remains Blumenberg's more modest notion of human "self-assertion" (138) and his counterintuitive claim that the idea of infinite, nonteleological progress is both "the only regulative principle that can make history humanly bearable," in that people do not thereby become mere means for a knowable end, and a methodological heuristic that "renders every absolute untenable" (35). Kracauer's own search for a standpoint between the Scylla of religious or teleological assuredness and the Charybdis of present-interest imperatives takes shape in the wake of the Blumenberg-Löwith debate.

Derrière-guard of the Avant-garde

The enemy of progressive history whose writings are most relevant to Kracauer's text is his friend and sometime critic Walter Benjamin. Like Kracauer, Benjamin was fascinated with the political significance of mass art forms such as photography and cinema, and sought ways to integrate the analysis of the superficial manifestations of popular commodity culture into a Marxian materialism that might otherwise disregard them. Indeed, Kracauer's 1922 essay "The Mass Ornament" (collected in Kracauer's book of the same title) can be seen as one of several sources for Benjamin's attempt to read the novelties displayed by the marketplace of bourgeois Paris as "wish images" that simultaneously transfigure "the inadequacies in the social organization of production" and evoke in occluded form the utopian "classless society" of the "primal past" (Benjamin, *Arcades Project* 4). On the one hand, behind both Kracauer and Benjamin here is Adolf Loos's brief but influential essay "Ornament und Verbrechen" ("Ornament and Crime"), delivered as a lecture in 1908 and subsequently published in various languages, a founding document in modern art's suspicion of ornament as a "symptom of backwardness or degeneracy" (Loos 170). Loos's claims would reappear in Benjamin's essay on Karl Kraus (Benjamin, *Selected Writings* 2:433–58) and in the *Arcades* (see Benjamin, *Arcades* 557 [S8a,1]). On the other hand, one finds the influence of Georg Simmel's idealist-vitalist critique of capitalism in *The Philosophy of Money* (1900), with its analyses of the rapidity of change and the "ceremonial fetishism" of the modern fashion industry, a text also quoted at length in the *Arcades* (see especially Benjamin, *Arcades* 226–27 [I7a,2]). (Benjamin, Kracauer, and Lukács had all been Simmel's students in Berlin, and Kracauer wrote a study of Simmel's work, *Georg Simmel: A Contribution to the Study of Contemporary Mental Life* [1919].)

The Kracauer of the 1920s prefigures Benjamin's later interest in bourgeois culture as a form of "distraction," as well as Adorno's notion of a "culture industry" (see Kracauer's 1926 essay "Cult of Distraction" in *Mass Ornament*). These essays provided a model for Benjamin's belief that capitalism, once allowed to develop—that is, decay—far enough in the production of its cultural ruins, would yield to a sudden, revolutionary awakening. At the moment of awakening, the commodity and the constricted life it supports would be redeemed, as figured in the utopian image that is "dialectics at a standstill"— the archaic fashion "novelty," the prostitute who is "seller and sold in one," the arcades themselves, "which are house no less than street" (Benjamin, *Arcades* 10). "The Mass Ornament" already hints at the thesis of a rational will to the domination of nature that in capitalism takes the form of new myth even as it destroys pre-rational beliefs—an argument that would appear not only in Benjamin's later writings but would become central to Horkheimer and Adorno's *Dialectic of Enlightenment* more than two decades later. (Here too, however, Simmel's *Philosophy of Money* is an important precursor, and Simmel's critique of the bourgeois notion that technology represents the domination of nature also makes its way into the *Arcades*, 661–62 [X7a,1].)

This period culminates in 1929–30 with Kracauer's most deliberately sociological analysis, *Die Angestellten* ("Salaried Employees"), in which German white-collar workers, caught between bourgeois aspiration and financial ruin during the depression, seek consolation in the distractions of popular culture, such as "pleasure palaces" and sports. The ethnographically inflected study (see Inka Mülder-Bach's splendid introduction to *The Salaried Masses*, which also points up the degree to which Kracauer anticipates postmodern trends in cultural theory opposed to any *grand récit* [*Salaried Masses* 4, 14]), built on firsthand interviews with *die Angestellten*, their union leaders, and their employers, is largely determined by Kracauer's suspicion of existing employee unions and their corporatist mentality, which embraces both "cultural goods" and an unmediated immersion in "nature" as medicines for a sickened work force. Kracauer remains indebted here to a Marxian analysis that insists on dissecting the contradictory response of entrepreneurs and employees alike to economic crisis. At the same time, he addresses the mass-cultural environment as a relatively autonomous but psychologically central realm of illusions—an approach that drew Benjamin's approval (see Benjamin's review, *Salaried Masses* 109–14).

But Kracauer also argued in a letter to Adorno in 1930 that the "disaster" hanging over Germany "is not just capitalism," which was obviously well advanced in France too; Germany seemed to be heading toward a fate very much its own (quoted in Mülder-Bach, introduction, *Salaried Masses* 19, n. 9).

The Salaried Masses ends with a remarkable commentary that looks forward to Kracauer's later discussion of history. Criticizing the trade-union belief that collective activity (such as speech-and-movement youth choruses) can itself be a source of political energy, Kracauer is driven to reflect on the inner nature of collectivism. "Collectivity in itself is just as empty as enterprise in itself, and merely the opposite pole of the entrepreneur's private initiative. The position remains the same whether you approve individual initiative, in the expectation that it will guarantee general well-being, or you acknowledge the masses as a fighting community, in the hope that it will realize aims worth struggling for. In both cases, you accept people without inquiring what relationship they have to the aims in question" (*Salaried Masses* 106). The conclusion both reaffirms Kracauer's emphasis on the contingent link between individual and collectivity and points inevitably to his later account of historical inquiry, which insists on a dialogue between the multiplicity of voices with their overlapping narratives and the necessity of subjective synthesis.

In subsequent works, especially in his social biography *Jacques Offenbach and the Paris of his Time* (1937) and the influential film study *From Caligari to Hitler* (1947), Kracauer effectively abandons his earlier theoretical commitment to, if not his vaguer sympathy with, the armature of Hegelian-Marxian universal history and turns to a far more empirical, and relatively nondialectical, study of the relations between the objects of mass culture and their social context. It is a shift that more than once drew sharply critical comments from Adorno and some disdain from Benjamin (see, for example, the letters between Benjamin and Adorno in Adorno and Benjamin, *Complete Correspondence* 183–87). In a late essay ("The Curious Realist: On Siegfried Kracauer"), Adorno recalls that Kracauer "mockingly called himself the derrière-guard of the avant-garde," and Adorno adds a needling epigram of his own—"Just proportion always carries its own penalty: moderationism" (*Notes* 62). Where Adorno famously remained suspicious of empirical examples to illustrate his theoretical claims, Kracauer now immersed himself in them, if perhaps with the loss of a more sweeping conceptualization of his material. In *From Caligari to Hitler,* for example, Kracauer interprets the "psychological" significance of German films of the Weimar era—their technical as well as thematic elements, though Kracauer's work later became one-sidedly linked to empirical "content analysis"—in terms of the development of a totalitarian consciousness that the films both reflected and shaped. It is a rich social-psychological survey of the collective German psyche of the era, albeit relatively unconcerned with immanent or historical contradictions. The book avoids the larger theoretical questions of capitalist development and Marxian teleology and remains focused on the emotional roots of the nation's social and political crisis, blocked out in discrete historical phases at times only four or five years long.

Adorno seems as much offended here by Kracauer's unabashed plot summaries and obvious enthusiasm for his material as he is by Kracauer's failure to connect Weimar psychology to a capitalist division of labor or to putatively similar totalitarian tendencies in American and Soviet filmmaking (*Notes* 74)—though Adorno ignores the rather different relations to capitalism in the latter two societies. Adorno's criticism was both brilliantly perceptive and unfair: the force and complexity of Kracauer's insights, however impure theoretically, made them something of a founding model for much subsequent analysis of film and mass media, as well as of Weimar culture itself. The decisive point is that, although still quite critical and progressive in his underlying intentions, Kracauer had became increasingly skeptical of utopian social transformation as well as of philosophical systems that would reduce individual experience to the articulate concepts of a narrative told in advance. His later work displays less the ironic pragmatism that bothered Adorno than a kind of disillusioned critical realism, with which the far more pessimistic Adorno should have had more sympathy than he was willing to acknowledge. For his part, Benjamin remained committed throughout the 1930s to the centrality of a negatively totalizing and messianic understanding of history and, even at the last, to the potential for utopian redemption flashing forth from the depths of bourgeois ruin. Kracauer, who found himself delayed in Marseilles in 1940 along with Benjamin and crossed successfully into Spain a few months after Benjamin's suicide—if that is in fact what it was—at Port Bou, had far less hope of ultimate salvation. But he also had less despair about the unforeseen possibilities of more quotidian forms of deliverance.

Benjamin's Messianism

Kracauer's late approach to history, that is, to "the last things before the last," supersedes formulations in "The Mass Ornament" that helped to shape Benjamin's own later work on history. But it also functions in various ways as a commentary on and revision of Benjamin's apocalyptic messianism in one of his last essays, "On the Philosophy of History" (often called the "Theses on the Philosophy of History"). There, in an oft-cited but difficult passage, Benjamin writes:

Zum Denken gehört nicht nur die Bewegung der Gedanken, sondern ebenso ihre Stillstellung. Wo das Denken in einer von Spannungen gesättigten Konstellation plötzlich einhält, da erteilt es derselben einen Chok, durch den es sich als Monade kristallisiert.

Der historische Materialist geht an einen geschichtlichen Gegenstand einzig und allein da heran, wo er ihm als Monade entgegentritt. In dieser Struktur erkennt er das Zeichen einer messianischen Stillstellung des Geschehens, anders gesagt, einer revolutionären Chance im Kampf für die unterdrückte Vergangenheit. . . .

Er erfasst die Konstellation, in die seine eigene Epoche mit einer ganz bestimmten früheren getreten ist. Er begründet so einen Begriff der Gegenwart als der "Jetztzeit," in welcher Splitter der messianischen eingesprengt sind. (Benjamin, *Schriften* 1:504–6)

To thinking belongs not only the movement of thoughts, but likewise their standstill. Where thinking suddenly stops in a constellation saturated with tensions, it gives the constellation a shock, through which thinking crystallizes itself as a monad. The historical materialist approaches a historical object only and exclusively where he confronts it as a monad. In this structure he recognizes the sign of a messianic standstill of events, or, put differently, a revolutionary chance in the fight for the oppressed past. . . .

He seizes the constellation in which his own epoch has joined with a quite definite earlier one. He thus establishes a concept of the present as the "now-time," in which splinters [or chips, or motes] of the messianic are sprinkled. (My translation; see also Benjamin, *Selected Writings* 4:396–97)

This can be compared rather directly to a similar passage in which Kracauer emphasizes in history less the emergence of an otherwise hidden opportunity for salvation than the appearance of a unique and compelling way to link particular events with general axioms.

Historical ideas appear to be of lasting significance because they connect the particular with the general in an articulate and truly unique way. Any such connection being an uncertain venture, they resemble flashes illumining the night. This is why their emergence in the historian's mind has been termed a "historical sensation" and said to "communicate a shock to the entire system . . . the shock . . . of recognition." They are nodal points—points at which the concrete and the abstract really meet and become one. Whenever this happens, the flow of indeterminate historical events is suddenly arrested and all that is then exposed to view is seen in the light of an image or conception which takes it out of the transient flow to relate it to one or another of the momentous problems and questions that are forever staring at us. (Kracauer, *History* 101; internal quotation from Isaiah Berlin, "History and Theory: the Concept of Scientific History," *History and Theory* 1, no. 1 [1960]: 1–31, at 24)

It would be instructive, I think, to reflect a bit on how Kracauer has subtly altered Benjamin's critique of empty time, and to consider what may have been lost, or gained, in the process.

The "Theses" can be read as a highly figural encoding of Marx's dialectical materialism, in which the vehicle of the metaphor is "theology." For example, in Marx, the revolutionary transformation of the present depends on the shock of total socioeconomic crisis, in which an unstructured proletariat suddenly crystallizes, as a political majority, in the act of making the revolution (see Marx and Engels 94). But a more plausible reading makes Marxian materialism into an instrument and function of theology—as Löwith might say, a secularized version of messianic eschatology. As Benjamin put it in an earlier draft of the "Theses": "In the idea of classless society, Marx secularized the idea of messianic time. And that was a good thing. It was only when the Social Democrats elevated this idea to an 'ideal' that the trouble began. The ideal was defined in Neo-Kantian doctrine as an 'infinite task.' . . . (Classless society is not the final goal of historical progress but its frequently miscarried, ultimately achieved interruption)" (*Selected Writings* 4:401–2). The apparent fusion of theology and Marxism in Benjamin's later thinking, which Benjamin himself did not consider inconsistent with his earlier work (see Scholem, *Walter Benjamin* 221–22), has understandably elicited a wide range of interpretations. (For a summary of the debate that emphasizes the degree to which Benjamin's Jewish messianism remained within the framework of historical materialism, see Traverso 167–87. For a reading of the "Theses" that emphasizes the way the two perspectives cancel one another, see Tiedemann, "Historical" 71–104. For a discussion of Benjamin's ambiguous location among various strains of pre-1914 Jewish messianism, both politically engaged and not—especially in relation to the influential strain expressed in Ernst Bloch's *Spirit of Utopia*—see Rabinbach; Tiedemann, "Dialectics." And for the blend of libertarian anarchism, mysticism, and romantic anticapitalism in Benjamin, see Löwy.) On the whole, Benjamin's utopianism/messianism has, like that of Bloch and many others, been considered one of the central elements that gives his work enduring appeal as cultural criticism: only by means of a critical judgment grounded in the possibility of utopian reconciliation can the manifest contradictions of cultural, social, and ultimately economic life in the present be confronted with a compelling counterfactual, and hence redemptive, image of the future. Whether for good or ill, however, it may be useful to note that neither the rescue and redemption of the cultural past nor the (nondialectical) rejection of historical progress is a particularly salient issue in Marx's work itself, and that messianism may serve to obscure critical judgment as much as to inspire it.

On the former point, at least, Marx is rather explicit. The great feudal and bourgeois revolutions of the past may indeed have borrowed their heroic and tragic quality from even earlier historical moments of crisis or transformation. "Luther donned the mask of the Apostle Paul, the revolution of 1789 to 1814 draped itself alternately as the Roman republic and the Roman empire";

Cromwell "borrowed speech, passions and illusions from the Old Testament" (Marx, *Eighteenth Brumaire* 15–17). And yet, as the "farce" of the failed revolution of 1848–51 in France demonstrates, while "awakening the dead" in this fashion may once have served to glorify new struggles by providing the illusion of universality to clearly limited events, it could only stunt "the social revolution of the nineteenth century" by imposing conceptual limitations on a global process. "Earlier revolutions required recollections of past world history in order to drug themselves concerning their own content. In order to arrive at its own content, the revolution of the nineteenth century must let the dead bury their dead. There the phrase went beyond the content; here the content goes beyond the phrase" (Marx, *Eighteenth Brumaire* 18). Marx's subtle reworking of Hegelian dialectic, where historical forms may be either more advanced than, or surpassed by, their content (as they were in Hegel's *Aesthetics*), will not of course shield his perspective from difficult questions: Is nineteenth-century revolution really as global as he thinks? Why only here and now does the invocation of the past as example and stimulus fail? What is clear, however, is that Benjamin did not take Marx's critique of "recollections of past world history" very much to heart.

Indeed, Benjamin's own citations of the French Revolution's evocation of ancient Rome would seem to work, albeit unwittingly, in the opposite direction: "awakening the dead" in order to transform the present remained a central theme of his work. In those earlier drafts of the "Theses," Benjamin would refute Marx precisely on the possibility of an eschatological cessation of history: "Marx says that revolutions are the locomotive of world history. But perhaps it is quite otherwise. Perhaps revolutions are an attempt by the passengers on this train—namely, the human race—to activate the emergency brake" (*Selected Writings* 4:402). The classless utopia is not then the consequence of "historical development," from which arises a "revolutionary situation"; it is a messianic possibility available in all times, in conjunction with a past that has heretofore been a "closed and locked" room, that arises from "political action, however destructive" (4:202).

Benjamin's language in the "Theses" is infused with hermetic references to the sixteenth-century messianic Kabbalism of Isaac Luria, who added to the older notion (one perhaps related to ancient Gnosticism) of the *tsimtsum*—the primal concentration or withdrawal and subsequent dissemination of God's light—two ideas central to Benjamin's final pronouncement on history: *shevirath ha-kelim*, or the "Breaking of the Vessels," and *tikkun*, or the mending of the world's defects and its restoration (see especially Gershom Scholem's summary of Luria's ideas in *Major Trends in Jewish Mysticism* 244–86). Lurianic Kabbalah held that the "vessels" or "bowls" (themselves composed of light) designed to hold the emanating divine light were instead shattered by it. The fragments of these vessels descended to earth, where as *kelipot* they became the shells or husks of all evil and disorder in the world. Along with these broken shards, however, a certain number of divine sparks of light—Luria counts 288—descended as well, embedded in the fragments. "In this way," writes Scholem, "the good elements of the divine order came to be mixed with the vicious ones" (Scholem, *Major Trends* 268), and these scattered "sparks" of the *shekhinah* (primal radiance of God) are to be separated from the dross of evil and restored to their proper place with the coming of the Messiah. In Benjamin, the *kelipot* or fallen fragments become allegories of, or perhaps are allegorized by, the fetishized commodity, husks of evil in which, with the profane illumination provided by a "dialectics at a standstill," the messianic chip that heralds the redemptive reversal or *tikkun* may be glimpsed in a transient flash, like the *Aufblitzen* of mimesis that Benjamin had earlier located in the fallen semiosis of purposive language (see "On the Mimetic Faculty," in Benjamin, *Selected Writings* 2:722).

Luria's teaching includes the notion of transmigration of souls, traces of which might appear in persons, animals, plants, or inanimate things as an "aura" radiating from the body (see Scholem, *Major Trends* 283)—an idea that appears at several points in Benjamin, especially in the essays "The Work of Art in the Age of Its Mechanical Reproducibility" and "The Storyteller" (both in Benjamin, *Selected Writings* 4:251–83, 3:143–67). Kabbalah effectively provides a foundation supporting Benjamin's investigations of the imagery of the worshipped commodity form as well as of the estranged or alienated intellect (such as Baudelaire's). Benjamin rooted the historical materialist's ability to read culture dialectically, as both fallen reflection and prophecy of transformation of the socioeconomic base, in the Lurianic vision of displaced, fragmented, lifeless things seeded (or sparked) with messianic light. That Luria's contribution to Kabbalist lore followed immediately upon the expulsion of the Jews from Spain, and perhaps reflected a new intensity in their sense of *galuth* or exile and their desire for restoration (see Scholem, *Major Trends* 284–86), no doubt found a resonance in Benjamin. It may also have suggested to him an odd irony, as he struggled to flee back to Spain in 1940.

The extent of Benjamin's debt to Jewish mysticism has been in some dispute, despite Gershom Scholem's views (see especially the two essays on Benjamin in Scholem's *On Jews and Judaism in Crisis*), not least because Scholem's own work, which in many ways defined the field of scholarship on the Kabbalah for the twentieth century, only took shape during and after Benjamin's lifetime. Benjamin's early work has been traced instead to the idealistic, reformist Youth Culture of Gustav Wyneken (see especially McCole

35–70), to the more diffuse wave of Jewish messianism that had captured the imagination of Benjamin's generation in the years before World War I (as seen in Rabinbach and in Löwy), and to the anticapitalism of German romantics such as the Schlegel brothers and Novalis (see Sayre and Löwy 55–57). Indeed, there is no reason not to extend this lineage to include the great chiliastic revolutionaries of the Protestant Reformation, from Luther himself to Thomas Münzer and Gerrard Winstanley, though Benjamin's chiliasm would be without a Christ. Nevertheless, Benjamin's writing from the beginning bears a relation to Kabbalah that is far more specific than his connection to Reformation chiliasts, the student-oriented Youth Culture or the broader currents of Jewish messianism surrounding him, and, as both McCole and Biale suggest, would seem to predate his acquaintance with Scholem. Benjamin knew the work of the early nineteenth-century mystical Catholic philosophers of history Franz von Baader, whose complete works he acquired in 1917, and that of Baader's and Friedrich Schelling's student Franz Joseph Molitor (see Baader; Molitor). Both Baader and Molitor comment on the Kabbalah (the latter quite extensively in a multivolume work, part of which Benjamin also acquired), and Benjamin refers to both in relation to the concept of *shekhina* in a letter to Scholem in May 1917 (Benjamin, *Correspondence* 86, *Gesammelte Briefe* 1:357; see also Biale 31–32, 72–73, 103–8, 196–98; Dieckhoff 16–50; Handelman 17, 101).

Scholem glosses in his notes an earlier hidden reference to Baader's version of *shekhinah* in a late-1916 letter from Benjamin to Herbert Blumenthal (*Gesammelte Briefe* 1:350). Benjamin implies in a subsequent letter to Scholem in June 1917 that he had been made aware of the work of at least Baader through a "small section" of a 1912 dissertation by an acquaintance, Max Pulver (Benjamin, *Correspondence* 89), and refers there again to Baader's account of *shekhinah* as well as to Baader's account of time and history. Scholem elsewhere notes that Benjamin "found Baader more impressive than Schelling," who would have been the leading source of German natural philosophy (see Scholem, *Walter Benjamin* 22). Oddly, Baader and Molitor have received little substantive attention in commentary on Benjamin. David Biale provides useful accounts of Molitor and to a lesser extent Baader in relation to Scholem, going as far as to suggest that Molitor, even with his Christological bias, may have been the most important early influence on Scholem's approach to Kabbalah (Biale 31–32). Biale also discusses Benjamin's affinity to Scholem on Kabbalist visions of language and history, though he provides only vague hints about Benjamin's knowledge of Kabbalah prior to meeting Scholem (see Biale 103–8, 196–98, 72–73). The most extensive English-language treatment of Benjamin's relation to Jewish thought does not mention Baader at all, and misidentifies Franz Joseph Molitor in its index as the music historian Raphael Molitor, a contemporary of Benjamin (see Handelman). In German scholarship, Reiner Dieckhoff, one of Scholem's students, establishes the most direct evidence linking Baader, Saint-Martin, and Molitor to Benjamin's early theory of language (presented in "Language as Such and the Language of Man" [1916]), all in the context of Benjamin's larger debt to mysticism of various sorts (Dieckhoff 16–50).

Like the conservatives Edmund Burke and Joseph de Maistre, Baader rejected Enlightenment philosophy, such as the religious skepticism of Kant and the humanist *contrat social* of Rousseau, insisting instead that the social and the religious are made of the same fabric, and that the Catholic Church should thus be directly involved in political life. The "anthropological" perspective of Baader's social theory also anticipates that of the more liberal Durkheim, however, since Baader favored the revival of medieval corporations and intermediary occupational associations, including those of the proletariat, to offset the individualistic excesses of industrial capitalism. A friend of and influence on Schelling, Baader drew heavily upon the earlier mysticism of Jakob Böhme and Louis Claude Saint-Martin, but he also elaborated a theory of historical time that emphasizes humanity as the sacrificial victim of history and the centrality of revelation.

Man begreift die Zeit nur als ein Opfer und warum die Schrift von einem Lamme spricht, welches seit Anfang der Zeit sich opfert.... Was nun aber die Herstellung einer solchen Theorie oder Philosophie der Zeit oder Geschichte und Societät betrifft, so ist vor allem die Einsicht festzuhalten, dass eine solche Theorie der Geschichte ohne jene einer Offenbarungsgeschichte schon darum nicht möglich ist, weil die Offenbarung als solche immer divinatorischer Natur oder die Zukunft anticipirend und in die zeitliche Gegenwart heim- oder herabziehend ist. (14:53)

One grasps time only as a victim [or sacrifice], and that is why Scripture speaks of a lamb, which sacrifices itself since the beginning of time.... Regarding the production of such a theory or philosophy of time or of history and society, it is important to hold fast to the insight that such a theory of history is impossible without a theory of a history of revelation, since revelation as such is by its very nature always divinatory, anticipating the future and drawing it home or down [i.e., transferred or copied as in an impression made from an etched plate] into the present time.

Though Benjamin avoided the idea of revelation per se, Baader's definition of revelation here correlates neatly with Benjamin's desire to read an anticipated or redeemed future in the commodities of the present. The passages from Baader to which Benjamin refers in his June 1917 letter to Scholem include discussions of the *shekhina* as the radiant home of the unmediated God (Baader

4:348); of the temporal as a fragment of the eternal and Böhme's view that in God the beginning and end are one (4:356); and of a second birth from a temporal day into an eternal one, as into an eternal Sabbath (4:340)—all notions that would remain with Benjamin until the "Theses."

Before the letter to Scholem in May 1917, there is no direct indication of Benjamin's acquaintance with the work of Molitor, whose own philosophy of history is far more concerned with the Kaballah (again as a mystical version of Christian doctrine) than is Baader's. But there is some internal evidence that Benjamin may have had access to Molitor's treatment of Kaballah—virtually the only substantive summary of Kaballah in German that would have been available to Benjamin before Scholem's scholarship—even prior to his meeting Scholem in 1915 and his subsequent acquisition of Molitor's writings. Several passages from Molitor's *Philosophie der Geschichte, oder Über die Tradition in dem alten Bunde und ihre Beziehung zur Kirche des neuen Bundes (mit vorzüglicher Rücksicht auf die Kabbalah)* [Philosophy of History, or On Tradition in the Old Testament and its Relation to the Church of the New Testament, with an excellent consideration of the Kaballah] (1834–57), bearing directly on Benjamin's own appropriations from Kaballah, will give a sense of what Benjamin found there.

Das wahre innere absolute Wesen der Gottheit ist unerkennbar für alle Creatur, das Geschöpf kann nur die Gottheit in ihrem Ausschein oder in ihren ספירות (S'phiroth) fassen. (Molitor 1:96n)

The true inner absolute being of divinity is unrecognizable for every creature, the creature can only grasp divinity in its shining forth or in its Sefiroth.

The Catholic Molitor claims that while there are ten Sefiroth (that is, ten emanations, appearances, spheres, stages, or gradations of the divine En-Sof, or hidden, infinite and innermost being of God), these are shaped into only three Parzuphim (personae or countenances; Scholem notes that both Cordovero and Luria list five [see Scholem, *Major Trends* 269–71]), so that Christ could be called the reflection or shining forth (one of three persons) of the Father.

But Molitor also refers directly to the Lurianic Kaballah that would become central to Benjamin's later ideas, and (I would argue) legible even in his earliest writing.

Dieses Leiden Christi dauert so lange fort, bis alle Glieder, deren Haupt er ist, aus den קלפה (Keliphoth) den Schlacken des Bösen wieder herausgezogen, oder diejenigen, welche sich nicht ziehen lassen wollen, vom Leibe abgetrennt und durch neue Glieder ersetzt worden sind. (Molitor 1:103n)

Christ's suffering continued until all the limbs, of which he is the head, had drawn back out of the *kelipot,* the slag or waste products of evil, or until those that would not allow themselves to extract had been separated from the body and replaced by new limbs.

In Kaballah, the Sefiroth are sometimes described as "limbs" of a central body, as of Adam Kadmon's (especially in the late thirteenth-century account in the *Sefer ha-zohar*—see Scholem, *Major Trends* 215). But the Sefiroth are equally the verse and word of scripture, the various names of God, and divine speech itself (Scholem, *Major Trends* 215–16). Molitor again invokes Lurianic imagery in his reference to the *kelim* or vessels that house the Sefiroth's atomized points of light and the idea of the *tsimtsum:*

Das Aeußere in diesen S'phiroth, oder das eigentliche Negative, geistig Leibliche, was die reelle Schiedlichkeit bildet, wird genannt die כלים Celim, Gefäße, als Gegensatz des einfachen Ezems oder des Willens der Selbstbeschränkung. (Molitor 2:159)

The outward appearance or exterior of these Sefiroth, or their properly negative, spiritual corporeality, that which forms their real separateness, is called the Kelim, vessels, as the antithesis of God's singular withdrawal [*Ezems = tsimtsum*] or will to self-limitation.

Both the *Zohar* and Luria are invoked in various places by Molitor (see, e.g., Molitor 1:80).

As early as a letter to Carla Seligson in September 1913, some two years before meeting Scholem, Benjamin displays a knowledge not only of the general account of Sefiroth and En-Sof in the Kabbalah, as provided by Molitor and Baader, but also of the more specific image of Luria's *kelipot,* those vessels or bowls of light that house the divine light, as they appear in Molitor (see Molitor 1:103n, 2:159). In a passage of the Seligson letter filled with Lurianic imagery that has been overlooked by previous accounts, Benjamin criticizes the desire for an institutional presence within Wyneken's youth movement and comments: "Almost everyone forgets that *they themselves* are the place where spirit actualizes itself. However, because they have made themselves inflexible, turned themselves into the pillars of a building instead of into the vessels or bowls [*Gefäßen, Schalen*] that can receive and shelter an ever purer content, they despair of the actualization we feel within ourselves. This soul is the *eternally actualizing soul*" (Benjamin, *Correspondence* 55, *Gesammelte Briefe* 1:175; Benjamin's italics). This influence can be felt again a bit later in his more often discussed essay "The Life of Students" (1915), where the notion of a messianic *Jetztzeit* in correspondence with earlier now-times is juxtaposed to mere bourgeois progress:

> The elements of the ultimate condition do not manifest themselves as formless progressive tendencies, but are deeply rooted in every present in the form of the most endangered, excoriated, and ridiculed ideas and products of the creative mind. The historical task is to disclose this immanent state of perfection and make it absolute, to make it visible and dominant in the present. This condition cannot be captured in terms of the pragmatic description of details (the history of institutions, customs, and so on); in fact, it eludes them. Rather, the task is to grasp its metaphysical structure, as with the messianic domain or the idea of the French Revolution. (Benjamin, *Selected Writings* 1:37)

In light of the Lurianic language in the letter to Seligson, the subsequent reference to *die Jetztzeit* in "The Life of Students" is in my view not simply an effect of the more diffuse Nietzschean and revolutionary spirit of the time or of Wyneken's Youth Culture. It is already a fairly specific Kabbalistic perspective, one that will remain intact to the end of Benjamin's career.

Indeed, one might argue that it was only because Benjamin later had somehow convinced himself that Communist discourse was *inherently* polysemic in precisely the sense of Talmudic interpretation that he could embrace Marxism at all. As he wrote to Max Rychner in 1931: "I have never been able to do research and think in any sense other than, if you will, a theological one, namely, in accord with the Talmudic teaching about the forty-nine levels of meaning in every passage of Torah. That is, in my experience, the most trite Communist platitude possesses more *hierarchies of meaning* than does contemporary bourgeois profundity, which has only one meaning, that of an apologetic" (Benjamin, *Correspondence* 372–73; Benjamin's italics). Such a perspective, however strained it might now appear, will be used finally to underwrite—or rather, to manipulate as a hidden agency—the increasingly untenable or equivocal prospect of a specifically Marxian political transformation in the late 1930s.

That Benjamin should have seen these unlikely correspondences between Kaballah, Christological mysticism, and materialist Marxism is itself a function of what we might call a secularized theological outlook, a political theology. Benjamin in fact sees intellectual correspondences throughout his reading. Hence, the critique of progress elaborated in the *Mikrocosmus* of Hermann Lotze, a neo-Platonist like Baader and Molitor, will be cited several times in the *Arcades*, resonating with the critique already developed in "The Life of Students" (see *Arcades* 478–81 [N13,2–N14a,5]), and will reappear in the "Theses" (*Selected Writings* 4:389). But it is the implied reference in "The Life of Students" to the *kelipot* that Benjamin may have gotten from Molitor—the slag or waste products of evil from which the spark of the divine is recovered with the coming of the Messiah—that is most significant, for this figure may be the most important hermeneutic gesture in all of Benjamin's writing. It is the central trope of the *Arcades*, it is the basic motif of Benjamin's approach to language, and it is with Benjamin up to the "Theses," where a now more fully developed Lurianic understanding of the *kelipot* can be invoked. In spite of the various phases or stages that critics have isolated in Benjamin's career—Youth Culture, spiritual withdrawal, and, later, Marxism—Benjamin's work remains very much of a piece when it comes to the theosophical strains he derived early on from Kaballah.

Differentiated and Bundled Time

Writing in a very different time and place, Kracauer mutes and revises Benjamin's debt to the Kabbalah, his messianism, and his revolutionary tone. For example, Kracauer still considers Marx's "substructure-superstructure theory" one of the "'right' generalizations" (*History* 101), as absolute as an historical idea can get without losing touch with its materials and becoming pure philosophy. But in claiming that "historical ideas are objective precisely because of their indebtedness to unmitigated subjectivity" (103)—that is, to the historian's imagination, experience, and accumulated knowledge, but also to his time and place—Kracauer also deprives historical materialism as a whole of whatever metaphysical or theosophical substance it may have had for Benjamin. Scholem recounts an early conversation in which Benjamin "conceded that no laws could be observed in history" yet simultaneously insisted (against Scholem's objections) on defining history as "the objective element in time, something *perceptibly* objective"—an "objective factor" that could be demonstrated "scientifically" (Scholem, *Walter Benjamin* 13). By contrast, Kracauer is not far from the early Frankfurt School's (never achieved) ideal of a "critical theory" that rejected both value-free positivism and Hegelian absolutism in favor of a more dynamic and skeptical hermeneutic. At the same time, Kracauer's philosophical interest in the intrinsic meaning of a concept such as temporality also recalls Husserl's and Heidegger's more extensive meditations on time and historicity, and Gadamer's on interpretation. But Kracauer's emphasis on the minor claims of an "unmitigated subjectivity," as opposed to the "sham profundity" (Kracauer, *History* 103) of existentialism—that is, his emphasis on what Heidegger would have called the merely "ontic" as opposed to the ontological—is in this regard more congruent with such work as Adorno's *Jargon of Authenticity.* Like Adorno, Kracauer criticized Benjamin precisely because of an "undialectical approach" where the nature of history itself was concerned. Kracauer notes that Benjamin "drives home the nonentity of chronological time without manifesting the slightest concern over the other side of the picture" (155). Yet Benjamin's presence can be felt throughout Kracauer's meditation on the inadequacy of homogeneous time. Though he claims to abandon Benjamin's "weak messianism," Kracauer preserves vestiges of the utopian buried within his own philosophy of history.

Kracauer has shifted the entire thematic of *die Jetztzeit*, or now-time, into a problem of hermeneutics, that is, into a heuristic that only approximates the totality and finality to which Benjamin aspired through it. Benjamin insists on the necessity to stop the flow of empty time if a redemptive possibility is to be rescued from the past in the face of false or illusory progress—that is, the sort of progress represented most immediately by a "vulgar-Marxist" conception of labor as the "exploitation of nature" and by a dogmatic social-democratic faith in progress that remained blind to the catastrophe of fascism (Benjamin, *Selected Writings* 4:393). Although, as Scholem suggests, the apocalyptic tone of the "Theses on the Philosophy of History" clearly owes something to its having been composed just after the Hitler-Stalin pact, the *Stillstellung* it emphasizes is a motif that runs throughout Benjamin's earlier writings in a variety of forms, from the sudden *tikkun*-like reversal of allegory in baroque *Trauerspiel* (Benjamin, *Origins of German Tragic Drama*), to the metempsychotic correspondences of Baudelaire and involuntary memory of Proust ("On Some Motifs in Baudelaire," in Benjamin, *Selected Writings* 4:313–55), to the semi-ecstatic "profane illuminations" of surrealism ("Surrealism," in Benjamin, *Selected Writings* 2:207–21), to the *Aufblitzen* (sudden flash) of "non-sensuous similarity" in the mimetic archive of language ("On the Mimetic Faculty," in Benjamin, *Selected Writings* 2:721). Indeed, the rejection of bourgeois progress and the commitment to a mystical-revolutionary-utopian notion of time at a standstill appear in Benjamin's very earliest work.

Even the rather mundane and (one would think) hardly forward-looking figure of the antiques collector, whose collection establishes an encyclopedia of related objects, is pressed into service as a prophetic *figura* of a mystical, but also potentially revolutionary, *Jetztzeit:* "Collecting is a form of practical memory, and of all the profane manifestations of 'nearness' it is the most binding. Thus, in a certain sense, the smallest act of political reflection makes for an epoch in the antiques business. We construct here an alarm clock that rouses the kitsch of the previous century to 'assembly'" (Benjamin, *Arcades* 205 [H1a,2]). The image of the alarm clock recurs at the end of "Surrealism," where it signals surrealism's Marxian potential, however compromised by the role of individual rather than mass intoxication, to substitute a political transformation for an historical view of the past (Benjamin, *Selected Writings* 2:218)—just the sort of present-interest history that worries Kracauer because of the universalist end encrypted in its putatively anti-universalist aims. Kracauer manages to preserve Benjamin's suspicion of the empty notion of progress implied by traditional historicism, but frees that suspicion from the mystical-religious dimension in which Benjamin locates it. Habermas, among others, has stressed Benjamin's counter-Enlightenment sensibility in this regard: for Benjamin, he writes, "we cannot be sure about even partial progress before the Last Judgment" (Habermas, "Walter Benjamin" 137). In Benjamin, the *nunc stans*, or arrested present of mystical knowledge, is itself the mythical prefiguration of that Last Judgment in the garb of materialist history (see, e.g., Witte 57; Wolin xlviii). Such *Jetztzeiten* fill history with meaning the way religious days of remembrance fill a calendar, each feast day being *the same day* every time it occurs.

In rescuing what I would call liturgical time from the ongoing disenchantment produced by the meaningless calendar of historicism, Benjamin's Gnostic or Kabbalist version of materialist history constructs simultaneous, messianic series of now-times, moments of crisis that run perpendicular to the empty time of false progress. "History is the subject of a construction whose site is not homogeneous, empty time, but time filled full by now-time [*Jetztzeit*]. Thus, to Robespierre ancient Rome was a past charged with now-time, a past which he blasted out of the continuum of history" (Benjamin, *Selected Writings* 4:395). Evoking and subtly altering in his own work the opening of Marx's *Eighteenth Brumaire,* Benjamin notes that the French Revolution, his primary example of a messianic *Jetztzeit* as early as the 1915 essay "The Life of Students" (Benjamin, *Selected Writings* 1:37), evoked Rome the way fashion evokes past costumes. But while fashion leaps into the past at the direction of the ruling class, Marxist practice does so "in the open air of history."

The sudden constellation of past and present moments becomes the dialectical ground of revolutionary action, but because such action cannot avail itself of any vision of the future or of progress, Benjamin's blasted history remains resolutely blind. Hence Benjamin's fondness for Paul Klee's *Angelus Novus,* with its "angel of history" blown backward into the future; and his affinity, in the "Critique of Violence," to Georges Sorel, whose anarchist general strike seemed to Benjamin the only sort of social violence that approached an acceptably "divine" or "sovereign" character, dependent on neither a "lawmaking" nor "law-preserving" purpose—that is, remaining blind, as does the messianic promise Derrida claims for deconstruction, to the future possibility of law itself (Benjamin, *Selected Writings* 1:236–52; see also Derrida, *Spectres* 28). Hence Benjamin's *rapprochement* with the conservatism of Carl Schmitt, in whose notion of sovereignty Benjamin found mirrored his own early interest (as revealed in the brief 1914 essay "The Religious Position of the New Youth") in Kierkegaard's meditations on the essential irrationality of choice and decision (see Benjamin, *Correspondence* 20, *Gesammelte Briefe* 3:558, *Gesammelte Schriften* 2:72–74, *Selected Writings* 1:252, *Selected Writings* 2:78; Kierkegaard, *Either/Or* 2:163–169, *Repetition*, 226–27; Schmitt, *Political Theology* 15). Hence too Benjamin's integration of a backward-focused political vision with Judaism, which prohibited the Jews from mystical prognostication and thereby "disenchanted the future" (*Selected Writings* 4:397), but at the same time emphasized both the backward glance of remembrance and the anticipation of the Messiah, who might appear at any moment.

The practical meaning of this backward political vision is made clear in the "Theses": a too-patient and progress-oriented social democracy hobbled the German working class by imagining it as the "redeemer of *future* generations," thus making it "forget both its hatred and its spirit of sacrifice, for both are nourished by the image of enslaved ancestors [*Vorfahren*] rather than by the ideal of liberated grandchildren" (Benjamin, *Schriften* 1:502, *Selected Writings* 4:394). It is a curious moment of near-mythic *ressentiment*, especially for a writer whose work is often directed against the power of myth. (After all, what anthropological status should be given to the term "ancestors"?) On the one hand, it concretizes religious abstractions such as the posterior horror of the "angel of history" in a political response of distinctly human dimensions. On the other hand, especially if we take those "ancestors" literally, it reduces the angel's sensibility to far more ambiguous terms, in which a mythic hatred inherited from the past, like the hunchback of religion, pulls the strings of historical materialism from beneath the stage. Indeed, such mobilizing "hatred" may have been felt more profoundly by the Hitler Youth bent on avenging fathers putatively sacrificed in the Great War than it was by the workers' movement, whose lack of a sense of urgency Benjamin castigated.

Kracauer deflates the mythic dimension of this contemporary alignment with a supposedly still vital (or ancestrally haunted) past by insisting instead that the constellation of present and past now-times is only what produces one of those contingent "'right' generalizations." Kracauer's now-times still harbor a utopian promise, but only in the sense that Proust's illuminating flashes of involuntary memory can be collected, through the obscuring continuity of a life history, into a series that mimics the closure and timelessness of art. Kracauer knows that history cannot be that work of art, except as fictional narrative or myth (see the related reflections on historical and novelistic narrative in LaCapra 1–14). Just as Benjamin invokes a liturgical temporality in which every Sabbath is a reminder of the coming Messiah, so Kracauer holds on to the secularized promise of redeemed now-times revealed in Proust's work. And it is finally Proust, the master of subjective, individual memory rather than objective and collective history, who provides Kracauer with the best approximation of the historian's utopian intent. Kracauer appropriates Proust as had Benjamin before him, but by remaining focused on the vicissitudes of individual response and unwilling to allegorize Proustian memory as universal history, Kracauer complicates the shift from esoteric insight to exoteric redemption that Habermas highlights in Benjamin's work—the shift from an auratic act of remembrance, increasingly threatened by mechanical reproduction and avant-garde technique, to the "open air" of collective transformation (see Habermas, "Walter Benjamin" 144–45).

Kracauer's suspicion of exoteric redemption finds expression finally in his version of historical discontinuity. For it is here that Kracauer gives a new meaning to what Benjamin had meant by the discontinuity implicit in a historical constellation of events. In Kracauer, homogeneous time is always in a complicated relationship with what he calls "bundles of shaped times" (*History* 154). Drawing from figures as diverse as Herder, Marx, Burckhardt, Dilthey, E. R. Curtius, Meyer Shapiro, Raymond Aron, and Maurice Mandelbaum, Kracauer observes that the notion of a historical period is often construed as possessing an unwarranted homogeneity and formal emptiness. For Kracauer, "empty time" is what makes possible the easy popular assumption of the coherent "period," and it is this assumption that must be dismantled. "The upshot is that the period, so to speak, disintegrates before our eyes. From a meaningful spatiotemporal unit it turns into a kind of meeting place for chance encounters—something like the waiting room of a railway station.... But understanding the whole society and large historical transformations affecting it is not therefore to be given up" (150). A given period must be broken down into independent "special histories," ranging from the social and the economic to the cultural, the aesthetic, and (one must assume, though Kracauer is not explicit about it) the scientific and technological as well.

Moreover, this internal discontinuity, which fractures each period designated by the dates of homogeneous history in a unique way, means that each period experiences its temporality in a different fashion—very much as

Kracauer in the 1960s acknowledges a sense of temporality very different in its urgencies from that of Benjamin in the 1930s.

> Each such period is an antinomic entity embodying in a condensed form the two irreconcilable time conceptions. As a configuration of events which belong to series with different time schedules, the period does *not* arise from the homogeneous flow of time; rather, it sets a time of its own—which implies that the way it experiences temporality may not be identical with the experiences of chronologically earlier or later periods. You must, so to speak, jump from one period to another. That is, the transitions between successive periods are problematic. (*History* 155)

Kracauer's conclusion begins to approach what Foucault argued about historical ruptures and the sudden transition between discursive epochs—though again, from the point of view of a hermeneutic conditioned by the possibility of progressive development rather than the arbitrariness of genealogy.

The core of Kracauer's description of "differentiated historical time" (*History* 146) is the tension, which in his view can only be worked out as a dialectic, between special and universal history, that is, between, on the one hand, the bundles of social or cultural expressions that obey internally maintained formal constraints—the production of social or economic interest, a movement in art, a tradition in philosophy—and which thus may be relatively asynchronous with regard to one another even as they share a similar chronology; and on the other, the way these different special histories of shaped or bundled time "tend to coalesce at certain moments which then are valid for all of them" (154). For Kracauer, the dialectical nature of the historical period is as compatible with the radical Marx as it is with the conservative Burckhardt or Ranke. And its truth always lies in an uneasy tension between temporal series of events that seem to obey logics independent of one another and the possibility of organizing the flow of history by periodization and the apprehension of continuity.

This is not to say that any underlying contemporary connection between different events, works, series, and so forth is little more than a convenient fiction and plays no further role in the determination of either the separate special histories or the tentative apprehension of historical development. In this sense, despite some resemblance between Kracauer's "special histories" and Lyotard's *petit récit*, nothing in Kracauer suggests Lyotard's hypostatization of "paralogy" or "dissension" in scientific progress. Because "someone always comes along to disturb the order of 'reason,'" claims Lytoard, "it is necessary to posit the existence of a power that destabilizes the capacity for explanation" (61). Likewise, Kracauer remains at some distance from Hayden White's metahistorical claims about the formal tropes and genres that govern, again somewhat arbitrarily, the emplotment of all historical narratives (see White)—a point that Kracauer himself makes in a reference to one of White's early essays (*History* 245, n. 34). Rather, it is to insist that the interpretation of past, present, and future alike is open to possibilities that cannot finally be encoded in advance by Enlightenment or progressive history, possibilities shaped by discontinuous bundles of time that historical actors and historians alike synthesize and reconfigure in imagining a discrete epoch. For Kracauer, the individual moments of such histories are not sedimented in Benjamin's liturgical constellations, as though infused with sparks of the messianic. Rather, such moments finally rest on the unpredictable effects of discontinuous histories and always-shifting understandings of temporality upon personal and collective consciousness alike. The historical narrative of progress is then not jettisoned, but it is historicized in turn: "The idea of progress presents itself differently from different periods whose succession may or may not amount to a progress" (202).

In his constant recourse to Proust, Kracauer is finally less than convincing. He realizes, it seems, that Benjamin's attempt to fuse the messianic and the material was doomed to fail, but he is unwilling to abandon completely the idea that historical insight might harness the past for constructive social change. In the opening epigraph of Benjamin's "Theses," which describes the chess-playing automaton, the puppet called historical materialism will win every game if it can enlist the services of theology, symbolized by a wizened hunchback pulling the puppet's strings beneath the table, safely hidden away from modernity's disenchanted eyes. Kracauer implicitly rejects the religious analogy but does not completely abandon a more secularized redemptive hermeneutics. His version of Proust, like Benjamin's, hopes to salvage a certain utopian element. But so does his more equivocal Benjaminlike identification with Kafka's portrait of Sancho Panza, who nightly feeds his "demon" or spirit with romances of chivalry. Named Don Quixote, the demon takes on an adventurous life of its own, one that Sancho Panza himself, now "a free man," followed "perhaps out of a sense of responsibility, and thus enjoyed great and profitable entertainment to the end of his days" (Kafka 430). Where Benjamin sees a foolish but fortunate assistant sending his master on ahead, so that "the burden is taken off the back," Kracauer finds instead something more like the historical imagination, which "points to a Utopia of the in-between—a terra incognita in the hollows between the lands we know" (Benjamin, *Selected Writings* 2:816; Kracauer, *History* 217).

For Kracauer, Benjamin's sense of arrested time is itself an obliquely aesthetic (that is, as Kant would have it, both subjective and universal) response to a disenchanted or secular understanding of time, a response that supplies a sense of "last things" where none can be justified otherwise. Understood in these terms, which are at points mirrored by Habermas's critique, Benjamin famously renounces the idealist "aura" of aesthetic autonomy in favor of the distracted bodily response of the proletariat at the movies (in "The Work of Art in the Age of Its Mechanical Reproducibility"), only to have a disavowed aesthetic response—the negative *telos* of universal history as universal decay—enter again by the back door of the mystical *Jetztzeit*. Benjamin's monads of religiously crystallized time absorb the transhistorical aura that technology had banished from the work of art itself.

In Benjamin's Wake

In 1972, Habermas responded to Benjamin's suspicion of progressive or Enlightenment history by insisting that we must disentangle notions of prosperity, liberty, and happiness, and by emphasizing the continuing value of Benjamin's unwillingness to accept an orthodox historical materialism that refused to admit the possibility of a "joyless" political emancipation, that is, one that generated economic prosperity but remained nevertheless meaningless and without emotional fulfillment (Habermas, "Walter Benjamin" 157). This unwillingness is exemplified in Benjamin's focus on the dialectical dream images of an otherwise empty bourgeois existence and in his commitment to a vision of substantive history, one knitted together by allegories and correspondences, rather than the "empty time" of Enlightenment rationalism and ameliorative socialism alike. Hence, for Habermas, "the liberation from cultural tradition of semantic potentials that must not be lost to the messianic condition is not the same as the liberation of political domination from structural violence" (155). And it is in demonstrating how to rescue those "semantic potentials" in tradition for the use of present-day social criticism that Benjamin's work proves significant. At the same time, Habermas recognized the inherently mythical nature of Benjamin's conflation of a theory of experience, or happiness, with materialist history, a conflation that implied a related identification of "ecstasy" and "politics" that "Benjamin could not have wanted." Habermas wants to preserve the idea of the "messianic condition" but acknowledges the ambiguity of all political theology at its heart.

Despite his wariness about the ease with which Benjamin's rescue of the past can slide into a regressive historical mythology all its own, however, Habermas concludes his analysis by noting that "without the influx of those semantic energies with which Benjamin's rescuing criticism was concerned, the structures of practical discourse—finally well-established—would necessarily become desolate.... Benjamin's conservative-revolutionary hermeneutics, which deciphers the history of culture with a view to rescuing it for the upheaval, may point out one path to take" (Habermas, "Walter Benjamin" 158–59). Not unlike Kracauer, Habermas wants to rescue Benjamin as relevant to the present day (in 1972, only three years after Kracauer's posthumous *History* appeared) by inverting Benjamin's priorities: instead of subordinating historical materialism to a theory of experience—which I would interpret primarily as a form of mystical religious belief—Habermas would harness Benjamin's theory of experience, his "rescuing critique," to the service of a progressive materialist history.

I want to emphasize the terms of Habermas's own version of critical rescue, one that insists (as I noted in chapter 1) on the "semantic energies" of the cultural past, because I believe that, despite the various shifts and reversals of "theory" in the humanities—let alone in Habermas's work—since 1972, approaches like that of Habermas are still dominant among those who invoke Benjamin as a model of cultural criticism, including those who simultaneously reject Habermas's critique of Benjamin. Although few today would fully embrace either the specific Kabbalistic resonance of Benjamin's messianic *Splitter* and the *Jetztzeiten* they would redeem, or the vision of wholesale revolutionary transformation Benjamin weds to them, Benjamin's legacy remains intact in the postmodern cultural critic's faith that a history brushed "against the grain" will reveal, like Foucault's "countermemory," moments of a forgotten past that can in turn seed the present with redemptive, transforming "energy." This is an assumption so deeply rooted in academic cultural criticism that it is generally passed by without comment: the "profane illumination" that Benjamin sought from history continues to underwrite a "weak messianism," though one that pays no heed to the religious or mystical significance of Benjamin's work even as it reproduces it. Derrida's *Spectres of Marx* is in a sense the abstract culmination of such criticism: Derrida has jettisoned all of Marx except for the anti-progressive history and the "messianism without a Messiah" theme he has borrowed from Benjamin.

Habermas makes explicit what is both promising and equivocal about Kracauer's late meditation on history. Kracauer is useful, in my view, to the degree that his sense of the discontinuous historical series of "shaped time," their tentative coalescing in the periods of a more universal history, the different ways temporality is experienced in these periods, and the necessity of a skepticism about "last things" all may at least help to remind us of the uncertain plurality of history that Benjamin's doctrine of *Jetztzeiten* both requires and negates. But Kracauer also wanted to retain vestiges of Benjamin's "rescuing critique," a strategy that Habermas embraces even as he revises it. The "semantic potentials" or "semantic energies" that Habermas invokes signify the counsel inherited from past "culture" in general but may also suggest the more substantive sources of meaning addressed in the previous chapter, such as specific religious traditions. As such, they may indeed help to generate moral and political values (or "potentials") for an otherwise "desolate" present, but always at the risk of a certain exclusive particularism. If we understand these values in Kracauer's terms, however, they can never be more than the discontinuous products of plural traditions that are themselves multiple and layered, and in the end always subjectively synthesized.

In her penetrating critique of Habermas's equivocal response to Benjamin's vision of history, Seyla Benhabib rightly points to the fact that Habermas remains caught between the modern, formal, Kantian ethics that will support his later notion of "communicative action" and the classical, but also potentially utopian, elaboration of "happiness" or "the good life" in terms of concrete needs and desires, both individual and social, which he encodes in his essay on Benjamin as the "semantic energies" of the cultural past (327–43). Benhabib's argument is, on the whole, quite congruent with the one I wish to develop here: that while admitting the importance of recovering the repressed or forgotten moments of tradition, especially as shaped by religion, for the elaboration of a more substantive notion of emotional fulfillment, one that lies beyond merely institutional notions of freedom and justice, Habermas nevertheless reverts to a fairly Hegelian understanding of the unified subject of history, and of the unified history produced by that subject.

In revising Habermas's tendency to fall back into a homogeneous understanding of history, which has often been blind to the special temporalities of class, gender, race, nation, religion, language, geography, and so on, Benhabib is finally not much interested in the epistemological plurality of history that Kracauer invokes. To be fair, her admittedly philosophical perspective is, by its very genre, far more concerned with "last things" than Kracauer the historian felt he had any right to be. Yet her critique demonstrates the persistence, as well as the limitations, of Benjamin's messianism in contemporary critical theory. Benhabib on the one hand admits that any modern revival of a unified, Aristotelian (or natural) conception of the "good life" would lead to "dogmatism," and that Kant's "Copernican Revolution," grounding norms in a rational democratic consensus, is irreversible (335). On the other hand, she is determined once again to rescue, in perhaps a more "utopian-anticipatory" (342) fashion than is Habermas, "the moment of transfiguration" represented by Benjamin's *Jetztzeit*, now as a final stage *within* the evolution of bourgeois universalism (329). It is a stage that for her vindicates earlier critical theory's insistence on transforming the meaning of the cultural tradition and "revolutionizing our needs and wants" (336). As Nietzsche delighted in observing, the final rectification of human desire—which can surely be placed among Kracauer's "last things"—has been the perennial goal of priest and philosopher alike, even if Benhabib elaborates that goal on the basis of Habermas's "communicative ethics" rather than Marcuse's more mythical distinction between true and false needs. What one might expect to remain provisional and plural through and through in what Blumenberg calls the infinite but not inevitable modern idea of progress gives way to the quasi-religious teleology embedded in "those moments of transfiguring experience" (343) that remain one of Benjamin's most enduring—and troublesome—legacies.

Since Habermas's critique, the nostalgic and mystical elements in Benjamin's conception of history have been more often called into question than not, if often then to be rationalized away in the more institutionally sanctioned revisionist project of reading the past against the grain of received wisdom. On rare occasions, however, one finds a wholesale critique of the redemptive strain in Benjamin's writing. Leo Bersani's *Culture of Redemption* correctly and refreshingly situates Benjamin's *Jetztzeit* in the context of his larger tendency to "see all history as a fall from Adamite being" (61). Bersani is not, however, primarily interested in questions of history. He focuses instead on literary art and the illusion of its "redemptive" interpretation. On this score, Bersani's larger argument is quite compelling—that art does not stand outside history and hence (as Plato suggested long ago) can't really correct or redeem it, and only the "philosophical" misreading or completion of art as redemption (or the equally philosophical "deconstructive criticism" that may secretly share the same goal) actually implies that art can (2, 62).

I would indicate only two problems with this approach where Benjamin is concerned. First, Benjamin's sense that art in itself can be redemptive is equivocal at best, since he clearly recognized that the modern fetishism of aesthetic novelty leads to an archaizing sameness. It is the primary theme of the 1935 essay "Paris, the Capital of the Nineteenth Century," where *l'art pour l'art* becomes the watchword of a "false consciousness" (see *Arcades* 11). Second—and this is a wider problem in contemporary cultural criticism, which often retains the substance of Benjamin's transforming "now-time" and "present-interest" view of the past even as it rejects or represses his mysticism—a version of Benjamin's consuming messianic temporality, which "*burns away history in a redemptive conflagration*" (Bersani 61; his italics), sneaks back in. As it does for Benhabib, a perfectly Benjaminian moment of "transfiguring experience" remains for Bersani even when art and culture have been subtracted. He replaces a redemptive idea of art with his own negative version of redemption in the idea of the "self-shattering and solipsistic jouissance" of sexuality, which he celebrates in Baudelaire, Bataille, and Flaubert—though its roots lie just as much in D. H. Lawrence, Marcuse, and Foucault.

Lest one imagine that this subject-consuming "jouissance" is truly as "solipsistic" and "socially dysfunctional" as advertised, Bersani observes instead that it is precisely such ego-dissolving sex that also dissolves "human beings' extraordinary willingness to kill in order to protect the seriousness of their statements" (4). In a sense, Bersani rescues Benjamin's redemptive "now-time" by embedding it ahistorically in the secularized mystique of Lawrence's and Bataille's sacrificial eroticism. It is admittedly a deconstructive idea of redemption, a subject-negating rather than subject-affirming redemption, but (as Bataille's own outline of revolutionary and historical potlatch, "The Notion of Expenditure," would show [see *Visions* 116–29]) it is hardly as critical of the utopian impulse to historical resolution as Bersani suggests. Bersani helpfully distances us from the grander allegorical narrative that drives Benjamin's work, but he does not thereby abandon the redemptive overcoming of historical time that is Benjamin's fundamental contribution to contemporary theory.

Rethinking Redemption

The difficulty that confronts the practice of cultural criticism in the postmodern present, a difficulty that Kracauer with his eye on multiplicity foretold, as it were, and Habermas tends to overlook, is not simply that the past must be rigorously sifted to cull semantic energies that will lend enduring significance to an ever more disenchanted present. The problem for contemporary cultural criticism is that the true diversity of the past actually yields an excess of these redemptive moments. Benjamin's *nunc stans* is not simply a correspondence between the present and any number of lost opportunities for transformation rescued from the past. His "now-time" is itself irreducibly plural and contradictory, and so is its messianic promise.

Benjamin's historical perspective may inspire a powerful ethical-political impulse to bring to light hidden or forgotten acts of oppression, to find a kind of memorial justice. And the deeper human need for redress of past and collective wrongs—as opposed to the more immediate and personal kind—should not be easily dismissed, though the force of the appeal for reparations that this need occasionally stimulates not surprisingly diminishes with the passage of time. Nevertheless, there are and have long been contradictory and competing versions of forgotten or repressed pasts produced by communities dedicated to redeeming historical loss for "present interests," and almost by necessity these have insisted upon an exclusive rather than inclusive vision: *Jetztzeiten* that justify so-called ethnic cleansing in remembrance of a nearly forgotten fourteenth-century military defeat; that fuel religious violence in the name of a seventh-century text or seventeenth-century persecution; that sanction militant communal aggression in the name of scripture, long-buried archeological evidence, destroyed religious sites, or the literary remains of ancestors whose heroic but suppressed fate is one day to be salvaged by a restored language and set of customs.

In the "Theses," Benjamin inverts the meaning of Nietzsche's claim that mankind's highest examples are the only rationale for the common mass of humanity by insisting that the "'cultural treasures'" are due not only to the "great geniuses," but to the "anonymous toil of others who lived in the same period." He then famously extends his observation into a maxim: "There is no document of culture which is not at the same time a document of barbarism" (*Selected Writings* 4:392). But the Achilles' heel of such a grand (if true) statement is that it can draw widespread assent only as long as it remains a generalization about history being written by the victors. The devil, as always, is in the details: Whose barbarism will be redressed? Whose trampled past will be redeemed? Who will pay the price? The last two hundred years especially have been powerfully shaped by such sentiments, often in the guise of nationalism. Most ironically, Nazi ideology, in the wake of the obvious injustices of Versailles reparations, raised those energies to new heights with its call to remember everything from long-lost Teutonic virtues to the "two million Germans who died [during World War I] all over the world for the idea of *Deutschland*" (Rosenberg 462). Benjamin's endorsement in the "Theses" of the idea that oppressed *Vorfahren* are a better motivation for political action than emancipated children finds numerous echoes in the present, and some are productive, but others bear a significance that Benjamin could not have wanted. His faith that all these energies are by nature constellations of a political theology built into history, "last things" emerging in a *Stillstand* rather than uncertain glimpses of an unknowable whole, shows—unfortunately—little diminishment.

This is an old story, as old as social solidarity itself, whether overtly religious or nominally secular. The reverse ethic—enduring terrible hardship in the present on the always-deferred promise that future generations will enjoy paradise, as Soviet ideology maintained for decades—is no more attractive, and it is in part what worried Benjamin in his day. Moreover, Benjamin's messianism is, after all, intended to be of a certain kind: universal, all-inclusive, and quite opposed to any ethnic, racial, or religious "special histories" that would remain distinct and exclusive in content. It is certainly true that Benjamin remained suspicious of Zionism throughout his life, from his early rejection of Buber's "'blood and experience' arguments" (Scholem, *Walter Benjamin* 29) to his persistent refusals to join Scholem in Israel—though one could claim even here that Benjamin was actually more orthodox than Scholem in waiting for the messianic event *before* returning to Jerusalem.

But we may be taking an illusory comfort in denouncing the narrow ethnic or nationalist perversions of messianic politics while endorsing the authentically emancipating forms supposedly elaborated in Benjamin's "Theses." Though complicated by those occasions when he referred specifically to Jewish history—and the last paragraph of the "Theses" may be one of the most telling instances—Benjamin seems for the most part to have divided the past rather neatly into polarized and (oddly) continuous legacies of oppressors and oppressed: those who carry off the spoils of civilization and transmit their heritage in an unbroken fashion, a heritage naively mistaken later for "the way it really was" by traditional historians, versus those others whose efforts and suffering constitute a true knowledge that was never directly recorded and must be restored, even if by mystical means. In the "Theses," directly below an aphorism by Nietzsche (from "On the Use and Abuse of History") concerning the need for a history that rejects the complacency of the "jaded idlers in the garden of knowledge," Benjamin writes: "The subject of historical knowledge is the struggling, oppressed class itself" (*Selected Writings* 4:394). Beyond the fact that this is hardly what Nietzsche had in mind, and derives directly from Lukács, what history demonstrates to a fault is that, as in Kracauer's understanding of temporality, oppression is likewise irreducibly multiple and layered over the long *durée,* uncontainable by the Lukácsian singularity and coherence Benjamin gives it (see Lukács, "Reification").

Religion, nationality, and race, for example, today still focus backward-looking eyes in ways that are often far more energizing than the class-based historical injustices spawned by the commodity fetish, even if we acknowledge with Kracauer the inescapable influence of economic life under modern capitalism. Moreover, the truly universal community would of necessity constitute a threat to many historically established forms of community—which is why acts of political "redemption" and attempts to rescue the past so often take place in the name of something fairly particular and exclusive, even when a universal community is the potential goal. By invoking in the last lines of the "Theses," perhaps the last lines of his entire theoretical project, a specifically religious refusal of magical prophecy, recollection of oppression ("the Torah and the prayers instructed them in remembrance"), and dream of deliverance ("for every second was the small gateway in time through which the

Messiah might enter" [*Selected Writings* 397]), Benjamin sought to suggest the larger, more inclusive vision of much Kabbalist mysticism. But these lines also ironically indicate that the universality of the historical materialism he allegorizes under the sign of religion here, at least as Marx had elaborated it, could be compromised by the religious specificity with which the "Theses" ends.

What actually lies beneath the veneer of a universal progress in barbarism masquerading, in Benjamin's account, as civilization, is a complex array of special histories, equivocal salvations, and competing injustices. Kracauer's unsolved dilemma—how to maintain an awareness of the plurality of nonsynchronous special histories as well as a commitment to an admittedly impure and partial ideal of progress, rather than to quasi-religious redemption—is very much still our own. (Even pragmatists such as Rorty mask the latter commitment by claiming some merely ethnocentric belief in the moral value of "continuing the conversation of the West" [394].) To be sure, Kracauer's last project may have been doomed from the start, since any theoretical account of the construction of his special histories and bundled times seems beyond his aim. Kracauer is inevitably thrown back on a critically self-conscious empiricism, albeit one guided by some good rules of thumb and skeptical optimism. Benjamin, by contrast, steeped in traditions of German mysticism from his earliest school days, throughout his life preferred the hermetic promise of total, messianic salvation to what we might call the secularizing *Verwindung* of a civilization contaminated by hidden or forgotten barbarism, or by forms of alienation that even Marx himself implied could not be fully extirpated. What Benjamin did not acknowledge is that history is replete with attempts to redeem barbarous pasts with paradises regained, and often the barbarism of paradise is even worse.

A gaze like that of Benjamin's angel of destructive progress, permanently fixed on the past and dedicated to the proposition that its inner truth is nothing but suffering, decay, and injustice—humanity as sacrificial lamb, as Baader (14:53) put it—will inevitably be both more discriminating and more mythic than the universal vision sought, perhaps in vain, by historical materialism. Like oppressed ancestors, the pain of history must on the one hand be fairly particular and personal to motivate the sacrificial hatred that would redeem it. On the other, it must be preserved by the durability of myth and legend against the consuming, but also necessary and useful, Nietzschean forgetfulness of individual complacency and "empty time." Kracauer's epistemological insecurity, which ensured his relegation to the rear stragglers of the advanced guard (Benjamin affectionately, if not uncritically, called Kracauer "a ragpicker at daybreak—in the dawn of the day of revolution" [Kracauer, *Salaried Masses* 114]), is also his best defense against history as myth, even (or perhaps especially) the Benjaminian sort of mythic anti-history that declares itself above all else the enemy of myth. In short, pretending that one can still invoke Benjamin's "now-time" without irony may be no better than the complacent bourgeois dream of automatic, unthinking progress. His *Jetztzeit* should be understood as possessing what Kracauer called "a time of its own," one that can have only the most equivocal significance for those who read Benjamin today.

3 * Durkheim's Modernity

From Theory of Religion to Political Theology

The complex tensions and intersections between rationality as a means to worldly ends and religious belief were of course at the center of modern social theory well before Benjamin and Kracauer. As Max Weber argued in the early years of the twentieth century, the rise of a capitalist economy guided by an increasingly powerful sense of instrumental rationality, accompanied by the division of labor and rationalization that had occurred—albeit at different speeds—in the realms of law, economics, and bureaucracy since the seventeenth century, was enabled in important ways by an "ascetic rationalism" that developed within Western religion itself after Luther and through which European Protestantism periodically tried to purge true religion of all vestiges of archaic magic (Weber, *Protestant* 182). Weber's perspective would seem to suggest that the intellectual of the twentieth century is above all an heir of Luther's and Calvin's Reformation and of Voltaire's Age of Reason, and hence of demystifying, humanizing, materialist, and politically leveling impulses, for which a supersensible and hierarchical belief in the sacred was supplanted by deist or anthropological reduction (as in the work of Feuerbach), if not by outright atheism. And although it is obvious that Weber's attitude to all this disenchantment was resolutely ironic, even critical—he noted that the concern for material goods fostered by the modern economic order had become an inescapable "iron cage" (181)—he did not imagine that the displacement or routinization of "charismatic" authority by more or less permanent social institutions was the prelude to catastrophe. Like Freud, one might say, Weber tragically acknowledged the discontent that secular rationality carried with it, as well as the need for some forms of professional charisma, but he did not long for a re-enchanted world.

Dialectic of Enlightenment versus Destruction of Reason

Some have suggested that the consequences of all this purposive rationality, democracy, and secular disenchantment are far more tragic than Weber allowed. Indeed Nietzsche—who may be numbered among the most influential critics of the Enlightenment's legacy, as it is embodied in the work of Descartes, Bacon, Newton, Locke, Kant, Condorcet, the English utilitarians, the ideals of science and democracy, and so forth—followed a Platonic line of political thought where democracy was concerned and predicted a rather more disturbing fate for the twentieth century. In the "Peoples and Fatherlands" essay of *Beyond Good and Evil* [1886]), Nietzsche declared that although future Europeans would be "extremely employable," they would also be in great need of a "master and commander":

While the democratization of Europe leads to the production of a type that is prepared for *slavery* in the highest sense, in single, exceptional cases the *strong* human being will have to turn out stronger and richer than perhaps ever before—thanks to the absence of prejudice from his training, thanks to the tremendous manifoldness of practice, art, and mask. I meant to say: the democratization of Europe is at the same time an involuntary arrangement for the cultivation of *tyrants*—taking that word in every sense, including the most spiritual. (Section 242; Nieztsche's italics)

To a large extent, Nietzsche's eerily accurate prophecy set the terms for future debate. The tyrannies of twentieth-century life wound up being every bit as impressive as its rationality. From the Nazi death camps and the Soviet gulag to the proliferation of totalitarian police states of the Right and Left, modern experience would seem to be overwhelmed by a barbarism all the more chilling for the unfeeling rationality, technological efficiency, and universalizing intentions enabling it.

Various commentators, in various traditions, pointed to this odd conjunction, perhaps too neatly summed up by Adorno and Horkheimer's thesis of a "dialectic of enlightenment"—that is, a hubristic confidence in the progress of humankind's ability to control the forces of nature, via instrumental reason, that finally assumes blind, mythic, and irrational dimensions, culminating in the totalitarian state. Any questioning of the imperative to dominate nature, Adorno and Horkheimer argued, any desire to maintain substantive (or charismatic) values unrelated to, or subversive of, scientific-technological purposes, would henceforth be branded irrational, nostalgic, and irrelevant.

The impersonal and ultimately mythic self-regard of modern rationality, and the absence of any concern for truth outside the parameters of technological control, were for Adorno and Horkheimer the intellectual sources of totalitarian regimes in Germany and the USSR, and of the pacification of all critical thinking in America by a mass-produced "culture industry."

At the same time, it is abundantly clear that, right beside the expansion of a disenchanted and scientific worldview, a powerful reaction against the Enlightenment arose within modern European culture (for a good recent overview of the topic, see McMahon). Although the most aggressive form of this reaction can be traced to radically conservative eighteenth-century religious romantics such as Joseph de Maistre (an odd amalgam of papist and mystic Freemason), it can be found equally within a renewed Roman Catholic orthodoxy (represented by the convert Cardinal Newman), an increasingly vocal and reform-minded Evangelicalism (such as that of the abolitionist William Wilberforce), and in traditions of pantheists after Spinoza, neo-Kantian metaphysicians after Fichte, natural philosophers after Schelling, existentialists after Kierkegaard, neo-Platonic spiritualists (such as the Kabbalist Madame Blavatsky) and theorists of mythic or racial *Volkscharakter* throughout the nineteenth and early twentieth centuries, some of them bearing fairly liberal and humane views, some not. As a result, against the prediction of Nietzsche and the critique of instrumental reason in Adorno and Horkheimer, where barbarism is understood to be the product of a calculating rationality run amok, one finds an opposing point of view that explains (or foresees) the twentieth-century success of tyranny as the consequence of irrational, mystical, and religious reaction rather than as an excess of unreflective technical skill and soulless social engineering.

Georg Lukács, whose early work tended to adopt the romantic, counter-Enlightenment argument against secular rationality, came in his later, ponderous (and post-Holocaust) *Destruction of Reason* to indict the resurgence of the irrational in modern life. He pointed especially to what he called a reactionary "religious atheism" in Schelling, Schopenhauer, Kierkegaard, and Nietzsche as the source of modernity's turn away from science (see, for example, his critique of the idealist-vitalist sociology of Georg Simmel, whose work had actually been an important influence on Lukács right up to his epoch-making Marxian essay on "Reification and the Consciousness of the Proletariat" of 1922 [Lukács, *Destruction* 448–49]). Lukács's later critical perspective was vitiated by his profound Marxist blindness to the barbarism of Stalin—Lukács in this period unfortunately tended to equate science and Soviet Marxism—but many anti-Stalinists and anti-Communists have shared his understanding and rejection of the modern embrace of irrationality.

Recently, it has fallen to the more moderate Jürgen Habermas to elaborate this perspective, in writings that argue for modernity as an incomplete or unfinished Enlightenment project (see Habermas's "Modernity: An Unfinished Project," and the debate it spawned, in Passerin d'Entrèves and Benhabib). For Habermas, the Enlightenment values of secular reason and democratic organization in the social or public sphere were undermined by modernity's return to a "new Paganism" in the realm of culture (see Habermas, *Philosophical Discourse*). Even Walter Benjamin, an important part of Habermas's own intellectual tradition, becomes problematic in his view, because Benjamin was so obviously influenced by Kaballah and the "religious atheism" that Lukács had outlined earlier (see Habermas, "Walter Benjamin"). In effect, for Habermas it is the continuation of romantic motifs, and a "pagan" religious perspective, however eccentric or cultic in form, that provides the key to understanding the extremes of twentieth-century political life. The charismatic Führer cult of Hitler and Stalin, the sacred character of the state, ecstatic varieties of collective experience, communal scapegoats, purgative national violence—all these point to quasi-religious, if not irrational, imperatives.

There are good reasons to agree with both the "excess of reason" and the "destruction of reason" characterizations of twentieth-century cultural life, but my primary concern in this chapter is to illustrate not the clarity of the opposition and of the debate I have just described but its radical instability, one that has already been suggested by the first two chapters. In his now classic overview of the generation of the 1890s in social theory, H. Stuart Hughes captured something of this instability when he referred to the "central paradox" emerging from the work of Dilthey, Durkheim, Bergson, Croce, Freud, Sorel, Weber, Gide, Thomas Mann, and many others: "more often than not, their work encouraged an anti-intellectualism to which the vast majority of them were intensely hostile" (Hughes 17). Like Hughes, I think the distinction between an Enlightened and a romantic modernity, or a secular and a mythic one, will not hold. And here, I do not mean simply that both religious and rational visions of modern history, independent of one another, eventually feed into parallel forms of political tyranny (as they do in Isaiah Berlin's comparison of Maistre and Tolstoy in *The Hedgehog and the Fox*). Nor am I primarily interested in rehearsing Jeffrey Herf's compelling argument in *Reactionary Modernism* that to account for something like Nazism, one ought to examine both irrational and rational forces, both a mythical consciousness fueling ecstatic mass rallies and a scientific-technological expertise willing to administer death camps, unconstrained by guiding moral principles. However accurate these notions of parallel paths to barbarism and the destructive conjunction of ordinarily distinct realms of myth and science may be, they still do not adequately address the degree to which religious and secular forms of thought were closely implicated in one another in the period, especially where the question of the social was at issue. The primary argument in what follows is that modernity is best understood through an elaboration of the twists and paradoxes of secularization—what we might call (adapting Heidegger) the *Verwindung,* or curative distortion, of the "ontotheological" tradition—that is, in the intimate and profoundly equivocal conjunction of a rational social imagination and a religious sensibility.

The Science of Religions

In the seventeenth and eighteenth centuries, the question of religion was, for both believers and blasphemers alike, to a large extent the question of theology. This is perhaps obviously true for defenses of Christianity, such as the Reverend John Orr's *Theory of Religion* (1762). Critical accounts of religion (which is to say, of "true" religion, or Christianity) also aligned theology and religion, from the early deism, or natural religion, of Edward Herbert (Lord Herbert of Cherbury, brother of the poet George Herbert) and Spinoza's *Ethics,* to the anticlerical Pierre Bayle and the libertine John Rochester, to the agnostic David Hume's *Dialogues Concerning Natural Religion* (1779) and Kant's summary account of the impossibility of ontological, cosmological, and physicotheological proofs of God's existence in the *Critique of Pure Reason* (1781). This is not to ignore the Enlightenment's wider interest in pagan or classical religions and in the historical and practical reasons for Christianity's triumph over them (in Gibbon's *Decline and Fall*), nor the lively discourse about myth and folkways (in Montesquieu and Herder), nor the flourishing investigations of the Orientalists (in William Jones and the Schlegels). Nor is it to overlook the early stirrings of an anthropological view of primitive religions—fetish, totem, and taboo first appear, at least in English, in the eighteenth century—or the millenarian fascination with occult and hermetic materials, including the Freemasonry that attracted Maistre, Mozart, and the American Founding Fathers alike (see, for example, Jacob). But it would be fair to say that the dominant problem of religion centered on the deists' watchmaker God, accompanied by the argument from design. Both are central to the academic debate in Hume's *Dialogues,* and to Kant's response in the *Critique of Pure Reason.*

At the same time, the study of religion *as* religion—that is, of separate traditions of belief and ritual quite apart from the theological truth involved in them—may be as old as the phenomenon of religion itself. In an appendix to *The Sacred and the Profane,* Mircea Eliade provides a remarkably brief and erudite history of the " 'history of religion' as a branch of knowledge" (216), a history that takes us back as far as Herodotus and the pre-Socratics and may have had its proper beginnings in Theophrastus (372–287 BCE), who, according to Diogenes Laertius, composed a history of religions in six books. Eliade moves briskly through a wide range of contributions, from Berosus, a priest of Bel under Alexander the Great; to Epicurus, Lucretius, the Stoics, Euhemerus (from whom we derive the term for the popular perspective that the gods were kings and heroes deified for their service to humanity), Polybius, and Strabo; to the Romans Cicero, Varro, Pausanias, Plutarch, Tacitus, Lucian; to the neo-Pythagorean reaction of Celsus and Porphyry; to the Christian "counterattack" under Tertullian, Clement, Origen, Eusebius, and Augustine; to medieval Catholic scholars challenged by Islam, the Islamic historians al-Biruni, ibn Hazm, and especially ibn Rushd (Averroës), and the Jewish scholars Saadia and Maimonides; to the Renaissance humanists' rediscovery of paganism, as seen in Ficino and the widespread interest in Hermes Trismegistus (see especially Yates here); to the great voyages of discovery of the fifteenth and sixteenth centuries and their consequences, especially the new comparative method of Jean François Lafitau, whose *Customs of the American Savages Compared to the Customs of the Earliest Ages* (1724) is often cited as one of the crucial milestones in the prehistory of modern Western anthropology, and of Charles de Brosses, who popularized Lafitau's term "fetishism"; to the Enlightenment's discussion of "natural religion" pursued by the French *philosophes* Voltaire, Diderot, and d'Alembert, and the German thinkers Wolf and Lessing; to Hume's more radical skepticism; and finally to mythologists such as Fontenelle, Dupuis, and Creuzer. But despite this long and complicated history, Eliade still argues that the history of religion emerged as a true "science of religions," that is, as an autonomous discipline, only with the work of Max Müller and his *Essay on Comparative Mythology* (1856).

Even before Müller, however, the question of religion, including religion in its Western or Judeo-Christian forms, became clearly separated for nineteenth-century intellectuals from the question of theology or divinity. Many reasons can be cited. Philosophy after Kant and Hume tended to insulate itself more rigorously from arguments about the existence and nature of God, which were left for the theologians to debate; the "natural supernaturalism" of the romantics (see Abrams) displaced the divine into nature itself; the authenticity of scriptural revelation had been thoroughly undermined for many elites by the work of Strauss and Feuerbach; and the received (biblical) accounts of earthly and hence human history had been shaken by the powerful geological evidence of Lyell. (The prime example of such accounts is the Irish Archbishop James Ussher's six-thousand-year chronology, built around Noah's flood, which had survived in the popular mind since the seventeenth century.) The coming of Darwin's natural selection in mid-century is generally seen as a watershed in the attack on a religious worldview, and for the broader or mass reception of religious doctrine this was undoubtedly the case. But among an intellectual elite most of the transformation had occurred well before Darwin. Max Weber borrowed his famous phrase about the "disenchantment of the world" from Schiller, who had used it a century earlier.

This separation of religion from theology, which largely abandoned the latter to the province of believers, did not at all put an end to an interest in the history of religion. Indeed, if we follow Eliade's chronology, the separation was both enabled by, and enabled in turn, a noticeable expansion in the critical or "scientific" study of religion. In fact, the study of religion as an entity in itself flourished as never before. In some ways, the real question is, why? Why were so many secular intellectuals—and the rather long list of just the major figures includes Strauss, Feuerbach, Müller, Mannhardt, Tylor, McLennan, Robertson Smith, Nietzsche, Frazer, Andrew Lang, R. R. Marrett, K. T. Preuss, Wilhelm Schmidt, Simmel, William James, Graebner, Frobenius, W. H. R. Rivers, Wilhelm Wundt, Weber, Durkheim, Lévy-Bruhl, and Freud, among many others)—concerned to elucidate the origins, the essential nature, and the history of religion, again quite apart from any discussion of the truth of revelation or speculative metaphysics? Why did these more "scientific" and materialist nineteenth-century intellectuals not conclude, as had Hume before them, that religion was nothing more than superstition, fed by gross ignorance and fear, manipulated by unscrupulous clerics? If religion, whether in its Judeo-Christian form or in its putatively inauthentic or less rationalized guises of Islam, Hinduism, Buddhism, animism, and so forth, was dependent upon mental error, why should further rational inquiry be expended on it? In 1844, Karl Marx famously dismissed religion as the "opium of the people" ("Contribution" 131). If many other nonreligious intellectuals of his time did not do the same, it is not, I think, simply because they felt that the third estate needed to be sedated by useful illusions—though this view has been perennially in evidence and was inherited by later cultural criticism, which tends to view the rise of an elite "culture concept" in the nineteenth-century as a clever substitute for the soporific of religion.

It is not only a matter of *why* intellectuals were so interested in a rational explanation of religious belief and ritual. There is also the fact that, for many of these same intellectuals, religion did not merely vanish once its material, social, or psychological beginnings and purposes were explained. Instead, they reimagined religious energy as something absorbed, sublimated, or transformed by secular ideas and behavior, from the redemptive power of mimesis to social solidarity, from the poetic word to the nation-state. In turn, the work of such secular intellectuals was itself often infiltrated by religious terminology. When Weber defines the nonrational appeal of a leader as *charisma* (originally a Greek term for a gift of grace from the gods) and Durkheim describes social solidarity as a consequence of *effervescence* (first applied in the seventeenth century to disorders of the blood, resulting in fever), they are paradoxically explaining social action by reference to religious or magical concepts—that is, prescientific from the perspective of their own times—even as they explain religious phenomena by rational social action.

The one thing we might say with some assurance is that, on the heels of the Enlightenment, the French Revolution, and a range of nationalist upheavals leading to 1848, the year of so many failed European rebellions, numerous thinkers of quite different religious and political persuasions were convinced that people needed to worship some transcendent force or idea if civilization was to survive the crises of legitimacy that afflicted it. Although this sort of conviction could be found across Europe, it had a special resonance in France, where a powerful strain of Catholicism crashed head on into the anticlericalism of the French Revolution. Among such conservatives as Chateaubriand, Lamennais, and Bonald, the demand for a return to the authority of the pope and a divinely sanctioned monarchy is perhaps hardly surprising, though mystical "throne and altar" types such as Maistre also acknowledged that government itself "est une véritable religion: il a ses dogmes, ses mystères, ses ministres; l'anéantir ou le soumettre à la discussion de chaque individu, c'est le même chose; il ne vit que par la raison nationale, c'est-à-dire par la foi politique, qui est un *symbole*" [is a true religion: it has its dogmas, its mysteries, its ministers; to abolish it or submit it to the discussion of each individual would be the same thing; it lives only through national judgment (or reason), that is to say, through political faith, which is a *creed* (or *emblem*)] (Maistre 1:376; Maistre's italics). Maistre's more liberal contemporary Fichte would argue a similar point in his *Addresses to the German Nation* (1808) about the as yet unborn German national mind. But an equally lively sense of the need for collective worship could be found among the radical revolutionaries and scientific reformers, as in the exemplary case of Robespierre, whose Enlightenment-inspired Cult of Reason in 1793 officially abolished the worship of God, only to be superseded by the Festival of the Supreme Being in 1794.

By the 1850s, the far more scholarly and methodical Auguste Comte, who rejected what he saw as the Protestant individualism, centralized state, and atheistic ideals of the Revolution, had ironically resurrected Robespierre's dramatic gesture in his own version of a grandiose Religion of Humanity or what he called "the Great Being," complete with a calendar of worship that today looks like nothing less than a humanist parody of Catholicism (see Lenzer 472–73, 465). Comte was in many ways the grandfather of modern sociology. He hoped to recover the moral influence formerly generated by private associations under medieval Catholicism, including family, church, guild, and estate, that the Revolution had banished. But he ended his career spinning out a quite fabulous secular religion—Huxley called it "Catholicism without Christianity" (see Lepenies 174)—one built on the belief that everything good and true about human civilization depended on worship based no longer on an outdated theology or a crisis-prone metaphysics but on the positivist (that is, scientific and materialist) credo of "Order and Progress" (Lenzer 448–49). Comte's calendar, and the program of education that went with it, attempted to forestall intellectual anarchy and political revolution by reorganizing moral life according to a "social physics" implied by the increasingly clear and reductive laws of astronomy, physics, chemistry, and physiology.

In effect, Maistre, Robespierre, and Comte all seemed to believe that had religion never existed, one would have needed, as Voltaire had once said of God, to invent it, or something very much like it. It was a belief central to the beginnings of sociology, as Wolf Lepenies has shown. (Psychologists and neo-Platonists would respond to somewhat different impulses but would intersect with the social theorists at various points.) Whether one sought a radically new order rooted in the rational state (with Robespierre), order and obedience based in the church (with Maistre), or order and progress in society itself (with Comte), a postreligious translation of religion appeared to be both inescapable and essential. Again, one can find this sort of reasoning, which is in certain ways a development of eighteenth-century deist thought, across Europe; but perhaps because of the French Revolution's lessons, what is striking is the degree to which a comprehensive, and quite substantial, entity called society was being elaborated in France as a replacement for religion. As Georg Simmel, one of the first German sociologists, observed in 1918, if the dominant idea of the Renaissance and eighteenth century had been nature, and that of the romantic period had been ego, then society "epitomized . . . the reality of life" for nineteenth-century thinkers (Simmel, *Conflict* 14). Though Simmel pointed to the vitalist concept of a *life*-energy as the new idea of the twentieth century, it would still be correct to say that he believed the fundamental problem to be the inner or moral life of a cohesive, self-sustaining society.

Most important of all, the nineteenth century's rediscovery of the religious character of social coherence in the wake of the French Revolution was in many ways what Robert Nisbet, linking Comte with Bonald, called a "deeply conservative movement" to ensure solidarity within national, republican, and increasingly disaggregated democratic societies (44). Lepenies has shown how important the later "Catholic" positivism of Comte (along with conservative social theorists such as Fustel de Coulanges and Le Play) would be for the radically conservative and Catholic French integral nationalists of the Third Republic: Charles Maurras and Henri Vaugeois, founders of the Institut de l'Action Française; Count Léon de Montesquieu-Fezensac, who held the first chair named for Comte at the institute; Maurice Barrès and Charles Péguy (40–46). But this rediscovery of the religious nature of the social was also linked to the desire for solidarity *among* the new independent nation-states of Europe, as Comte's broader vision of a pan-European—and, finally, racially defined—moral order linking France, Italy, Spain, Britain, and Germany reveals (see Löwith 67–82).

This is, I think, at least one good reason for the flourishing of a sociological "theory of religion" between 1840 and World War I: the era's great consolidation of the nation as an "imagined community" (in Benedict Anderson's terms) demanded a model of nontheocratic collective consciousness, one that would depend on specific regimes of national education but that also, in its more liberal guises, looked forward to a unified Europe or "Western Republic" quite opposed to the East (B. Anderson; Lenzer 472–73, 448). (Such social theory is certainly related to the deeper and older problem of "original sin" and the fallenness of humankind, as Christopher Herbert has argued, though it is clearly not necessarily dependent, as he also suggests, on Puritan or Wesleyan anxiety over unregulated desire. Indeed, right-wing Roman Catholics such as Bonald, Maistre, and Donoso Cortés, and their twentieth-century inheritors Maurras and Schmitt, all held distinctly Hobbesian views of humanity while being, like Comte, staunchly anti-Protestant.) Comte's "religious" theory of society leads inexorably to the writings of Emile Durkheim—who was, significantly, the secular (and Jewish) intellectual against whom Maurras, Barrès and friends most dedicated their efforts, and whose work drew especially upon the more liberal, internationalist trends in Comte's.

Durkheim's Hypostasis

Durkheim provides a useful key to the modern intersection of secular reason and secularized religion, a key to what we might call modern culture's love-hate relationship with religion. His work is crucial for understanding how scientific and materialist investigations of religion were at times shaped in turn by the power of religious thought. Durkheim's early sociology, as seen in *De la division du travail social* (1893), followed Comte in arguing for the moral importance of intermediary social groups, such as professional associations, unions, civic clubs, and the like. Durkheim held an affirmative view of the modern capitalist ("organic") division of labor, which promoted individualism, as opposed to the primitive rigidity of homogeneous ("mechanical") society. But he also argued for a new corporatism, a revival of the classical Roman *gens*—*collegium* and *sodales*—as a remedy for the anomic propensities within capitalism. The underlying problem of the sociology of religion, however, was there all along. After 1894 and his reading of English anthropologists concerned with totemic religions, especially McLennan, Robertson Smith, and Frazer, Durkheim became increasingly concerned with the idea that religious belief is primarily a transfiguration or symbolization of social life.

Durkheim's later account of religious belief, presented in full as *Les formes élémentaires de la vie religieuse: Le système totémique en Australie* (1912), is in its own scholarly way a paradigmatic example of modern ambivalence about the nature of religion. His central thesis is based, erroneously, on the supposed primacy of the clan—a primitive version, as it were, of the Roman *gens* and medieval guild—in ethnographies of Australian aboriginal culture. Durkheim argues that the totemic representations of clan solidarity should be understood as the "elementary forms" of religious thinking in general, and that these forms are thoroughly social in origin, meaning, and function. Religion for Durkheim is not primarily a means of representing the natural world, for its persistence would then be incomprehensible, because in this respect it is "barely more than a fabric of errors." Rather, Durkheim concludes, "religion is first and foremost a system of ideas by means of which individuals imagine the society of which they are members and the obscure yet intimate relations they have with it" (*Elementary* 227).

Durkheim does not limit this characterization to primitive religion, which is why after him his analysis also came to occupy a fundamental position in the study of myth, magic, society, and language, especially in French thought from Mauss and Bataille to Lévi-Strauss and Derrida. The totemic clan is finally for Durkheim the historical source of our ability to classify and order the world of our perceptions, thus generating our epistemological distinctions and ordering concepts (the A and not-A of Aristotelian logic; the Kantian categories of space, time, and causality; the idea of "force"; national flags) as well as our moral sensibility, as reflected in Durkheim's most basic moral distinction between the sacred and the profane. All societies consecrate certain concepts the transgression of which amounts to a kind of sacrilege—for example, the idea of progress or "free discussion" in modernity (*Elementary* 215). Ultimately, language itself is a storehouse of "collective representations" (436), and thus for Durkheim more a representation of social solidarity than a mirror of nature or an instrument of practical communication. The "impersonality" and "stability" of collectively accepted ideas is what makes for "logical" thought, what characterizes "truth" (437). And in this sense the truths of modernity are functionally equivalent to the impersonality and stability of totems and the religious forces behind them.

On one level, Durkheim is no relativist. He admits that modern rational and scientific concepts, shaped by individual testing and critique, have a precision and clarity—and hence a realistic validity—that the religion of primitive clan consciousness does not. On another level of abstraction, however, such a distinction is one of degree only, so that primitive and modern collective representations are equal in kind. Steven Lukes has argued that Durkheim's last project was a contradictory critique of William James's pragmatism, in which Durkheim simply "did not distinguish between the truth of a belief and the acceptance of a belief as true" (Lukes 495). For Lukes, Durkheim criticized pragmatism for abandoning any claim to the realism of true beliefs, but then simultaneously based all claims to validity on the social origin and authority of beliefs, including (one must assume) the claims of his own sociology. Yet Lukes's observation that Durkheim confused philosophically valid truth claims with mere social belief still manages to miss the crucial element of Durkheim's late work on religion, which is that Durkheim did not in fact feel the need to make the sort of analytical distinctions—between "truth" per se and "society"—that Lukes emphasizes. In Durkheim, the socioreligious (totemic) origin of all rational categories of thought posits an enigmatic ambivalence at the core of human understanding itself.

Such ambivalence runs throughout Durkheim's approach to religion. On the one hand, religion is the expression of a shared need for social cohesion. It is an interpretation that a particular society makes about its own collective identity, which could be taken to imply that the members of such a society possess an inchoate sense of their collective identity prior to their "religious" representation of it. In this case, the totem is expediently chosen from among nearby animals or plants, as Durkheim at times suggests, to symbolize a group character based on perceived kinship that individuals already feel "by nature," as it were. Thus, Durkheim writes, "the god of the clan, the totemic principle, can be none other than the clan itself, but the clan hypostatized [*hypostasié*] and imagined in the physical form of the plant or animal that serves as totem" (*Elementary* 208; translation modified). The sacred, one could say, is the social whole projected exoterically as a symbol embodying the group's essence or moral substance, as the older philosophical meaning of the Greek *hupostatos*—that is, a metaphysical foundation or principle—would suggest, though Durkheim may be using the term simply in its modern guise of any abstraction given material form. "Nowhere can a collective feeling become conscious of itself without fixing upon a tangible object" (238). Religious thinking in this sense is simply an effort to give concrete embodiment to what is already felt to be the moral essence of the group.

But Durkheim treats religion at the same time as if it were the self-constituting activity of the group, independent of any prior or more "natural" relations or intuited moral substance. This suggests that every collective unity is right from the start a function of, and could not come into existence without, religious thinking. In this latter case, collective identity is produced only out of a certain "ecstatic" state that arises spontaneously, and inexplicably, from the close interaction of individuals (*Elementary* 228). This sacred emotion, or "effervescence" (220), induces within distinct individuals the sense that there is something greater than the sum of their separate existences—hence the etymologically appropriate "ex-stasis," as Durkheim notes. The hypostatized "something" over and above them, but also within them, represented by the totem is what in fact produces their social existence: it is religion that transforms the natural world of the senses, in which "everything is disparate and discontinuous" and in which beings do not merge with one another, into the very different one in which "the people of the clan, and the various beings whose form the totemic emblem represents, are held to be made of the same essence" (238).

In this latter sense, group kinship thus comes from sharing "the same name"—that is, the same symbolic essence—rather than "definite blood relations" (122) or other intuited identity, and it is the name that endows the kinship. "Hence," Durkheim writes, in a revision of Feuerbach's simpler anthropomorphism, "it is man who makes his gods, one can say, or at least, it is man who makes them endure; but at the same time, it is through them that he himself endures" (345). In the first case, religion is merely a conceptual intensifier of existing and more basic human relationships, which may be the bonds of kinship, but could just as easily be those of practical survival or trade. It would thus be an intensifier of solidarity, and thus perhaps useful to the group, but not necessarily essential. In the second case, the social group as such really cannot be thought of outside the category of religion, and all social existence requires some form of religious thought. In this second case, it is the sense given to the Greek *hupostasis* by the Christian doctrine of the incarnation—the union of Christ's human and divine natures in one person—that may be most relevant to Durkheim's meaning, for there would be some grounds for saying that individuals, via an initial effervescent delirium and totemic representation, incarnate the social as a religious object.

The ambiguity is fundamental to Durkheim's thought, and not, I think, just a product of misreading (as Pickering 231–35 argues): "For the principle features of collective life to have begun as none other than various features of religious life, it is evident that religious life must necessarily have been the eminent form and, as it were, the epitome of collective life. If religion gave birth to all that is essential in society, that is so because the idea of society is the soul of religion" (Durkheim, *Elementary* 421). Durkheim at one point calls the totem the "flag of the clan" (222), and the symbolic force of a national flag illustrates the ambiguity well enough. Is a national flag a symbolic, though not really sacred, representation of more instrumental and material relationships that actually supply the underlying substance, or essence, of national identity; or is the flag a sine qua non of national identity itself, in the sense that it is really "sacred" objects such as the flag that in fact create, in the strong sense of that term, the substance of national identity. (Responding to this sort of confusion about totemism itself, Lévi-Strauss argued that in fact totemism exists only in the rather rare situations where two quite distinct human propensities—identification with animals and grouping by kinship—coincide; see *Totemism* 11.)

Durkheim's argument is revised via Marcel Mauss by Lévi-Strauss's later reduction of magic, and hence of any collective universal (a "supplementary ration" or "floating signifier"), to a peculiar quasi-Kantian structure of language and mind (Lévi-Strauss, *Introduction* 63). It was a reduction that compelled Lévi-Strauss to characterize his own science as nothing more than a myth about other myths (*Raw* 12). But I am most interested here in emphasizing the major, and paradoxical, consequence of Durkheim's eminently secular and rational approach to a sociological theory of religion. By making religious thinking and collective representations, along with collective life itself, two sides of the same coin—and by placing his nebulous notion of "effervescence" at the origin of both—Durkheim implies that there is something religious or magical about all secular concepts at the very moment that he reduces all religious (or magical) thought to a social rationale. Durkheim first deploys the notion of "effervescence" in *Le suicide* (1897) to describe the passions aroused by the industrialized marketplace (*Suicide* 255–56; see also Crapanzano 391, n. 2). But it soon becomes Durkheim's most significant, obscure, and magical concept, approaching a vitalism that his methods otherwise rigorously exclude. (In his book *Three Faces of God*, Donald Nielsen in fact argues, inconclusively in my view, that Durkheim was indeed a closet vitalist.) Durkheim intends the notion of "effervescence" to be a social and scientific explanation of the origins of primitive magic and religion. But "effervescence," as T. S. Eliot observed very early on, is finally no explanation at all, and would seem to represent the incorporation of magic as explanation into Durkheim's own sociology (see Eliot, "Review" 158–59; see also Schrempp 24). (Years later, Lévi-Strauss would make a similar critique of Mauss's explanation of magic.)

There has been uneasiness about Durkheim's "effervescence" and his "group theory" of religion for some time, especially since the triumph of totalitarian regimes in the 1930s. Durkheim's model of religion and society was if anything too scientifically plausible in its own day. If we can borrow the major thermodynamic metaphor of the nineteenth century, it was as if Durkheim had come to imagine society as the caloric effect of the energy produced by the effervescent collision of individual psychic atoms. Much of the criticism has been aimed at Durkheim's supposedly hidden dependence on an irrational "crowd psychology," as developed by his more psychologically oriented rivals Gustave Le Bon and Gabriel Tarde (for a history of such reaction, see Pickering 395–403; see also Parsons 321). Such dependence had to be hidden because Durkheim claimed that he would invoke only social explanations of social phenomena (see *Rules*, chap. 2).

This is a complex issue, but even Durkheim's defenders admit that "effervescence" is mysterious. Whether Durkheim's theory of the effervescent origins of collective solidarity, like other modern versions of ecstatic community, is somehow proto-fascist, as Vincent Crapanzano argues, is a difficult question—not least because of the centrality of race in much (though not all) fascist ideology and its complete absence in Durkheim, and, as in Comte the overtly internationalist, pan-European thrust of Durkheim's ideas (Crapanzano 112–13). But a loose connection is hard to ignore, as Mauss noted in a letter of 1939 replying to Svend Ranulf, who had provocatively labeled Durkheim, along with Tönnies and Comte, one of the "scholarly forerunners of Fascism" (Ranulf 30–35). As quoted by Ranulf, Mauss observed "that all this is a real tragedy for us, a very powerful verification of things that we [Mauss and Durkheim] have indicated, and the proof that we should have expected this verification by evil rather than a verification by goodness" (34; my translation). Raymond Aron reported a comment made by Léon Brunschvicg in the 1930s: "Nuremberg [the site of Nazi rallies] is religion according to Durkheim, society adoring itself" (see Lukes 339, n. 71).

In fact, quite apart from Ranulf's limited purview, and certainly independent of (even directly opposed to) the disastrous political sympathies of the

1930s, the conjunction of secular, rational social theory and quasi-religious thinking is widespread by the end of the nineteenth century. (For a good overview of "secular religion," Fabian socialism, and vitalism in Britain during the Edwardian era, see Rose 1–116.) The idea of a "civic religion" is of course ancient, found in Weber's axiom of comparative analysis of religious traditions—"it is a universal phenomenon that the formation of a political association entails subordination to its corresponding god"—and the complex interactions among household, tribal and local gods, along with the "synoikism" (or syncretism) in the religion of the *polis* wrought by conquest, are central to his discussion (see Weber, *Economy* 413, 416). The rationalization and universalizing of primitive civic religions, especially via monotheism, and the subsequent rationalization of economic and social life effectively supplanted or secularized the power of such civic religions.

And yet the trajectory taking us from Comte to Durkheim suggests that something like civic religion returns, now not in the guise of fidelity to a local deity, or even to monotheistic authority (though the latter allegiance surely persisted), but rather as a religion of the social itself—a political theology based on nothing more than the sacred character of social life, of society as a religious object. The ambiguities in Durkheim's late work might then help us see how the various intellectual traditions meeting in the early twentieth century—from Simmel's vitalism, to James's psychology of religious experience, to the disenchanted sociology of Durkheim—produce a rich and suggestive, but also highly unstable, merging of social theory and religious thought. It is an intersection that was often redemptive in appeal, even if, for Lukács, Ranulf, Aron, and others, it would later appear quite questionable. I want to illustrate the ambiguity of this "religion of society" that Comte and Durkheim invent with a brief anecdote about the early twentieth-century Cambridge anthropologist Jane Harrison.

Jane Harrison and Social Redemption

On November 25, 1912, Jane Harrison gave a lecture to the Heretics, an avowedly secular and left-leaning (Fabian) society at Cambridge University designed "to promote discussion on problems of Religion, Philosophy, and Art." The very existence of such a society is an interesting part of the intellectual history of the period. The Heretics had little concern to promote religion of any sort, its by-laws expressly forbidding "all appeal to Authority" (Harrison 40), by which it meant primarily sacred scripture. Its list of "Honorary Members" included (beyond Harrison herself) a veritable who's who of the day's leading intellectuals, several of them members of the Bloomsbury circle around Virginia and Vanessa Woolf—people such as the classicist Francis M. Cornford; the mathematician Ernest William Hobson; the political theorist Leonard T. Hobhouse; the economist John Maynard Keynes; the philosophers John Ellis McTaggart, George Moore, and Bertrand Russell; the anthropologist W. H. R. Rivers, the playwright George Bernard Shaw; and the historian G. M. Trevelyan. Its president was C. K. Ogden, then only twenty-three years old, the editor, critic, aesthetician, and psycholinguist who would later write *The Meaning of Meaning,* which had a large impact on Anglo-American literary criticism at mid-century. Ogden also came to be concerned with questions of overpopulation and "uncontrolled breeding." Indeed, eugenics was as important a part of progressive Edwardian social thought as the rethinking of religion: both were central to a New Liberal understanding of social, racial, and national progress (see Freeden).

Central to the anthropological character of the Heretics was a trio known as Cambridge Ritualists, comprising Harrison, Cornford, and the translator and theater producer Gilbert Murray. Drawing together Nietzsche's early revaluation of the "primitive" components of Greek thought in *The Birth of Tragedy from the Spirit of Music,* Sir James Frazer's grand synthesis in *The Golden Bough* of the evolution of myth from magic to religion to science, and Durkheim's sociology of religion, the Ritualists were in many ways the culmination of a longer nineteenth-century trend blurring earlier Enlightenment distinctions between primitive and classical Greek culture (see Pecora, *Households* 41). In *From Religion to Society* (1912), for example, Cornford demonstrates that a form of secularization was crucial to the rise of Greek philosophy, which represented no clean break with earlier Greek religion and mythology. On the contrary, Cornford writes, "there is a real continuity between the earliest rational speculation and the religious representation that lay behind it"; philosophy directly inherits "certain great conceptions—'God,' 'Soul,' 'Destiny,' 'Law'"—from the "unreasoned intuitions of mythology" (Cornford xiii). In a sense, what Cornford shows in some detail is that Western thought in its pre-Christian or "pagan" forms is *already* engaged in secularization.

Harrison's putative topic that November was "Unanimism," a term referring to the spiritual ideals of the short-lived literary community l'Abbaye, founded a few years earlier in France as a "monastery without an Abbot" (Harrison 4). But her real concern was the problem of "conversion." Borrowing from William James, F. M. Davenport, Bertrand Russell, and especially Durkheim, Harrison saw the conversion experience as a form of initiation. Like Russell and Durkheim—and like the Unanimists in France (whose leading figure, Jules Romains, was a follower of Durkheim, and also of Bergson)—Harrison evacuates the notion of theology in order to explore in a more secular fashion a group theory of religion. For Harrison, conversion initiates the individual not into divine mysteries but "into his tribe, his social group" (25). She further claims that the release from self and the submergence of the ego in Durkheim's "collective consciousness" is not only the basic organizing principle of all forms of community but *the* redemptive force in modern society. (Durkheim's *Elementary Forms* was just being published in France at this time, though Durkheim's and Mauss's basic ideas on religion had been disseminated earlier in essays such as "De quelques formes primitives de classification" [1901–2].) The Unanimist literary collective is an example for Harrison of the new secular religion of modernity, visible in peace societies, socialism, and new forms of cooperative association situated between private enterprise and state bureaucracy, such as those that Comte and Durkheim had promoted. Perhaps, her audience might well have thought, modernity's "atheistic" sense of religion could be discovered in the Heretics themselves, who in effect formed a cooperative professional association of intellectuals—though in France the Unanimists could also draw on a long-established tradition of associative or guild socialism and syndicalism going back to Fourier and Proudhon.

What is astonishing, however, despite the refusal of all scriptural "authority" in her discussion and among the Heretics, is how quickly and easily Harrison turns near her conclusion to ideas that, in the wake of Nazism, fascism, and Soviet Communism, have a religiously authoritarian resonance Harrison surely did not intend and perhaps could not have imagined. She notes that her study of Unanimism's Durkheimian sense of religion has in fact helped her to understand and approve "the ethics of Conformity," the democratic basis of "Conservatism," and "the extraordinary reverence paid to the official" (33–34). On the last point, Harrison's own "conversion" has been a telling one: though she used to think the political official "a *quasi* comic figure, something of the dressed-up doll," she now sees in him "the real pathos and grandeur of the sacrificial victim. He is sacred through suffering. He commands, but only by obeying" (34). This religious apotheosis, in the language of secular anthropology, of a once-laughable officialdom is in some ways surprising, not least because of the skeptical, rational, and liberal spirit of Harrison's own work and of her distinguished, freethinking audience. It depends, I think, on Harrison's deeper sense of the democratic character of charismatic national authority. Of course, not one of Harrison's listeners could have known how far a "dressed-up doll" such as Adolf Hitler would go in exploiting precisely those sentiments Harrison invokes to describe the sacred, self-sacrificing leader. Harrison's enlightened attempt to understand the secular nature of religious commitment leads her to consider a small and esoteric literary movement such as Unanimism as an exoteric emblem of larger redemptive trends in the early twentieth century. Like Robespierre's Cult of Reason and Comte's Religion of Humanity, and supported by Durkheim's sense of the religious character of all social solidarity, Harrison's vision of the new secular religion of modernity is vaguely socialist, internationalist, and utopian. But it is also, as only hindsight can comprehend, an eerily accurate forecast of a terribly painful political reality, where conformity to a collective consciousness and reverence for the Christlike "pathos and grandeur" of a Führer became the prelude to pan-European nightmare.

As noted earlier, this quasi-religious regard for the idea of society was widely shared in the early decades of the last century. Harrison's case suggests it was not at all confined to overtly "messianic" intellectual climates—for example, the middle European and largely Jewish and socialist cultural formation prior to 1914, which included such figures as Georg Lukács, Martin Buber, Walter Benjamin, and Ernst Bloch (see Rabinbach). Nor does Harrison's perspective have any direct connection to the proto-fascist, anti-Semitic royalism of such people as Maurras, a religious disbeliever who nevertheless found salvation only in a return to religious forms of authority—though both Harrison and Maurras would be important sources for T. S. Eliot. What Harrison's lecture in 1912 illustrates is that the argument for a submergence of self in a collective identity of religious dimensions could also be derived from the secular exploration of the nature of religious belief. Harrison thus emerges as the bearer of a secular rationality that strangely helps to reopen a Pandora's box of religious impulses.

In the larger sweep of twentieth-century culture, Harrison's brief lecture is no more than a blip on the historian's radar screen; indeed, there has been no scholarly discussion of it. But it provides us with a window into her time that resonates in powerful ways with a host of more prominent figures. Some of these figures—for example, Georges Bataille—were very much a part of a Durkheimian tradition in social theory, and Bataille's thinking, including his own *Théorie de la religion*, reproduces especially in its conclusion the central equivocation over religious and "scientific" modes of thought and sociality (including a Nietzschean excursus on the military origins of Islam). Occult ideas are clearly a powerful strain in this story, and mystically oriented "secret societies" of one sort or another were plentiful. But even more significant is the degree to which such little *Gemeinschaften*, ranging from nineteenth-century millenarian sects to Bataille's own surreal version of a secret society, Acéphale, consciously elaborated a Durkheimian conviction that the religious *symbole*, both emblem and creed and often carried by quite arbitrary vehicles, was a functional requirement of any sort of group coherence. (Acéphale was in this sense just a more ironic version of Romains's equally "headless" Unanimist collective decades earlier.)

Some of these sects were clearly "pagan" or occult in character; some were simply dissenting versions of organized Christian belief; some were politically charismatic and revolutionary in character; and some, like those of Bataille's and Caillois's circle, were what could only be called ironic experiments in the *performance* of religious symbolization and community (see, for example, the documents in *Encyclopaedia Acephalica*). Acéphale's notion of a "secret society" in fact embraced all of the above, from the charismatic organization of the Society of Jesus to the occult authority of the Ku Klux Klan. Bataille's mystical collective comprised artists, intellectuals, and philosophers, but the essential mystery of the endeavor referred to the nature of society rather than to the wisdom imparted by occult doctrine (see especially Hollier; Richman). Bataille did have fairly esoteric notions about solar energy, blood sacrifice, and ecstatic behavior. But these notions did not derive primarily from occult sources—they came from a respectable tradition of anthropology, ethnology, and sociology before him (see especially the early essays in *Visions of Excess*).

Others, such as T. S. Eliot, registered the force of Durkheim's ideas at a greater remove and arrived at a similar blurring of the secular and sacred on the grounds of quite different traditions of thought. Eliot not only knew Durkheim's work, but appeared from early on to value Durkheim's ideas on religion and community even more than those of Lévy-Bruhl, whose work on a *mentalité primitive* is so often cited as a primary ethnological influence on Eliot (on Durkheim's role, see Bush; Manganaro; Menand and Schwartz). Eliot's early and admiring reviews (1916 and 1918) of Durkheim's *Elementary Forms*, though they show how clearly Eliot understood both the strength and weaknesses of Durkheim's theory of religion, also suggest that, for Eliot, Durkheim's totemic explanation of "group consciousness" was actually best seen as "no theory at all": it was instead a demonstration of what was "incapable of explanation" about collective consciousness, of the "inexplicable" realm that opens up as modern, secular social psychology probes "the limits of individual psychology" (see Eliot, "Review" 158–59).

Nevertheless, Durkheim's ideas are remarkably persistent in Eliot's work, both pre- and post-conversion. In the much later *Notes towards the Definition of Culture* (1949), Eliot substitutes the word "culture" for the phrase "association and community" used in the first review of Durkheim (see "Durkheim" 314). But the substance and logic of Eliot's remarks remain remarkably close to Durkheim's perspective, despite the early criticism. In the later text, Eliot writes of his difficult "conception of culture and religion as being, when each term is taken in the right context, different aspects of the same thing" (*Notes* 28). He acknowledges that "the identity of religion and culture" (68) is most complete in primitive societies, where there is "no clear distinction between religious and non-religious activities" (67). But he concludes in good Hegelian or, better, Freudian fashion that although modern social differentiation and the consciousness it allows make impossible or totalitarian any return to an immanent primitive unity of thought (which Durkheim had called "mechanical solidarity"), so that religion and culture now often stand opposed, nevertheless "we do not leave the earlier stage of development behind us.... The identity of religion and culture remains on the unconscious level" (68).

One could argue that Eliot's decision in this late essay to adopt "the point of view of the sociologist" (Eliot, *Notes* 69) is crucial in understanding both his supposedly more intimate relationship to religion after his own 1927 conversion to Anglo-Catholicism and his earlier "profane" work, and that we should regard what might appear to be merely an expression of nostalgia for a more organic moment in past European civilization instead (or perhaps, also) as an eminently Durkheimian conception of social coherence, in which religion is a function of collective life, but in which the collective representations of the profane world also then emerge as unconsciously religious in character. As Dominick LaCapra has observed, "For Durkheim, sociology itself had the task of providing a theoretical foundation for religion. Thus Durkheim made the almost Thomistic effort to reconcile reason and faith, but in a secularized fashion adapted to the needs of modern society" (*Durkheim* 289). LaCapra's insight about the implicit Thomism in Durkheim is important for much of modernist thinking around him. Like his final refusal to distinguish between pragmatist contexts and rationalist notions of validity, Durkheim's understanding of the social origins of religious belief was in practice inseparable from a sense of the social *as* sacred, a moral and epistemological equation that would have at the very least unpredictable and at times volatile consequences for twentieth-century political life. At the same time, this equation signaled for Durkheim that religious thinking promised, through the historical expansion of collective horizons, a kind of realism and validity through which the effervescence of particular cultures would lead eventually to a new "international life" able to "universalize religious beliefs" (Durkheim, *Elementary* 446).

The royalism and anti-Semitism of a text such as *After Strange Gods*, of which even Eliot himself was soon ashamed, makes any deeper comparison of Eliot with the republican, Jewish, and politically liberal if still morally conservative Durkheim problematic. My point is rather that the intellectual bonds and looser resemblance linking Durkheim's complicated account of religion and society with Romains's Unanimism, Harrison's redemptive treatment of conversion, Bataille's Acéphale, and Eliot's conception of the "inexplicable" religion-culture dyad reorients us in relation to the problem of religion and secularism in early twentieth-century intellectual life generally. In this sense, *The Waste Land* is a text devoted to religious sociology, rather than to occult, existential, or negative theological reflection, precisely because a functional, and causally ambiguous, relationship between social coherence and religious ritual lies at the center of its meaning. Speaking from the perspective of a religious sociologist, and again in vaguely Hegelian tones, Eliot treated "the culture of a people as the incarnation of its religion" (*Notes* 32). Durkheim, speaking as a sociologist of religion, said much the same thing, as long as we understand the word "religion" to mean at the same time the incarnation of communal solidarity. The tension between Eliot's and Durkheim's attitudes, which is itself a version of an underlying ambiguity in the relation between religion and community that, borrowing from Heidegger, we might describe as part of the *Verwindung,* or curative distortion, of the secularization process in modernity, exemplifies a modern obsession with the elementary forms of religious thought—in effect, with a "theory of religion"—rudiments that appeared to be at the same time the wellsprings of Western civilization and the basis for a redemption of that civilization (see Heidegger, *Identity* 32–33, 36–37). The discovery of the social behind the sacred, which at the same time opened the way for the transformation of the social into the sacred, was an indispensable part of the flourishing of a modern sensibility, from the most esoteric secret societies to the literary icons.

Modern culture's tortuous approach to religion can be reduced to three main paths, all of them in some sense responses to a militantly secular Enlightenment: the return to orthodoxy; the unstable concatenation of natural philosophy, *Lebensphilosophie,* and vitalism that Lukács called "religious atheism"; and the sociology of religion. Although these three paths to, and through, religion can be at times quite rigorously distinguished, at other times they appear oddly complementary. The orthodox Action Française of Charles Maurras and Durkheim's sociology of religion represent directly opposed understandings of the meaning of religion and, not incidentally, directly opposed responses to the Dreyfus affair. Yet both helped to elaborate a modern understanding of the immanent sacred content of social life. A direct heir to these strands of thought among related others is T. S. Eliot, whose often-discussed "classicism" and rejection of the romantic cult of self-expression (akin in different ways to that of both Maurras and Durkheim) is at the same time traceable to the also clearly romantic—or at least virulently anti-Enlightenment—thinking of Maistre. For Bataille and Eliot alike, though in obviously different ways, an original coincidence of social-secular and religious elements persists in spite of the triumph of modern instrumental reason, and for both this almost-forgotten coincidence is the key, as it is for Harrison, to social redemption.

Approaching the problem of religion and modernity in this way suggests that Julien Benda's notion of a *trahison des clercs*, elaborated elsewhere by both Raymond Aron and Isaiah Berlin (in his *Crooked Timber*), and most recently revised and updated by Mark Lilla (in *The Reckless Mind*) as the overweening hubris and passion of the "philotyrannical intellectual," may obscure more than it reveals. It may be true, in a handful of cases, that modern Western intellectuals betrayed their sober, professional obligation to the rational truth, that is, to impartial and secular scholarship, in order to achieve real political authority—which Lilla calls "the lure of Syracuse," after Plato's failed mission to educate Dionysius in Sicily (see Lilla, "Lure"). Both Heidegger, a "religious atheist" who briefly joined the Nazi Party, and Lukács, with his tortured "scientific" allegiance to Stalin and his nasty experience as a Hungarian revolutionary, might fit this model. But T. S. Eliot would be a rather awkward example, and Jane Harrison does not fit the model at all, though her approach to sacred forms of political authority is arguably as disturbing as anything in Heidegger and certainly has the merit of greater clarity. Most of all, almost every discernible intention in what Durkheim wrote would seem to contradict what Benda saw as the tyrannous consequences of the loss of intellectual autonomy. Against Benda and his followers, I have tried to argue that we should focus less on the problem of individual intellectual responsibility—which, however important, is surely a difficult concept in every age, and every cultural location—and look instead to what I have characterized as the necessarily distorting consequences of Western secularization, in which the volatility in the equation of the sacred and the social is built into the terms of the discourse. It is this discourse, I believe, that constitutes the broader foundations of the political theology of the age.

Carl Schmitt's Political Theology

In 1922, some eleven years before he joined the Nazi Party as Hitler came to power, Carl Schmitt declared that "all significant concepts of the modern theory of the state are secularized theological concepts not only because of their historical development—in which they were transferred from theology to the theory of the state, whereby, for example, the omnipotent God became the omnipotent lawgiver—but also because of their systematic structure, the recognition of which is necessary for a sociological consideration of these concepts" (*Political Theology* 37). On the surface, the kinship of this comment to Durkheim's claim that "nearly all the great social institutions were born in religion" (*Elementary* 421) is purely accidental. Schmitt's perspective, after all, was nurtured by his Catholic upbringing and Hobbesian-Maistrian conservatism, and it perhaps owed even more to the proto-existentialism and vitalism of Kierkegaard, whose regard for the essential irrationality of all decisions played so large a role in Schmitt's thinking about political sovereignty. Kierkegaard had a similar view of the relationship between religion and politics, though his terms were inverted, and one of his prophecies from 1848 wound up (along with epigraphs from Sade and Nietzsche) on the first page of the first issue of Georges Bataille's short-lived but very significant journal, *Acéphale:* "Ce qui avait visage de politique et s'imaginait être politique, se démasquera un jour comme mouvement religieux" [What wore the face of politics and imagined itself to be political, one day will be unmasked as a religious movement] (see *Acéphale* 1, no. 24 [June 1936]; see also Hollier 164). Drawing a link in this way between Schmitt and Bataille via Kierkegaard may not mean much—like Nietzsche, Kierkegaard has been a highly problematic source for both right- and left-wing political critique, Walter Benjamin included. The more interesting question may be: In what sense can Schmitt's ultimately anti-Semitic understanding of the religious roots of the political be said to parallel Durkheim's? After all, Durkheim's focus on the importance of civil society, and especially his early work's pluralist celebration of the voluntary professional associations, trade unions, and corporations of civic life rather than the duties and necessity of political sovereignty, would at first glance seem to be the sort of thing that Schmitt decried as "radically self-contradictory, namely, liberal bourgeois democracy," that is, the very opposite of the dictatorial realism needed to preserve the state in a time of crisis (*Political Romanticism* 13).

Schmitt found much to admire as well as to criticize in Comte's effort to found a "positivistic" church (see *Roman Catholicism* 19), even as he rejected Proudhon's atheism. His Hegelian critique of the "political romanticism" of German egoists and ironists—people such as Friedrich Schlegel and Adam Müller—masked another sort of romantic politics, one that anchored itself in the same seventeenth-century patriarchal royalism that Maistre admired, and that looked further back to the guild socialism and feudal organization of occupational and religious associations admired by Comte as well as by Durkheim (see Schmitt, *Political Romanticism*). Indeed, if one looked at Schmitt's writings of 1932–34, while Hitler was coming to power, what one finds is not further discussion of his well-known friend-enemy polarity, nor a celebration of sovereign decisionism, both of which are usually taken to be Schmitt's most salient proto-Nazi concepts. (One should note, nevertheless, that Schmitt in fact originally saw decisionism as the exceptional means—the necessary state of exception—for saving the Weimar constitution from both the Left and Right radicalism of his time, an idea given renewed political life whenever a nominally democratic regime, such as that of Algeria or Tunisia, suspends constitutional guarantees to forestall the election of an antidemocratic political party. In this sense, one could say that Schmitt's notion of the irreducibility of decisionism is the abiding conceptual aporia of all constitutional democracies.) What one finds instead in Schmitt's work, as he joins Hitler's cause, is an elaboration of a deeply Durkheimian theme: the essential role of intermediary civic, religious, and professional associations, situated between private enterprise and the state as legally sanctioned "concrete orders" and assuring a social continuity that would require only infrequent "decisionist" interventions of the sovereign's authority (see Schmitt, *Über die drei Arten* 7–40).

Durkheim's own view of the political state, which like Schmitt's insisted that the state be a necessary regulative mechanism separate from society, was so close to Schmitt on this point that Durkheim at times sounds like a distant source: "We should then define political society," Durkheim had written, "as one formed by the union of a greater or lesser number of secondary social groups, subject to the same one authority which is not itself subject to any superior authority duly constituted" (*Professional Ethics* 45). In fact, Durkheim was a source of sorts, mediated by the work of the French Institutionalists (Joseph T. Delos, Maurice Hauriou, and Georges Renard), and in particular by that of the vitalist Hauriou. Hauriou interpreted Durkheim as making "objective" law (which in English was called common law, defined by custom and tradition, as opposed to the subjective French Code civil) supreme "by ranking the social milieu above individuals" (97). Hauriou's definition of a corporate social institution builds upon, but also subtly distorts, Durkheim's notion of the *conscience collective:* an institution is "an enterprise that is realized and endures juridically in a social milieu; . . . a power is organized that equips it with organs"; and among the group's members, "manifestations of communion occur that are directed by the organs of the power and regulated by procedures" (99). Not unlike Harrison, Hauriou thus interprets Durkheim's "collective consciousness" in a prescriptive way and then emphasizes the leading role of "superior minds" for directing the "average opinion" of the social milieu, reasserting a specifically Roman Catholic content behind Durkheim's phrase. "Communion in an idea is Ariel; the collective consciousness, Caliban. Communion in an idea includes an agreement of wills under the direction of a chief" (108). It is along these lines that Hauriou then provided the logic behind Schmitt's ideas (see Schmitt, *Über die drei Arten* 54–57).

Schmitt's was in the end a far more feudal, monolithic, and totalitarian model than Durkheim's, poised as it was as a defense against perceived social decay and emphasizing protection in return for obedience and one-party rule, even if for both men the sovereign state provided defense against external threats as well as moral finality for a set of autonomous social institutions (see especially Schmitt, *Staat*). Whereas Schmitt stressed that the state's interest to "decide" among rival choices or factions was purely a matter of social self-preservation having nothing to do with democracy or the extension of the individual's rights, Durkheim saw the state primarily as an instrument to preserve the interests of the individual against the functionally necessary and salutary, but potentially all-consuming, tendencies of secondary and professional associations. Schmitt's institutionalism was also not really what was wanted by Hitler's SS, who correctly saw Hegel's constitutional estates resurfacing in Schmitt's prose. But the striking descent of Durkheim's thinking, via Hauriou, to Schmitt's political theology underlines the equivocating interpenetration of theoretical models at this time, when the essentially religious content of social life emerged as a central axiom of analysis. The strange, distorted kinship between Schmitt and Durkheim—the *Verwindung* of secularization that so marks religion, national consciousness, and modernity—suddenly makes almost predictable the appearance of those opening Kierkegaardian lines merging religion and politics, with their direct relationship to Schmitt's thinking, in the otherwise deeply Durkheimian pages of *Acéphale*.

The Highest Form of Psychic Life

Unlike Schmitt, Durkheim was one of the most self-aware, liberal, humane, and tyrannophobic intellectuals of his day. The assimilated son of a rabbi, he was appalled at the crass chauvinism and racism of his nominally Christian countrymen during the Dreyfus affair, which perhaps lent some urgency to his interest in the mechanics of social solidarity. He envisioned a democratic socialist future in which individualism and international cooperation would grow in tandem and harmony. That is, Durkheim is very much a model for the *bien-pensant* European of today's European Union. And yet there are passages in his *Elementary Forms of the Religious Life*, like the following one near its conclusion, that seem profoundly ambiguous when we read them today. The ambiguity stems from the fact that here Durkheim seems to be imitating—whether deliberately or accidentally is unclear—the primitive clan consciousness he purports to explain: whereas totemic religion was formerly the symbolic hypostasis of a putatively "real" society, "society" itself now appears to be the grand hypostasis of Durkheim's sociology.

En résumé, la société n'est nullement l'être illogique ou alogique, incohérent et fantastique qu'on se plaît trop souvent à voir en elle. Tout au contraire, la conscience collective est la forme la plus haute de la vie psychique, puisque c'est une conscience de consciences. Placée en dehors et au-dessus des contingences individuelles et locales, elle ne voit les choses que par leur aspect permanent et essentiel qu'elle fixe en des notions communicables. En même temps qu'elle voit de haut, elle voit au loin; à chaque moment du temps, elle embrasse toute la réalité connue; c'est pourquoi elle seule peut fournir à l'esprit des cadres qui s'appliquent à la totalité des êtres et qui permettent de les penser. Ces cadres, elle ne les crée pas artificiellement; elle les trouve en elle; elle ne fait qu'en prendre conscience. (Durkheim, *Formes élémentaires* 633–34)

In conclusion, society is in no sense the illogical or alogical, incoherent, and fantastic being that too often one likes to consider it. Quite the contrary, the collective consciousness is the highest form of psychic life, since it is a consciousness of the consciousnesses. Placed outside of and above individual and local contingencies, it sees things only in their permanent and essential aspect, which it fixes in communicable ideas. At the same time that it sees from above, it sees farther; at each moment in time, it embraces all known reality; that is why it alone can furnish the mind with the frames that are applicable to the totality of beings and that make it possible to think of them. It does not create these frames artificially; it finds them within itself; it only becomes conscious of them. (My translation; see also Durkheim, *Elementary* 445)

We know what Durkheim wants to say here: that no one of us alone is responsible for the concepts and categories we use, that we create "knowledge" or "truth" out of the intellectual conventions shared by individuals within a given society and linguistic community, for otherwise both communication and reason would be impossible. And it makes a great deal of "secular" sense. This positivist view, after all, is basic to the social-constructionist perspective dominating literary and cultural criticism at the present time.

But looking back on a century in which the conversion experience that for Jane Harrison happily subordinated the individual to the sacred authority of society also enabled unspeakable horrors, it is hard to treat this remarkable apotheosis of the social simply as the scientific analysis Durkheim no doubt intended. For it requires only a small shift in perspective to read the passage not as description, but as prescription: to conclude that if society depends for "order and progress" on a collective consciousness and moral consensus indistinguishable from religious belief, then the more enveloping the consciousness and more complete the consensus, the better the society. Though Durkheim certainly was concerned elsewhere to safeguard individual conscience, generally through the intervention of the state, against the power of social institutions to shape and even coerce opinion, there is nothing here in his account of *conscience collective* that would reflect John Stuart Mill's earlier and deeper anxieties. "Protection . . . against the tyranny of the magistrate," Mill wrote, "is not enough; there needs protection also against the tyranny of the prevailing opinion and feeling; against the tendency of society to impose, by other means than civil penalties, its own ideas and practices as rules of conduct on those who dissent from them. . . . There is a limit to the legitimate interference of collective opinion with individual independence" ("On Liberty" 7). Mill is obviously hypostasizing "society" in his own critical way here too. But he is a long way from Durkheim's more positivistic point of view, in which individual consciousness, both epistemic and moral, is largely void of content without the collective consciousness that provides it with structural categories or "frames" and, hence, with "communicable ideas" themselves.

The epistemic primacy of "the social" outlined by Durkheim in such passages is often implicitly embraced today by cultural criticism, even as it is leavened by the search for articulations of difference. But it would be wrong to think of the view expressed here as nothing more than an echo of premodern or "mechanical" solidarity that can be found only in highly traditional and fundamentalist contexts, or that haunts highly rationalized societies only on their peripheries (or, as with Nazism, in their most extreme forms). Whenever we deny all philosophical nativism (of the sort assumed by Chomsky's linguistics, for example) and imagine the individual mind as nothing more than the sum of its social (and generally primarily linguistic) inputs, we are not far from Durkheim.

And yet it is important to realize that the *pre*scriptive sense of Durkheim's conclusion could arise not because amoral monsters gained tyrannical power and irrational ideas about race became widely popular, though there is obviously much truth to this reasoning; nor because philosophers such as Heidegger and Lukács and Schmitt decided to go to "Syracuse" and abandoned their scholarly humility in pursuing the sirens of universal truth and power, even if this is what some of them did. The prescriptive sense also emerged from within the paradoxes of a secular social theory that explored the religious depths of social identity, from what we might call a deeper impulse in modern intellectual work in which secular analysis, demanding a coherence increasingly threatened by the disenchantment of religious and even philosophical certainties, elaborated an abstraction called society as the very foundation of consciousness, a super-subject possessing a creative force and a moral authority that are nothing short of magical, nothing less than divine—in short, a political theology. Secular intellectuals of eminently good will, searching for an understanding of the moral life of nations without the compass of religious dogma, elaborated this plausible abstraction as the new foundation of consciousness. In the light of Durkheim's social rationality, the totalitarian drift of the twentieth century's nation-state correlates neither with the ironic fulfillment nor with the reactionary destruction of Enlightenment secularism, but with a twilight world where secular rationality rediscovers the putatively religious character of its origins and functions.

Durkheim may be one of the best lights we have for illuminating the reconvergence of sociopolitical and religious frames of understanding in the last century, though not so much for what his theory explicitly claims as for what it represents despite its better intentions. Especially when placed in the context of the larger flowering of theory of religion and "religious atheism" at the end of the nineteenth century, the vision of modernity that emerges from Durkheim's late work requires the reconciliation of the religious and the social, now on the putatively empirical and secular bases of sociality itself, rather than (like the work of Maistre and Bonald) on the strength of renewed papal authority, or (as in classical Greece and Rome) on the tutelary gods of a civic religion. What the nineteenth century achieves, I am arguing, and what becomes so evident in Durkheim, is an understanding of the social that derives its religious content from the inner workings of society itself. This "immanent" view of sacred sociality no longer needs to refer to forces or gods or duties outside the social, for the effervescent magic produced by the social organism is all that is required to explain the reverence that individuals have—and, for some, ought to have—for it.

If this broader sense of political theology is properly understood, there is no reason to connect the liberal Durkheim in any way to the sort of virulent social philosophy that one finds in Alfred Rosenberg's *Myth of the Twentieth Century*. To do that, one would have to inject discourses of biological race, historically continuous ethnicity, and mythic consciousness—discourses that appear nowhere in Durkheim's writings and that it was the main thrust of his functionalism as well as his internationalist humanism to rebut. It would be equally difficult to imagine Durkheim as an ideologue of utopian socialism or state communism, though he remained far more sympathetic to the former than the latter. Instead, I would regard Durkheim's work on religion as a powerful expression of a particular historical moment in the evolution of the idea of society, an expression of the degree to which, for much good but also for much ill, mass or collective identity came in nineteenth- and twentieth-century European life to possess a near-sacred significance in its own right and to demand a near-sacred allegiance that tended to trump all other forms of meaning and all other claims of affiliation.

4 * Arnoldian Ethnology

Nation Between Religion and Race

> What the French call the *science des origines*, the science of origins,—a science which is at the bottom of all real knowledge of the actual world, and which is every day growing in interest and importance....
> MATTHEW ARNOLD, *On the Study of Celtic Literature*

In the light shed by current trends in "cultural studies," Matthew Arnold's pre-Weberian version of society and culture would seem to be precisely that which must be contested: a grand edifice housing only those Europeans responsible for what *Culture and Anarchy* calls "the best that has been thought and known in the world" (Arnold 5:113), dead white males whose "desire after the things of the mind simply for their own sakes and for the pleasure of seeing them as they are" (5:91) provides an elite heritage of disinterested, secular reflection to guide the rest of us. And to a large extent, this view of Arnold is correct, albeit terribly reductive. What may be too quickly overlooked in demonizing him, however, is the degree to which an element of Arnold's work that has always been something of an embarrassment for his interpreters—Arnold's confusing and inconsistent approach to the relationships between race (or nation), religion, and culture, especially culture understood as a secular ideal—continues to be an embarrassing problem for us today. Arnold was clearly egalitarian when it came to the dissemination of "sweetness and light" (5:99), and he was hardly a purist when the issue was race, emphasizing instead the hybrid vigor of the English. He had a strong sense of the centrality of religious traditions but was a champion of what we would today call secular humanist ideals. He strongly disliked the dominant bourgeois mentality of his time, limited as it was to "the concern for making money, and the concern for saving our souls" (5:186), and showed a distinct affection for lost, oppressed, or simply non-English cultural traditions. He was also thoroughly interdisciplinary and transnational in his methods, eschewing any systematic codification of knowledge that might hinder the interpretive play of the mind. In this last sense, especially, Arnold was a key practitioner of what Edward Said meant by "secular criticism."

In all of this, Arnold is more our contemporary than many would now care to admit. His difficulties in exploring the relationships between race, nation, religion, and culture thus should have a peculiar claim on our sympathies, for they are not as far removed from our own complicated obsessions with such terms as they might seem. Like the Celtic sensibility Arnold found buried within the English soul, Arnold's ethnology represents a conceptual knot that has refused to go away in spite of all sincere attempts to ignore it. In what follows, I want to suggest that Arnold resolved, or perhaps avoided, the dilemma concerning secularization formulated by Jean-Claude Monod as outlined in my introduction—*avant la lettre,* as it were—but that he did so at a heavy price. For Arnold, one might say, the choice lay between secularization as the "worlding" or translation of a Judeo-Christian tradition, in which the modern machinery of utilitarian reform and democratic enfranchisement that seemed to him so threatening could be described as the intemperate, oppositional consequence of religiously derived enthusiasms, laws, and obedience (which Arnold called Hebraism) in worldly economic and political affairs; and secularization as the wholesale "retreat of religion" in the face of a purely rational and enlightened construction of human ideas and institutions guided by attenuated Aristotelian notions of virtue and right reason (which Arnold called Hellenism). Arnold's solution involved making use of both accounts of secularization, but only by resorting to notions of racial disposition—one essentially religious in nature, and one rational—that would have a career in subsequent decades he could have neither foreseen nor desired.

Secularizing St. Paul

It is easy to forget today that almost a third of Arnold's writing focused on religion—much of it dedicated to the proposition that the dissenting sects of Protestant Britain had reduced themselves to an irrational theological dogmatism (derived largely from Calvin) by ignoring the natural morality and desire for righteousness exemplified by the life of Christ, which was for Arnold the true message of Christianity. In texts such as *Literature and Dogma* (1871–73) and *God and the Bible* (1875), Arnold elaborates at length both his deeply rooted humanism and his powerful distrust of the enthusiasm of the dissenting traditions, largely following the skeptical approaches of German biblical criticism after Schleiermacher. (Arnold is reported to have said, "I *thrive* on religious exegesis" [7:436].) However, it is his approach to Paul, in *St. Paul and Protestantism* (1869–70), that may provide the clearest sense of what was at stake in Arnold's account of secularization. For it is here that the traditional distinction between the letter of Jewish law and the spirit of Christian morality is most salient. As Paul wrote, in what are among his most consequential verses, "our sufficiency is of God;/Who also hath made us able ministers of the new testament; not of the letter, but of the spirit: for the letter killeth, but the spirit giveth life" (II Corinthians 3:5–6, King James Version). Arnold's humanism is firmly rooted in these lines.

The errors of dissenting Protestantism, in Arnold's view, are due to a misapprehension of the import of Paul's rhetoric, a focus on what is ancillary in Paul (the ideas of election, justification by faith, and utter dependence on God's grace, most pronounced in Paul's Letter to the Ephesians) and a glossing over of what is most important: Paul's deeply human and eminently practical moral sense, his desire to die to sin and, by enlisting reason and sympathy in equal portions, to pursue an *"an unseen power of goodness . . . through identification with Christ"* (Arnold 6:44). Arnold's Hellenic, neo-Aristotelian reading of Paul is itself designed to correct the errors of Calvin and his followers, which arose because of their fundamental inability to interpret—or, perhaps, see past—the Semitic nature of Paul's rhetoric.

The Hebrew genius has not, like the Greek, its conscious and clear-marked division into a poetic side and a scientific side; the scientific side is almost absent.... The admirable maxim of the great mediaeval Jewish school of Biblical critics: *The Law speaks with the tongue of the children of men,*—a maxim which is the very foundation of all sane Biblical criticism,—was for centuries a dead letter to the whole body of our Western exegesis, and is a dead letter to the whole body of our popular exegesis still. (6:21)

Despite later Jewish scholarship, in other words, the Semitic nature of Paul's language remained an obstacle. What Paul "Orientalises" with a "vivid figure of rhetoric," such as the possibility of election, the Calvinists with their more Hellenic propensities take as a "formal scientific proposition." This is no fault of Paul, but of the Calvinists. When Paul "Judaises," however, it is due to what seems to be a more profound racial defect: "he uses Jewish Scriptures in a Jew's arbitrary and uncritical fashion, as if they had a talismanic character; as if for a doctrine, however true in itself, their confirmation was still necessary, and as if this confirmation was to be got from their mere words alone, however detached from the sense of their context, and however violently allegorised or otherwise wrested" (Arnold 6:22). Paul's remarks on the metaphysical (rather than practical and human) side of Christ, on Christ as Logos, as well as his appropriation of Christ as the Jewish Messiah, "of whom the heart of the Jewish race was full, and on whom the Jewish instructors of Paul's youth had dwelt abundantly"—all this was for Arnold "added by Paul from outside to his own essential ideas concerning" the true, historical Jesus (6:41).

What Arnold enjoins us to do, in effect, is to read around the nonscientific (or non-Hellenic), Oriental, and Judaic character of Paul's language to the natural—that is, secularized Christian—morality embedded in it. But it is important to recognize that Arnold's focus on Paul's "appeal to reality and experience" (Arnold 6:29), which is the "scientific" core of his writing, is a double-edged sword when one considers the broader issue of secularization. On the one hand, it emphasizes, in a fashion that we could today only consider salutary, enlightened, and progressive, that the true force of Paul's message lies in his "profound practical religious sense, and rests upon facts of human nature which experience can follow and appreciate" (6:50). The importance of Paul as an interpreter of Christ's message consists precisely in the degree to which Paul "does not begin outside the sphere of science" (6:29) and thus forecasts Diderot's sense of a natural religion that transcends in its universal appeal all forms of scriptural revelation. On the other hand, Arnold achieves this eminently enlightened and nonsectarian reading of Paul only because he can trace that which obscures the natural and universal significance of Paul's ethical spirit—that is, his "arbitrary and uncritical" use of language, emphasizing its "talismanic" character—back to its Semitic roots.

If by Hebraism Arnold meant "an exclusive attention to the moral side of our nature, to conscience, and to doing rather than knowing" (6:21), what saved that impulse to righteousness from dogmatism, and what had been sorely lacking in the interpretive skills of Calvin and his followers as they mistook Judaic figures of speech for Hellenic science, was the ability to see Paul's message as distorted by his own Jewish background and training. The secular, more universal morality of any acceptable version of Hebraism emerges in Paul, perhaps the most influential convert from Judaism to Christ, on a vague and only implicit linguistic-racial basis: the more Paul is the authentic embodiment of an enlightened secular Christian morality, the less he Judaises, the less he is really a Jew. The irony here is curious, but I think fundamental: it is as if, at least for Arnold, emphasizing the "natural" moral bases of religious thought and undermining their sources in scriptural revelation entailed the idea that the structures of feeling of entire nations (or linguistically determined races) were also natural, given, and innate. In blunter terms, it is as if Arnold's work opened up the possibility that it was the early nineteenth century's final undoing of scriptural revelation via textual critique, historicization, and humanization that in part enabled a view of religious truth and cultural-national identity that was more or less racial in character. Which is to say, in some sense, that in Arnold all the modernizing benefits of secularization, including the potential end of sectarian zealotry and conflict, are subtly, perhaps accidentally, but inextricably tied to the rise of racial thinking. Race then surprisingly emerges in Arnold's ethnology as something like the inadvertent substitute for a no-longer-tenable received religion. But to see more precisely how this process works in Arnold, we need to turn to his earlier writing, in which the whole complex dyad of the Hebraic and the Hellenic first emerges.

Between Religion and Race: Hellenes and Hebrews

The opposition between Hellene and Hebrew in Arnold's writing is a remarkably persistent trope in post-Enlightenment thought. Arnold's rhetoric both echoes prominent strains in romantic (especially German) literature and philosophy and is in turn reproduced by a large segment of the modernism to follow. Such rhetoric depends on the belief that ancient Greece represented a condition of natural harmony, grace, spontaneity, vitality, and freedom, a condition that needed to be recovered, on a higher plane, in a modern world plagued by excessive spiritual strivings and an ascetic narrowness of mind. It is a perspective essential to Winckelmann's art history, apotheosized a century later by Pater. As Lionel Gossman describes it, this "philhellenism or neohumanism" (Gossman 4) was widespread in German writing, from Wolf and the Humboldts to Goethe, Schiller, Hölderlin, Hegel, and Heine (the widely credited source of Arnold's views on the topic), for many of whom the worship of Hellas paralleled an even more ubiquitous desire to rediscover the innocence and wholeness lost in the Mosaic legend of the fall of man. It lay behind Byron's—and many other educated Europeans'—support for Greek independence from the Ottoman Empire and was elaborated in another, more estranging key by Nietzsche toward the end of the century. Moreover, as Gossman observes, this affection for Greece was often both anti-Semitic (or at least anti-Judaic, opposed to Judaism as a religion) and anti-Christian in character.

But the distinction between a higher, disinterested curiosity linked to the pagan Greeks and the philistine (or Evangelical) pragmatism of England's merchant classes is also fundamental to English romanticism in the poetry of Wordsworth, Shelley, and Byron, and it is reproduced in the neoromantic modernism of Pater, Wilde, Hardy, and Forster (see DeLaura; Gottfried). Joyce playfully manipulated the Hellene-Hebrew dichotomy as the basis of his great mock epic—"Jewgreek is greekjew. Extremes meet," we read in *Ulysses* (episode 15, lines 2097–98)—but only because, like many others around him, he accepted on some deep level the ethnological assumptions it embodied (see

Ellmann, *Joyce* 395). D. H. Lawrence turned the distinction into something palpable in the bodies of his characters and in their relation to an instinctual life repressed by modernity as a whole. In *Lord Jim*, Conrad specifically labels Cornelius, who is among the most abject examples of pathological *ressentiment* in all of his work, "the Nazarene" (Conrad, *Lord Jim* 173). The word echoes Heine's use of the term to describe the "natural disposition" (Heine 94; quoted and translated in Gossman 17) of ascetic Jews and Christians alike in their difference from life-affirming Hellenes. Conrad puts the epithet, a common Islamic term for Christians, in the mouth of Jim's faithful and obedient Malay servant, Tamb' Itam, but its explicit identification with *ressentiment* is central, as it is in Heine, to Conrad's meaning.

Gossman more or less absolves Arnold of any overt complicity in the racially based anti-Semitism or religiously based anti-Judaic tendencies of his time—rightly, I think, at least on the whole. In this, Matthew would prove to be quite separate from his father, Thomas, who had profoundly influenced him in so many other ways, and whose rather strong anti-Semitic opinions were voiced publicly. Moreover, for Gossman, even the distinction between Hellenism and Hebraism in *Culture and Anarchy* is less a dialectic of opposites (as it is in Heine's thinking) than a flexible and pragmatic search for synthesis (as is seen in Heine's own German-Jewish background), a "spiritual balance" (Arnold 5:173) that appears all the more plausible because of Arnold's characteristic lack of conceptual rigor. Arnold may indicate at times that Hellenism is itself the essence of true "culture" while Hebraism tends toward narrow enthusiasm and unthinking action, but for Gossman it is really the awkward accommodation of playful intelligence and righteous morality that Arnold is after, an "inclusive, pluralistic vision of 'culture'" (Gossman 36) that parallels an English parliamentary tradition dedicated less to organic unity than to imperfect consensus amid difference.

Gossman's approach also persuasively detaches Arnold's thinking from the more fully elaborated notions of racial identity and racial consciousness available at this time—if only by default of Arnold's fuzzy concepts—and emphasizes instead what *Culture and Anarchy* calls the intellectual, emotional, or ideological "impulse" (Arnold 5:178), "bent," "force" (5:179), or "tendency" (5:180) that would urge the behavior marked either as Hellenism or Hebraism. For example, Arnold's Hebraism would seem to depend less on any notion of innate racial composition—it makes no reference to the anatomy or mental capacity of Jews—than on a moral imagination, supposedly traceable back to scriptural revelation, that is, to Jewish law, and powerfully sustained in the modern period by Christian Evangelical fervor. Hebraism thus appears to be a learned perspective, based on the evidence of sacred texts, rather than a racial inheritance, a perspective that in its unhealthy or extreme forms turns moral rectitude and practical efficacy into ends in themselves. It is also a perspective that, it seems, can be moderated by other learned perspectives, such as Hellenism, which are equally textual in kind. In this view, culture as Arnold imagines it does not demand the modification of any particular "natural dispositions," racial or otherwise, but only the secularizing abandonment of the ideology of religious certainty, or what *Culture and Anarchy* calls "strictness of conscience"—which can of course take many forms, but most often implies an unthinking adherence to written law—in order that an alternative tendency toward disinterested inquiry, or "spontaneity of consciousness" (Arnold 5:176), can flourish unconstrained by moral and political imperatives.

This way of reading *Culture and Anarchy* has been a fairly dominant one, even among those, such as Lionel Trilling (in *Matthew Arnold*) and Raymond Williams (in *Culture and Society*), who criticize the shortcomings of Arnold's logic and political sentiments. Who could object for long to Arnold's ambiguous terminology, once it is understood as simply demanding a practical (parliamentary) balance between pluralism and righteousness, between free inquiry and ethical concern? (For a usefully skeptical view of what this practical balance represents, however, see Graff.) Seen in the broadest terms, and with little dependence on the ghosts of Aristotelian entelechy in Arnold's notion of a guiding faculty of reason, Hellenism is in many ways equivalent to what one expects from an enlightened, secular worldview. Indeed, George Stocking provides an anthropological historian's support for the view that Arnold's sense of the word "culture" is actually much closer to the usage of modern relativist anthropology, which at least strives to detach itself from racism and ethnocentrism, than was that of Arnold's contemporary E. B. Tylor, who is generally credited as the source of anthropology's culture concept. Tylor, a nonconformist, positivist, and utilitarian who would have been a perfect example of Arnold's dissenting Philistine, elaborated an evolutionary, developmental notion of culture or civilization in the singular. Different peoples and races could be normatively ranked along a universal though obviously not uniform progression toward the material and moral condition of Tylor's own time and place. Arnold, with his neoromantic alienation from modern Western society and its rationalist machinery, instead develops what for Stocking is a sense of culture as "an integrative, organic, holistic, inner manifestation" (Stocking 796), a view that was supposedly more likely than Tylor's to imply modern anthropology's relativism. In fact, Stocking does not mention race at all in his discussion of Arnold. Gossman's recent account of the German romantic roots of Arnold's thinking, certainly among the most thorough yet provided, may emphasize more than have most Arnold's "pragmatic" if "conservative" view of the state and his affection for Hebraism. But Gossman is in good company when he finds little in *Culture and Anarchy* that suggests biological race as a cultural determinant and much that prefigures later efforts at pluralism, whether humanist or anthropological. Previous and equally comprehensive accounts of Arnold's sources for *Culture and Anarchy*, like that of David J. DeLaura, likewise do little to explore the race-culture link in Arnold's work itself.

Writing more than half a century earlier, Lionel Trilling could not have been more opposed to certain of Gossman's interpretations. For Trilling, Arnold's state is an "essentially mystic conception" (Trilling 255), a "liberal" myth that ignores the realities of power; and Arnold's Hellenism is clearly the implicitly favored impulse, a proper human end to which Hebraism should serve only as a (modestly pursued) means. Like Gossman, however, Trilling's reading of *Culture and Anarchy* suggests neither a specifically "racial" content (242) nor any anti-Semitism; Trilling even notes in a footnote how far Heine's Greek-Jew distinction was accepted by many Jewish intellectuals of Heine's era, such as Moses Hess (256n). Trilling's book, however, has room to discuss a work by Arnold that neither Gossman nor Stocking mentions at all—*On the Study of Celtic Literature*—and here the problem of race in Arnold is squarely faced, even as the problem of religion (and secularization) would seem to be occluded: "Science, the anthropology of his day, told him that the spirit of a nation—what we might call its national *style*—is determined by 'blood' or 'race' and that these are constants, asserting themselves against all other determinants such as class, existing social forms, and geographical and economic environment" (232–33). As Trilling's brief survey of the essay demonstrates, the evidence for Arnold's belief in inherited racial characteristics is very strong. Still, Trilling's rightly critical focus on the Victorian assumptions about race in *Celtic Literature* does not go very far in exploring its significance for interpreting the complex knots of religion, nation, and enlightened thought in *Culture and Anarchy*.

A little more than a decade after Trilling's discussion, Frederic Faverty published *Matthew Arnold, the Ethnologist*, a study that takes the racial assumptions so evident in *Celtic Literature* as keys to Arnold's work, *Culture and Anarchy* included. Although, for Faverty, "it must be admitted at the start that Arnold was no systematic racialist" (Faverty 1), it is also clear that "like his contemporary, Taine, he sought always for the dominant trait (pensée maîtresse) in the race or nation under discussion" (186). Faverty accepts much of what animates Gossman's approach—that Arnold rejected the anatomical absurdities propagated in books such as Emile Burnouf's *La science des religions*, with its grotesque caricature of Semitic anatomy; that Arnold actually displays a "a profound admiration" (174) for Hebraism and found it a necessary component of a balanced human perfection; and that, whether discussing Indo-Europeans or Semites, Arnold generally pointed out virtues and defects alike. But for Faverty, these virtues and defects were still racial dispositions, at least in their origins, and his conclusion is as harsh as criticism of Arnold gets: "To the unfounded assumptions of the racial hypothesis Arnold lent the weight of a distinguished name. His pronouncements upon the Celt, the Saxon, and Jew have not gone unheard; they have told upon the world's practice" (191–92). Faverty's penetrating work has been too often ignored in major Arnold studies, even though, as Ruth apRoberts noted a few years back, his "rich study . . . is by no means dated" (apRoberts 97; see also Graff 191; Lloyd 145, n. 11). Faverty's own currency aside, how should we address today the very real problem of Arnold's relationship to the ethnological assumptions of his day, a problem raised more obviously by a work such as *Celtic Literature* than by any of Arnold's other writings? And to what extent should Arnold's sentiments in *Culture and Anarchy* be assimilated to those in *Celtic Literature*, published serially in the *Cornhill* in 1866, only one year before the earliest elements of *Culture and Anarchy* began appearing there? As recent work on culture and race has begun to demonstrate, these are questions with continuing relevance for current criticism (see Young 55–89.)

Celtic Hauntings

The difficulty facing any attempt to reconcile the ethnological assumptions in *Celtic Literature* with the underlying religious-secularization motifs of *Culture and Anarchy* is not hard to see. Stocking is quite impressed, for example, when Arnold admits that he could easily have been an aristocratic Barbarian. "Place me in one of his great fortified posts . . . with all pleasures at my command, everyone I met smiling on me, and with every appearance of permanence and security before me and behind me,—then I too might have grown, I feel, into a passable child of the established fact, of commendable spirit and politeness, and . . . a little inaccessible to ideas and light" (Arnold 5:144; quoted in Stocking 795–96). Though Stocking oddly does not state it bluntly, what he really seems to admire here is simply Arnold's sense that a different environment, a different "way of life" or set of customs, would have produced a different person, a notion supposedly both more in tune with modern anthropology and quite different from Tylor's emphasis on a fixed evolutionary sequence. That Arnold is talking here more about *class* within a nation than about races or nations, and that a recognition of environmental influence in this narrow context need not necessarily contradict more broadly based assumptions about racial inheritance—all this goes by unobserved in Stocking's essay. Yet Stocking's point is still a good one: Arnold's humanism implies in such passages that "human beings shared a capacity for various types of development" (Stocking 795), including development based on the inculcation of either Hebraistic or Hellenistic tendencies, a capacity that much of the anthropology of his time seemed to be repressing.

By contrast, what Trilling confronts in *Celtic Literature* would seem to be a direct and conscious refutation of all that Stocking claims about Arnold. "Modes of life, institutions, government, climate, and so forth,—let me say it once for all,—will further or hinder the development of an aptitude, but they will not by themselves create the aptitude or explain it. On the other hand, a people's habit and complexion of nature go far to determine its modes of life, institutions, and government, and even to prescribe the limits within which the influences of climate shall tell upon it" (Arnold 3:353). It is a refutation especially pertinent to Stocking's argument in that, as Trilling points out, Arnold's target here seems to be Henry Thomas Buckle, whose emphasis on "the non-racial determinants of culture" (Trilling 235) implies something far closer to some shared "capacity for various types of development" than is suggested by Arnold's rather frankly biological "complexion of nature." In rejecting Buckle, of course, Arnold is surely not implying the evolutionism that inspired Tylor; but he is clearly rejecting the essential elements of Stocking's "modern" anthropological perspective.

One possible impediment to comparing *Culture and Anarchy* with *Celtic Literature* in this way is that Arnold was never much bothered by inconsistency. Like Emerson across the Atlantic, Arnold's mind was perhaps too deliberately free of the hobgoblins of systematic thought to concern itself with the ethnological niceties described by Stocking. In the introduction to *Celtic Literature,* Arnold admits the "provisional character" (Arnold 3:387) of his remarks quite openly, and he goes so far in the published version of his lectures as to include footnotes by Lord Strangford that time and again point out the errors (or worse) propagated by Arnold's superficial knowledge of philology, Celtic and otherwise. Oddly, Arnold apparently felt no need either to correct his text for publication or to refute Strangford; the contradictions and mistakes remain unresolved.

If the text of *Celtic Literature* itself can be so riddled with contradictions, it is all the more reason to think that the gap between *Culture and Anarchy* and his study of the Celts mattered little to Arnold. Though *Culture and Anarchy* develops a liberal, inclusive, and secularizing view of culture as "a harmonious expansion of *all* the powers which make the beauty and worth of human nature" (Arnold 5:94), *Celtic Literature*'s pseudo-scientific ethnological categories are at times not that far from those of Joseph Arthur de Gobineau: "As there are for physiology physical marks, such as the square head of the German, the round head of the Gael, the oval head of the Cymri, which determine the type of a people, so for criticism there are spiritual marks which determine the type, and make us speak of the Greek genius, the Teutonic genius, the Celtic genius, and so on" (3:340). *Culture and Anarchy* focuses in large part on a sense of culture as "cultivation," on what the German romantics had called *Bildung*, both as a search for inward perfection and as an egalitarian drive "to make the best that has been thought and known in the world current everywhere, to make all men live in an atmosphere of sweetness and light" (5:113)—a principle that has seemed to a great many to be still unsurpassed as a secular humanist ideal. By contrast, *Celtic Literature* is dedicated to an account of culture as a set of identifiable physical, linguistic, and spiritual characteristics that seem to derive more from a medieval theory of the humors than from any positivist or evolutionary Victorian ethnology. The difficult question raised by the tension between the two texts is an unsettling one: to what extent does the secularizing and humanist force of *Culture and Anarchy* somehow depend on the (now almost forgotten) ethnological assumptions of *Celtic Literature?*

Arnold uses and italicizes the word "humour" both in *Culture and Anarchy*, where the English nation is described as "eminently Indo-European by its *humour*" (Arnold 5:174), and in *Celtic Literature*, where the unique "*humour*" of the English appears to be Germanism awkwardly leavened by "hauntings of Celtism" (3:360). The phlegmatic Germans (Arnold actually refers at one point to "the Saxon's phlegm" [3:348]) are dull, steady, and "humdrum," even "ignoble," yet methodical in their "patient fidelity to Nature,—in a word, *science*" (3:341). The sanguine Celts are sentimental and lively (3:343), yet lacking in patience or self-control (that is, "feminine"—hence their chivalry); they are close to "natural magic," prone to "extravagance and exaggeration" (3:347), "ineffectual in politics" (3:346), and "*always ready to react against the despotism of fact*" (3:344). Even the body's organs display the difference: the German "has the larger volume of intestines," while the Frenchman (whom Arnold also considered fundamentally Celtic, even beyond Brittany) "has the more developed organs of respiration" (3:343). Arnold's larger purpose was to illustrate, against much philo-Teutonic and anti-Celtic opinion in England at this time, the degree to which the English have inherited elements of both racial dispositions. In *Celtic Literature*, Arnold's ethnology is in fact different from Tylor's evolutionism, though not, as Stocking observes of *Culture and Anarchy*, because it is more modern in its functionalism and relativism, but rather because it is profoundly anachronistic in its conception of national-racial "spirit." Hegel's grand typologies of national *Geist* in the *Philosophy of History* seem no more untimely, and we should recall that in *Friendship's Garland* Arnold, referring in passing to *Celtic Literature*'s typologies, comically explains his Hellenism through Arminius's notion of *Geist* as "intelligence" (Arnold had been reading Hegel's *Phenomenology of Spirit;* see Arnold 5:42, 5:76–77).

Further difficulties of interpretation arise from the fact that *Celtic Literature* is clearly a work of borrowed scholarship. Throughout his career, Arnold lifted ideas and terminology from continental writers whose work was less known in England. Ernest Renan wrote essays on Marcus Aurelius, Spinoza, and the Celts, and so did Arnold. On this score, however, *Celtic Literature* may be in a class by itself. Arnold's debt to Renan's "La poésie des races celtiques," published as part of his *Essais de morale et de critique* in 1859, has long been recognized, though Renan's essay is a far more sentimental and nostalgic survey of Celtic attributes than is Arnold's attempt at ethnological science. It was from Renan, himself a Breton Celt, that Arnold took what was perhaps the germ of his essay: the belief that, in Renan's words, "le chevalrie,—cet idéal de douceur et de beauté posé comme but suprême de la vie,—n'est une création ni classique, ni chrétienne, ni germanique, mais bien réellement celtique" [chivalry—that ideal of sweetness and beauty posited as the highest end of life—is a creation neither classical, nor Christian, nor Germanic, but truly Celtic] (Renan, *Essais* 385). Already in Renan the Celtic sensibility has become an antidote, as it were, for that of a dominant Germanic Christendom. But as Faverty demonstrates, Arnold borrowed just as extensively from Henri Martin's *Histoire de France,* passages of which, like that on the Celt's resistance to the "despotism of fact," found numerous echoes in *Celtic Literature.* Add to this Arnold's debts to Amédée Thierry's *Histoire des gaulois* for the emphasis on philology and anthropology—Arnold could have taken his sense of the main groups within the Celtic race, Welsh-Cornish and Breton (the Cymric) versus Scottish and Irish (the Gaelic), from either Thierry or Renan (see Arnold 3:498, editor's note to p. 292, lines 31–38; Faverty 123)—and W. F. Edwards's *Recherches sur les langues celtiques* for the remarks on the physiological evidence of Celtic inheritance in England (Faverty 36), and *Celtic Literature* begins to break apart into something of a scholarly collage. Is the problem then that Arnold's interest in the Celts, stimulated mainly it seems by a visit to Brittany and a subsequent visit to Wales, where he attended an Eisteddfod, or Bardic Congress, at Llandudno, was based on a hastily assembled, if still comprehensive, hodgepodge of ethnological writing—for which Arnold himself can hardly be held fully responsible?

Neither a high tolerance for inconsistency nor hasty scholarship, however, is finally very satisfying as an explanation for the twists and turns in Arnold's ethnology. To tackle the second point first, Arnold's scholarship was always much broader than it was deep—and this should not seem odd in a critic so devoted to the idea that intellectual machinery, including the tendency to the overspecialization of thought, was the curse of his time. Indeed, Arnold is very much our contemporary in this regard, for it is precisely Arnold who should be seen as the great progenitor of the post-1968 demand for interdisciplinary and nonsystematic humanistic inquiry, at least in the Anglo-American world. Much in contemporary "cultural studies" reproduces the cursory quality of Arnold's anthropological and philological thought along with his breadth of vision. The issue, then as today, is less how to excuse this combination of qualities than to understand what it enables or overlooks, for both good and ill.

By the same token, Arnold's inconsistent approach to the concept of culture should itself be seen less as a simple failing to be explained away than as a crucial hinge in this thinking. It is far more likely that Arnold did not recognize any real contradiction between the ideal of a secular criticism expressed in *Culture and Anarchy* and the ethnological-racial opinions of *Celtic Literature* than that he did and ignored them. Or perhaps, as I have already suggested, the former in some way depended on the latter, at least for Arnold. Once again, Arnold should perhaps be considered our contemporary, for it is precisely his equivocations that haunt, albeit in strongly disavowed forms, contemporary humanistic reflection on culture. Arnold's sense of culture is somehow both cultivated secular disposition and biologically rooted aptitude, both what *Culture and Anarchy* calls a "study of perfection" whose inwardness is itself real only if it implies "a *general* perfection, embracing all our fellow-men with whom we have to do" (Arnold 5:215) and, in *Celtic Literature,* a "complexion of nature" (3:353) displayed by a racial-national stock even when blended with others in diverse physical and social environments.

The concept of culture for Arnold is in fact fluid and dynamic, and it tacks back and forth between these positions and through several intervening ones with some ease. This conceptual sliding or equivocation is mediated by the host of metaphors—"impulse," "bent," "force," "tendency"—that do so much work in *Culture and Anarchy* within the tension between religion and secularization. For with such terms, Arnold can talk about a wide variety of things in either of two, often unspecified, causal sequences: either learned, if deeply rooted, sensibilities that have been cultivated by scriptural-religious, literary, and philosophical traditions; or religious, literary, and philosophical traditions that are themselves primarily the consequence of racial-national "genius" or "spirit," a natural—that is, biologically given—complexion of consciousness that can be traced, in varying depths, wherever a "people" migrate and intermarry. Although *Culture and Anarchy* would appear to be indebted primarily to the first causal sequence (hence its continuing viability in contemporary thought, and especially its relevance to what Edward Said calls "secular criticism") and *Celtic Literature* to the second (hence its relative invisibility today), it is important to recognize that both types of arguments are present in varying degrees in both essays. Once we take seriously Arnold's claim that the new "science of origins" is indeed the foundation of "all real knowledge of the actual world," the fact that these two causal chains are inextricably linked in his thinking becomes difficult to ignore, and becomes perhaps not unexpected at all.

Secular Culture and Race

If any piece of scholarship illustrates how far the road to hell can be paved with good intentions, *Celtic Literature* is it. Perhaps the most difficult problem of all in addressing the essay is that it embodies manifestly good intentions— that is, good from the perspective of much current opinion—quite in spite of its now discredited racial assumptions. Arnold not only seriously promoted the value of studying Celtic literature and myth at a time when its mostly ill-informed proponents had been subjected to withering (and often justified) attack, he also called at the end of his essay for a "chair of Celtic" (3:384) at Oxford or Cambridge. (Among his listeners at the last of Arnold's Celtic lectures was John Rhys, who would be the first to occupy such a chair when it was established in 1877 at Jesus College [Arnold, editor's note, 3:493]). If we are to believe such figures as W. B. Yeats and Andrew Lang, Arnold's essay, along with the writings of James Macpherson and Renan, had a formative influence on the Celtic Revival (see Faverty 152–53; Kelleher) that would soon transform—we might say reinvent—the literary history of Ireland, even if Arnold, like Joyce, displayed little of the revival's enthusiasm for Gaelic language and folklore. Moreover, in essays such as "Irish Catholicism and British Liberalism," Arnold supported the Irish Catholic demand for a religiously sectarian Catholic university (Arnold 8:321–47), though the ethnographic grounds for his support become clearer in an essay on the great conservative political theorist Joseph de Maistre: "Just as every plan of government is a baneful dream, unless it be in harmony with the character and circumstances of the nation, so it is with education" (9:101). Whatever Arnold's shortcomings in accepting a race-religion-culture nexus, his essay deployed such thinking toward ends that would be widely praised in the modern academy: the revival of a neglected and oppressed cultural tradition and the institutionalization of its study within the university.

Yet Arnold's brief excursions through Brittany and Wales, which reminded him of something in his Cornish mother, and presumably in himself—Renan also saw Bretagne through the eyes of his mother and his childhood—produced complicated results. His pointed interest in Celtic matters was at heart one more expression of his profoundly romantic attraction to things (such as classical grace and medieval humors) that had come to seem irrelevant to the utilitarian sensibility, technological progress, and science of the secular modern world. This attraction could extend from solitary, sentimental melancholics, such as the autobiographical hero of Etienne Pivert de Senancour's *Obermann*—"l'expression d'un homme qui sent et non d'un homme qui travaille" [the expression of a man who feels and not a man who works] (Senancour I), we read in its first sentence—to entire peoples around whom the aura of lost nobility could be imagined to glow in direct proportion to their worldly disappointment.

"For ages and ages," Arnold notes in *Celtic Literature*, "the world has been constantly slipping, ever more and more, out of the Celt's grasp. 'They went forth to war,' Ossian says most truly, '*but they always fell*'" (Arnold 3:346). The line Arnold cites here from James Macpherson's largely invented *Poems of Ossian*, which is perhaps the single most important influence on the reawakened European interest in folk culture and oral tradition throughout the late eighteenth and nineteenth centuries, including that of German romantics such as Herder (see Chapman, *Gaelic Vision* 29–52, 83–84), also serves as Arnold's epigraph. It is hard not to conclude that what Arnold saw in the Celts, partly in himself, but also in the Irish, whom many of the English would have considered a distinctly alien race at this time, was an all but forgotten poetic sensibility, the value of which lay precisely in its manifest unsuitability for worldly success in Arnold's day. In elaborating this melancholic Celtic nobility, Arnold largely followed the lead of Macpherson, who, like Walter Scott in his popular *Waverley* novels, reflected more closely the mood of Scottish clansmen after the failed rebellion of 1745 than he did a heritage of Celtic poetry (see Smart 26–29). "For the sword which they were no longer able to yield," writes Faverty in summary of Macpherson's image of the Celts, "they substituted the harp. They were a dying race, but like the swan, they would sing a beautiful lament before they expired" (Faverty 149). Arnold's crucial difference from Macpherson, however, lies in the fact that in *Celtic Literature* we find a mechanism, racial inheritance, by which the virtues of that beaten breed might survive in the English—if only, like so many other anthropological "survivals," in latent form.

Arnold's *Celtic Literature* is thus riddled with a nostalgia equal to, if more temperate than, Renan's, for which the lost cause of the Celts becomes a salutary reminder of a "style," "grace," and "delicate magic" absent from the Teutonic (Saxon) character of the modern English Philistine. All the attributes Arnold cites had become part of a commonly accepted discourse on the Celts from Macpherson on, though Arnold would turn that discourse to his own purposes: "The Celt's quick feeling for what is noble and distinguished gave his poetry style; his indomitable personality gave it pride and passion; his sensibility and nervous exaltation gave it a better gift still, the gift of rendering with wonderful felicity the magical charm of nature" (Arnold 3:374). In *Culture and Anarchy*, the "extraordinary grace" demanded by feudalism's "struggling society" from England's "land-holding class," whose charismatic dominance provided "cohesion" and an "ideal or standard for the rest of the community," disappears from the "luxurious, settled and easy society" of the modern aristocratic Barbarians (5:203). But that grace, that style and magical charm, are never really lost in Arnold. They are constantly recaptured on other grounds, in phrases such as "sweetness and light," in the spontaneous play of the secular mind that marks Hellenism, but also in the racial heritage of Celtic poetry, as if that secular mind held within it elements not that different from those of the Celt's racial spirit.

Arnold's point is both retrospective and very much of his moment. He wants to illustrate the deep undercurrents of this often-overlooked Celtic influence in English literary history: Shakespeare, Milton, Byron, Wordsworth, and Keats are all called to testify to its workings. But he also wants to demonstrate to an uncomprehending and increasingly dominant philistine, dissenting, and puritanical middle class that there is a vestigial "humour" of romance, poetry, and magic flowing in its veins, a sort of secular Celtic humor that could substitute for what aristocratic England has lost, once it is recognized as innate. For *Celtic Literature*, the repressed "hauntings of Celtism" (Arnold 3:360) in the Englishman's character, which prompt his characteristically "self-conscious" and "embarrassed" nature, or what George Sand called his "typical awkwardness" (3:360–61), are appropriate reproductions of the haunting, magical qualities of Celtic poetry itself—as if the poetry had been designed all along to remind the English that something intimately their own needed to be recovered from the mists of their racial past and used as a bulwark against the religious philistinism of their time.

Unsurprisingly, it is this uncanny nostalgia that gives *Celtic Literature* its convoluted politics, for however admirable (in part) the noble Celtic sensibility might be, it remains resolutely a thing of the past, forever cursed by a worldly impotence and "feminine" (Arnold 3:347) lack of discipline that binds it irrevocably to the British Empire. In this regard, Arnold's treatment of the Celt illustrates Lord Lytton's view that Irish virtues may "win affection but never esteem" (quoted in Faverty 146)—just like the virtues bestowed on women by a supposedly Celt-invented code of chivalry. To be sure, *Celtic Literature*, like *Culture and Anarchy*, has a distinctly ameliorative social program, demonstrating "traces of kinship, and the most essential sort of kinship, spiritual kinship, between us and the Celt, of which we had never dreamed" (Arnold 3:335). At a time when, fifteen years after the Great Hunger in Ireland, relations between the English and Irish were at a particularly low ebb, distrust was the rule, and the rather stark choice between "coercion" and "separation" (Lloyd 142) seemed to be all that was left, Arnold's essay tried to demonstrate that "we English, alien and uncongenial to our Celtic partners as we may have hitherto shown ourselves, have notwithstanding, beyond perhaps any nation, a thousand latent springs of possible sympathy with them." Arnold's grand goal is nothing less than a transformation of English character, "substituting, in place of that type of Englishman with whom alone the Celt has too long been familiar, a new type, more intelligent, more gracious, and more humane"—a type more open, as it were, to a secularized "sweetness and light." And yet Arnold is in no way calling here for more Irish (much less Welsh!) autonomy; like most of the English, Arnold had no sympathy even for the maintenance of the Welsh and Gaelic languages if these challenged the hegemony of English. He demands just as great a transformation of character from "the Celtic members of this empire," who would thereby better realize "that they are inextricably bound up with us" (Arnold 3:395). Arnold's twin appeals to the English and Celts of the empire for political moderation, however balanced they may at first seem, are in fact quite asymmetrical.

Arnold's appeal to the English presumes what to him would be historically obvious: the English are the hardier (politically and spiritually dominant) stock, both by virtue of their sound Teutonic basis (or primary humor) and by virtue of their heterosis, that is, of the various racial humors that have been bred into that basis. Like the physical hybrid, the cultural hybrid in Arnold would appear to be richer and stronger for its admixture—a fairly progressive thesis, after all, at a time of strong national and racial chauvinism: "just what constitutes special power and genius in a man seems often to be his blending with the basis of his national temperament, some additional gift or grace not proper to that temperament" (Arnold 3:358; on the broader question of the hybrid in the nineteenth century, see Young 1–28). Philology, physiology, and poetry all point toward an "affinity of race" (Arnold 3:335) between the English and the Celts, but it is only the English who seem to have benefited historically from the numerous invasions and conquests that united one race with another in Britain, precisely because the English are themselves the happy racial consequence of earlier cross-breeding, a point made in a more satirical vein by Daniel Defoe's poem of 1701 on the prejudice against William III's foreignness, "The True-Born Englishman." The Celts were the original, passive ("feminine"), and absorbed stock, "insensibly getting mixed with their conquerors"—the Saxons, the Romans, the Normans—"their blood entering into the composition of a new people, in which the stock of the conquerors counts for most, but the stock of the conquered, too, counts for something" (Arnold 3:338). It would thus appear that those Celts who fled westward into Wales, Scotland, and Ireland to avoid destruction or servitude, and who thus retained some degree of racial purity, paid a high price on the world's stage, both because of the weakness of their racial stock and because of the lack of any tempering influence. Had Arnold, when writing *Celtic Literature*, enjoyed the benefit of hearing Renan's later lecture *Qu'est-ce qu'une nation?* delivered at the Sorbonne in 1882, he would have found sentiments that both confirmed and usefully undermined his ideas about the Celts and the English: "Ethnographic considerations have thus been for nothing in the constitution of modern nations.... The truth is that there is no pure race, and that to make politics depend upon ethnographical analysis is to sustain it upon a chimera. The most noble countries, the English, the French, the Italians, are those where the blood is most mixed" (Renan, *Nation* 37; my translation). Arnold agreed, but only up to a point, for Renan's chimera did in fact matter to him in 1866.

Unlike the later Renan, moreover, Arnold is far from treating all forms of racial simplicity or complexity in the same way, and the only real marker of racial health is Darwinian in nature—the superior worldly and spiritual success of the race. Like the Celt, for example, the German nature is "all of a piece" (Arnold 3:361), yet the Germans have enjoyed political and cultural prosperity, in spite of their racial *Gemeinheit* (vulgarity), dullness, and lack of poetry, because of the relative strength of their stock, a strength based in a "*steadiness with honesty*" (Arnold 3:341) and shared by the English (in the form of "*energy with honesty*") through Saxon conquest. The French, by contrast, are a blend in which Frankish-German and Latin have been superimposed on "an undoubtedly Celtic basis" (3:349). But the French suffer much more from their Celtic inheritance than do the English, precisely because the Celtic humor *remained* the basis of the French stock. Once again, the final arbiter of cultural complexion is nothing less than blood: "Gaul was Latinised in language, manners, and laws, and yet her people remained essentially Celtic. The Germanisation of Britain went far deeper than the Latinisation of France, and not only laws, manners, and language, but the main current of the blood, became Germanic" (3:338).

What Arnold actually means here is unclear. Did the Romans simply not procreate much with their Celtic hosts in Gaul? Were the Saxons far more thorough in producing offspring through the Celts of Britain? Should the Saxons be considered true colonizers, settling and intermarrying among the native population that did not flee, and the Romans mere imperialists? "They were no colonists," Marlow says of the Romans in *Heart of Darkness*, "their administration was merely a squeeze, and nothing more, I suspect" (Conrad, *Heart of Darkness* 10). It is an open question, made all the more puzzling by the fact that, following such logic, the English could be considered more Norman (that is, Latin-Celt) than anything else—a possibility Arnold, despite his rejection of all strident English philo-Teutonism and his elaboration of Norman influences, does not address. Arnold endorsed the sentiment that France was "famed in all great arts, *in none supreme*" (quoted in Faverty 137), and it seems only through its Latin (rational) humor that France had been able to overcome its Celtic flaws—though elsewhere even this Latin inheritance appears to be marked by sensuality (see Arnold 10:155). The English, by contrast, appear to have inherited only Latin virtues from the Normans, who brought with them the imperial Roman gifts for oratory and orderly administration.

The dizzying combinations of racial traits that Arnold is able to distinguish perhaps point to a salient characteristic of all such arguments: Arnold's genealogies are primarily ways of rationalizing the social and political realities of his day, of explaining and perhaps justifying English authority even as he contests its cruder exercise, challenges its narrow-minded (and often narrowly religious) chauvinism, and admits—or rather, celebrates—an awkward hybrid vigor that is essential to the secularizing benefits of Hellenism. Some current ethnological approaches to the question of the Celt deny that the term has any racial or ethnic coherence at all. Malcolm Chapman reminds us that it was only after William Jones's elaboration, in 1786, of the relation of Sanskrit to Greek and comparative philology's subsequent reconstruction of an "Indo-European" (or "Indo-Germanic") genealogy of languages that language began to be taken as a key to the genealogy of "peoples, races, nations, and cultures" (Chapman, *Celts* 14–16), a key much exploited in an age of rising nationalism, but with little historical justification. The near-mystical romantic link between language, race, nation, and religious sensibility could thus be mapped in both evolutionary and geographical terms and, following Barthold Niebuhr, in terms of European history itself. For Chapman, "the Celt" is one of the most influential and persistent, but least credible, genealogical units of the age. Like others before him, he finds little evidence that, for much of its supposed history, the Celt ever embodied the concatenation of physical, spiritual, and linguistic characteristics that is assumed by romantic Celtic studies and Matthew Arnold alike. Chapman comes close to endorsing the idea that "there is no such thing as Celt" (Chapman, *Celts* 251), that the term may really be no more than a name for attributes, such as charm, grace, and poetic sentiment, imposed by all industrialized metropolitan societies on their "folk" (another late eighteenth-century invention) peripheries. (For a very early predecessor of Chapman's argument, see the 1867 review of *Celtic Literature* by Fagan.)

What is clear in Arnold is that a racial "basis," a people's original "complexion of nature" or humor, will have a determining influence on its culture and religious sensibility unless that basis has been saturated with and overcome by the blood of a conquering race. At best, a people will be able to temper the vices of its racial basis with the virtues of its racial cross-breeding. The phlegmatic, puritanical Teutonism of the English can thus be enlivened by Celtic sentiment and magic; the Celtic extravagance, femininity, and eternal readiness "to react against the despotism of fact" inherited by the French can be held in check, but only barely, by Roman laws and bureaucracy. Even here, of course, the asymmetry persists, for England is blessed both with a more wholesome Teutonic "basis," despite its vices, than the French, and with a greater resource, in its vestigial Celtic humor, for tempering that basis than the Germans. England's greatest danger may be too much dull, plodding moral rectitude, but France must constantly beware an explosive rebellion against fact—a dangerous tendency that France, with its seemingly endless political upheavals in the nineteenth century, could be said to share with the Irish Celts it was often asked to support against England.

Arnold's notions of racially based traits and cultural cross-breeding might appear to be of little relevance to the larger rise of "multicultural" pedagogy in recent years and to contemporary notions of cultural hybridity and cross-cultural aesthetic practice. After all, these modern meditations on what Arnold called the "science of origins" would seem to have been amply inoculated against all that plagues Arnold's ethnology by a repudiation of the biological-racial inheritance of cultural traits and by a more thoroughgoing relativism. Like John Stuart Mill, Andrew Lang, Yeats, and Renan, most of Arnold's readers today are likely to reject the theory of "inherent natural differences" (Mill, *Principles* 324) supporting *Celtic Literature* as an outmoded explanation for both individual character and cultural traditions (see Lang; Renan, *Nation* 37; Yeats), just as surely as they would reject the traditions of strict scriptural interpretation against which Arnold inveighed.

Yet, like many people in casual conversation, then and now, these earlier writers were hardly always free in practice from using national-racial assumptions to explain cultural or political aptitudes, despite their stated beliefs. Mill's attitude was primarily developmental rather than racial: like the similar views of Marx on Oriental despotism, Mill's view that "despotism is a legitimate mode of government when dealing with barbarians" ("On Liberty" 263) may be a convenient notion for imperial designs, but it is not necessarily racially based. However, when Mill indicts the "despotism of Custom . . . over the whole East" (318) and notes that China, "stationary" for thousands of years despite earlier eras of progress, will only be "farther improved . . . by foreigners," it is not hard to imagine that Mill's readers, despite his better intentions, would take this situation as having something to do with an innate Chinese racial disposition unleavened by contact with other dispositions, since it is only the sheer "diversity of character and culture" (320) found most obviously in Europe that, with proper nurturing, will save the nations and individuals of Europe from a similar fate. It should thus not be surprising that highly sublimated versions of Arnoldian racial inheritance, along with what may be the practical impossibility of strict relativism, continue to haunt uses of the word "culture" in contemporary cultural criticism, just as surely as the assumptions of a coherent and continuous Celtic personality have persisted in ways that critics such as Chapman rightly find unwarranted.

When we refer to a culture, in purely secular terms, as having a coherence based on a national or regional or group identity over time, as elaborated in a particular language, literary tradition, and set of customs—whether these are designated Irish, French, German, or one of a number of newer ethnic American "communities"—does our usage in fact limit such a sense of culture to something like what Pierre Bourdieu calls a learned, and hence quite functionally motivated and hierarchically structured, *habitus* (Bourdieu 167)? Or is this sense of culture fundamentally different from that of Bourdieu's sense of class? Do we not at such times also imply that culture is an expression, as Arnold put it in *Celtic Literature*, of a people's innate "genius" (Arnold 3:325) or soul, a "natural disposition" composed of intellectual, emotional, and psychological tendencies passed on by blood? By the same token, when we value the cross-fertilization enabled by transnational flows of ideas and capital, and champion the discursively (rather than racially) hybrid character of cultures around the globe as a salutary form of resistance to oppressive notions of racial and cultural purity, can we always prevent our rhetoric from subtly implying something not so different from what Arnold openly stated—that there really are distinct or simpler or purer cultural "humours" to be so blended in the first place, that the heterogeneous mix of self and other promoted by cosmopolitan modernity, if it is to represent a salutary and fully secularized cultural vigor, must have begun with near-innate aptitudes and sensibilities?

The exemplary paradoxes of Arnold's work suggest that even when contemporary cultural criticism elaborates the vicissitudes and complexities of modern cultural or ethnic sensibility, it may still inadvertently end up dragging along the ghosts of blood inheritance. It can be argued that religiously based forms of solidarity were just as important to nascent nineteenth-century nationalism as the affiliations of racial kinship, and that both have been central in turn to anti-colonial struggles for political emancipation. But in Arnold, it would appear that the effort to arrive at the standpoint of an adequately secularized cultural criticism in some sense required the elaboration of natural and *national Geist* in place of strong religion. This is a substitution that may yet reverberate throughout the contemporary focus on ethnic-cultural "difference," even when terms as bald as "blood" and "race" are never used.

At one point in *Celtic Literature,* Arnold cites linguistic evidence—faulty, as Strangford's note shows—to demonstrate that "the hearth comes to mean home. Then from home it comes to mean the group of homes, the tribe; from the tribe the entire nation; and in this sense of nation or people, the word appears in Gothic, Norse, Celtic, and Persian, as well as in Scythian" (Arnold 3:331). Arnold's bad philology notwithstanding, I would suggest that clear echoes of such *volkisch* (and indeed ancient) thinking, implying that the race or nation is in fact the family writ large, can be heard throughout the modernism that triumphs in Arnold's wake, and that vestiges of it survive well into contemporary critical thought. Current usage of the word "ethnicity," for example, as in "ethnic American literatures"—English literature no longer qualifying, of course, as ethnic, though an Englishman's ethnicity was in no sense to be taken for granted among the Victorians—at times does much of the equivocating work that Arnold's "impulse," "bent," "force," and "tendency" do. Ethnicity can enable precisely the same conceptual slippage, the same back-and-forth shuttle of meanings between an arbitrarily transmitted custom and a racial inheritance that manifests itself as an expression of the soul, as a vague but intractable "sensibility" passed on by blood kinship. As Robert J. C. Young has argued, "The ethnological basis of Arnold's cultural politics, and the way in which racism, ethnology and culture slide so easily into each other, might also give us pause about current ways in which we champion ethnicity, and promote a culturally defined ethnic, as opposed to a biologically defined racial, identity" (Young 88). In a recent issue of *PMLA* devoted to ethnicity, Sander Gilman notes: "Ethnicity as it is used in the humanities is a North American sociological concept that is defined against the categories of race and class"; yet, it often "comes very close to definitions of race in sociology and physical anthropology" (Gilman 19). Still, none of the essays collected in the issue openly confronts the potential problems raised by using such a term as "ethnicity," with its vague connotation of inherited characteristics, in a causal relation to culture.

In practice, I would argue, ethnicity often allows the disavowed ghost of blood-carried cultural humors to occupy the otherwise sanitized (or non-"essentialist") precincts of contemporary cultural studies. For the last two decades or so, and partly in response to the racial and imperialist role that the idea of culture had played in earlier scholarship, anthropologists have been coming to the conclusion that the "culture concept" inherited from Tylor and so central to cultural anthropology in the earlier twentieth century is far too much of an hypostasis, too amorphous and even dangerous, to be of use any longer for scholarly work (for a good overview, see Buzard). But the demand that we eschew the word "culture" altogether, because it supposedly designates nothing *but* ghosts (see Michaels), is liable to foreclose the need to elaborate the sort of rhetorical intersections among religion, nation, and race that we find in Arnold. Hence, I do not mean to claim that neither "race" nor "culture" matters, but rather that the relationship between them is as arbitrary (if historically maintained or contrived) and nonnatural as the relationship between race and language—a fact all too easy to forget once race, language, and culture are recognized as powerful instruments of social and political power, while the religious bases of social solidarity once so important to figures like Weber and Durkheim are consumed by the secularizing forces of modernity. Just as, in the present age of globalization and anti-Western resistance to it, the secularization thesis itself is very much in question, Arnold's complex meditations on the nation situated in the transition from religion to race may have much to tell us about the unintended consequences of the secularizing impulse.

From Religious Transmission to Racial Kinship

However much I agree with readers such as Gossman that Arnold's use of the words "Hebraism" and "Hellenism" would seem to be free of any overt anti-Semitism, I remain convinced that the lingering resonance of *Celtic Literature*'s view of race in *Culture and Anarchy* cannot be ignored, and that these must of course reflect back in turn on what Arnold meant by Hebraism and Hellenism in the first place. The Celts and the Saxons belonged, we should remember, to the same racial family tree, in spite of their differences: both were Indo-European, and it seems that it is the Celtic aptitude for sentiment and beauty that makes the Saxon all the more truly "Hellenic." The Hebrews and English belonged to completely different racial trees for Arnold, despite the similarity of their moral tendencies. To be sure, Arnold found the vulgar caricatures of the Semite in Gobineau and Burnouf worthy of ridicule and certainly rejected, in *Literature and Dogma,* Burnouf's thesis that Christ, like other northern Jews of Galilee, was really Aryan (that is, Indo-European or Indo-Germanic). Arnold thus dismissed Bernouf's claim that Christianity was a metaphysical doctrine imported from Persia and India rather than the practical religion of the southern Jews of Jerusalem and Judea, those true Semites guided by legal literalism, incapacity for abstraction or science, and small brains (see Arnold 6:239–40; see also Faverty 172). But what cannot be disputed is that Arnold followed the lead of Renan, in texts such as his *Histoire du peuple d'Israel,* in thinking of Indo-European and Semite as distinct racial groups with distinct humors, aptitudes, and complexions of nature. Arnold refused Burnouf's idea that Christianity was Aryan in origin. But he admitted "that Israel shows no talent for metaphysics," even if religious greatness arises from the fact that "he [i.e., Israel] does *not* found religion on metaphysics" (Arnold 6:241). Renan had insisted that the Indo-Europeans excelled at intellectual, political, and military achievement, while the Semites were responsible for the development of religious belief. Arnold's own conceptions are not far off.

In language that echoes *Celtic Literature*'s "science of origins," Arnold observes in *Culture and Anarchy* that "science has now made visible to everybody the great and pregnant elements of difference which lie in race, and in how signal a manner they make the genius and history of an Indo-European people vary from those of a Semitic people. Hellenism is of Indo-European growth, Hebraism of Semitic growth; and we English, a nation of Indo-European stock, seem to belong naturally to the movement of Hellenism." And yet Arnold goes on to point out that there is an "essential unity of man" marked by the "affinities we can perceive, in this point or that, between members of one family of peoples and members of another" (Arnold 5:173). The racial affinity, or *likeness,* of the English Protestants and the Jews is one such affinity—Renan and Taine had also noticed a similar seriousness, strength, and simplicity of spirit (see Faverty 173)—and it is a likeness reflected in the religious continuity of Hebraism, from the Jews to the English Evangelicals.

But the thesis that Arnold's Hebraism represents no more than a relatively smooth continuum of transmitted religious and moral tradition from Judaism to Christianity, as implied by Trilling, Stocking, Gossman and many others, actually does not at all contradict the notion that for Arnold the English and the Jews represent quite distinct innate racial aptitudes. The Aryan English and the Semitic Hebrews resemble one another to an extraordinary degree, and they share a religious tradition, but they are hardly the same racially. It is precisely because the English are racially rooted in their Indo-European humors that Arnold can reasonably expect them, as in "St. Paul and Protestantism," to redress the "over-Hebraising of Puritanism" (Arnold 6:7), a task that includes Arnold's attempt to translate the great convert St. Paul "for us modern and Western people" (6:23) in a way that corrects "the defect in the critical habit of himself and his [Jewish] race" (6:22).

What seems superficially to be merely a single transmitted tradition of religious and moral ideas in Arnold's essay turns out to be instead the evolutionary emergence of a "likeness in the strength and prominence of the moral fibre" in the English and Hebrew people. "Eminently Indo-European by its *humour*," by its power of "imaginatively acknowledging the multiform aspects of the problem of life" and hence of resisting "over-certainty," the English race also has in its practical and moral life "a strong share of the assuredness, the tenacity, and intensity of the Hebrews" (Arnold 5:174). English Puritanism may be called a form of Hebraism because Christianity in its origins "transformed and renewed" (5:187) the Hebraism of the Jews. But Puritanism as the continuation of a religious and moral tradition must at the same time be distinguished from the racially given moral complexion of the English as an Indo-European people. Puritanism is in fact the consequence then both of a religious law externally transmitted (with modifications) from the Jews by converts like Paul, and of a quite distinct and racially given moral aptitude in the English, albeit an aptitude equal to that of the Jews. As such, the impulse or tendency toward Puritan Christianity is driven first of all by "the conscience and moral sense of our race" (Arnold 5:174), and by "our race" Arnold means "the English nation." This "moral sense" echoes, or resembles, the racial humor of the Jews only because of some much older racial connection, implied by "the essential unity of man," in prehistory. Conceived in racial rather than religious terms, Jewish morality and English (Indo-European, Hellenic) morality are not consecutive points on the same line of evolutionary descent, as are Judaism and Christianity; they are actually two distinct, if similar, evolutionary products linked by a common, but much older and unnamable, ancestor.

Matthew Arnold may have differed from Thomas on the literal truth of the Bible story, but the son followed the father on the need to make Christianity over into a more English, or Indo-European, phenomenon. As he wrote in a letter to his mother on Christmas day, 1867:

Bunsen used to say that our great business was to get rid of all that was purely Semitic in Christianity, and to make it Indo-Germanic, and Schleiermacher that in the

Christianity of us Western nations there was really much more of Plato and Socrates than of Joshua and David; and, on the whole, papa worked in the direction . . . of Bunsen and Schleiermacher, and was perhaps the only powerful Englishman of his day who did so. . . . Perhaps the change of times and modes of action being allowed for, my scope is not so different from his as you and I often think. (Arnold, editor's note, 6:456)

Baron Bunsen, it should be noted, was responsible for the theory "of the coexistence of two races among the Jews, one black, the other of a dark color" (Faverty 172), an earlier version of the theory that Arnold had rejected in Burnouf. Arnold may have insisted on the idea that Christianity as a religion indeed originated among the Jews rather than the Aryans, and from practical moral experience rather than metaphysical speculation. After all, it is precisely Christianity as deeply felt ethical perfection rather than as mechanical legalism, literal history, or divine intervention that earned Arnold's admiration and acceptance. But it is the Hellenic humor of the Indo-European races that in Arnold is most often called upon to make Christianity into the instrument of such perfection.

And Arnold did not hesitate when needed, as in his treatment of the Liberal proposal to allow marriage to "one's deceased wife's sister" (Arnold 5:206), to remind his readers that the worst parts of Hebraism were, in fact, Semitic: "the delicate and apprehensive genius of the Indo-European race" cannot allow itself to be "hoodwinked" by a "divine law expressed for them by the voice of any Oriental and polygamous nation like the Hebrews" (5:208). Hebraism as a religious concept—or rather, as the idea of religion itself—cannot in practice be divorced for Arnold from the opposed racial bases, Semitic and Indo-European, that give it its peculiar complexions and limitations. Neither, finally, can the idea of Hellenism—the idea of a secularizing humanism—be separated in Arnold from race, for it is composed of Indo-European tendencies lacking in the Semitic peoples. Culture, then, far from being only that inward perfection of spirit spread among the peoples of the earth by means of cultivation, or education, is always in Arnold anchored, whether vulgarly or vaguely, in a theory of racial inheritance, a theory that both explains culture's origins and determines the natural aptitudes of those who are to be cultivated.

5 * The Modernist Moment
Virginia Woolf Voyages Out

In light of the vicissitudes of secularization explored in the previous chapters, how then should we today situate a modern, secular writer's texts in relation to her culture's—and more specifically, her nation's—religious traditions? This has, in a certain sense, been a problem of modern*ism* from the beginning. Ever since T. S. Eliot's early essay "*Ulysses,* Order, and Myth" (1923), an important strain of English and American criticism has tended to subsume early twentieth-century attitudes toward religion of various kinds under the rubric of a synthetic or anthropological—but also often impersonal and ironic—manipulation of mythopoetic devices (Eliot, *Selected Prose* 175–78; for a good recent example of this approach, see Martz, though in fact the critical literature on this point is vast). At the same time, the older and, for criticism of Western literature up to the eighteenth century, still quite central question of the writer's specific religious beliefs—or at least, of the degree to which the writer's imagination was shaped by religiously defined traditions of thought—in no sense disappeared for twentieth-century literature, and here a wide range of sources, from Eliot's later criticism (especially in *Notes towards the Definition of Culture*) to the historicism of Erich Auerbach and the phenomenology of Paul Ricoeur and Hans Gadamer, has served as guides. (For a very small handful of representative examples spread over the last five decades, see Wilder, Miller, Scott, Abrams, Hartman, Coulson, Brooks, Hanson, Ker, and the essays collected in Gunn, *Literature,* and in Tennyson and Ericson). About the significance, and the right way to measure the significance, of religion for the secular literature of a secular age, from, say, Baudelaire to Beckett, there has been little agreement, however. (Gunn provides good summaries of twentieth-century trends in the critical history of religion and literature in *Interpretation* 9–51, *Culture* 173–96.)

Modernity and the Secular Writer

Pointing to the wealth of religious imagery in the superficially quite secular writers of the Edwardian era, including Yeats, Joyce, T. S. Eliot, Lawrence, Forster, Ford, James, Shaw, Synge, and Pound, Richard Ellmann once concluded that in rejecting Victorian perspectives, "the Edwardians were looking for ways to be religious about life itself" (Ellmann, *Edwardians* 196). By contrast, Gabriel Josipovici has emphasized "the paradox of solipsism and communion" embedded in all profane modern literature, insisting that the fragmented remnants of the religious tradition contained in texts as different as T. S. Eliot's "Gerontion" and Alain Robbe-Grillet's *Le voyeur* actually enabled readers "to experience the limits of our world and so to sense what lies beyond, the absolutely other, distinct from me and my desires" (Josipovici 302, 307; cited in Gunn, *Interpretation* 223–24). From yet another perspective, J. Hillis Miller has argued that religion understood to be simply a historical reflection of the writer's social environment was devoid of any intrinsic meaning: "Religious themes in literature are without religious significance unless they spring from a direct relationship between the poet and God, however much they may take a form dictated by the age" (Tennyson and Ericson 43). It was the broader, more philosophical-anthropological approach to literature's entanglement with myth and ritual that left a lasting mark on literary theory. Northrop Frye's *Anatomy of Criticism* (1957) was the *summa litterarum* of this mode of interpretation, through which nominally secular literature could be seen as reproducing the metaphoric, generic, and structural gestures of sacred scripture, which was itself secularized—or at least bracketed off phenomenologically from theology—as a translation or completion of a poetry of reality (I adapt the phrase from the title of Miller's early book) built into the nature of things. "The culture of the past," Frye wrote, "is not only the memory of mankind, but our own buried life, and study of it leads to a recognition scene, a discovery in which we see, not our past lives, but the total cultural form of our present life" (Frye 346). Though Frye was an ordained minister of the United Church of Canada, his work became a rich though now often-overlooked source for postmodern ironists and Marxists alike—Hayden White and Fredric Jameson are perhaps his two most significant inheritors (see Jameson 69–74; White 7–11).

But Frye was in other ways the last of his breed. It is not simply that his easy confidence in the meaning of those capacious pronouns "our" and "we" seems increasingly today as though it belongs to a rather different world of thought, one in which "the memory of mankind," defined by "*our* own buried life" and "*our* past lives," is a function of a largely Eurocentric (and male) set of neurons. It is also that Frye imagines a totality called mankind as having, if not one transcendental or religious reality, at least a structure of consciousness defined by mythical and metaphorical endowments, and in the West by a scriptural "great code" that is the semiotic template of the Judeo-Christian mind. Even before Frye, and increasingly after, a Nietzsche-inspired reaction had begun to castigate the putatively secular humanism of modernism, along with much of its critical reception, as an insufficiently skeptical and radical project. In Heidegger, Sartre, Löwith, Derrida, and Foucault, what had appeared to Eliot to be modern high culture's ostensible refusal of religious faith was on closer inspection belied by the evidence of a disavowed accommodation with religion in the closet: historicist teleology, primitivism, the repressed question of Being, logocentrism, and so forth. And yet this postmodern critique—especially that associated with, but also criticized by, Derrida—has itself often echoed its existential fathers' vaguely religious (or negative-theological) concerns, primarily those of Kierkegaard, Heidegger, and, increasingly today, Levinas (for different examples of such criticism, see Gordon; Leonard; M. Taylor; Wolosky).

What is remarkable from the present vantage point is how routinely the strains of negative theology, at times embraced and at times disavowed, deeply embedded in the antihumanism and antihistoricism of the mid-century linguistic turn in French philosophy have been overlooked by those who seek in opposition to it a neoromantic spiritual and aesthetic renewal (see, for example, Falck). Clearly, the postmodern has also meant a return to questions of political theology, which have intensified in the wake of various forms of religious revival at the end of the cold war and in response to new pressures toward globalization (see Derrida, *Acts,* especially 40–101, 230–98). Even Jameson found it necessary decades ago to argue at the end of *The Political Unconscious* that Marxism did not need to renounce its similarity to religious belief—a kinship Ernst Bloch had celebrated earlier and Karl Löwith had treated as evidence of Marxism's failure—precisely because, as Durkheim, Eliot, and Schmitt had in different ways insisted, the social and the religious were very much the same kind of thing (see Jameson 285, 292; see also Bloch; Durkheim, *Elementary;* Löwith; Schmitt, *Political Theology*).

So the much-decried limitations of Frye's perspective (or of the later T. S. Eliot's, for that matter) should not be taken to mean that the underlying issues of religion and secularization in modern Western literature have been superseded by other matters such as language or representation, as has perhaps too often been assumed during the last quarter century. There may be other ways of talking about the cultural processes at work, not so much by focusing on the persistence of hidden or private religious belief or on the paradoxical projection of a *via negativa* from the depths of doubt, but rather by investigating what we might call the survival of desacralized religious dispositions, attitudes, strategies of response, and improvisations, that is, of secularized religious habitus, alongside or rather as an integral part of social class, in spaces intellectually dominated by the disavowal of belief (on the idea of class habitus, see Bourdieu 78–83). Looking at the problem in this way, that is, as a problem of the reproduction of historical structures of collective space, may also help us understand how sociality itself reappeared as a near-sacred category of thought during the process of secularization in the West.

I am thus not simply, or primarily, concerned with pursuing the great Joycean paradox of resistance to religion, in which the mind of an individual, whether that of protagonist or author, seems to be "supersaturated" with the faith in which he says he disbelieves (Joyce, *Portrait* 240)—a formula that works well enough both for Stephen Dedalus and for Joyce himself, since Joyce both exemplified and documented the enduring conceptual force of religious institutions. Rather, I am interested in the ways that certain infrastructures of collective life in the early twentieth century, from the family to the professional association to the hypostatized idea of society itself, might remain supersaturated with the religion in which the group's members say they disbelieve. In a sense, my larger goal is to find new, and perhaps unexpected, meaning in T. S. Eliot's difficult "conception of culture and religion as being, when each term is taken in the right context, different aspects of the same thing" (Eliot, *Notes* 28). My choice of Virginia Woolf is presented as no more than one example among many where both the nature of secularization and its larger political significance can be underlined and reexamined.

Published in 1915, *The Voyage Out* is Woolf's first novel. After what may have been seven rewritings in as many years, it turned out to be a remarkable and remarkably strange book indeed. Whatever the novel may owe to Woolf's life during its composition—including several romantic flirtations, the death of a beloved brother, a marriage proposal that went sour, a nervous breakdown, marriage, and then a second nervous breakdown—it is in many ways an awkwardly managed storehouse of imagery and characters on which most of Woolf's mature work would draw. *Mrs. Dalloway*'s Richard and Clarissa Dalloway first appear here, along with the parental substitutes Helen and Ridley Ambrose, who would later be transformed into Mr. and Mrs. Ramsay in *To the Lighthouse*. So does the nearly ubiquitous image of a rising and falling wave, perhaps the governing trope of Woolf's fictional and nonfictional worlds, with its bipolar cycles of gregariousness and inwardness, hope and despair, mania and depression. But the book is also, especially when compared with a completed earlier draft titled *Melymbrosia*, a striking demonstration of the great stylistic shift we have come to call modernism in the English novel. And since there are about as many modernisms as there are important early twentieth-century modernists, the book also sheds light on the specific nature of this shift in Woolf's work.

My claim is that, in Woolf's case, the question of modernism as literary technique can be superimposed on the question of secularization, and, further, that Woolf's version of both owes a great debt to the author's reaction to her family's religious heritage, specifically her translation of its Evangelical Clapham Sect Protestantism. By translation, I mean something like the transmutation of an embodied structure of household and clan relationships—forms of social habitus—into a textual practice that encodes the perceptual phenomena of this habitus as literary style. Already during Woolf's lifetime, David Daiches had argued that modernism's stylistic esotericism was a direct result of the withering of exoteric belief systems, for which a compensation of sorts was to be found in innovative literary technique:

Public belief becomes a matter of technique, and when it ceases to exist writers have often to find new technical devices to compensate for the loss of a device no longer available. To convey the individual sensibility of the writer directly and impressively to the reader, without first referring it to common notions which link reader and writer and in terms of which the meaning can be objectified and universalized, demands new kinds of subtlety in expression, which we find in, for example, the novels of Virginia Woolf. (Tennyson and Ericson 83)

Daiches's view cannot finally be sustained in its entirety: his argument is weakest when it invokes the unexamined though still widely held view that "meaning" is somehow thinner or less available or more fragmented in modernist literature because that literature more heavily depends on something like a private language for its medium. As almost seven decades of commentary on Woolf's work after Daiches's remarks have revealed, Woolf's novels are not quite as devoid of "common notions" as they may have at first appeared to be, nor is her language (nor that of any other modernist, for that matter) anywhere near as "private" or inscrutable as once thought.

Nevertheless, Daiches's sense that religion as a public matter permeates literary technique—quite apart from, and perhaps in contradiction to, authorial expressions of faith or its absence—may usefully remind us that religion need not only be grasped as inward experience (to use William James's famous definition; see James 42; for an updated James, see C. Taylor), but as a complex array of social rituals and representations against or within which various secularisms may take shape. I argue that Woolf has in effect secularized her religious heritage as a style that enacts its own "transcendental theory" of consciousness and sociality. But consciousness and sociality are intimately related here, and they emerge together, as in Durkheim, from the household, clan, and finally national bases of collective identity (see Durkheim, *Elementary* 99–126).

Associated Minds: From Clapham to Bloomsbury

Woolf's great-grandfather and grandfather were part of a circle of people who gathered in the village of Clapham, just outside the old City of London, around the abolitionist, missionary, and philanthropist William Wilberforce and his cousin and fellow reform-minded Parliamentarian Henry Thornton in the late eighteenth and early nineteenth centuries. (Clapham Church was replaced in 1815 by St. Paul's Cathedral, but the neighborhood was not fully enveloped by London until the twentieth century.) The group included Charles Grant, Edward Eliot, Zachary and Selina Macaulay, Grenville Sharpe, John Shore, William Smith, and the rector of Clapham church, John Venn, as well as regular visitors such as William Pitt and Hannah More. The sect may have been reformist, but its members were part of a well-established elite. Henry Thornton was at one point governor of the Bank of England; his grandfather Robert was among the first generation of wealthy merchants to settle in Clapham at the beginning of the eighteenth century, and his father, John (uncle of William Wilberforce), was born there in 1760. The Venn family had been ministers in the Church of England since 1595; Henry Venn was briefly the curate at Clapham before his son John took over. Charles Grant was director of the East India Company. Woolf's great-grandfather, James Stephen, married into the Wilberforce family, and her grandfather, Sir James Stephen, able under-secretary in the Colonial Office and later professor of modern history at Cambridge, married into the Venn family. The fellowship was characterized superficially by the Evangelical Methodism of Wilberforce's Wesleyan piety and Thornton's Calvinism. But the group remained members of the Church of England even after John Wesley's break with it (see Rudolf 89–142).

Evangelical thought in the nineteenth century was organized around a loose collection of primary themes, at the center of which was the Calvinist emphasis on original sin and the doctrine of election. But the determinism of such doctrine was much tempered by the inexplicable miracle of God's grace, which is after all what made evangelizing itself both possible and required.

In his famous account of the "Protestant ethic," Max Weber observed that Calvin's rather harsh doctrine, which seemingly robbed believers of any chance to influence their eligibility for salvation, at the same time stimulated a powerful psychological reaction. Believers could still reasonably hope to find evidence of election in their worldly circumstances, in the success, enabled by divine grace, of their worldly endeavors, ranging from the conversion of others to the rewards of the marketplace. The success of like-minded peers and friends, all engaged in a noble cause, could only intensify the assurance that one was of the elect—hence both the ideological strength of the Clapham Sect, as well as the disapproval it occasionally drew from those who derisively referred to Wilberforce and associates as "saints." In his splendid biography of Leslie Stephen, Noel Annan argues that Evangelicalism "was the single most widespread influence in Victorian England" (146; for a more recent account that stresses a transconfessional, antipapal "Protestantism" as central to British identity, see Colley). And Evangelical faith stressed personal experience over philosophical intellection. In particular, it emphasized both the emotional response to one's helplessness before a God who was as much judge as savior and the duty of the individual to make clear moral judgments in turn. Indeed, knowledge of God was itself a matter of emotional response, not theological reflection—it was the "inner light" that removed guilt and doubt alike (see Annan, *Leslie Stephen* 146–52). But it also placed an enormously heavy burden on the individual's responsibility to find that light (as Durkheim thought was exemplified by the apparently higher rates of suicide in Protestant countries; see *Suicide*).

Clapham was, by almost all accounts, a rather generous and convivial version of Evangelical thought, which tended to harden and narrow in later years. Despite, or perhaps because of, its puritanical rejection of personal ambition and the vulgar desires of the flesh, the Clapham Sect was actually quite practical, worldly, and full-bodied in its efforts to make an earnest, muscular Christianity serve society as a whole. Wilberforce's chief work, *A Practical View of the Prevailing Religious System of Professed Christians in the Higher and Middle Classes in this Country Contrasted with Real Christianity* (1797), went through some fifteen editions, and the Clapham Sect had a very wide political influence. It was perhaps the main force behind the abolition of the slave trade, which occurred twenty years after Wilberforce first proposed it in Parliament.

But the fellowship that gathered in Clapham was also committed to using the British Empire for the purpose of promoting social reform and Christianity around the globe. As Sir James Stephen remarked of Claphamite missionary efforts, "the religion of Christ was conquering and to conquer.... If anything in futurity could be certain, it was the dominion, over the whole earth, of the faith professed by every nation which retained either wisdom to investigate, or energy to act, or wealth to negotiate, or power to interpose in the questions which most deeply affect the entire race of man" (J. Stephen 582). Wilberforce argued successfully for the right to introduce Christian missionaries to India, via the East India Company, against staunch opposition in a Parliament that did not want to alienate native rulers. There is no exaggeration in saying that the missionary self-righteousness of the Evangelical spirit became at times the primary moral justification for some of the worst abuses of British imperialism, especially in India. And yet it was the devout Evangelical William Gladstone who, at century's end, tried to thwart the expansion of empire promoted by Disraeli and Queen Victoria, emphasized trade rather than force, supported Home Rule for Ireland, and denounced the rising tide of jingoism during the European scramble for Africa. The contradiction between the high Evangelical ideal and the brutal imperial reality of the civilizing mission was intractable, however. It is a latter-day Wilberforcean Evangelicalism that is soundly ridiculed by Conrad in *Heart of Darkness*, even though the empire in question there is Belgian. The naive idea that Kurtz or Marlow could be an "emissary of light, something like a lower sort of apostle" (12) and the missionary ideals of the "International Society for the Suppression of Savage Customs" (50) are presented by Conrad primarily as products of feminine sentimentality and self-serving sympathy. Woolf will agree with Conrad about the illusions of empire, but she will all the same salvage refined versions of sentiment and sympathy that derive from her family's Evangelicalism.

Significantly, Clapham's high moral purposes rested less on theological discourse than on a pronounced sense of what Durkheim called social effervescence (*Elementary* 216–25). The Clapham fellowship's members lived near one another, they constantly entertained, they intermarried, they were intimately involved in one another's families, and they spread this enthusiasm for social solidarity well beyond the village. In effect, Clapham may be better described as a clan, or rather, as a series of interrelated households, in which what I have elsewhere called the household's sumptuary and liturgical rites loomed large (see Pecora, *Households* 52–57). As one historian of the sect wrote in 1952, "Others of the group who did not own houses in Clapham visited and lived with their co-labourers—especially during the heat of the [anti-slavery] crusade—with an easy informality which seems almost incredible in this day" (Howse 15). What the Clapham Sect implicitly evangelized almost as much as the word of a reform-minded God were the quite real social benefits of belonging to a high-minded, well-off, and philanthropic clan such as the Clapham Sect.

Though their festivities were, as Sir James Stephen wrote, not "exhilarating," it was still the case that "Clapham Common, of course, thought itself the best of all possible commons. If the common was attacked, the whole homage was in a flame. If it was laughed at, there could be no remaining sense of decency among men. The commoners admired in each other the reflection of their own looks, and the echo of their own voices" (J. Stephen 536). Annan refers to an "intellectual aristocracy" (*Leslie Stephen* 5)—a phrase he traces to J. K. Stephen, son of Fitzjames Stephen—in the early nineteenth century, made up of Evangelicals such as those at Clapham, Quakers such as the Cadburys, Gaskells, and Foxes, and Unitarian or philosophical radicals such as the Wedgewoods, Darwins, Martineaus, Huxleys, and Stracheys. These formed a new class that included professional civil servants, colonial administrators, headmasters, school inspectors, museum curators, and journalists. "Thus they gradually spread over the length and breadth of English intellectual life criticising the assumptions of the ruling class above them and forming the opinions of the upper middle class to which they belonged. They were the leaders of the new intelligentsia," an unusually stable intelligentsia rooted in several generations of intertwined academic families (Annan, "Intellectual Aristocracy" 244).

Woolf perfectly encapsulated the continuing presence of Clapham's socioreligious habitus and high moral self-regard in her own generation when she described the Alardyce clan of her second novel, *Night and Day:* "The Alardyces had married and intermarried, and their offspring were generally profuse, and had a way of meeting regularly in each other's houses for meals and family celebrations which had acquired a semi-sacred character, and were as regularly observed as days of feasting and fasting in the Church" (37). Bloomsbury before and just after World War I had its own large component of Cambridge Apostles, servants of empire, and scions of England's intellectual aristocracy: Woolf and her sister Vanessa, Leonard Woolf, Clive Bell, Lytton Strachey, Duncan Grant, John Maynard Keynes (perhaps the most influential economist of the era), Desmond McCarthy, Roger Fry, and, perhaps less central, E. M. Forster, another descendant of the Clapham Sect (see Q. Bell). It is important to see that the members of this moral household—or, more precisely, collection of related households, which were far more intimately entwined than the families around Clapham Common—all likewise basking in the mutual reflection of their looks and the mutual echo of their voices, in large part represented the historical secularization of the earlier Clapham Sect habitus.

Alasdair MacIntyre has in fact used precisely this line of descent, which takes us from Clapham Commons to Bloomsbury, as a prime example of what he means by the complete collapse of any rational moral tradition in modernity. What incoherently comes to supplant an Aristotelian sense of substantive moral thought and human virtue is what MacIntyre calls "emotivism" or "intuitionism": "a rhetoric which serves to conceal behind the masks of morality what are in fact the preferences of arbitrary will and desire" (MacIntyre 71). MacIntyre argues that each succeeding generation of moral protagonists from Clapham to Bloomsbury, while refusing to admit that its own morality was arbitrary, leveled precisely the charge of arbitrariness at those it presumably superseded, capped finally by G. E. Moore's incoherent synthesis of intuitionism, utilitarianism, and aesthetics.

So the Evangelicals of the Clapham Sect saw in the morality of the Enlightenment a rational and rationalizing disguise for selfishness and sin; so in turn the emancipated grandchildren of the Evangelicals and their Victorian successors saw Evangelical piety as mere hypocrisy; so later Bloomsbury, liberated by G. E. Moore, saw the whole semi-official cultural paraphernalia of the Victorian age as a pompous charade concealing the arrogant self-will not only of fathers and clergymen, but also of Arnold, Ruskin and Spencer; and so in precisely the same way D. H. Lawrence "saw through" Bloomsbury. (MacIntyre 71–72)

For MacIntyre, this moral devolution neatly demonstrates that no rational and conscious moral consensus in modernity is possible (252), and that only a return to a pre-Hobbesian, pre-individualistic Aristotelian sense of virtue in active support of durable moral and intellectual traditions will save us from complete chaos.

I am less concerned here with MacIntyre's conclusions about moral philosophy—though ultimately I find them unsatisfying—than with what I take to be a lacuna in his account of the Clapham-to-Bloomsbury road. As he will himself point out near the conclusion of his book, "the possession of a historical identity and the possession of a social identity coincide.... What I am, therefore, is in key part what I inherit, a specific past that is present to some degree in my present. I find myself part of a history and that is generally to say, whether I like it or not, whether I recognize it or not, one of the bearers of a tradition" (MacIntyre 221). When vital, as opposed merely to being preserved for observation (as they are, supposedly, after Burke), such traditions are full of rational conflict. And this conflict, which is itself a socially and historically embedded argument about the proper goods that constitute the tradition, extends over generations. More to the point, this means that the narratives of individual lives are "generally and characteristically embedded in and made intelligible in terms of the larger and longer histories of a number of traditions" (222). It is the loss of the "virtues"—such as truthfulness, courage, justice, and the ability to acknowledge the tradition in the first place—that for MacIntyre destroys the tradition, and hence the moral rationality it sustains.

When looked at more carefully in terms of MacIntyre's notions of socially embedded but contentious traditions of thought, however, the path from Clapham to Bloomsbury is not quite the complete fragmentation of a moral sensibility into arbitrary impulses and intuitions that he claims it represents, though that is certainly what one might derive from reading Moore out of context (which is, ironically, just the sort of reading in moral thought that MacIntyre warns us against). Rather, understood dialectically as the secularization of a religious tradition, a secularization embedded in a social class and national consciousness—and it is significant that MacIntyre does not say much about the paradoxes of secularization—there is little that seems arbitrary or capricious. Moreover, if we take seriously MacIntyre's claim about how the narrative of an individual life is embedded in the narrative of a cultural tradition, Woolf's work emerges as far less a merely willful anomaly than a powerful representation of the way those two social and historical narratives—individual and cultural—are as completely intertwined with one another as MacIntyre claims.

In fact, for Annan, there is almost a direct line between the coterie gathered in Clapham and that of Bloomsbury, and it is this line that I want to highlight (see Annan, *Leslie Stephen* 152–62). Woolf's father, Leslie Stephen, raised as a member of the third generation of Claphamite thought, suffered a crisis of faith and embraced atheism (or "agnosticism"). But his turn to utilitarianism in mid-century is less a simple rejection of Claphamite ideals than it is a rigorous secularization—a point Nietzsche never tired of making about utilitarianism—since both Evangelicalism and utilitarianism in the event emphasized ethical experience over religious metaphysics, a sort of common moral sense over scholastic rationality. Moreover, his rigorous moral calculus, derived from what he took to be human nature, tended to denigrate the role of imagination even beyond what had been found in earlier Claphamite thinking. Most important, especially for my purposes here, Annan argues that although each generation of Clapham Sect heirs rejected a larger proportion of the Evangelical heritage, the "spirit of the coterie" remained strong (157). The fourth generation, that of Bloomsbury, on the surface waged a full-scale "intellectual revolt against Christianity" (159), in which the central idea of original sin at the heart of Evangelicalism was replaced by a return to the older, vaguer Enlightenment ideal of reasonableness, the earlier sexual restraint was abandoned, and art was morally rehabilitated via the synthesis of neo-Kantian aesthetics, philosophical realism, and utilitarian ethics in Moore, whose work appears briefly in *The Voyage Out*, and whose *Principia Ethica* Woolf read (see Levy 274–76). But underneath, the spirit of the coterie, or what I would broaden to include the idea of the clan and professional association, remained.

That spirit was exclusive, wary of the unconverted, filled with the assurance of its own rightness, and suspicious of power and wealth unconnected with a higher moral purpose. Keynes himself described Bloomsbury as having a religion: "Our religion," he wrote in a memoir, "closely followed the English puritan tradition of being chiefly concerned with the salvation of our own souls . . . We claimed the right to judge every individual case on its merits, and the wisdom, experience, and self-control to do so successfully. This was a very important part of our faith" (Keynes, *Two Memoirs* 84–97; quoted in Annan, *Leslie Stephen* 160). In effect, and not at all metaphorically, Bloomsbury wanted to see itself, just as had Clapham, as numbered among the elect; imbued with a certain, albeit theologically detached, inner light; driven to proselytize both moral reform and a finely delineated moral awareness; in possession of a moral sensibility based, as in Clapham, more on personal experience than on systematic metaphysics, so that what MacIntyre understands as simple moral "emotivism" or "intuitionism" emerges less as the arbitrary product of modernity's irrational self-will than (even in Moore) as a worldview embedded in a specific Evangelical tradition of thought; and finally, afflicted with an oppressive sense of responsibility to find the light in a world distant from God, where one's fate depended less on following unquestioned ecclesiastical authority than on finding the morally right emotional response to any particular person or event. In all these ways, I think, but especially in this last sense, Woolf's personal psychic narrative became powerfully intertwined with the cultural narrative of her (largely disavowed) religious tradition.

Seen in this way, Woolf's debts to her Evangelical heritage go well beyond her father's enduring sense of duty in the face of religious disbelief, which is often the way it is understood (see, for example, Lee, *Novels* 3, 6). I believe the echoes of Clapham in Woolf's immediate family (as in that of the Alardyces) and in Bloomsbury had a more formative role in Woolf's work. And although, as Lee suggests, Bloomsbury is a latter-day version not only of Clapham, but of nineteenth-century intellectual circles more generally, from the Lake Poets to the Pre-Raphaelite Brotherhood, the particular resonance with Clapham is significant precisely because it illustrates so well the unusually close kinship of overtly religious sects and those aesthetic or intellectual coteries that were nominally secular. Bloomsbury may have been irreverent, sexually daring, and skeptical, but its effervescent, high-minded reformism translated and secularized the social formation of James Stephen's Clapham fellowship. Though the Clapham Sect may have been distinctly puritan and ascetic in its doctrinal morality, its members were actually rather worldly in practice. Their high morality in a sense enabled an open and guiltless pleasure in a rather exclusive sort of sociality.

It is thus no accident, as *Night and Day* already suggests, that a Claphamlike house party, where seemingly trivial entertainment is grounded in a deeply serious, even religious, belief in the moral significance of social effervescence, plays a central role in two of Woolf's major works—*Mrs. Dalloway* and *To the Lighthouse*. In a diary entry for January 6, 1915, Woolf lamented "the dressing & the journey" involved in attending a party at Gordon Square, but then acknowledged "that with the first chink of light in the hall & chatter of voices I should become intoxicated, & determine that life held nothing comparable to a party. I should see beautiful people, & get a sensation of being on the highest crest of the biggest wave—right in the center & swim of things" (*Diary* 1:10). Many years later, the elite at the parties Woolf attended were more aristocratic than intellectual, but she was still "enthralled," as she put it in "Am I a Snob?" (1936), by "social festivity" (*Moments* 210).

Both *Mrs. Dalloway* and *To the Lighthouse* are also marked by a stinging critique of the Evangelicalism and imperialism of Woolf's Claphamite forebears—Miss Kilman's ascetic faith in *Mrs. Dalloway* and Mr. Ramsay's mindless recitation of Tennyson at the beginning of *To the Lighthouse* are oft-cited examples. But the multilayered character of this critique can be neatly illustrated by Woolf's response to a speech in 1919 by Annie Besant, the noted neo-Malthusian, Fabian socialist, and theosophist, in support of Indian Home Rule. (Besant had been elected president of the Indian National Congress late in 1918, though she was soon replaced by Gandhi.) "It seems to me more & more clear that the only honest people are the artists, & that these social reformers & philanthropists get so out of hand, & harbor so many discreditable desires under the disguise of loving their kind, that in the end there's more to find fault with in them than in us. But if I were one of them?" (*Diary* 1:293). In fact, Woolf *is* one of them, however ambivalently. Woolf's "distaste for the Fabian type" (1:276)—typified for her by figures such as Sidney and Beatrice Webb, Noel Buxton, and Robin Page Arnot, was vaguely Nietzschean. She thought they all looked "unhealthy & singular & impotent" and noted that "the idea that these frail webspinners can affect the destiny of nations seems to me fantastic" (1:26). Yet Woolf routinely attended Fabian events, which were latter-day versions of the sort of Clapham Sect public meeting held earlier at Exeter Hall and central examples of the wider secular religion and vitalism driving social reform at the time (see Rose 16–30), to which she generally found it "well worth going." And it should be remembered that Fabianism, as seen in the figure of George Bernard Shaw, had itself embraced Nietzsche's critique of unhealthy bourgeois impotence as well as a highly questionable eugenics program to combat it. In any case, after one gathering of the unhealthy and impotent at Essex Hall in 1915, Woolf happily declared herself a Fabian.

Woolf's critique of Clapham Sect religious ideology, prompted in part by the atheism of her father, need not be seen then as a rejection of the larger clan mentality or habitus that I have outlined so far. Woolf manages to recuperate the underlying structure and moral seriousness of the Clapham fellowship while ridding it of its evangelically and imperially colonizing fervor. Gillian Beer has articulated this dialectical nuance in Woolf precisely as a form of rewriting, of translation: Woolf "did not simply reject the Victorians and their concerns, or renounce them. Instead she persistingly re-wrote them" (Beer 140). This rewriting is worth emphasizing. Woolf's Nietzschean critique of religious *ressentiment* and impotence—a critique that may have come to Woolf more through Shaw, Hardy, Conrad, and her father than through Nietzsche's work itself—is finally what separates Woolf's attenuated debt to Evangelical thought from that of George Eliot. Eliot's idea of organic social sympathy, derived from Strauss's, Feuerbach's, and Comte's anthropological reduction and rehabilitation of religiously based morality, still depended on a certain muted asceticism. Such sympathy "requires ... the development of the kind of self Eliot considered ideal, the 'self that self restrains' in the interests of some larger, corporate identity" (Gallagher 56). Woolf's refusal of the ascetic ideal, by contrast, complicates her own similar Evangelical inheritance: society in Woolf is not predicated on organic metaphors, selves are not caught in webs of causal determinations, and sacrifice (like that of Septimus Warren Smith in *Mrs. Dalloway*) does not necessarily bring redemption. Even Eliot's and Woolf's contrasting views of their shared vocation reflect this dichotomy. Eliot prized the professional writer who would make an honest living from her diligence and hard work—she is the authorial embodiment of Max Weber's Protestant ethic—while Woolf insisted that an inheritance of five hundred pounds a year was required to free the writer from the pressures of employment in the marketplace. And yet, I would argue, although Evangelicalism as an institution is surely more legible in Eliot's writing than it is in Woolf's, the habitus of Claphamite sociality embedded in Bloomsbury is nevertheless a powerful, if sublimated, element in the making of Woolf's fiction.

The significance of the Clapham fellowship's ideal of a proliferating social sympathy for Woolf's work thus has less to do with compassion, or with the negation of the egoistic self in the service of a higher cause, than with the fellowship members' psychological (and elective) affinity, mutual understanding, and association of minds. It is a social ideal that was very much a part of Clapham's nonconformist rejection of hypocritical complacency and conventional belief, especially as represented by the Church of England. Sir James Stephen saw both how persistent that nonconformist moral position would be for later generations, and how perfectly secularized its religious presuppositions would become in the context of later "societies" of reformers.

Exeter Hall [a metonym for Evangelicalism and a large hall in the Strand, London, which opened in 1831, housed religious and philanthropic meetings, and was the home of England's Young Men's Christian Association, or YMCA] also prophecies. As to the events which are coming upon us, she adopts the theory of her Claphamite progenitor. In reducing theory to practice, she is almost as much a Socialist as Mr. Owen himself. The moral regeneration which she foretells is to be brought about neither by church, by workhouse, by monk, by hero, nor by the purifying of St. James's. She [i.e., Exeter Hall, or Evangelicalism] believes in the continually decreasing power of the individual, and the as constantly augmenting power of associated, minds. . . . Ours is the age of societies. For the redress of every oppression that is done under the sun, there is a public meeting. (J. Stephen 583, 584)

Stephen's declaration that "ours is the age of societies" is a rather exact prefiguring of Durkheim's belief, in the early years of the twentieth century, that the intermediary professional associations of modern, "organic" (that is, individualistic yet interdependent) society performed a crucial task maintaining collective morality and solidarity in the face of the disruptions and anomie that would occasionally plague industrial, capitalist economies (see especially Durkheim, preface to the second edition of *Division* xxxi–lix).

These intermediary societies, even those without the philanthropic ideals of a Clapham Sect, were thus microcosms of the utopian potential of society writ large, and Durkheim saw them as such. They were necessary steppingstones in the achievement of a kind of universal religion, that is, of the pacifist internationalism that dominated reform movements in the decade leading up to World War I and that persisted among the antiwar intelligentsia in the years leading up to World War II. Woolf's *Three Guineas* is at heart the record of her continuing ambivalence toward such societies, an ambivalence predicated now not on their "impotence" and "discreditable desires," noted in the earlier example of Annie Besant's Fabians, but rather on the failure of such largely male organizations to understand the history and current condition of women as an essential part of the world's ills. Nevertheless, even in *Three Guineas*, Woolf does not really discredit the utopian idea of the association embraced earlier by her grandfather and father and later by Durkheim—she translates it, as Beer suggests, into one to which she could sincerely belong, that famous international, or antinational, "society of outsiders." And this society of outsiders would itself be largely a secularized version of the Clapham Sect: "By criticizing religion they would attempt to free the religious spirit from its present servitude and would help, if need be, to create a new religion based, it might well be, upon the New Testament, but, it might well be, very different from the religion now erected upon that basis" (Woolf, *Three Guineas* 113). Woolf's sentiments here are not exactly those of Wilberforce—but it is not hard to see how Woolf's desire to "free the religious spirit" from its servitude to false or inadequate forms is part of the same reformist vision that Wilberforce embodied.

This lifelong tendency in Woolf's thinking to gravitate toward an ideal of associated minds in the abstract, that is, to fellowship outside any and all existing modes of institutional affiliation, implies that although Woolf (like Durkheim) would insist on the nonsectarian and even utopian potential of such societies (indeed, of society itself), the most acceptable form her secularized relationship to the Clapham Sect could take would be equally abstract and outside of reality—that is, it would be in her fiction. Annan observes that Evangelicalism "is a religion for men of this world" (*Leslie Stephen* 151) and that the Clapham Sect "had the confidence to change the world" (152), a confidence that permeated generations of reform-minded utilitarians, such as Leslie Stephen, in the later nineteenth century: "And so a young Evangelical who developed a turn for philosophy was likely to be drawn towards the Utilitarians who professed to base their conclusions on an empirical examination of human experience" (148). Yet this confident, even at times radical, worldliness was never finally free of the sense that the world contaminated, that one's bodily participation would be justified, or redeemed, only through constant self-examination and introspection. Borrowing William Hazlitt's phrase for the purely contemplative life, Annan also notes that the diary of Clapham's Henry Thornton was that of a man "in this world, not of it" (151; see also Hazlitt 6:91). The ambivalence is crucial, for Wilberforce and company were very much inclined to meddle in worldly affairs, even as they needed to feel somehow apart from it; and the fellowship of Clapham Common—like that of Bloomsbury later, in my view—was an important form of mediation.

This same ambivalence about the call, and pleasures, of worldliness and the defensive need for constant self-examination can be appropriately applied to Woolf. It is in Woolf's fiction that we should look for the most significant translation of the structure of Evangelical sociality, a secularizing translation that would appear finally as the disembodied embodiment of Evangelical vision filtered through her father's utilitarianism. That translation is what emerges in Woolf's writing as style or technique. None of Woolf's novels better exhibits her critical appropriation of her religious inheritance, purging the Clapham Sect of its project for universal conversion and power while preserving its quasi-ecstatic ideal of associated minds, its embrace of a worldly sociality outside of conventional institutions, and the vestiges of its puritanical discomfort with the individual body, than does *The Voyage Out*.

Religion, Gender, Empire, and the Secular Imagination

The plot of the novel concerns the story of an innocent young woman's "coming out"—hence the title—into society, into adulthood, and into the world beyond England. Rachel Vinrace is so naive that she does not know why her father forbids her to walk around London alone, or why strange women can be seen cruising the streets of Piccadilly at night, until sexual awareness suddenly dawns after the rakish older politician Richard Dalloway makes an unexpected pass at her. As Rachel's widowed father, Willoughby, says to his sister-in-law, Helen Ambrose, "I should be very glad ... if you could see your way to helping my girl, bringing her out,—she's a little shy now,—making a woman of her, the kind of woman her mother would have liked her to be" (*Voyage* 86). Rachel has insisted on accompanying her father, a merchant captain, on one of his voyages to South America. (Captain Vinrace imports goats—"music depends upon goats" [*Voyage* 17], he cryptically reminds his daughter—though the meaning of the phrase is only decipherable in earlier drafts of the novel.) While her father makes his way up the Amazon, Rachel stays with her maternal aunt and uncle at their run-down villa in the English seaside resort colony of Santa Marina, where Woolf, who had no personal experience of South America, curiously imagines tigers roaming at night and "elephants coming down in the darkness to drink at pools" (*Voyage* 112). In the course of her stay, Rachel falls in love, or at least thinks she does, with Terence Hewet, who proposes and is accepted. But after a sightseeing trip with other members of the colony to a primitive Indian village in the interior, Rachel falls suddenly, tragically ill with fever and dies—on the verge, as it were, of womanhood, marriage, and perhaps a larger role in her father's ambitions for political office. But this bare-bones sketch of the plot tells us nothing about Rachel's deeper, and at times quite surreal, anxieties concerning sex, marriage, and maternity.

Rachel is sexually awakened early in the voyage by Richard Dalloway's kiss, an event that is described in free indirect discourse as providing her with a strange "exultation" in which "life seemed to hold infinite possibilities she had never guessed at," so that "something wonderful had happened" (*Voyage* 75).

But the coerced awakening has profoundly ambiguous consequences. Rachel is also disturbed by it and afterward feels uncomfortable in Richard's presence. At night, she dreams of walking down a long, narrowing, damp tunnel that opens up into a vault, trapping her there alone with a "little deformed man who squatted on the floor gibbering, with long nails" whose face "was pitted and like the face of an animal," while "the wall behind him oozed with damp, which collected into drops and slid down" (*Voyage* 75). The imagery seems to represent Rachel's confused—at the time, Freudians would surely have said "hysterical"—impression of her own womb, as if it were a sewer inhabited by filth, disease, and perhaps death: Rachel lies "still and cold as death" during the dream. (Louise De Salvo, who has perhaps done more than anyone else to illuminate the composition and symbolism of the novel, traces the image of a threatening womb back to Sir Thomas Browne's *Religio Medici*, to which the text alludes at one point.) The little deformed man—who is transformed into little deformed women playing cards when the dream recurs during Rachel's fatal illness (*Voyage* 344)—at least initially suggests a vampiric, or perhaps piratical, male sexuality. Startled, Rachel lies awake imagining that "all night long barbarian men harassed the ship; they came scuffling down the passages, and stopped to snuffle at her door" (*Voyage* 76). But the squatting animal-like figure of her dream is perhaps the distorted image of a fetus as well. As if to supply an exclamation point for the nightmarish appearance of Rachel's reproductive interior, even after Rachel's death and the all-too-successful engagement of the vapid Susan Warrington, the novel's final pages satirically present the elderly literary historian Miss Allan reading a reputedly clever modern (and fictitious) novel titled simply *Maternity* (*Voyage* 384). Although both the sexual and the maternal themes have been much discussed in the criticism, especially in the light of Woolf's own childhood molestation at the hands of George Duckworth (who wound up being the publisher of the novel), there is another theme—religion—that, beyond de Salvo, has surprisingly received almost no attention at all, and that will be my primary focus here.

The nearly complete indifference of critics to any analysis of the role of religion in the novel is all the more curious given the fair number of religiously oriented details in it. The heroine is named Rachel, evoking the childless second wife of Jacob in Genesis; the biblical Rachel, who has had about all she can stand of the endlessly fertile Leah (Jacob's first wife and Rachel's older sister, whom Jacob is tricked into marrying first) finally tells her husband, "Give me sons, or I shall die," only to end up in fact dying during the birth of her second son. The novel is set primarily in a tourist hotel that has been converted from a monastery. And there is a ship named

Euphrosyne, which, though it is both the name of one of the three classical Graces (joyfulness) and a satirical reference to a bad book of poetry published earlier by Leonard Woolf, Lytton Strachey, Clive Bell, and their Cambridge Apostle friends, is finally a reference to Saint Euphrosyne, who lived out her final days in a monastery as a holy and venerated transvestite monk (see DeSalvo 60). Terence Hewet's aunt is a "religious fanatic" also named Rachel (*Voyage* 144). St. John Hirst, the disaffected atheist who gives Rachel the first volume of Gibbon's *Decline and Fall* (176) and ostentatiously reads Sappho in church (239), winds up confiding to her on their inland tour that the "indecent" (280) poem on God he is composing has kept him awake at night, "and the awful thing was that he'd practically proved the fact that God did exist" (289). And the fashionable, worldly nationalist and imperialist Clarissa Dalloway curls up to sleep with a "little white volume of Pascal which went with her everywhere" (49).

There is also a lengthy satire of a Church of England religious service, held in the hotel's cryptlike chapel, which neatly encapsulates within it an outline history of religion as it had come to be elucidated in Woolf's day. That service includes a hodgepodge of a Wilberforcean sermon by the minister, Mr. Bax, which on the one hand stimulates in Rachel a "violent" hatred of Christian hypocrisy, causing her to reject "all that she had before implicitly believed" (*Voyage* 238), and on the other compels her to contemplate a higher, "beautiful idea," an idea that Mr. Bax's rhetoric and the perfunctory belief of those around her cannot adequately capture. It is perhaps significant that the chapel service satire was among the very first things Woolf composed and that it remained lightly edited as the text evolved, while the names Rachel and *Euphrosyne* appear only in the final version, indicating Woolf underlined the religious thematic of the novel as it neared completion.

It is not difficult to see why the book's religious motifs, even when they have been duly noted and glossed, have attracted little serious attention. There is very little sustained critical discussion of religion in any of Woolf's work, primarily because Woolf seems on the whole so hostile to conventional religious belief. When religious belief as such does appear in Woolf, it is usually the butt of satire, either for its banality (as in the case of Mr. Bax) or for its predatory desire to dominate. The most famous case in Woolf's work is surely the Evangelical Miss Kilman, the poor, educated, but embittered governess of Clarissa's daughter Elizabeth in *Mrs. Dalloway,* whose perhaps too obvious name suggests both the social *ressentiment* that finds its fulfillment in asceticism and faith and an angry undercurrent of repressed lesbianism in her affection for Elizabeth. In *The Voyage Out*, Helen Ambrose, worried about the religious influence of the nurse employed to care for her young children while she is away, responds to Willoughby Vinrace's assurance that "a little religion hurts nobody" with the quip: "I would rather my children told lies" (*Voyage* 22). Indeed, Woolf's dislike of religious *ressentiment* is crucial in her treatment of Mr. Bax too, since it is his disturbing citation of a particularly vengeful psalm passage from the Book of Common Prayer that could be said to trigger Rachel's critical response to her previously unexamined Christian faith. But Bax's citation of the psalms is disturbing only for his complacent chapel audience, and that is why it has been either ignored or misunderstood. (DeSalvo reads the sermon simply as "fire and brimstone," which for me misses the point of both of the quoted psalm and the entire chapel scene.) In the larger context of what I see as Woolf's quick but sharp elaboration of the evolution of religion, the citation makes perfect sense.

In fact, religion in Woolf's novels is almost never a straightforward affair of satire or renunciation. *To the Lighthouse,* written at what could be called the peak of Woolf's career as a novelist, provides good examples of the complexity. On the one hand, Woolf's perspective in this novel seems no less "rationalist" than that of Helen Ambrose and is perfectly aligned with that earlier character's deep suspicion of unwanted religious influence. As Mrs. Ramsay, illumined by the stroke of the lighthouse, meditates on eternity and the underlying unity of things, isolated fragments of speech stored in her memory begin to surface, most startlingly among them, "We are in the hands of the Lord." Mrs. Ramsay's response indicates what would seem to be Woolf's own resistance to the unwanted vestiges of her religious heritage: "But instantly she was annoyed with herself for saying that. Who had said it? Not she; she had been trapped into saying something she did not mean" (*Lighthouse* 97). Yet this event, not unlike other vaguely Proustian instances of suddenly recovered memory in the novel, is in no way the whole story.

As Hermione Lee suggests, *To the Lighthouse* "continually hovers on the edge of becoming a fairy tale, or, more ambitiously, a mythical or even Christian allegory." She points to the most salient religious motifs in that novel: the Madonna and Child tableau that structures its opening (and closing) and Lily's Christlike "it is finished" when she completes her painting and imagines that Mr. Ramsay has finally reached the lighthouse (Lee, *Novels* 127–28; *Lighthouse* 309). Lee understands these elements not as "religious" in terms of confessional, Christian belief, but, following Frye, in terms of mythopoetic conventions, especially those of a pre-Christian paganism: as in a fairy tale, Mrs. Ramsay is "seen by others as a superhuman figure with goddess-like creative powers" (*Novels* 128). In Lee's view, as in that of many others, Woolf may draw upon this mythopoetic heritage to give formal structure to her work—a perspective congruent with T. S. Eliot's on Joyce—but it is hardly central in substantive terms. Indeed, Lee concludes by utterly collapsing any distinction between the broader moral-philosophical perspective of Virginia Woolf and that of her utilitarian father: "The artist [that is, Lily, but also Woolf] here rejects the passive form of worship (such as Christianity) for what she considers a more arduous responsibility. So Leslie Stephen, saying, like Mr. Ramsay, 'There is no God,' turned from the 'muscular Christianity' of his early years to a rationalist philosophy of responsibility and endurance, but retained the Evangelical belief in the 'supreme importance of the individual's relation to the good'" (Lee, *Novels* 136–37; the internal quote is from Annan, *Leslie Stephen* 123). But to identify Woolf and her father to this extent is also to gloss too quickly over all that she felt worthy of parody in Leslie Stephen himself, as he becomes the unfeeling, unseeing, and self-centered egoist Mr. Ramsay, constantly in need of reassurance, whether about his rank among philosophers or about the excellence of his boots.

On the contrary, Woolf's argument with her father was about more than his often angry demeanor or dismissive egoism—it was about the solipsism, narrowness, and sheer bullying of a purer utilitarian rationalism itself, one that could easily appear to be a larger threat to the imagination (as Dickens demonstrated to great effect in *Hard Times*) than the inner light, emotional experience of God, and effervescent, if still exclusive, sociality of her Claphamite forebears. The mythopoetic transformation of Mr. Carmichael, "looking like an old pagan god, shaggy, with weeds in his hair and the trident (it was only a French novel) in his hand" into Poseidon at the end of *To the Lighthouse* (309) may be a direct response to Leslie Stephen's gloss on Wordsworth's "The World Is Too Much with Us" in his introduction to *English Thought in the Eighteenth Century*. If we consider the Wordsworth passage in its entirety, it appears to have an intimate connection to the plot of Woolf's novel itself. Stephen's response to Wordsworth's familiar sonnet is nothing short of astonishing in its unwillingness to suspend disbelief, though it is an unwillingness justified on purely secular and scientific (not religious) grounds.

The sight of Proteus and Triton might restore to the world the long-vanished charm. Now, as far as science is concerned, we are tempted to say that Wordsworth is simply wrong. The Greek mythology gave an inaccurate representation of the facts. . . . A slight acquaintance with the law of storms is far more useful to the sailor than any guess about a mysterious being, capriciously riding the waves, and capable, perhaps, of being propitiated by charms. From the purely utilitarian point of view, we are the better off the closer the correspondence between our beliefs and the external realities. But, further, we are tempted to say the same even in a poetical sense. Why should Wordsworth regret Proteus and Triton? Because the Greek inferred from the sea the existence of beings the contemplation of whose power and beauty was a source of delight to him? But, in the first place, the facts are to Wordsworth what they were to the Greek. If the Greek thought the sea lovely in color and form, the color and the form remain. The imaginary being in whom the phenomena were embodied could only be known through the phenomena. . . . Why not love the sea instead of loving Proteus, who is but the sea personified? And, secondly, we must add that the dream reflects the painful as well as the pleasurable emotions. . . . The sailor, imagining a treacherous deity lurking beneath the waves, saw new cause for dread, and would often have been glad enough to learn that Proteus was a figment. (L. Stephen 14–15)

One is tempted to say that here is the literal mind run amok, firmly supported by Humean skepticism, ruthless naturalism, and a peculiar distaste for illusion of any sort, however pleasing. It is no wonder the utilitarian mind exasperated Dickens.

Stephen's larger argument—that the necessary disenchantment of the world produced by the dawn of scientific reason is understandably depressing—in itself may seem perfectly sound, even today. Many share Wordsworth's desire to hold on to a "creed outworn," no less than to a fetish or a flag, in order to represent their deeper emotions, at least as long as they have no access to a more rational replacement; no respectable materialist account of culture, whether Marxian or otherwise, could begin from a position very far from this. But in Stephen's case, the almost complete incomprehension of the workings of poetic language meant an intolerance of the human imagination as well: "The idols gradually lose their sanctity; but they are cherished by poets long after they are disowned by philosophers, and the poet has the greatest immediate influence with the many. In the normal case, therefore, we may assume that the imagination exercises, on the whole, a retarding influence" (L. Stephen 17). It is not hard to understand why a daughter with literary ambitions would have difficulty with these views. It is also not hard to understand how she might build a novel around a sailing philosopher with perhaps too much faith in "the law of storms" and too little in the imaginary beings who haunt our dreams. This is not to say that Woolf, in revolt against her father's philistine dearth of wit, simply returned in some wholesale way to myth, fetishes, and religion, pagan or otherwise. The end of *To the Lighthouse* has just as much subtlety and irony in it as the end of Wordsworth's sonnet. But it is to say that the workings of the imagination are for Woolf deeply embedded in a history of religious belief and secularization, and in a network of familial and clan relationships (from Clapham to Bloomsbury) that formed a remarkably durable social and moral habitus. Woolf's novels are in this sense all about the ways imagination survives disenchantment, which is to say that they are also about the ways religious thought and practice are inextricably embedded in the secular social and literary forms that would transcend them.

The second reason religion has been overlooked by Woolf criticism is perhaps even more compelling: for many readers, there are simply more important things in her work to talk about, especially concerning gender, sexuality, and the subjugation of women. This makes perfect sense, and it would have been rather odd had the critical response been otherwise. And yet, the problem of religion is not distinct from that of gender, at least in *The Voyage Out*. It is crucial to analyze how religion and especially religious symbolization work in the novel if we are to understand how Woolf imagined that she could rise above the more disturbing qualities of fleshly bodies, bodily functions, sexual congress, carnal desire (at least of the heterosexual sort), bourgeois marriage, motherhood, and the long history of men's domination of women that all the other things seem to underwrite, without at the same time reproducing the *ressentiment* and life-denying asceticism of the Miss Kilmans of the world. (Kathryn Bond Stockton has focused on the largely unexplored link between religious feeling and lesbian desire in the earlier novels of Charlotte Brontë and George Eliot, and although her argument is perhaps too theoretical for my purposes here, it sheds some light on what may have been at stake for Woolf in the presentation of Miss Kilman.) In *The Voyage Out*, there is no third way for Rachel. As if unconsciously avoiding the fate of her biblical namesake, Rachel is self-consumed by fever before marriage and motherhood are able to destroy her. But this is not all that happens, and Rachel's full response to Mr. Bax's sermon and in certain ways the sermon itself contain the germs of Woolf's larger literary project, one that reaches its most robust form years later in the "transcendental theory" (*Dalloway* 231) of Clarissa Dalloway and the divine madness of Septimus Warren Smith in *Mrs. Dalloway*, and in the abstract aesthetics of Mrs. Ramsay's life and Lily Briscoe's vision in *To the Lighthouse*. Woolf's search for a third way, balanced on the fence as it were between carnal embodiment and ascetic *ressentiment*, and perhaps between heterosexual and lesbian desire as well, begins oddly enough with hapless Mr. Bax.

There is yet one more reason that religion has been ignored in *The Voyage Out*, and that is the more recent, and again quite understandable, turn to the role of empire in the novel. Like *Mrs. Dalloway*, which is in many ways a rewriting of the "Wandering Rocks" episode of Joyce's *Ulysses*, *The Voyage Out* is a fairly self-conscious rewriting of Conrad's *Heart of Darkness*. Marianne DeKoven's extended comparison of the two books (in *Rich and Strange*, 85–138) is perhaps the fullest treatment of the issue, but it has been acknowledged for some time (see Pitt 141–54). The comparison depends primarily on the deracinating voyage of an innocent idealist to an unknown continent, the atmosphere of faded empire in the down-at-heels English colony, and a trek inland to see a primitive tribe, which is where Hewet's proposal, Rachel's acceptance, and the beginning of her tragic end occur. There is even a story told about a famous explorer, named Mackenzie, "who went farther inland than any one's been yet" and wound up dying of fever in a hut identified by the tourists' guide, Mr. Flushing (*Voyage* 288).

One could say that Woolf's novel is more parody of Conrad than recasting, since the true heart of darkness in her novel turns out to be that most familiar institution of all—marriage. (We recall that it is precisely this institution, or at least the Intended who is to celebrate it with Kurtz, that Marlow's final lie is designed to preserve.) But the comparison also involves little details such as those attached to Mr. Pepper, who is a sort of universal intellectual (or rather, typical Cambridge dilettante) with a passion for Homeric Greek, undiscovered monsters of the sea, and long-winded stories. In the first chapter, just as the *Euphrosyne* gets under way, Mr. Pepper leaps onto his seat with his feet tucked under him, in a direct imitation of Conrad's Marlow: "Drawn up there, sucking at his cigar, with his arms encircling his knees, he looked like the image of Buddha, and from this elevation began a discourse, addressed to nobody, for nobody had called for it, upon the unplumbed depths of ocean" (*Voyage* 17). Woolf is of course just as serious about deflating the pretensions of empire as is Conrad, but she is also keen on letting the hot air out of Conrad's most famous narrative device, the Buddha-posing Charley Marlow himself.

And yet, there is a point at which Woolf's homage to Conrad raises interesting questions for her own work, not least at the point where she translates Marlow's famously redemptive and religious idea of civilization— "something you can set up, and bow down before and offer a sacrifice to...." (*Heart* 10)—into the "idea" that floats "somewhere above" Rachel during Mr. Bax's sermon, "the idea which they could none of them grasp, which they pretended to grasp, always escaping out of reach, a beautiful idea, an idea like a butterfly" (*Voyage* 237). If the butterfly here in turn suggests those rare specimens sought by Stein in Conrad's *Lord Jim*, there is good reason, since the *Euphrosyne*, and by metonymic extension Rachel herself, are figured early in Woolf's novel in language that suggests the redemptive "Eastern bride" sought by Tuan Jim: "She [the *Euphrosyne*] was a bride going forth to her husband, a virgin unknown of men; in her vigour and purity she might be likened to all beautiful things, worshipped and felt as a symbol" (*Voyage* 27–28). The "beautiful idea" that later floats into view above Rachel in the hotel chapel is a version of this idea, which appears in authorial perspective.

It is as if the secularization of religious into aesthetic symbol that Woolf is elaborating at the novel's opening will be reenacted by Rachel herself in the chapel. The question is, what sort of "idea" is Rachel's, or Woolf's, and is it simply a matter of turning real objects into abstract and disembodied "symbols" floating in the air around us?

Mr. Bax Leads the Congregation

The service and sermon are worth a closer look. On a Sunday, the starched and suddenly pious English guests make their way downstairs into "the old chapel of the monks" (*Voyage* 235), where the Roman Catholic Mass, confession, penance, and worship of saints' images that had occupied the place for centuries has been replaced by the spare benches, tasteful footstools, small brass-eagled pulpit, and ugly carpeting of Protestantism. The already secularizing transition from the pseudo-magic of Catholic idolatry to the sober rationalism and "peaceful atmosphere" (*Voyage* 236) of the English Church, established by the reading of the Lord's Prayer, is broken when Mr. Bax quotes lines strung together from Psalms 56 and 58.

"Be merciful unto me, O God," he read, "for man goeth about to devour me: he is daily fighting and troubling me.... They daily mistake my words: all that they imagine is to do me evil. They hold all together and keep themselves close.... Break their teeth, O God, in their mouths; smite the jaw-bones of the lions, O Lord: let them fall away like water that runneth apace; and when they shoot their arrows let them be rooted out." (*Voyage* 236; Woolf's ellipses)

DeSalvo glosses the passage as a reference to "the wrath befalling sinners" (133). The psalms cited by Bax are in fact clear expressions of what Nietzsche decried as the *ressentiment* fueling the Judeo-Christian tradition. In a more oblique way, the passage also has a particular resonance for Rachel, who has lost sleep worrying about barbarian men "troubling her" and who may desire a kind of vengeance in return.

Woolf clearly intends this psalm citation to be read as a representation of archaic *ressentiment,* since it is precisely at this point that members of the congregation, especially the more worldly men, feel "the inconvenience of the sudden intrusion of this old savage. They looked more secular and critical as they listened to the ravings of the old black man with a cloth round his loins cursing with vehement gesture by a camp-fire in the desert" (*Voyage* 236). The service has thus leapt back into the prehistory of religion, well before monkish Catholicism, to the moment of primitive shamanism—to the priestly caste in which the roots of the psalms' more articulate *ressentiment* can be located. The "old black man" in the desert is perhaps a reference to the aboriginal priests of Australia, whose religious life in a series of texts beginning with the nineteenth-century anthropologist Robertson Smith had been recently described as the most primitive form of religion yet discovered. After this journey back to primitive religion, Mr. Bax rapidly brings his listeners forward through the evolution of religion, accompanied by "the sound of pages being turned as if they were in a class": a passage from the Old Testament leads to the "sad and beautiful figure of Christ" and to the modern-day worshippers' attempt to fit Christ's "interpretation of life upon the lives they lived" (*Voyage* 236). It is at this point that Rachel, frustrated with the sloppiness of Bax's sermon—it was like "an unsatisfactory piece of music badly played" (*Voyage* 237)—begins to listen critically for the first time. And it is at this point, amid the "forced solemnity," acquiescence, and emotional pretense of the service, that Rachel's "beautiful idea" floats into view.

One would expect, given what has preceded it, that the sermon would be presented in a satirical light, and to a large extent it is. Mr. Bax rambles on amiably, very much like a latter-day Clapham Sect preacher, about English duties of fraternal sympathy to the natives when on holiday. Woolf compares the sermon to an article that would appear in the weekly newspapers, and Bax's unthinking glibness in claiming that the success of English rule in India depended on "a strict code of politeness" (*Voyage* 240) would have been apparent to any reader familiar with the turmoil and growing violence threatening the Raj in the years just before World War I. Most criticism of the scene has taken the satire at face value, and little more has been said about Bax's words. In his peroration, however, Bax enlarges his discourse on sympathy into an extended metaphor designed to provide the moral lesson of the day, and in doing so, I think, oddly begins to approach, without ever reaching, the meaning of Rachel's "beautiful idea" (see also Rose 44–45). Bax's metaphor is on the one hand a version of Clapham Sect moral solidarity:

"As a drop of water, detached, alone, separate from others, falling from the cloud and entering the great ocean, alters, so scientists tell us, not only the immediate spot in the ocean where it falls, but all the myriad drops which together compose the great universe of waters, and by this means alters the configuration of the globe . . . so is a marvel comparable to this within the reach of each one of us, who dropping a little word or a little deed into the great universe alters it; yea it is a solemn thought, *alters* it, for good or for evil." (*Voyage* 240–41)

In the context of Woolf's parody of Bax's Evangelical confusion about empire, the organic metaphor, not unlike what we might find in George Eliot, is just one more sign of the ceremony's emptiness.

And yet, the immersion of all in all that it describes, which depends on the emotional as well as mental extension of the individual beyond the boundaries of bodily existence, promises Rachel (and Woolf too) a mechanism for transcending the more disturbing, even monstrous, elements of human flesh and human desire without at the same time falling into the equally pernicious *ressentiment* and asceticism of primitive shamans and people like Miss Kilman. I am thus claiming, first, that Rachel's "beautiful idea" is the next stage of rationalization and secularization in the genealogy of religious thought that has been presented during the chapel service, taking us from aboriginal rage against the elements, to an Old Testament desire for revenge against one's enemies, to the still all too physically embodied icon-worship of the Roman Church, to the spare architecture and pleasantries of Protestantism, to Bax's clumsy articulation of Clapham Sect social responsibility, and finally to some more ethereal realm of pure phenomena, where bodies and emotions, as if beaten to an airy thinness, enter into a communion that the afternoon's "loathsome exhibition" (*Voyage* 242) of conventional religious sentiment cannot grasp. Second, I am claiming that this "idea" evolves into one of Woolf's most important narrative motifs. Not unlike Wilberforce himself, Rachel compares the "prevailing religious system of professed Christians in the higher and middle classes" with some more authentic idea of human fellowship and finds the former a sham. Indeed, Woolf liked the underlying substance of Bax's metaphor so well that she repeated its central idea near the end of her last novel, *Between the Acts*, as the Reverend Streatfield comments on the decidedly comic historical pageant that has just ended: "To me at least it was indicated that we are members of one another. Each is part of the whole. Yes, that occurred to me, sitting among you in the audience.... We act different parts; but are the same" (192). Like Bax, Streatfield is treated ironically: immediately after this he launches into an account of the money raised by the pageant for the church fund. But like Bax's too-grand metaphor, Streatfield's awkward Evangelical intervention captures something central in Woolf's work and thought in which, not unlike the metamorphic protagonist of *Orlando* or the nearly indistinguishable voices of *The Waves*, "we act different parts; but are the same."

Usually taken for comic relief, Bax's religious service is important because it winds up correcting a vision of disembodied detachment that occurs to Rachel at the beginning of the novel, even before Richard Dalloway's kiss stimulates a nightmarish disgust with her own body.

To feel anything strongly was to create an abyss between oneself and others who feel strongly perhaps but differently. It was better to play the piano and forget all the rest. The conclusion was very welcome. Let these odd men and women—her aunts, the Hunts, Ridley, Helen, Mr. Pepper, and the rest—be symbols,—featureless but dignified, symbols of age, of youth, of motherhood, of learning, and beautiful often as people upon the stage are beautiful.... Reality dwelling in what one saw and felt, but did not talk about, one could accept a system in which things went round and round quite satisfactorily to other people, without often troubling to think about it, except as something superficially strange.... Inextricably mixed in dreamy confusion, her mind seemed to enter into communion, to be delightfully expanded and combined, with the spirit of the whitish boards of deck, with the spirit of the sea, with the spirit of Beethoven Op. 111, even with the spirit of poor William Cowper there at Olney. Like a ball of thistledown it kissed the sea, rose, kissed it again, and thus rising and kissing passed finally out of sight. (*Voyage* 32)

It is a splendid passage, and it of course looks ahead to similar passages in Woolf's later novels. But what is missing in this case, and quite obviously so, is any "communion" between Rachel and another living being. People have been turned into symbols on a stage, who can be "beautiful" without Rachel's having to feel strongly about them or to be emotionally linked or responsive to them, while her own confused consciousness can protect itself by finding a kind of inhuman immersion in objects, works of art, and dead writers, all comfortably outside her body. (One sign of Woolf's youthful defensiveness as a writer in *The Voyage Out* may be the wealth of literary allusions sprinkled throughout it, a device used more sparingly in her later works.) Richard Dalloway's kiss a few pages later comes as a shock to Rachel's system because it is so unlike her detached and theatrical mental vision of kissing the sea.

It is not as if the possibility of being a distinct and inviolate individual does not appeal to Rachel when her Aunt Helen reassures her of her uniqueness after learning about Dalloway's aggressiveness: "The vision of her own personality, of herself as a real everlasting thing, different from anything else, unmergeable, like the sea or the wind, flashed into Rachel's mind, and she became profoundly excited at the thought of living. 'I can be m-m-myself,' she stammered, 'in spite of you, in spite of the Dalloways, and Mr. Pepper, and Father, and my Aunts, in spite of these?'" Helen "gravely" responds in soothing tones: "In spite of every one" (*Voyage* 83–84). But the idea of remaining "unmergeable" finally will not work for Rachel, any more than it will for Woolf: the excitement of "living" as oneself, free of the social expectations and constraints that may be imposed on one, must also be done in one's own body, often in contact, whether wanted or not, with other bodies, a body that is heir to the flesh and its desires and its shame, as well as to its potential, like the rained-upon earth in Mr. Bax's sermon, for bearing fruit.

Moreover, Rachel fears that the solipsism of feeling "strongly," exemplified by Walter Pater's impressionism, will preclude the emotional connection and mental association with others that she also craves. Rachel's most intimate sense of her own body, her most complete embodiment, comes as she slips beneath the waves of delirium during her fatal illness: "She was completely cut off, and unable to communicate with the rest of the world, isolated alone with her body" (*Voyage* 342). Rachel's recurring experience of this delirium is that she is drowning, "curled up at the bottom of the sea" (*Voyage* 353), momentarily surfacing, and then sinking again. The powerful and endlessly fascinating thing about Woolf's work, beginning with *The Voyage Out*, is Woolf's attempt to make a virtue out of her own necessity, to transform the deathly, drowning anxiety of being isolated and inviolate into a poetics of association that represented for her a higher stage of what I can only call religious consciousness, a stage somehow beyond the flesh and ascetic disavowal alike. That this higher stage may only come permanently at the price of one's own identity, of one's own life, is perhaps made most explicit later in *The Waves*. Structured by the seemingly discontinuous theatrical declamations of a clan of friends held together by the absent sacrificial victim of empire, Percival, *The Waves* ends by suggesting that the association of minds occurs now only in the writer, Bernard, no longer "thrown up and down on the roar of other people's voices, singing the same song," but rather in an "endless throwing away, dissipation, flooding forth without our willing it," which is to say, "a sort of death" (279).

Out of Body Experience

Though there are a number of places one might go to examine Woolf's more mature formulation of this higher religion, Clarissa's "transcendental theory" in *Mrs. Dalloway* is perhaps the clearest. The later novel as a whole reprises a number of themes first broached in *The Voyage Out*. Like Rachel, the shell-shocked Septimus Smith identifies more easily with the great writers of the past and believes they all share a loathing toward and despair over the embodied human condition; for Septimus, even Shakespeare found that the "business of copulation was filth" (*Dalloway* 134). Like Helen Ambrose, Clarissa Dalloway's chief objection to religion is its tendency to pursue "Conversion," which "feasts on the wills of the weakly, living to impress, to impose," offering help, but desiring power (151). When combined with the ideal of proportion trumpeted by the conformist psychiatry of Sir William Bradshaw, conversion becomes the basic trope of empire—in India, in Africa, even in London. For Clarissa, a conversion-minded woman such as Miss Kilman makes both love and religion "detestable" (191).

So it is all the more significant that when, late in the novel, Peter Walsh recalls a conversation he once had with Clarissa Dalloway on an omnibus in London, the words he remembers her speaking elaborate a more refined and less overtly moralized version of the circulation of imaginative sympathy found in Mr. Bax's sermon. It is as if one had taken Bax's extended metaphor for modern, rationalized, and secularized religious feeling, where the individual is immersed in the great ocean of humanity, and evacuated it of any cruder Evangelical sense of proportion and conversion, that is, of empire, still lurking within it.

But she said, sitting on the bus going up Shaftesbury Avenue, she felt herself everywhere; not "here, here, here"; and she tapped the back of the seat; but everywhere. She waved her hand going up Shaftesbury Avenue. She was all that. So that to know her, or any one, one must seek out the people who completed them; even the places. Odd affinities she had with people she had never spoken to, some woman in the street, some man behind a counter—even trees, or barns. It ended in a transcendental theory which, with her horror of death, allowed her to believe, or say that she believed (for all her skepticism), that since our apparitions, the part of us which appears, are so momentary compared with the other, the unseen part of us, which spreads wide, the unseen might survive, be recovered somehow attached to this person or that, or even haunting certain places after death... perhaps—perhaps. (*Dalloway* 231–32)

It should thus be no surprise at the end of the novel that during her party, Clarissa both feels the unseen presence of the suicide Septimus Smith and, though they have never met, thinks his thoughts: "and the words came to her, Fear no more the heat of the sun.... She felt somehow very like him—the young man who had killed himself. She felt glad that he had done it; thrown it away. The clock was ticking. The leaden circles [of Big Ben's tolling] dissolved in air. He made her feel the beauty; made her feel the fun" (*Dalloway* 283–84). Septimus Smith's influence on Clarissa Dalloway may not be precisely what the more prosaic Mr. Bax had in mind—there is no organic relationship between them, indeed, no relationship at all—and yet their minds and emotions are associated. In a sense, Mr. Bax's fumbling service, which takes us from the old savage of primitive *ressentiment* almost to the ungraspable butterfly of the religious idea itself, and his sermon, which buries its own beautiful idea of sympathy in the English ideology of the good colonizer, together represent the awkward beginning of Clarissa's—and Virginia Woolf's—transcendental theory of human consciousness.

One would not be mistaken in thinking that there is something of hermetic philosophy in all this, some hint of neo-Platonism, Kabbalism, spiritism, and the more empirical investigations of the era's Society for Psychical Research (on the last, see Rose 4–5). Clarissa Dalloway's sense that "our apparitions, the part of us which appears, are so momentary compared with the other, the unseen part of us, which spreads wide" surely echoes mystical concepts of migratory souls, unseen auras, and communication with the dead. We should recall as well that the immortality of the soul, even when divorced from the manifold of "appearances," retained a philosophical validity for Cambridge philosophers such as the Hegelian J. E. McTaggart and his pupil Moore and remained a staple of the Apostles' conversations (see Levy 162). Hermione Lee has suggested that moments of emotional transport in Woolf's novels, beginning with Rachel's intimate physical confrontation with Helen Ambrose during the tour to the native village, describe moments "of emotion in terms of a physical orgasm" (Lee, *Novels* 45). In that climactic and much-discussed passage (*Voyage* 294–95), for example, Woolf presents a series of disjointed phenomena, as if Rachel were drowning in the murky waters of a bodily awareness now ecstatically freed from the continuity of cause and effect as well as from coherent individuation, rather like the "dissevered syllables" of Hewet's repeated name or the "broken fragments of speech" that float down to the ground when Helen congratulates Hewet on his engagement. In a sense, at the moment she is enveloped by Helen's body, Rachel "drowns" in a bodily awareness that is *not* simply isolated and deathly, as it will be in her later illness.

Like a surreal version of Henry Thornton, Rachel is here very much in the world but not of it: swooning into an unconceptualized bodily rapture ("speechless and almost without sense") and at the same time outside herself. Perhaps the best way of describing the transcendental relations enjoyed by such figures as Mrs. Dalloway, Mrs. Ramsay, and Lily Briscoe would be as a highly refined form of religious ecstasy, something akin to that of St. Theresa of Ávila (who shares the name of Rachel's deceased mother and who had been so important for George Eliot), in which it is the dissolution of normally contained bodily states in a larger identification with the other, rather then the ascetic abnegation of the flesh, that is achieved. That religious ecstasy has itself been interpreted as a sublimation of orgasm—orgasm without the individualized, corporeal body, as it were—only underlines its appropriateness for Woolf. Yet I think what Woolf means at these moments is in fact closer to religious ecstasy, however poor a vehicle for it Rachel may seem to be.

My resort to the term "ecstasy" here is not arbitrary. In a passage in "A Sketch of the Past," Woolf manages to suggest in a few lines much of what I have tried to synthesize in this chapter. Woolf speaks at one point of her tomboyish shame at looking at herself in the hall mirror when growing up. Not surprisingly, it is her startling revelation that this sense of shame may have been caused by her sexual molestation as a child that has captured most of our critical attention. But just before this revelation, Woolf suggests that her feeling of shame may indeed have been an ancestral emotion: "I am almost inclined to drag in my grandfather—Sir James, who once smoked a cigar, liked it, and so threw away his cigar and never smoked another. I am almost inclined to think that I inherited a streak of the puritan, of the Clapham Sect." Even more significant is the fact that Woolf's professed response to this puritan inheritance is hardly straightforward. "Yet this did not prevent me," she writes, "from feeling ecstasies and raptures spontaneously and intensely and without any shame or the least sense of guilt, so long as they were disconnected from my own body" (*Moments* 68). The dissociative experience Woolf describes here—a psychological phenomenon popularized in 1905 by Morton Prince—may or may not be linked to her sexual abuse. But it is precisely this ecstatic projection beyond both the body and the ascetic denial of it that Woolf will try time and again to capture in her fiction. It was her brother-in-law Clive Bell, after all, who had declared, two years before the publication of *The Voyage Out:* "Art and Religion are, then, two roads by which men escape from circumstance to ecstasy. Between aesthetic and religious rapture there is a family alliance" (C. Bell 92). I want to suggest that such emotional dissociation, where one feels "raptures" so long as they are disconnected from one's own body, owes an even greater "family alliance" to the Clapham Sect of Woolf's grandfather than she was able to say, and that the religious association of hearts and minds that typified Claphamite social effervescence was an integral part of Woolf's search for an adequate literary style, for a dissociative textual practice that she could call her own. In effect, Woolf's sense of her inherited emotional disposition will be integrated with her sense of an inherited social habitus—Bloomsbury and the Fabian Society as heirs to the Clapham Sect—and both will be integrated in turn with Woolf's own dissociative response to the trauma of her half-brother's molestation of her as a child. It is as if the private and public currents of her life, the complementary drives toward esoteric dissociation and exoteric association, weirdly mirror one another, without any simple causal relationship existing between them.

Woolf's Secular Modernism

Erich Auerbach once famously described the "reflection of multiple consciousnesses" in Woolf's writing as the half-mournful, half-celebratory consequence of Woolf's embrace of the "random moment." In Auerbach's view, the seemingly spontaneous Proustian or Bergsonian or Paterian moment of consciousness, "which is comparatively independent of the controversial and unstable orders over which men fight and despair," punctuates the novels of Woolf and other modernists less as a consequence of philosophical or literary influence than as the product of the manifold "crises in adjustment" within modern society, the "widening" of horizons in World War I, indeed the collapse of existing religious, philosophical, ethical, and economic principles, and with them the wholesale disintegration of Enlightenment ideals of democracy, progress, and liberalism (Auerbach 549, 552, 550). Elaborating upon the shifting temporalities and seemingly unanchored perspectives of the opening scenes in *To the Lighthouse*, Auerbach's reading becomes a sweeping interpretive tour de force about the arrival of modernism as a whole.

Under his scrutiny, the stylistic innovations that mark Woolf's work, and modernism more broadly, reflect the fragmentation of a Judeo-Christian cultural tradition through which, especially between the era of Dante and the nineteenth century, classical stylistic decorum had become as democratized as society, the divine had been fully incarnated via Christ in humanity, and the rich tapestry of everyday life had come finally to be represented in the realistic novel in all its manifold and organic interconnectedness. In the disintegration of a "clearly formulable and recognized community of thought and feeling" amid increasing factionalism, the rise of "mutually hostile groups," and "strange alliances" around the time of World War I and just after, the sense of narrative continuity that required "reliable criteria" also disintegrated into "multiple and multivalent reflections of consiousness" (551). In Auerbach's view, the great humanist narrative collapses in ruins with Woolf, Joyce, Proust, and Eliot, as the isolated, if intensely felt, moment of awareness finally cuts itself loose—like Pater's solipsistic, transitory impression, and the deracinated Kurtz of Conrad's *Heart of Darkness*—from the durable cultural and religious traditions that once gave it meaning.

But this is not all bad for Auerbach, for it is precisely through the writer's concentration on the stream of intensely personal yet random moments of experience, detached as never before from the sectarianism and disorder fragmenting public life, that a new and more "elemental" sense of the "things which men have in common" can arise. This dissolution of external order and emphasis on an "unprejudiced ... representation of the random moment in the lives of different people" (Auerbach 552), no matter how exotic they may have once seemed, is for Auerbach the clearest sign pointing toward a radically simplifying and unifying solution to all the catastrophic disorder that had roiled Europe between 1914 and the time of the publication of *Mimesis*. Moreover, Auerbach manages to see an underlying kinship between the modernists' multifaceted, unprejudiced focus on the random moment of experience and his own critical methodology, which focused intently on specific (and seemingly random) moments in specific (and seemingly random) texts in order to allow them, in the truest sense of the German romantic tradition, to stand as perfect microcosms of entire and coherent historical epochs.

Auerbach's views have been often enough criticized, though his larger sense of the meaning of modernist fragmentation remains a sort of critical truism. There is much to recommend it. Yet something as complex by nature as literary technique is overdetermined from the start, and we imagine such coherent historical causalities and significances only at some cost to a potentially richer account of the fictive imagination. What I want to suggest in concluding is that what Auerbach sees in Woolf is not simply a direct reflection or transcendence of a world shattered by strife and a time out of joint. There are of course places, such as the "Time Passes" episode of *To the Lighthouse*, where the ravages of war and the consequent breaking of what Woolf calls the "mirror" of nature—a mirror of consolation found in "solitude on the beach" (202)—are represented as a disruption, and perhaps a transformation, of human history. Yet the welter of overlapping and interpenetrating multiple perspectives that is so striking in Woolf's mature work, especially in *To the Lighthouse*, seems to have had different and more deeply embedded roots in the Evangelical heritage that Woolf half-satirizes and half-recuperates—her version, we might say, of Heidegger's *Verwindung*, or recuperating distortion, of tradition—in the novel she published during World War I, *The Voyage Out*. When after the war Woolf famously observed that "human character changed," she was referring to the relatively uneventful December of 1910, which for her marked a point at which relations between masters and servants, husbands and wives, and parents and children were democratized, accompanied by "a change in religion, conduct, politics, and literature" (see "Mr. Bennett" 320–21; for a more sweeping account of European cultural revolution in 1910, see Harrison). But it is obvious that this change was hardly as sudden, wholesale, or transforming as Woolf's hyperbole implied, and that she translated the social forms of her family's secularizing religious pilgrimage with great deliberateness.

In this sense, I think what Auerbach is actually describing in his account of Woolf's focus on the moment of experience is precisely an effect of the secularization of religious feeling that accompanies modernization, and not simply a direct reflection of a fragmented modern world. It is no accident that in the later novel, it is "the atheist Tansley," Mr. Ramsay's too-earnest graduate student, who, like St. John Hirst, is most directly ridiculed as a narrow chauvinist and who is most obviously in need of emotional rescue. And it is no accident that in almost direct, but also redemptive, opposition to the desiccated Tansley we find Mrs. Ramsay, for whom the titular lighthouse that seems so long out of reach for her husband becomes the secular source of a neo-Evangelical "inner light": "Often she found herself sitting and looking, sitting and looking, with her work in her hands until she became the thing she looked at—that light, for example" (*Lighthouse* 97). It is immediately following this infusion of light that Mrs. Ramsay imagines herself "in the hands of the Lord," but no one attentive to the Evangelical significance of the sudden arrival of such illumination would be as surprised by the sentiment as is the annoyed Mrs. Ramsay.

And it is in response to this "steady light, the pitiless, the remorseless, which was so much her, yet so little her, which had her," not unlike the divine word, "at its beck and call," that Mrs. Ramsay experiences her own orgasmic-ecstatic moment, though one carefully restricted to a luminous manipulation of the organs of her mind.

But for all that, she thought, watching it with fascination, hypnotized, as if it were stroking with its silver fingers some sealed vessel in her brain whose bursting would flood her with delight, she had known happiness, exquisite happiness, intense happiness, and it silvered the rough waves a little more brightly, as daylight faded, and the blue went out of the sea and it rolled in waves of pure lemon which curved and swelled and broke upon the beach and the ecstasy burst in her eyes and waves of pure delight raced over the floor of her mind and she felt, It is enough! It is enough! (*Lighthouse* 99–100)

One might say that Mrs. Ramsay's most erotic union—perhaps the most graphically erotic consummation in all of Woolf's fiction—is with the lighthouse's light; and yet that union is itself inseparable from the religious context in which it occurs, as if the erotic were to be taken quite immediately as a reoccupation of the answer position that had once been provided by the inner light of religious experience. Struggling with the vestiges of a faith she finds insufficiently authentic, fascinated by two rooks she has named Joseph and Mary squabbling just outside her window, sitting still at the center of a vortex of swirling perceptions, reflections, and memories, Mrs. Ramsay is the enabling muse, as it were, of her own little clan or coterie, whose members are, both like and unlike those gathered earlier on Clapham Common, absorbed in the reflection of their own looks, and the echo of their own voices.

Mrs. Ramsay's world will be replaced by Lily's in the course of *To the Lighthouse,* and in that way Woolf may be telling us that the associated minds gathered around Mrs. Ramsay will henceforth gather only in art, or rather books (such as her own)—a point made explicit near the end of *The Waves.* But in a passage that rather neatly reproduces the sense of Mr. Bax's banal Claphamite peroration, in which individuals, like drops of water, are said to be morally immersed in and throughout the whole of humanity, we are also told that Mrs. Ramsay, reflecting on her extended household one evening, was flattered "to think how, wound about in their hearts, however long they lived she would be woven . . . and she felt . . . that community of feeling with other people which emotion gives as if the walls of partition had become so thin that practically (the feeling was one of relief and happiness) it was all one stream" (*Lighthouse* 170). No doubt, such a passage was what made Woolf worry that *To the Lighthouse,* perhaps her favorite novel, would be condemned by the critics as "sentimental," no more than an elegy for familial ghosts (see Lee, *Virginia* 476, 482). But what we should surely acknowledge is that Mrs. Ramsay's consoling self-reflections in *To the Lighthouse* are no less sentimental or banal than Mr. Bax's liturgical peroration, which is generally understood as outright satire by Woolf's critics. The Evangelical echoes in Mrs. Ramsay's reflections, as well as Woolf's willingness to include them, without irony, despite her concerns about sentimentality, suggest that Woolf had a far more intimate relationship to her Clapham Sect heritage than we normally acknowledge.

Moreover, it is crucial to recognize that this heritage does not dissipate into the thin air of the book's "Time Passes" entr'acte upon Mrs. Ramsay's death and the epoch-shattering war years. For the religious heritage is subtly reproduced, and perhaps intensified, in Lily Briscoe, who clearly comes to "reoccupy" (to adapt Hans Blumenberg's term) Mrs. Ramsay's own secularized religious position (see Blumenberg, *Legitimacy* 65). After all, it is Lily who labors over an abstract (which is to say, secularized) portrait of a Madonna and Child throughout the novel, a portrait in which the human figure has been reduced to an inhuman geometry, but a geometry that we are told Mrs. Ramsay herself understands as transcendent reality, as a "wedge of darkness" that spreads everywhere, in all things. And it is Lily, watched over by Mr. Carmichael's pagan homosexual Poseidon, who, linking the completion of her painting with the thought that Mr. Ramsay has finally reached the lighthouse, quotes Christ's "It is finished" (*Lighthouse* 309) at the end of the novel, without irony, without wondering (as had Mrs. Ramsay earlier) where her words came from.

The deeper psychological dilemma Woolf faced, whatever its ultimate etiology, may have been how to be free of one's body while neither denying it nor abandoning the pleasures of sociality it provided, and her solution became a form of psychic "rapture" that periodically surfaces throughout her work. But this rapture, this ecstatic association with others, has a long heritage in English Evangelical thought, at least in the sort of Evangelical sociality embraced by Clapham village, where the emphasis on the powerful emotional response kindled by "inner light" is intimately joined to the wider pleasures of associated minds. Whatever else it may be, Woolf's modernism was in many ways a textual reenactment—a phenomenological dramatization—of all those reflected looks and echoed voices on Clapham Common, but also in Bloomsbury, in the parties at Gordon Square and (later, perhaps sitting next to Noel Coward) at Argyll House, and in a multitude of extended households and reform associations, from a Fabian Society meeting to an imaginary society of "outsiders." None of these liturgies of associated minds managed, for anything more than a few precious moments, to approach the "beautiful idea" fluttering over Rachel Vinrace in *The Voyage Out,* or to assuage the doubt and despair that troubled most of Woolf's protagonists and finally destroyed Woolf herself. But this is why, perhaps, Woolf was at various points in her life so determined to find a way of netting her own beautiful idea of quasi-religious ex-stasis—the chance to stand outside or beside herself, to allow herself to be both permeated and absorbed by others—in the disembodied and slightly more permanent medium of her prose.

Woolf's life and work, from the youthful struggle with her father's rationalism to her participation in Bloomsbury and the writing of her novels, remain embedded in a world shaped by the religious, which is to say also philosophical and cultural, forms of her Claphamite ancestors. We should no more ignore the significance of this religious context, even in its secularized versions, than we should ignore the persistent relevance of Woolf's class position, toward which she showed almost equal ambivalence. One could also say that it is precisely the secularized Evangelical sociality of Woolf's life and writing that most overtly defines them as English, or perhaps British, in the modern era. The cultural aristocracy that in so many ways learned its peculiar forms of social solidarity, or collective consciousness, on the Clapham-to-Bloomsbury road also did much to define the public nature of modern English national identity, one that would not substantially alter until well after World War II, as the collapse of empire and what Tom Nairn once called "the break-up of Britain" began to introduce completely new forms of religious practice, and, as Salman Rushdie's work would demonstrate, new modes of secular response.

Conclusion

Humanism and Globalization

In *The Civilization of the Renaissance in Italy* (1860), Jacob Burckhardt located the birth of humanism in fourteenth-century Italy, and the terms of his analysis became a sort of truism for elite modern European culture. Renaissance humanism in Burckhardt's eyes meant that mankind rejected the medieval "veil ... woven of faith, illusion, and childish prepossession," in which "man was conscious of himself only as a member of a race, people, party, family, or corporation [e.g., the Church]." Instead, the humanist embraced an "*objective* treatment ... of all the things of this world" and a "*subjective*" appreciation of himself "as a spiritual *individual*" (129). In short, for Burckhardt and for many others, humanism as it developed within medieval Catholicism (in such men as Erasmus and More) and the Reformation that followed broke up the hegemony of corporate (Roman Catholic) spirituality—as well as its material basis, if we assume that the expropriation of church property and its transfer into private hands played a necessary role in this process. The invention of this seemingly self-sufficient and secular individual generated in turn for Burckhardt the inquisitive—and acquisitive—mind that could think in and for itself, an autonomous mind possessing a worldly, cosmopolitan perspective no longer dominated by what Francis Bacon had called the idols of the tribe, and open to what Matthew Arnold called Hellenism. (For a substantial and sophisticated updating of Burckhardt's main claims, one that responds to criticism such as that of Huizinga and some Marxian scholarship, see Burke, especially 1–26, 192–200; see also Huizinga.)

In this sense, humanism also came to be indistinguishable for modern Western thinkers from what we today call secularization, since it was only by means of an intellect liberated from the unchallenged authority of tradition, especially from what had become intertwined religious, cosmological, and political traditions and their corporate investiture, that true knowledge of the material universe and of human beings alike would be possible. It would not be too much to say that without something like Burckhardt's sense of a cosmopolitan individual capable of challenging any and all forms of collective authority, indeed morally driven to do so, Said's notion of "secular criticism" would be impossible. The more widespread embrace of what Blumenberg calls modest human "self-assertion," which is what for Burckhardt entails a private as opposed to corporate (that is, both public and political) spirituality, signaled as well a deeper sense of the individual's sustained and growing power over his or her own destiny on earth. That a new form of corporate identity—the modern nation-state—served in many ways to repair the veil of corporate identity rent by humanist individualism is hardly mentioned by Burckhardt, but it is an essential part of the story all the same. With Protestantism's fragmentation of papal political authority, the nation-state, and hence the possibility of a sharper distinction between church and state, between Calvin's "two kingdoms" of spiritual and secular authority, also took root more or less permanently in Europe.

Burckhardt himself found the nascent form of these new intellectual and moral qualities in the cult of personality and ambition in the princely courts of the despotic Italian city-states, abetted by the rediscovery of Greek and Roman classical literature—Machiavelli is his main point of reference. Later, as Habermas shows, this courtly humanism would migrate into the bourgeois public sphere of the eighteenth-century salons, coffeehouses, newspapers, private aesthetic judgment, and public opinion, so that "civil society came into existence as the corollary of a depersonalized state authority" (Habermas, *Structural* 19). It is through this migration that, as I noted in my introduction, culture and cultural criticism come finally to oppose themselves, in Adorno's conception, to all that is "official." But Burckhardt's grand vision of the cosmopolitan individual already contains this resistance to the official *in nuce*, and it is worth citing in detail, for it is here that the centrality of Burckhardt's version of humanist tradition, rooted in the figure of Dante, becomes clearly legible for later theorists of the secular, cosmopolitan intellectual, such as Auerbach and Said. (The literature on cosmopolitanism itself is growing, but see especially A. Anderson; Berman; Brennan; Hohendahl; Robbins; Tan.)

The cosmopolitanism which grew up in the most gifted circles is in itself a high stage of individualism. Dante, as we have already said, finds a new home in the language and culture of Italy, but goes beyond even this in the words, "My country is the whole world" [*De Vulgari Eloquentia*, book 1, chapter 6]. And when his recall to Florence was offered him on unworthy conditions, he wrote back: "Can I not everywhere behold the light of the sun and the stars; everywhere meditate on the noblest truths, without appearing ingloriously and shamefully before the city and the people. Even my bread will not fail me." The artists exult no less defiantly in their freedom from the constraints of fixed residence. "Only he who has learned everything," says Ghiberti [*Secondo Commentario*, chapter 15], "is nowhere a stranger; robbed of his fortune and without friends, he is yet the citizen of every country, and can fearlessly despise the changes of fortune." In the same strain an exiled humanist writes: "Wherever a learned man fixes his seat, there is home" [Malagola, *Codro Urceo*, chapter 5]. (Burckhardt 132–33)

Burckhardt goes on to note that such a conception of the deracinated yet empowered individual recalls the older Roman saying *Ubi bene, ibi patria* (where one is happy, there is one's home), a saying deliberately inverted by Rousseau when he wanted to emphasize to the Polish cultural elite the value of strong national identity as a way of resisting the dismemberment of their lands by more powerful states in the late eighteenth century: "You must turn a certain execrable proverb upside-down, and bring each Pole to say from the bottom of his heart: *Ubi patria, ibi bene* [where one's home is, there one is happy]" (Rousseau 14).

The complex tensions between Burckhardt and Rousseau might be imagined as a sort of template for the equally complicated tensions today between, on the one hand, the cosmopolitan humanist, either of Western or non-Western provenance, who consciously or otherwise may bear the imprint of a certain imperial project in the humanist desire to feel at home everywhere, even as this desire is held out as a model for rising above all religious or communal particularisms; and, on the other hand, the national or populist intellectual, who often provides a powerful check against the hegemony of secularizing and modernizing Western thought, all the while tending to provide in turn rationales for the deeper claims of religious-ethnic identities, some openly tolerant, some less so. It is a tension that has been very much at the center of contemporary debates about the role of secular, humanist discourse in a postcolonial, and now global, cultural environment.

In all this, however, Burckhardt also provided an implicit rationale for studying what we in America commonly call "the humanities" (*Geisteswissenschaften* in German, or *les sciences humaines* in France)—that is, literature, philosophy, history, and the arts, which is to say all the things that have come since Burckhardt and Arnold to be addressed by the term "cultural criticism." The reasons for this link between the humanist's individual and the humanities are diverse, but fundamental. First, up to the nineteenth century, all the liberal arts, including what we would today call humanistic and scientific disciplines, could be understood as practices that claimed to make the intellect more objective, more enlightened, less clouded by dogma and illusion, for they all promoted what Arnold called the disinterested endeavor "to make the best that has been thought and known in the world current everywhere" (Arnold 5:113). Second, and rather ambiguously given the simultaneous rise of European imperialism from the fifteenth century on, the humanities shaped an autonomous, freethinking, and worldly spirit who would be at home everywhere, which Burckhardt called an "all-sided man," or *l'uomo universale* (134). This worldly or universal spirit was subsequently reduced to cliché, but it became in many ways the basis for a humanistic education, one that promoted a high degree of literacy, familiarity with learned thought beginning with the ancients, and, at least by the eighteenth century and the rise of comparative philology, a rather lively, if also often controlling, interest in the languages, myths, belief systems, and literatures of European and non-European cultures alike. Indeed, this worldly humanistic spirit can still be found at the core of what we mean today by secular criticism.

This notion of humanism has been durable for the secular intellectuals who embody it, but it has always had some significant detractors. On one side, many religious thinkers have naturally been suspicious of its emphasis on secular learning and the putative benefits of individual reflection, though it seems clear that Protestant Christian religious belief has in fact been quietly integrated with humanist commitments throughout modern European history. On the other side, many contemporary thinkers have rejected the term human*ism* precisely because it seems (quite despite its antiauthoritarian elements) to foster anew a dogmatic, quasi-religious, and ultimately imperial notion of human nature that is putatively based only the predilections of an elite group of Europeans. To fully understand the grounds for this more recent rejection of humanism, we need to go back to Nietzsche's stinging critique of the resentful will to power within the Judeo-Christian tradition, Heidegger's late deconstruction of a human-centered idea of Being, Foucault's wholesale suspicion of the Enlightenment's ideals of man and his rights (later revised), Derrida's deconstruction of Western philosophy as "white mythology" (see Derrida, *Margins* 268–69), and finally to a full century of non-Western critics of Western secular humanism, from Mohandas K. Gandhi and Rabindranath Tagore to Ashis Nandy and Talal Asad, who have linked this secular humanism to the global dominance of Western power and its ideal of the capitalist-centered nation-state.

The effects of this now well-established critique of humanism on the American academy are palpable, and so, in my view, have been its intellectual benefits. The critique has, even at a minimum, provided a critical self-consciousness often lacking in the West's more complacent versions of its humanist tradition. But I am not convinced that the modern challenge to humanism should be considered quite the radical departure from humanism's ideals that many, both pro and con, assume it is; nor am I convinced that such a departure, were it to be sufficiently radical, would be sustainable, or finally desirable. So the problem I want to pose here is this: to what extent can (or should) the line of thought taking us from Burckhardt's understanding of humanism to Said's idea of secular criticism, a line that presumes, albeit in different ways, the awakening of the spiritual individual whose modest ambitions toward self-assertion include at some level what Hobbes called the desire for power after power, become an adequate model for a global understanding of the humanities? Like Ashis Nandy, who follows Gandhi in this regard, and to a lesser extent Talal Asad, some powerful critics of Western humanism have explicitly rejected the universal cultural validity of this ideal of the inquisitive/acquisitive secular individual. It seems clear enough, however, that the notion of a secularized study of the humanities is still the dominant one in Western universities, which simply assume its value.

* * *

Tracing the link between the modern humanities and secular European humanism in this way thus raises interesting problems when we try to resituate the humanities, and the cultural criticism built on them, in a global context. The historian Dipesh Chakrabarty, who has been an important contributor to the Marxist-oriented Subaltern Studies project in India, acknowledges that Western modernity, including the ideals of science, liberal democracy, individualism, universal human rights, and so forth, should not simply be dismissed in favor of the sort of wholesale critique one finds in Nandy and, to a lesser degree, Asad. At the same time, Chakrabarty puts quite bluntly the problem confronting any attempt at a truly global version of the humanities, one that complicates the Subaltern Studies project of "'Indians' 'representing themselves in history.'". He continues:

I have a more perverse proposition to argue. It is that insofar as the academic discourse of history—that is, "history" as a discourse produced at the institutional site of the university—is concerned, "Europe" remains the sovereign, theoretical subject of all histories, including the ones we call "Indian," "Chinese," "Kenyan," and so on. There is a peculiar way in which all these other histories tend to become variations on a master narrative that could be called "the history of Europe." In this sense, "Indian" history itself is in a position of subalternity; one can only articulate subaltern subject positions in the name of this history. (Chakrabarty 27)

(Chakrabarty's understanding of modern "history" as a discipline constructed even outside of Europe according to European narratives of development leading to the nation-state finds strong support in Pransenjit Duara's analysis of Chinese historiography and Pascal Casanova's recent argument that makes similar claims, on the basis of Pierre Bourdieu's notion of the symbolic or cultural field, where global literary history is concerned; see Casanova; Duara.)

At the heart, I think, of Chakrabarty's lament over the intractable problem of narrating a history of India that would *not* simply be a variation, as he puts it, of some "master narrative called 'the history of Europe'" (and he says this fully cognizant of our postmodern suspicion of all such master narratives), one finds a group of literary genres that have been central components of Western thought for two centuries, some for much longer. "Many of the public and private rituals of modern individualism," writes Chakrabarty, "became visible in India in the nineteenth century. One sees this, for instance, in the sudden flourishing in this period of the four basic genres that help express the modern self: the novel, the biography, the autobiography, and history. Along with these came modern industry, technology, medicine, a quasi-bourgeois (though colonial) legal system supported by a state that nationalism was to take over and make its own" (Chakrabarty 34). I want to accentuate what remains only modestly touched upon in Chakrabarty's argument: that the humanities—embodied for me not only in the four genres he cites but in the broader history of ideas that produces Burckhardt's narrative of *l'uomo universale*—are a fundamental element of the quasi-fictional (if also "quasi-bourgeois") "history of Europe" that shadows global history at this point, and that the idea of "variations" on a master narrative of history leading to secularization, modernization, individualism and the liberal traditions of the nation-state includes in some fundamental way variations on the idea of the humanities. (Indeed, this point is congruent with Blumenberg's claim, addressed in chapter 1, that the shift toward a modern Protestant ideal of modest "self-assertion" began with the breakdown of an Aristotelian aesthetic order even before the collapse of Aristotelian cosmological and moral orders.)

Chakrabarty invokes Homi Bhabha's widely cited idea of "mimicry," in which the formerly colonized subject can only be imitative—albeit always with significant and resistant differences—of the dominant European subject (see Bhabha), though one should note that his point also recalls, albeit in a more sophisticated and ambiguous way, the earlier idea of colonial mimicry that

V. S. Naipaul once so controversially emphasized. Like Bhabha, Chakrabarty will insist that we see this mimicry as part of the contested and contradictory terrain on which European identity came to imagine itself. What he calls the task of "provincializing Europe" thus involves preserving the promise of a democratic modernity—this, after all, is still part of the socialist vision of Subaltern Studies—while emphasizing the destructive ambivalence and even repression that have in fact been inseparable from the West's humanist Enlightenment.

This worthy goal has been central to what is called postcolonial studies for some time now. Yet in the end, Chakrabarty's proposed "provincializing" of Europe remains profoundly ambivalent, even contradictory. On the one hand, he admits that "political modernity" is "impossible to *think* of anywhere in the world without invoking categories and concepts, the genealogies of which go deep into the intellectual and even theological traditions of Europe" (Chakrabarty 4). This predicament leads, in his account, to a certain kind of evolutionary historicism—that is, to the sense that whatever developed first in European modernity would unfold later, at a slower pace, in the modernizing of the non-Western world. On the other hand, Chakrabarty wants to escape from this Eurocentric historicism, which he sees as caught up in something more like a "reified" or "virtual" Europe than a real one, by resurrecting forgotten or repressed forms of belief, knowledge, and social habitus, especially the religious dogmas and customary practices of tribal groups, peasants, and workers, and the harder-to-isolate habits of educated elites that other Indian Marxists, following the European historicism of scholars such as Eric Hobsbawm, tend to relegate to the category of the "prepolitical." By recuperating seemingly trivial social rituals of the past such as *adda* (or public conversation, from mere gossip to political discussion), Chakrabarty implies the existence of something like a specifically Indian or at least Bengali sense of civil society that Hobsbawm's terminology is bound to ignore (see Chakrabarty 180–213). The point, as I understand it, is instead to see that an Indian modernity would necessarily be both somehow like a European modernity and very much unlike it—that is, we should not expect it to be either "bourgeois" in the European sense or built around the same European categories (like those of Burckhardt) of "spiritual" individualism.

Chakrabarty thus usefully reminds us, for example, that the "subaltern" so often invoked by "subaltern studies" has often been motivated by customary and, behind these in so many ways, religious impulses that Marxist cultural critics have had a hard time even acknowledging, let alone analyzing. And yet, Chakrabarty himself can point to little beyond vague hints of "other possibilities of human solidarity" in the subaltern religious cultures that have been repressed by Western modernity (45). He emphasizes that the persistence of the old gods and spirits are important as "social facts," as what differentiates Indian modernity from that of the West, but also routinely disavows the largely conservative role they now tend to play in modern society. He wants to draw some sustenance for the future (not unlike Habermas vis-à-vis Christianity in my first chapter) from the sense of fellowship embodied in past indigenous customs but in the end presents little that would be of use in the pursuit of social justice, a task that in his own account must remain very much determined by a European tradition of civil and human rights. After all, he notes, the premodern social practices can today only appear "superstitious" and "anachronistic if not reactionary" (253).

In this sense, Chakrabarty's search for a non-Western modernity with which he can still feel politically comfortable constantly dances along the edge of what he calls a "politics of despair" (Chakrabarty 45). He offers little hope, for example, that today's academy could ever adequately accommodate the non-Western sense of modernity he is hoping to find. The task of imagining the modern world as "radically heterogeneous" turns out to be "impossible within the knowledge protocols of academic history, for the globality of academia is not independent of the globality that the European modern has created" (46). But then, Chakrabarty gives no indication that any other "knowledge protocols," somehow found outside academic history, would work as well for him. Chakrabarty's book, methodologically governed as it is by Marx on capitalism in its first half and by Heidegger on a nontotalizing (and non-Marxian) sense of history in its second half, is itself powerful testament to just how difficult any radically heterogeneous sense of global modernity would be. For Chakrabarty, whose native language and culture are Bengali, a global humanities still takes shape under the umbrella of a debate between Marx and Heidegger, that is, between a Western historicism on the one hand, in which the essential question is the uneven transition to capitalism and then to socialism, and an equally Western (and universalizing) philosophy of existence on the other, in which the essential question of the human relation to Being requires a step back from a philosophical project that unfolds from Plato's ideas to the materialist modernity of Hobbes, Adam Smith, and Karl Marx, a step back from what Heidegger calls "the onto-theological constitution of metaphysics" in the West that leads finally to a secular global technocracy.

Some of Chakrabarty's points here are not entirely new. Indeed, one could claim that the postcolonial perspective as a whole, from figures such as C. L. R. James and Frantz Fanon to Edward Said, was founded (and will perhaps founder) on the dilemma of a belated non-Western Marxism, which entailed simultaneously embracing the European Enlightenment's narrative of progressive modernization while trying to imagine trajectories of development that would not simply turn out to be "variations" of a singular European master narrative. My point is not so much to pose a counter to the models of Chakrabarty or Bhabha or Said, but rather to insist upon the larger process of "secularization," which is an important and often neglected part of thinking about cultures in global terms, and to insist on the problem of the humanities posed within such models. That is, the idea of the humanities, far more than we might want to admit in the contemporary academy, is hinged at one end with the humanist secularization central to European modernity, which is to say it is inextricably dependent on the simultaneous transformation and overcoming of the Christian worldview it inherits; and at the other to the quasi-autonomous field of self-regulating and competing cultural spheres that we commonly call the "civil society" of the modern nation-state. Those disciplines we label the humanities thus tend to drag a certain notion of humanist "spiritual individual" along with them, and they tend to lead to, and flourish best in, civil societies where there is a relatively durable separation and competition among the various intellectually productive social systems of modernity, such as the aesthetic, the cultural, the religious, the economic, the political, the legal, the bureaucratic-administrative, and so forth—that is, wherever one would find all the things that Habermas associates with the coming of a "public sphere" in eighteenth-century Europe and, ultimately, the modern capitalist nation-state.

A radical globalizing of the humanities—one that penetrated to the very roots of the European humanities in the hope of transforming them—thus might not be such a straightforward thing. Such radical intellectual globalization could not simply be understood, in my view, as the expansion of horizons or the promulgation of greater inclusiveness. Neither inclusiveness nor contrapuntal, transnational reading necessarily entails a perspective through which the production of secular culture and secular cultural criticism is made problematic, so that it becomes part of what is to be critically elaborated from the start. For if we take what Chakrabarty says seriously—and I think he is basically right in his diagnosis of the issue—then the institutional presence of what used to be called the humanistic disciplines is not at all a neutral fact of academic life, no matter how global its reach. That institutional presence still embraces, for example, the production of the "spiritual individual" so dear to Burckhardt, which is to say the individual who practices what Said calls a "secular criticism" built around the autonomy of individual conscience and a libertarian intransigence in the face of religious, social, and political authority. The humanities, even as traditionally constituted, thus represent at one end a highly politicized sort of activity, at least once they are understood in Chakrabarty's terms as a central component of the master narrative of European modernization. To put the matter more directly, there is a central dilemma at the heart of any attempt to imagine a truly global study of the humanities in the West. Can the humanities as formal academic disciplines really become transformed by globalization, or will the globalization of the humanities mean primarily that even more (and more subtle) variations of a European master narrative are going to be written? In the terms so controversially posed by the social theorist Francis Fukuyama in 1989, at the start of the current debate over globalization: Will a global version of the humanities effectively mean the "end of history" for the humanities, since it will henceforth produce only further variations, as Chakrabarty put it, of an older European master narrative? Or will a global humanities mean instead a radically new beginning, one that might ultimately suggest a radically new role for humanistic study, including cultural criticism, in the twenty-first century?

* * *

I do not think anyone is in a position to answer these last questions. But by way of conclusion, I want to insist that Chakarbarty's ambivalent turn to what Habermas would call the "semantic potentials" latent in his own indigenous religious traditions suggests a strong parallel to the situation of the Western intellectual in tension—at times unconsciously—with equally indigenous religious traditions, and that this parallel, this kinship through secularization, is important to acknowledge when we speak, perhaps far too glibly, of the "secular" Western intellectual. I have tried in the preceding chapters to offer one admittedly rather cursory way of reopening the question of secularization within European (or Judaic and Christian) modernity, one that is intended in turn to suggest the possibility of a more inclusive model of cultural criticism across the boundaries of religion and nation even as it "provincializes" secularism per se. That is, only by trying to look behind, or step back away from, what has ironically come to be fairly dogmatic categories of thought in our own time—"secularism" and "secular criticism" in particular—in favor of a messier, more paradoxical, yet clearly ongoing process of secularization can we begin to appreciate an odd and seldom emphasized parallel between a figure such as Habermas, with his appeals to what would seem to be no longer viable religious "structures of thought," as if these were somehow still indispensable to his secular social and political philosophy, and a figure such as Chakrabarty, who feels equally driven by the need to locate semantic potentials—durable sediments of value and meaning—in religious modes of thought and practices that (even for Chakabarty) have only the most tenuous relationship to the project of secular political modernity that he finds himself dedicated to furthering. In short, despite the immense and significant difference between the meaning of secularization in the West and the meaning of secularization in global terms, there may yet be similarities of response across religious-political boundaries that provide a ground of sorts for a richer account of secularization, and hence of modernity.

In his remarkably sensitive and careful approach to the question of *laïcité islamique* in modern Algeria, for example, Henri Sanson argues that it is not inappropriate, either empirically or theoretically, to speak of the "laïc" and of "laïcité" when treating Islamic societies, even though the terms themselves are rooted in French usage and history. Though the terms "secular" and "secularity" in English (which can be traced to the thirteenth and fourteenth centuries respectively, though "secularization" and "secularism" are eighteenth- and nineteenth-century coinages) have histories rather different from those of their French counterparts, the terms "laïc" and "laïcité" bear some of the same ambiguities as the English terms: they refer historically to the laity, or the non-sacerdotal part of a religious confession, but have come to include offices and institutions—for example, schools—with no religious affiliation, and hence to imply sociopolitical conditions that embrace a clearer distinction between private faith and public administration in the modern French republic than had obtained under the ancien régime. (The English "secularism" today, though not so much its nineteenth-century usage, connotes in common parlance a stronger sense of anti-religious feeling or worldliness than does "laïcité," and indeed one might more likely find "secularism" simply translated as "sécularisme.") Nevertheless, it is the ambiguity of the term "laicité"—one mirroring in certain respects the tension in the term "secularization" elaborated by Monod in my introduction and threaded throughout the previous discussions, juxtaposing the transposition or transformation of religious thought with its overturning—that enables Sanson to articulate the nuances of a process of secularization in Algeria's predominantly Islamic society, one in which *laïcité* develops not outside of (*dehors*) religious confession but within it (*dedans*) (see Sanson 11). (For a different but similarly sophisticated approach to the rise of secularism—or *laiklik*, also borrowed form the French *laïc*—from *within* Islamic Turkey and not only as an importation from the West, see Silverstein.)

More specifically, it is the way Sanson further elaborates his decision "à mettre en rapport läicité et islamité"—to place secularity and Islam in contact—that I want to highlight. "Such a choice imposes itself on us, moreover, in consideration of the double will, manifest in Algerian society, to have Islam as a transcendent norm, or further, as a principle of belonging, of reference, of justification, of finality on the one hand, and, on the other, to have secularity as a practical norm, or further, as a principle of action, with all that this entails in terms of calls for independence, for liberty, for reason, and for conscience" (Sanson 8). The details and context of the emergence of this *double volonté* in Algerian society, in which tribal Arabic, Islamic, and colonial French lines of thought and practice intersect, occupies Sanson's subsequent discussion. In Islamic Algeria, secularization—to the extent that we are justified in using the term at all—is thus embedded in fairly specific conditions, conditions that are also remarkably different from those out of which secularization in the West developed. The presumptive specificity of secularization in the West, which has played a central role in this book's discussions, is something about which Sanson is no less aware than was Max Weber.

Sanson's goal, then, is to emphasize something particular that might be called *laïcité islamique* and to work through its development *within* the structures of Islamic religious belief, structures that remain politically dominant in Algeria in ways that Catholicism clearly does not in France. But I would want to recall all the same (and with no claim of originality whatsoever) that secularization in the West, despite its manifest differences from the Algerian situation outlined by Sanson, *also* arose as much *dedans* as *dehors* its confessional framework, as much via translation and transformation of religious conceptions as via overturning—and certainly without any radical new beginnings (which, as Blumenberg shows quite decisively in my view, should not be expected from intellectual history in any case, Foucault notwithstanding). Moreover, I would argue that those who have tried to rethink the problem of secularization outside the West, and beyond the Weberian assumptions of universal applicability (such as Nandy especially, but to a more moderate extent Chakrabarty, Viswanathan, and even Asad), have in different ways been all too quick to hypostatize Western society as *already* fully secularized society, to discount the degree to which the "double will" Sanson finds in Islamic Algeria still operates, sotto voce, in Western thought, and hence to overlook much of the ambivalence and contradiction that can be found, in different ways, in the writings of Arnold and Woolf, Benjamin and Kracauer, Durkheim and Habermas.

That none of these Western thinkers overtly expects to keep Christianity (or that modern hybrid conflation "Judeo-Christianity") "as a transcendent norm, or further, as a principle of belonging, of reference, of justification, of finality" is obvious. And this is indeed an important difference from what Sanson describes in Algeria, where the political situation has only worsened since Sanson's study, and where the secular socialist state and Islamic militants accuse one another of responsibility for the killing of 100,000 or more civilians during the civil strife of the 1990s. But it is also important to acknowledge the degree to which the appeals of Western intellectuals, from Arnold to Said, to secular criticism take shape for them too *within* the context of religious questions and religious answers, answers at the very least "reoccupied" by secular ideas; and to acknowledge further that even the most overtly secular among them can still maintain his belief that there is "no alternative" to the "continual critical reappropriation and reinterpretation" of the Judeo-Christian legacy if "universalistic egalitarianism," "human rights," "democracy," and so forth are to be maintained (Habermas, *Religion* 149). Just as important, I would argue that most of the rigorous and unflinchingly secular post-Said critiques of the West's dogmatic hubris, at least where knowledge of its others is concerned, have been less than willing to acknowledge the extent of their own implication in the specificity of secularization in the West, the extent to which secular, humanist cultural criticism has been shaped, at times down to its core concepts, by a process that, again, has evolved as much within the confessional lines of religion in the West as outside them.

It should be clear that there is no need to conflate or confuse the specificity of secularization in modern postcolonial Algeria with the specificity of secularization in Arnold's England, Durkheim's France, Benjamin's Germany, or Habermas's EU—and each national situation in Europe, it should be clear, is itself fairly specific. There is, in any case, no easily achieved generality or universality to be had along these lines. But there is also nothing to be gained intellectually by erecting impassable walls between them. And there are very good reasons to recognize certain similarities along a spectrum that runs from Nandy, who maintains the possibility of interconfessional tolerance independent of secularization, to Chakrabarty, who wishes to mine his Bengali past for beliefs and attitudes that might make a necessary modernity in India seem less like an empty imitation of secular Europe, to Habermas, who believes that secular Europe will itself be an empty, desiccated shell of managerial forms unless it remains somehow nourished by the "semantic potentials" of its religious legacy. Moreover, understanding this spectrum in Kracauer's terms as layered strata of "special histories" that nevertheless retain their own temporalities, the different contemporary versions of secularization represented by Nandy, Chakrabarty, Habermas, and even Said can be seen both as the discontinuous products of plural traditions that are themselves multiple and layered, and at the same time as "coeval" (I borrow the term from Fabian 37–69) or "bundled" products of a singular modernity that retains the marks of its subjective synthesis.

"Whatever and however we may try to think, we think within the sphere of tradition," Heidegger wrote at the end of his late essay "The Principle of Identity." "Tradition prevails when it frees us from thinking back to a thinking forward, which is no longer a planning. Only when we turn thoughtfully toward what has already been thought, will we be turned to use for what must still be thought" (Heidegger, *Identity* 41). What I would like to imagine, then, is a version of secular cultural criticism newly engaged by the tensions and inconsistencies in the secularization story, both as that story has unfolded—and continues to unfold—in the West, and as it occurs in different guises and with clearly different results outside the West. But in either case, what is important (as Asad and others before him noted) is that the static and totalizing concept of secularism—connoting an already achieved and reliably reproducible intellectual standpoint—be supplanted with a dynamic understanding of secularization, that is, with a process that has remained, at least up to the present, in some ambiguous relationship with religious tradition, neither translation and transformation, nor radical overturning and forgetting.

Bibliography

Abrams, M. H. *Natural Supernaturalism: Tradition and Revolution in Romantic Literature.* New York: W. W. Norton, 1971.
Acéphale: Religion, sociologie, philosophie, 1936–39. Paris: Editions Jean-Michel Place, 1980.
Adorno, Theodor. *Aesthetic Theory.* Ed. Gretel Adorno and Rolf Tiedemann. Trans. Robert Hullot-Kentor. Minneapolis: University of Minnesota Press, 1997.
———. *The Jargon of Authenticity.* Trans. Knut Tarnowski and Frederic Will. Evanston, IL: Northwestern University Press, 1973.
———. *Notes to Literature.* Vol. 2. Ed. Rolf Tiedemann. Trans. Shierry Weber Nicholsen. New York: Columbia University Press, 1992.
———. *Prisms.* Trans. Samuel and Shierry Weber. Cambridge, MA: MIT Press, 1984.
Adorno, Theodor, and Walter Benjamin. *The Complete Correspondence, 1928–1940.* Ed. Henri Lonitz. Trans. Nicholas Walker. Cambridge, MA: Harvard University Press, 1999.
Ali, Tariq. *The Clash of Fundamentalisms: Crusades, Jihads and Modernity.* London: Verso, 2002.
Almond, Gabriel A., R. Scott Appleby, and Emmanuel Sivan, eds. *Strong Religion: The Rise of Fundamentalisms around the World.* Chicago: University of Chicago Press, 2003.
Anderson, Amanda. *The Powers of Distance: Cosmopolitanism and the Cultivation of Detachment.* Princeton, NJ: Princeton University Press, 2001.
Anderson, Benedict. *Imagined Communities: Reflections on the Origin and Spread of Nationalism.* Rev. ed. London: Verso, 1991.
Annan, Noel. "The Intellectual Aristocracy." *Studies in Social History.* Ed. J. H. Plumb. London: Longmans, Green, 1955, 241–87.
———. *Leslie Stephen: The Godless Victorian.* London: Weidenfeld & Nicolson, 1984.

apRoberts, Ruth. "Frederic E. Faverty's *Matthew Arnold, the Ethnologist*." *The Arnoldian* 15, no. 1 (1987–88): 95–98.

Aquinas, Thomas. *An Aquinas Reader: Selections from the Writings of Thomas Aquinas*. Ed. Mary T. Clark. New York: Fordham University Press, 1988.

Aristotle. *The Complete Works of Aristotle*. Rev. Oxford translation. 2 vols. Ed. Jonathan Barnes. Princeton, NJ: Princeton University Press, 1984.

Arnold, Matthew. *Complete Prose Works*. 11 vols. Ed. R. H. Super. Ann Arbor: University of Michigan Press, 1960–77.

Aron, Raymond. *L'opium des intellectuels*. Paris: Calmann-Lévy, 1955.

Asad, Talal. *Formations of the Secular: Christianity, Islam, and Modernity*. Stanford, CA: Stanford University Press, 2003.

———. *Genealogies of Religion*. Baltimore, MD: Johns Hopkins University Press, 1993.

Auerbach, Erich. *Mimesis: The Representation of Reality in Western Literature*. Fiftieth anniversary ed. Trans. Willard R. Trask. Intro. Edward W. Said. Princeton, NJ: Princeton University Press, 2003.

Baader, Franz von. *Sämmtliche Werke*. 16 vols. Ed. Franz Hoffman, Julius Hamberger, Anton Lutterbeck, F. von Osten, and Christoph Schlüter. Leipzig: Herrmann Bethmann, 1851–60.

Bacon, Francis. *The Great Instauration; and, New Atlantis*. Ed. J. Weinberger. Arlington Heights, IL: Harlan Davidson, 1980.

Barker, Eileen, James A. Beckford, and Karel Dobbelaere, eds. *Secularization, Rationalism, and Sectarianism: Essays in Honour of Bryan R. Wilson*. Oxford: Clarendon Press, 1993.

Bataille, Georges. *Théorie de la religion*. Paris: Editions Gallimard, 1973.

———. *Visions of Excess: Selected Writings, 1927–1939*. Ed. Allan Stoekl. Trans. Allan Stoekl, with Carl R. Lovitt and Donald M. Leslie Jr. Theory and History of Literature 14. Minneapolis: University of Minnesota Press, 1985.

Bataille, Georges, and Michel Leiris, Marcel Griaule, Carl Einstein, Robert Desnos, et al. *Encyclopaedia Acephalica*. Ed. Alastair Brotchie. Trans. Iain White et al. London: Atlas Press, 1995.

Beer, Gillian. *Arguing with the Past: Essays in Narrative from Woolf to Sidney*. London: Routledge, 1989.

Bell, Clive. *Art*. New York: Frederick A. Stokes, 1914.

Bell, David A. *The Cult of the Nation in France: Inventing Nationalism, 1680–1800*. Cambridge, MA: Harvard University Press, 2001.

Bell, Quentin. *Bloomsbury*. London: Omega, 1974.

Bellah, Robert. *Beyond Belief: Essays on Religion in a Post-Traditional World*. New York: Harper & Row, 1970.

Benda, Julien. *La trahison des clercs*. Paris: B. Grasset, 1927.

Benhabib, Seyla. *Critique, Norm, and Utopia: A Study of the Foundations of Critical Theory*. New York: Columbia University Press, 1986.

Benjamin, Walter. *The Arcades Project*. Trans. Howard Eiland and Kevin McLaughlin. Cambridge, MA: Belknap Press of Harvard University Press, 1999.

———. *Correspondence of Walter Benjamin*. Ed. Gerschom Scholem and Theodor Adorno. Trans. Manfred R. Jacobson and Evelyn M. Jacobson. Chicago: University of Chicago Press, 1994.

———. *Gesammelte Briefe*. 4 vols. Ed. Christoph Gödde and Henri Lonitz. Frankfurt am Main: Suhrkamp Verlag, 1995.

———. *Gesammelte Schriften*. Ed. Rolf Tiedemann and Hermann Schweppenhäuser. Suhrkamp Verlag, 1972–89.

———. *Origins of German Tragic Drama*. Trans. John Osborne. London: Verso, 1985.

———. *Schriften*. 2 vols. Ed. Theodor Adorno and Gretel Adorno. Frankfurt: Suhrkamp, 1955.

———. *Selected Writings*. Vol. 1: 1913–26. Ed. Marcus Bullock and Michael Jennings. Trans. Edmund Jephcott et al. Cambridge, MA: Belknap Press of Harvard University Press, 1996.

———. *Selected Writings*. Vol. 2: 1927–34. Ed. Michael Jennings, Howard Eiland, and Gray Smith. Trans. Edmund Jephcott et al. Cambridge, MA: Belknap Press of Harvard University Press, 1999.

———. *Selected Writings*. Vol. 3: 1935–38. Ed. Michael W. Jennings, Marcus Bullock, Howard Eiland, and Gary Smith. Trans. Edmund Jephcott et al. Cambridge, MA: Belknap Press of Harvard University Press, 2002.

———. *Selected Writings*. Vol. 4: 1938–40. Ed. Howard Eiland and Michael Jennings. Trans. Edmund Jephcott et al. Cambridge, MA: Belknap Press of Harvard University Press, 2003.

Berger, Peter L. *The Sacred Canopy: Elements of a Sociological Theory of Religion*. Garden City, NY: Doubleday, 1967.

———, ed. *The Desecularization of the World: Resurgent Religion and World Politics*. New York: William B. Erdmans, 1999.

Berlin, Isaiah. *Against the Current: Essays in the History of Ideas*. Ed. Henry Hardy. Princeton, NJ: Princeton University Press, 2001.

———. *The Crooked Timber of Humanity*. London: John Murray, 1990.

———. *The Hedgehog and the Fox: An Essay on Tolstoy's View of History*. London: Grove, Weidenfeld & Nicolson, 1953.

Berman, Jessica. *Modernist Fiction, Cosmopolitanism, and the Politics of Community*. Cambridge: Cambridge University Press, 2001.

Bersani, Leo. *The Culture of Redemption*. Cambridge, MA: Harvard University Press, 1990.

Bhabha, Homi. "Of Mimicry and Man: The Ambivalence of Colonial Discourse." *October: The First Decade, 1976–1986*. Ed. Annette Michelson et al. Cambridge, MA: MIT Press, 1987, 317–26.

Biale, David. *Gershom Scholem: Kabbalah and Counter-History*. Cambridge, MA: Harvard University Press, 1979.

Bloch, Ernst. *Spirit of Utopia*. Trans. Anthony Nassar. Stanford, CA: Stanford University Press, 2000.

Blumenberg, Hans. *The Legitimacy of the Modern Age*. Trans. Robert M. Wallace. Cambridge, MA: MIT Press, 1985.

———. "On a Lineage of the Idea of Progress." *Social Research* 41 (1974): 5–27.

Bourdieu, Pierre. *Outline of a Theory of Practice*. Trans. Richard Nice. Cambridge: Cambridge University Press, 1990.

Brennan, Timothy. *At Home in the World: Cosmopolitanism Now*. Cambridge, MA: Harvard University Press, 1997.

Brooks, Cleanth. *Community, Religion, and Literature*. Columbia: University of Missouri Press, 1995.

Brown, Callum G. "A Revisionist Approach to Religious Change." *Religion and Modernization: Sociologists and Historians Debate the Secularization Thesis.* Ed. Steve Bruce. Oxford: Clarendon Press, 1992, 31–58.

Bruce, Steve, ed. *Religion and Modernization: Sociologists and Historians Debate the Secularization Thesis.* Ed. Steve Bruce. Oxford: Clarendon Press, 1992.

Burckhardt, Jacob. *The Civilisation of the Renaissance in Italy.* Trans. S. G. C. Middlemore. London: Swan Sonnenschein, 1904.

Burke, Peter. *The Italian Renaissance: Culture and Society in Italy.* Rev. ed. Princeton, NJ: Princeton University Press, 1987.

Burnouf, Emile. *The Science of Religions.* Trans. Julie Liebe. London: S. Sonnenschein, Lowrey, 1888.

Bury, J. B. *The Idea of Progress.* New York: 1932.

Bush, Ronald. "The Presence of the Past: Ethnographic Thinking/Literary Politics." *Prehistories of the Future: The Primitivist Project and the Culture of Modernism.* Ed. Elazar Barkan and Ronald Bush. Stanford, CA: Stanford University Press, 1995, 23–41.

Buzard, James. "Notes on the Defenestration of Culture." *Disciplinarity at the Fin de Siècle.* Ed. Amanda Anderson and Joseph Valente. Princeton, NJ: Princeton University Press, 2002, 312–31.

Calvin, John. *Institutes of the Christian Religion.* 2 vols. Trans. John Allen. Philadelphia: Presbyterian Board of Christian Education, 1935.

Casanova, Pascal. *The World Republic of Letters.* Trans. M. B. DeBevoise. Cambridge, MA: Harvard University Press, 2005.

Cassirer, Ernst. *The Philosophy of the Enlightenment.* Trans. Fritz C. A. Koelln and James P. Pettegrove. Princeton, NJ: Princeton University Press, 1951.

Chadwick, Owen. *The Secularization of the European Mind in the Nineteenth Century.* Cambridge: Cambridge University Press, 1990.

Chakrabarty, Dipesh. *Provincializing Europe: Postcolonial Thought and Historical Difference.* Princeton, NJ: Princeton University Press, 2000.

Chapman, Malcolm. *The Celts: The Construction of a Myth.* New York: St. Martin's Press, 1992.

———. *The Gaelic Vision in Scottish Culture.* London: Croom Helm, 1978.

Cohen, H. Floris. *The Scientific Revolution: A Historiographical Inquiry.* Chicago: University of Chicago Press, 1994.

Colley, Linda. *Britons.* New Haven, CT: Yale University Press, 1992.

Connell, Matt. "Through the Eyes of the Artificial Angel: Secular Theology in Theodor Adorno's Freudo-Marxist Reading of Franz Kafka and Walter Benjamin." *Trajectories of Mysticism in Theory and Literature.* Ed. Philip Leonard. London: Macmillan, 2000, 198–218.

Conrad, Joseph. *Heart of Darkness.* Ed. Robert Kimbrough. New York: Norton, 1988.

———. *Lord Jim.* Ed. Thomas Moser. New York: Norton, 1968.

Cornford, F. M. *From Religion to Philosophy: A Study in the Origins of Western Speculation.* Princeton, NJ: Princeton University Press, 1991.

Coulson, John. *Religion and Imagination: "In Aid of a Grammar of Assent."* Oxford: Clarendon Press, 1981.
Crapanzano, Vincent. "The Moment of Prestidigitation: Magic, Illusion, and Mana in the Thought of Emile Durkheim and Marcel Mauss." *Prehistories of the Future: The Primitivist Project and the Culture of Modernism.* Ed. Elazar Barkan and Ronald Bush. Stanford, CA: Stanford University Press, 1995, 95–113.
Crusius, Irene, ed. *Zur Säkularisation geistlicher Institutionen im 16. und im 18./19. Jahrhundert.* Göttingen: Vandenhoeck & Ruprecht, 1996.
Davie, Grace. *Religion in Modern Europe: A Memory Mutates.* Oxford: Oxford University Press, 2000.
DeKoven, Marianne. *Rich and Strange: Gender, History, Modernism.* Princeton, NJ: Princeton University Press, 1991.
DeLaura, David J. *Hebrew and Hellene in Victorian England.* Austin: University of Texas Press, 1969.
Derrida, Jacques. *Acts of Religion.* Ed. Gil Anidjar. New York: Routledge, 2002.
———. *Of Grammatology.* Trans. Gayatri Chakravorty Spivak. Baltimore, MD: Johns Hopkins University Press, 1976.
———. *Margins of Philosophy.* Trans. Alan Bass. Chicago: University of Chicago Press, 1982.
———. *Spectres of Marx: The State of the Debt, the Work of Mourning, and the New International.* Trans. Peggy Kamuf. New York: Routledge, 1994.
DeSalvo, Louise A. *Virginia Woolf's First Voyage: A Novel in the Making.* Totowa, NJ: Rowman & Littlefield, 1980.
Diderot, Denis. *Oeuvres.* 5 vols. Ed. Laurent Versini. Paris: Robert Laffont, 1994.
Dieckhoff, Reiner. *Mythos und Moderne: Uber die verborgene Mystik in den Schriften Walter Benjamins.* Cologne: Janus Presse, 1987.
Dobbelaere, Karel. "Secularization: A Multi-Dimensional Concept." *Current Sociology* 29, no. 2 (1981): 1–216.
Duara, Prasenjit. *Rescuing History from the Nation: Questioning Narratives of Modern China.* Chicago: University of Chicago Press, 1995.
Du Bois, W. E. B. *The Souls of Black Folk.* New York: Penguin, 1989.
Durkheim, Emile. *The Division of Labor in Society.* Trans. W. D. Halls. New York: Free Press, 1984.
———. *The Elementary Forms of Religious Life.* Trans. Karen E. Fields. New York: Free Press, 1995.
———. *Les formes élémentaires de la vie religieuse: Le système totémique en Australie.* Paris: Presses Universitaires de France, 1968.
———. *Professional Ethics and Civic Morals.* London: Routledge, 1957.
———. *Rules of Sociological Method.* Ed. Steven Lukes. Trans. W. D. Halls. New York: Free Press, 1982.
———. *Le suicide: Etude de sociologie.* Paris: Quadrige-PUF, 1930.
Durkheim, Emile, and Marcel Mauss. "De quelques formes primitives de classification." *L'année sociologique* 6 (1901–2): 1–72.
Edwards, W. F. *Recherches sur les langues celtiques.* Paris: Imprimerie royale, 1844.
Eliade, Mircea. *The Sacred and the Profane.* Trans. Willard R. Trask. New York: Harper & Brothers, 1959.

Eliot, T. S. *After Strange Gods*. London: Faber & Faber, 1934.

———. "Durkheim." Review of Emile Durkheim, *The Elementary Forms of the Religious Life*, trans. J. W. Swain (London: George Allen & Unwin, 1915). Reprinted in Louis Menand and Sanford Schwartz. "T. S. Eliot on Durkheim." *Modern Philology* 79, no. 3 (February 1982): 309–15.

———. *Notes towards the Definition of Culture*. New York: Harcourt, Brace, 1949.

———. "Review of Emile Durkheim, *The Elementary Forms of the Religious Life*, trans. J. W. Swain." *Monist* 28, no. 1 (January 1918): 158–59.

———. *Selected Prose of T. S. Eliot*. Ed. Frank Kermode. New York: Harcourt Brace Jovanovich, 1975.

Ellmann, Richard. *James Joyce*. Rev. ed. Oxford: Oxford University Press, 1983.

———, ed. *Edwardians and Late Victorians*. English Institute Essays, 1959. New York: Columbia University Press, 1960.

Fabian, Johannes. *Time and the Other: How Anthropology Makes Its Object*. New York: Columbia University Press, 1983.

Fagan, Henry Stuart. "Notices of Books." *Contemporary Review* 6 (1867): 257–61.

Falck, Colin. *Myth, Truth and Literature: Towards a True Post-Modernism*. 2nd ed. Cambridge: Cambridge University Press, 1994.

Faverty, Frederic. *Matthew Arnold, the Ethnologist*. Evanston, IL: Northwestern University Press, 1951.

Ferry, Luc. *L'Homme-Dieu, ou le sens de la vie*. Paris: Grasset, 1996.

Fichte, Johann Gottlieb. *Addresses to the German Nation*. Trans. R. F. Jones and G. H. Turnbull. Westport, CT: Greenwood Press, 1979.

Fish, Stanley. *The Trouble with Principle*. Cambridge, MA: Harvard University Press, 2001.

Fletcher, Richard. *The Cross and the Crescent: Christianity and Islam from Muhammad to the Reformation*. New York: Viking Books, 2004.

Foucault, Michel. *Histoire de la folie*. Paris: Librairie Plon, 1961.

———. "Nietzsche, Genealogy, History." *Language, Counter-Memory, Practice*. Ed. Donald F. Bouchard. Trans. Donald F. Bouchard and Sherry Simon. Ithaca, NY: Cornell University Press, 1977, 139–64.

Freeden, Michael. *The New Liberalism: An Ideology of Social Reform*. Oxford: Clarendon Press, 1978.

Frye, Northrop. *Anatomy of Criticism*. Princeton, NJ: Princeton University Press, 1957.

Gallagher, Catherine. "George Eliot and Daniel Deronda: The Prostitute and the Jewish Question." *Sex, Politics, and Science in the Nineteenth-Century Novel*. Ed. Ruth Bernard Yeazell. Selected Papers from the English Institute, 1983–84, new series, no. 10. Baltimore, MD: Johns Hopkins University Press, 1986, 39–62.

Gauchet, Marcel. *The Disenchantment of the World: A Political History of Religion*. Trans. Oscar Burge. Princeton, NJ: Princeton University Press, 1997.

Geertz, Clifford. *The Interpretation of Cultures*. New York: Basic Books, 1973.

Gehlen, Arnold. "Die Säkularisierung des Forstschrifts." *Einblicke*. Vol. 7. Ed. K. S. Rehberg. Frankfurt: Klostermann, 1978.

Gellner, Ernest. *Nations and Nationalism*. Ithaca, NY: Cornell University Press, 1983.

Giddens, Anthony. *Capitalism and Modern Social Theory: An Analysis of the Writings of Marx, Durkheim, and Max Weber*. Cambridge: Cambridge University Press, 1971.

Gilman, Sander. "Ethnicity-Ethnicities-Literature-Literatures." *PMLA* 113 (1998): 19–27.
Gordon, David J. *Literary Atheism*. New York: Peter Lang, 2002.
Gossman, Lionel. "Philhellenism and Antisemitism: Mathew Arnold and his German Models." *Comparative Literature* 46 (1994): 1–39.
Gottfried, Leon. *Matthew Arnold and the Romantics*. London: Routledge & Kegan Paul, 1963.
Graff, Gerald. "Arnold, Reason, and Common Culture." Mathew Arnold, *Culture and Anarchy*. Ed. Samuel Lipman. New Haven, CT: Yale University Press, 1994, 186–201.
Gunn, Giles. *The Culture of Criticism and the Criticism of Culture*. New York: Oxford University Press, 1987.
———. *The Interpretation of Otherness: Literature, Religion, and the American Imagination*. New York: Oxford University Press, 1979.
———. "On Edward W. Said." *Raritan* 23, no. 4 (Spring 2004): 71–78.
———, ed. *Literature and Religion*. New York: Harper & Row, 1971.
Habermas, Jürgen. "Citizenship and National Identity: Some Reflections on the Future of Europe." *Praxis International* 12, no. 1 (April 1992): 1–19.
———. *Legitimation Crisis*. Trans. Thomas McCarthy. Boston: Beacon Press, 1975.
———. *Nachmetaphysiches Denken*. Frankfurt am Main: Suhrkamp, 1988. Cited in "Transcendence." Trans. Eric Crump and Peter P. Kenny. *Religion and Rationality: Essays on Reason, God, and Modernity*. Ed. Eduardo Mendieta. Cambridge, MA: MIT Press, 2002, 79.
———. *Philosophical Discourse of Modernity*. Trans. Frederick Lawrence. Cambridge, MA: Harvard University Press, 1987.
———. *The Postnational Constellation: Political Essays*. Trans. Max Pensky. Cambridge: Polity Press, 2001.
———. *Religion and Rationality: Essays on Reason, God, and Modernity*. Ed. Eduardo Mendieta. Cambridge, MA: MIT Press, 2002.
———. *The Structural Transformation of the Public Sphere: An Inquiry into a Category of Bourgeois Society*. Trans. Thomas Burger, with the assistance of Frederick Lawrence. Cambridge, MA: MIT Press, 1989.
———. *Theory and Practice*. Trans. John Viertel. Boston: Beacon Press, 1973.
———. "Walter Benjamin: Consciousness-Raising or Rescuing Critique." *Philosophical-Political Profiles*. Trans. Frederick G. Lawrence. Cambridge, MA: MIT Press, 1983, 129–63.
Handelman, Susan A. *Fragments of Redemption: Jewish Thought and Literary Theory in Benjamin, Scholem, and Levinas*. Bloomington: Indiana University Press, 1991.
Hanson, Ellis. *Decadence and Catholicism*. Cambridge, MA: Harvard University Press, 1997.
Harrington, Austin. "Ernst Troeltsch's Concept of Europe." *European Journal of Social Theory* 7, no. 4 (2004): 479–98.
Harrison, Jane. *Unanimism: A Study of Conversion and Some Contemporary French Poets. Being A Paper Read before "The Heretics" on November 25, 1912*. Cambridge: Express\ Printing, 1913.
Harrison, Thomas. *1910: The Emancipation of Dissonance*. Berkeley: University of California Press, 1996.

Hartman, Geoffrey. *Criticism in the Wilderness: The Study of Literature Today.* New Haven, CT: Yale University Press, 1980.
Hauriou, Maurice. "The Theory of the Institution and the Foundation: A Study in Social Vitalism." *The French Institutionalists: Maurice Hauriou, Georges Renard, and Joseph T. Delos.* Ed. Albert Broderick. Trans. Mary Welling. Cambridge, MA: Harvard University Press, 1970.
Hazlitt, William. *The Collected Works of William Hazlitt.* 12 vols. Ed. A. R. Waller and Arnold Glover. London: J. M. Dent, 1902–4.
Hegel, G. W. F. *Phenomenology of Spirit.* Trans. A. V. Miller. Oxford: Oxford University Press, 1977.
———. *The Philosophy of History.* Trans. J. Sibree. New York: Dover, 1956.
Heidegger, Martin. *Identity and Difference.* Trans. Joan Stambaugh. New York: Harper & Row, 1969.
———. *Poetry, Language, Thought.* Trans. Albert Hofstadter. New York: Harper Colophon, 1971.
Heine, Heinrich. "Ludwig Börne: Eine Denkschrift." 1841. *Werke und Briefe.* Ed. Kans Kaufmann. 10 vols. Berlin: Aufbau-Verlag, 1962, 6:83–229.
Herbert, Christopher. *Culture and Anomie: Ethnographic Imagination in the Nineteenth Century.* Chicago: University of Chicago Press, 1991.
Herf, Jeffrey. *Reactionary Modernism: Technology, Culture, and Politics in Weimar and the Third Reich.* Cambridge, MA: Harvard University Press, 1984.
Hill, Christopher. *Puritanism and Revolution: Studies in the Interpretation of the English Revolution of the 17th Century.* New York: Schocken, 1964.
Hohendahl, Peter Uwe, ed. *Patriotism, Cosmopolitanism, and National Culture: Public Culture in Hamburg, 1700–1933.* Amsterdam: Rodopi, 2003.
Hollier, Denis. *Le Collège de sociologie.* Paris: Editions Gallimard, 1979.
Horkheimer, Max, and Adorno, Theodor W. *Dialectic of Enlightenment.* Trans. Edmund Jephcott. Stanford, CA: Stanford University Press, 2002.
———. *Dialektik der Aufklärung.* New York: Social Studies Association, 1944.
Howse, Ernest Marshall. *Saints in Politics: The Clapham Sect and the Growth of Freedom.* Toronto: University of Toronto Press, 1952.
Hughes, Stuart H. *Consciousness and Society: The Reorientation of European Social Thought, 1890–1930.* New York: Vintage Books, 1958.
Huizinga, Johan. *The Waning of the Middle Ages: A Study of the Forms of Life, Thought, and Art in France and the Netherlands in the XIVth and XVth Centuries.* Trans. F. Hopman. London: E. Arnold, 1937.
Hume, David. *Dialogues Concerning Natural Religion.* Ed. Stanley Tweyman. London: Routledge, 1991.
Huntington, Samuel P. *The Clash of Civilizations and the Remaking of World Order.* New York: Simon & Schuster, 1996.
Israel, Jonathan I. *Radical Enlightenment: Philosophy and the Making of Modernity, 1650–1750.* Oxford: Oxford University Press, 2002.
Jacob, Margaret. *Living the Enlightenment: Freemasonry and Politics in Eighteenth-Century Europe.* Oxford: Oxford University Press, 1992.
James, William. *The Varieties of Religious Experience: A Study in Human Nature.* New York: Mentor/New American Library, 1958.

Jameson, Fredric. *The Political Unconscious: Narrative as a Socially Symbolic Act.* Ithaca, NY: Cornell University Press, 1981.
Joyce, James. *A Portrait of the Artist as a Young Man.* Ed. Chester Anderson. New York: Penguin Books, 1977.
———. *Ulysses.* Ed. Hans Walter Gabler. New York: Vintage, 1986.
Kafka, Franz. "The Truth about Sancho Panza." *The Complete Stories.* Ed. Nahum Glatzer. New York: Schocken Books, 1976.
Kant, Immanuel. *Critique of Pure Reason.* Trans. F. Max Müller. Garden City, NY: Anchor Books, 1966.
Keddie, Nikki. "Secularism and the State: Towards Clarity and Global Comparison." *New Left Review* 226 (October–November 1997): 21–40.
Kelleher, John V. "Matthew Arnold and the Celtic Revival." *Perspectives of Criticism.* Ed. Harry Levin. Cambridge, MA: Harvard University Press, 1950, 197–221.
Ker, Ian Turnbull. *Catholic Revival in English Literature, 1845–1961: Newman, Hopkins, Belloc, Chesterton, Greene, Waugh.* Notre Dame, IN: University of Notre Dame Press, 2003.
Kierkegaard, Sören. *Either/Or.* 2 vols. Ed. and trans. Howard V. Hong and Edna H. Hong. Princeton, NJ: Princeton University Press, 1987.
———. *Fear and Trembling, Repetition.* Ed. and trans. Howard V. Hong and Edna H. Hong. Princeton, NJ: Princeton University Press, 1983.
Kosmin, Barry, and Seymour P. Lachman. *One Nation under God: Religion in Contemporary American Society.* New York: Harmony Books, 1993.
Kracauer, Siegfried. *From Caligari to Hitler: A Psychological Study of the German Film.* Princeton, NJ: Princeton University Press, 1947.
———. *History: The Last Things before the Last.* Completed and ed. Paul Oskar Kristeller. New York: Oxford University Press, 1969.
———. *The Mass Ornament: Weimar Essays.* Trans. and ed. Thomas Y. Levin. Cambridge, MA: Harvard University Press, 1995.
———. *Orpheus in Paris: Offenbach and the Paris of His Time.* Trans. Gwenda David and Eric Mosbacher. New York: Vienna House, 1972.
———. *The Salaried Masses: Duty and Distraction in Weimar Germany.* Trans. Quintin Hoare. London: Verso, 1998.
LaCapra, Dominick. *Emile Durkheim: Sociologist and Philosopher.* Ithaca, NY: Cornell University Press, 1972.
———. *History, Politics, and the Novel.* Ithaca, NY: Cornell University Press, 1987.
Lang, Andrew. "The Celtic Renascence." *Blackwood's Edinburgh Magazine* 161 (1897): 181–92.
Laslett, Peter. *The World We Have Lost.* London: Methuen, 1971.
Lee, Hermione. *The Novels of Virginia Woolf.* London: Methuen, 1977.
———. *Virginia Woolf.* New York: Alfred A. Knopf, 1998.
Lehmann, Hartmut. *Protestantisches Christentum im Prozess der Säkularisierung.* Göttingen: Vandenhoeck & Ruprecht, 2001.
Lenzer, Gertrude, ed. *Auguste Comte and Positivism: The Essential Writings.* New York: Harper & Row, 1975.
Leonard, Philip, ed. *Trajectories of Mysticism in Theory and Literature.* London: Macmillan, 2000.

Lepenies, Wolf. *Between Literature and Science: The Rise of Sociology.* Trans. R. J. Hollingdale. Cambridge: Cambridge University Press, 1988.
Lévi-Strauss, Claude. *Introduction to the Work of Marcel Mauss.* Trans. Felicity Baker. London: Routledge & Kegan Paul, 1987.
———. *The Raw and the Cooked.* Trans. John and Doreen Weightman. Chicago: University of Chicago Press, 1969.
———. *Structural Anthropology.* Vol. 2. Trans. Monique Layton. Chicago: University of Chicago Press, 1983.
———. *Totemism.* Trans. Rodney Needham. Boston: Beacon Press, 1963.
Levy, Paul. *Moore: G. E. Moore and the Cambridge Apostles.* Oxford: Oxford University Press, 1981.
Lewis, Bernard. *What Went Wrong?* Oxford: Oxford University Press, 2002.
———. *Islam and the West.* New York: Oxford University Press, 1993.
Lilla, Mark. "The Lure of Syracuse." *New York Review of Books* 48, no. 14 (September 20, 2001): 81–86.
———. *The Reckless Mind: Intellectuals in Politics.* New York: New York Review Books, 2001.
Lincoln, Bruce. *Holy Terrors: Thinking about Religion after September 11.* Chicago: University of Chicago Press, 2003.
Lloyd, David. "Arnold, Ferguson, Schiller." *Cultural Critique* 1 (1985): 137–69.
Loos, Adolf. *Ornament and Crime: Selected Essays.* Ed. Adolf Opel. Trans. Michael Mitchell. Riverside, CA: Ariadne Press, 1998.
Lotze, Hermann. *Mikrocosmus: Ideen zur Naturgeschichte und Geschichte der Menschheit; Versuch einer Anthropologie.* 3 vols. Leipzig: S. Hirzel, 1876–80.
Löwith, Karl. *Meaning in History.* Chicago: University of Chicago Press, 1949.
Löwy, Michael. "Jewish Messianism and Libertarian Utopia in Central Europe." Trans. Renée B. Larrier. *New German Critique* 20 (Spring–Summer 1980): 105–15.
Lübbe, H. *Säkularisierung: Geschichte einen ideenpolitischen Begriffs.* Freiburg: Alber, 1965.
Luhmann, Niklas. "Positives Recht und Ideologie." *Soziologische Aufklärung: Aufsätze zur Theorie sozialer Systeme.* Köln: Westdeutscher Verlag, 1970, 178–203.
———. "Soziologie des politischen Systems." *Soziologische Aufklärung: Aufsätze zur Theorie sozialer Systeme.* Köln: Westdeutscher Verlag, 1970, 154–77.
Lukács, Georg. *The Destruction of Reason.* Trans. Peter Palmer. Atlantic Highlands, NJ: Humanities Press, 1981.
———. "Reification and the Consciousness of the Proletariat." *History and Class Consciousness.* Trans. Rodney Livingstone. Cambridge, MA: MIT Press, 1968.
Lukes, Steven. *Emile Durkheim: His Life and Work.* New York: Harper & Row, 1972.
Lyotard, Francois. *The Postmodern Condition: A Report on Knowledge.* Trans. Geoff Bennington and Brian Massumi. Theory and History of Literature 10. Minneapolis: University of Minnesota Press, 1984.
MacIntyre, Alasdair. *After Virtue.* 2nd ed. Notre Dame, IN: University of Notre Dame Press, 1984.
Macpherson, James. *Poems of Ossian.* 3 vols. Trans. James Macpherson. London: W. Miller, J. Murray, & J. Harding, 1805.
McCole, John. *Walter Benjamin and the Antinomies of Tradition.* Ithaca, NY: Cornell University Press, 1993.

McLeod, Hugh. *Secularisation in Western Europe, 1848–1914.* London: Palgrave Macmillan, 2000.

McMahon, Darrin M. *Enemies of the Enlightenment: The French Counter-Enlightenment and the Making of Modernity.* Oxford: Oxford University Press, 2002.

Mailloux, Steven. "Contingent Universals: Religious Fundamentalism, Academic Postmodernism, and Public Intellectuals in the Aftermath of September 11." *Cardozo Law Review* 24, no. 4 (2003): 1583–1604.

Maistre, Joseph de. *Etude sur la souveraineté.* In *Oeuvres complètes, I–II.* Geneva: Slatkin Reprints, 1979, 1:311–554.

Manent, Pierre. *The City of Man.* Trans. Marc A. LePain. Princeton, NJ: Princeton University Press, 1998.

Manganaro, Marc. "'Beating a Drum in a Jungle': T. S. Eliot on the Artist as 'Primitive.'" *Modern Language Quarterly* 47, no. 4 (December 1986): 393–421.

Martí, José. *The America of José Martí: Selected Writings of José Martí.* Trans. Juan de Os. New York: Funk & Wagnalls, 1954.

Martin, David. *A General Theory of Secularization.* Oxford: Blackwell, 1978.

Martin, Henri. *Histoire de France, depuis les temps les plus reculés jusqu'en 1789.* 17 vols. Paris: Furne, 1855–60.

Martz, Louis L. *Many Gods and Many Voices: The Role of the Prophet in English and American Modernism.* Columbia: University of Missouri Press, 1998.

Marx, Karl. "A Contribution to the Critique of Hegel's 'Philosophy of Right.'" *Critique of Hegel's Philosophy of Right.* Trans. Annette Jolin and Joseph O'Malley. Ed. Joseph O'Malley. Cambridge: Cambridge University Press, 1970.

―――. *The Eighteenth Brumaire of Louis Bonaparte.* Trans. anon. New York: International, 1981.

―――. "On the Jewish Question." *Selected Writings.* Ed. Lawrence Simon. Trans. Lloyd Easton and Kurt Guddat. Indianapolis, IN: Hackett, 1994, 1–26.

Marx, Karl, and Frederick Engels. *The German Ideology, Part 1.* Ed. C. J. Arthur. Trans. W. Lough. New York: International, 1977.

Menand, Louis, and Sanford Schwartz. "T. S. Eliot on Durkheim." *Modern Philology* 79, no. 3 (February 1982): 309–15.

Michaels, Walter Benn. *Our America: Nativism, Modernism, and Pluralism.* Durham, NC: Duke University Press, 1995.

Milbank, John. *Theology and Social Theory: Beyond Secular Reason.* Oxford: Blackwell, 1990.

―――. *The Word Made Strange: Theology, Language, Culture.* Oxford: Blackwell, 1997.

Mill, John Stuart. "On Liberty." *The Basic Writings of John Stuart Mill.* New York: Modern Library, 2002, 3–119.

―――. *Principles of Political Economy, with Some of Their Applications to Social Philosophy.* London: Longmans, Green, 1909.

Miller, J. Hillis. *Poets of Reality.* Cambridge, MA: Harvard University Press, 1965.

Molitor, Franz Joseph. *Philosophie der Geschichte, oder Über die Tradition in dem alten Bunde und ihre Beziehung zur Kirche des neuen Bundes (mit vorzüglicher Rücksicht auf die Kabbalah).* 3 vols. in 2. Münster: Theissingschen Buchhandlung, 1834–39.

Monod, Jean-Claude. *La querelle de la secularization de Hegel à Blumenberg.* Paris: Librairie Philosophique J. Vrin, 2002.

Nairn, Tom. *The Break-Up of Britain.* London: New Left Books, 1977.
Nandy, Ashis. "The Politics of Secularism and the Recovery of Religious Tolerance." *Mirrors of Violence: Communities, Riots, and Survivors in South Asia.* Ed. Veena Das. Delhi: Oxford University Press, 1990, 69–91.
———. *The Romance of the State and the Fate of Dissent in the Tropics.* Oxford: Oxford University Press, 2003.
Needham, Joseph. *Science and Civilization in China.* 7 vols. Cambridge: Cambridge University Press, 1954.
Nielsen, Donald A. *Three Faces of God: Society, Religion, and the Categories of Totality in the Philosophy of Emile Durkheim.* Albany: State University of New York Press, 1999.
Nietzsche, Friedrich. *Beyond Good and Evil.* Trans. Walter Kaufmann. New York: Vintage Books, 1966.
———. *On the Genealogy of Morals.* Trans. Walter Kaufmann and R. J. Hollingdale. New York: Vintage Books, 1969.
———. *The Use and Abuse of History.* Trans. Adrian Collins. Indianapolis, IN: Bobs-Merrill, 1957.
Nisbet, Robert A. "The French Revolution and the Rise of Sociology." 1943. *Emile Durkheim: Critical Assessments.* Ed. Peter Hamilton. 4 vols. London: Routledge, 1990, 1:38–48.
Nussbaum, Martha. *Women and Human Development: The Capabilities Approach.* Cambridge: Cambridge University Press, 2000.
Orr, John, Archdeacon of Ferns. *The Theory of Religion, in its Absolute Internal State: In Three Parts. I. Of the Nature and End of Religion, its Rise and Progress in the Human Mind, and the Improvement and Reinforcement which it receives from the Revelation of the Gospel. II. Of the Evidences of Nature and Revealed Religion in general; with a Review of some of the most material Objections, which have been urged against them. III. Of the Excellence and Importance of True Religion, With A Conclusion, in relation to the Persons, who disbelieve, or doubt of the Truth of Religion, and likewise to those who profess to be Believers of it.* London: A. Millar, 1762.
Parsons, Talcott. *The Structure of Social Action.* New York: McGraw-Hill, 1937.
Passerin D'Entrèves, Maurizio, and Seyla Benhabib, eds. *Habermas and the Unfinished Project of Modernity.* Cambridge, MA: MIT Press, 1997.
Pecora, Vincent P. *Households of the Soul.* Baltimore, MD: Johns Hopkins University Press, 1997.
———, ed. *Nations and Identities: Classic Readings.* Malden, MA: Blackwell, 2001.
Pew Research Center for the People and the Press. "Among Wealthy Nations . . . U.S. Stands Alone in its Embrace of Religion." *Pew Global Attitudes Project.* Survey report released December 19, 2002. Available online at http://www.people-press.org/reports.
Pew Research Center for the People and the Press and Pew Forum on Religion and Public Life. "Religion and Politics: Contention and Consensus." Survey report released July 24, 2003. Available online at http://www.people-press.org/reports.
Pickering, W. S. F. *Durkheim's Sociology of Religion: Themes and Theories.* London: Routledge & Kegan Paul, 1984.
Pitt, R. "Exploration of Self in Conrad's *Heart of Darkness* and Woolf's *Voyage Out.*" *Conradiana* 10, no. 2 (1978): 141–54.

Popper, Karl. *The Poverty of Historicism*. London: Routledge & Kegan Paul, 1957.
Porter, Roy, and Simon Schama. *Flesh in the Age of Reason: The Modern Foundations of Body and Soul*. New York: W. W. Norton, 2004.
Prince, Morton. *The Dissociation of a Personality: A Biographical Study in Abnormal Psychology*. London: Longmans, Green, 1905.
Prüfer, Sebastian. *Sozialismus statt Religion: Die deutsche Sozialdemokratie vor der religiösen Frage, 1863–1890*. Göttingen: Vandenhoeck & Ruprecht, 2002.
Putnam, Hilary. "Wittgenstein on Religious Belief." *On Community*. Ed. Leroy S. Rounder. Notre Dame, IN: University of Notre Dame, 1991, 56–75.
Rabinbach, Anson. "Between Enlightenment and Apocalypse: Benjamin, Bloch and Modern German Jewish Messianism." *New German Critique* 34 (Winter 1985): 78–124.
Ranulf, Svend. "Scholarly Forerunners of Fascism." 1939. *Emile Durkheim: Critical Assessments*. Ed. Peter Hamilton. 4 vols. London: Routledge, 1990, 1:23–37.
Rawls, John. *Political Liberalism*. New York: Columbia University Press, 1993.
Renan, Ernest. *Essais de morale et de critique*. Paris: Calmann-Lévy, 1924.
_____. *Histoire du peuple d'Israël*. 5 vols. Paris: Calmann-Lévy, 1889–93.
_____. *Qu'est-ce qu'une nation?* Paris: Pierre Bordas et fils, 1991.
Richman, Michèle H. *Sacred Revolutions: Durkheim and the Collège de Sociologie*. Minneapolis: University of Minnesota Press, 2002.
Riesterer, Berthold P. *Karl Löwith's View of History: A Critical Appraisal of Historicism*. The Hague: Martinus Nijhoff, 1969.
Robbins, Bruce. *Feeling Global: Internationalism in Distress*. New York: New York University Press, 1999.
Rorty, Richard. *Philosophy and the Mirror of Nature*. Princeton, NJ: Princeton University Press, 1979.
Rose, Jonathan. *The Edwardian Temperament, 1895–1919*. Athens: Ohio University Press, 1986.
Rosenberg, Alfred. *The Myth of the Twentieth Century*. Trans. Vivian Bird. Newport Beach, CA: Noontide Press, 1982.
Rousseau, Jean-Jacques. *The Government of Poland*. Trans. Willmoore Kendall. Indianapolis, IN: Bobbs-Merrill, 1972.
Rudolf, R. de M., I.S.O. "The Clapham Sect." *Clapham and the Clapham Sect*. Clapham, London: Clapham Antiquarian Society & Edmund Baldwin, 1927, 89–142.
Said, Edward W. *Beginnings: Intention and Method*. New York: Columbia University Press, 1985.
_____. *Culture and Imperialism*. New York: Alfred A. Knopf, 1993.
_____. *Orientalism*. New York: Vintage Books, 1979.
_____. *Reflections on Exile and Other Essays*. Cambridge, MA: Harvard University Press, 2000.
_____. *The World, the Text, and the Critic*. Cambridge, MA: Harvard University Press, 1983.
Sanson, Henri. *Laïcité islamique en Algerie*. Paris: Editions du Centre National de la Recherche Scientifique, 1983.
Sayre, Robert, and Michael Löwy. "Figures of Romantic Anti-Capitalism." *New German Critique* 32 (Spring–Summer 1984): 42–92.

Schiller, Friedrich. *On the Aesthetic Education of Man, in a Series of Letters*. Trans. Reginald Snell. New York: Frederick Ungar, 1983.
Schmitt, Carl. *Political Romanticism*. Trans. Guy Oakes. Cambridge, MA: MIT Press, 1986.
———. *Political Theology: Four Chapters on the Concept of Sovereignty*. Trans. George Schwab. Cambridge, MA: MIT Press, 1985.
———. *Roman Catholicism and Political Form*. Trans. G. L. Ulmen. Westport, CT: Greenwood Press, 1996.
———. *Staat, Bewegung, Volk: Die Dreigliederung der Politischen Einheit*. Hamburg: Hanseatische Verlagsanstalt, 1935.
———. *Über die drei Arten des Rechtswissenschaftlichen Denkens*. Hamburg: Hanseatische Verlagsanstalt, 1934.
Scholem, Gershom G. *Major Trends in Jewish Mysticism*. Rev. ed. New York: Schocken Books, 1941.
———. *On Jews and Judaism in Crisis: Selected Essays*. Ed. Werner J. Dannhauser. New York: Schocken Books, 1976.
———. *Walter Benjamin: The Story of a Friendship*. Trans. Harry Zohn. New York: Schocken, 1981.
Schrempp, Gregory. "Aristotle's Other Self: On the Boundless Subject of Anthropological Discourse." *Romantic Motives: Essays on Anthropological Sensibility*. Ed. George W. Stocking Jr. Madison: University of Wisconsin Press, 1989.
Scott, Nathan A., Jr. *Negative Capability: Studies in the New Literature and the Religious Situation*. New Haven, CT: Yale University Press, 1969.
Senancour, Etienne Pivert de. *Obermann*. Paris: Libraire E. Droz, 1931.
Shapin, Steven. *The Scientific Revolution*. Chicago: University of Chicago Press, 1996.
Silverstein, Brian. "Islam and Modernity in Turkey: Power, Tradition and Historicity in the European Provinces of the Muslim World." *Anthropological Quarterly* 76, no. 3 (2003): 497–517.
Simmel, Georg. *The Conflict in Modern Culture and Other Essays*. Trans. K. Peter Etzkorn. New York: Teacher's College Press, Columbia University, 1968.
———. *The Philosophy of Money*. Trans. Tom Bottomore and David Frisby. London: Routledge & Kegan Paul, 1978.
Sironneau, Jean-Pierre. *Sécularisation et religions politiques*. La Haye: Mouton, 1982.
Smart, J. S. *James Macpherson: An Episode in Literature*. London: David Nutt, 1905.
Smith, Adam. *The Theory of the Moral Sentiments*. Ed. Knud Haakonssen. Cambridge: Cambridge University Press, 2002.
Smith, Anthony D. *National Identity*. London: Penguin, 1991.
———. *Nationalism and Modernism: A Critical Survey of Recent Theories of Nations and Nationalism*. London: Routledge, 1998.
Stark, Rodney. *For the Glory of God: How Monotheism Led to Reformations, Science, Witch-Hunts, and the End of Slavery*. Princeton, NJ: Princeton University Press, 2003.
Stephen, Sir James. *Essays in Ecclesiastical Biography*. London: Longmans, Green, Reader, & Dyer, 1868.
Stephen, Leslie. *Selected Writings in British Intellectual History*. Chicago: University of Chicago Press, 1979.

Stocking, George. "Matthew Arnold, E. B. Tylor, and the Uses of Invention." *American Anthropologist* 65 (1963): 783–99.
Stockton, Kathryn Bond. *God between Their Lips: Desire between Women in Irigaray, Brontë, and Eliot*. Stanford, CA: Stanford University Press, 1994.
Strauss, Leo. *Natural Right and History*. Chicago: University of Chicago Press, 1953.
———. *What Is Political Philosophy? and Other Studies*. Glencoe, IL: Free Press, 1959.
Tan, Kok-chor. *Justice without Borders: Cosmopolitanism, Nationalism, and Patriotism*. Cambridge: Cambridge University Press, 2004.
Taylor, Charles. *Varieties of Religion Today: William James Revisited*. Cambridge, MA: Harvard University Press, 2002.
Taylor, Mark C. *Tears*. New York: State University of New York Press, 1990.
Tennyson, G. B., and Edward E. Ericson Jr., eds. *Religion and Modern Literature: Essays in Theory and Criticism*. Grand Rapids, MI: William B. Eerdmans, 1975.
Thierry, Amédée. *Histoire des gaulois, depuis les temps les plus reculés jusqu'à l'entière soumission de la Gaule à la domination romaine*. 2 vols. Paris: Hachette, 1835.
Tiedemann, Rolf. "Dialectics at a Standstill: Approaches to the *Passagen-Werk*." Walter Benjamin. *The Arcades Project*. Trans. Howard Eiland and Kevin McLaughlin. Cambridge, MA: Belknap Press of Harvard University Press, 1999, 929–45.
———. "Historical Materialism or Political Messianism? An Interpretation of the Theses 'On the Concept of History.'" *Philosophical Forum* 4, no. 1–2 (1983–84): 71–104.
Traverso, Enzo. *The Marxists and the Jewish Question: The History of a Debate, 1843–1943*. Trans. Bernard Gibbons. New Jersey: Humanities Press, 1994.
Trilling, Lionel. *Matthew Arnold*. New York: Harcourt Brace Jovanovich, 1977.
van der Veer, Peter, and Hartmut Lehmann, eds. *Nation and Religion: Perspectives on Europe and Asia*. Princeton, NJ: Princeton University Press, 1999.
Vattimo, Gianni. *The End of Modernity: Nihilism and Hermeneutics in Post-Modern Culture*. Trans. Jon R. Snyder. Cambridge: Polity Press, 1988.
Viswanathan, Gauri. *Masks of Conquest: Literary Study and British Rule in India*. New York: Columbia University Press, 1989.
———. *Outside the Fold: Conversion, Modernity, and Belief*. Princeton, NJ: Princeton University Press, 1998.
Waché, Brigitte. *Religion et culture en Europe occidentale au XIXe siècle*. Paris: Belin, 2002.
Wallace, Robert M. "Progress, Secularization and Modernity: The Löwith-Blumenberg Debate." *New German Critique* 22 (1981): 63–79.
Wallis, Roy, and Steve Bruce. "Secularization: The Orthodox Model." *Religion and Modernization: Sociologists and Historians Debate the Secularization Thesis*. Ed. Steve Bruce. Oxford: Clarendon Press, 1992, 8–30.
Ward, Graham. *Theology and Contemporary Critical Theory*. New York: St. Martin's Press, 1996.
———. *True Religion*. Malden, MA: Blackwell, 2003.
Weber, Max. *Economy and Society: An Outline of Interpretive Sociology*. 2 vols. Ed. Guenther Roth and Claus Wittich. Trans. Ephraim Fischoff et al. Berkeley: University of California Press, 1978.
———. *The Protestant Ethic and the Spirit of Capitalism*. Trans. Talcott Parsons. London: Routledge, 2001.

---. *The Religion of India: The Sociology of Hinduism and Buddhism*. Trans. Hans H. Gerth and Don Martindale. Glencoe, IL: Free Press, 1958.
White, Hayden. *Metahistory: The Historical Imagination in Nineteenth-Century Europe*. Baltimore, MD: Johns Hopkins University Press, 1973.
Wilder, Amos N. *Theology and Modern Literature*. Cambridge, MA: Harvard University Press, 1958.
Williams, Raymond. *Culture and Society, 1780–1950*. New York: Columbia University Press, 1983.
Witte, Bernd. "Paris–Berlin–Paris: Personal, Literary, and Social Experience in Walter Benjamin's Late Works." Trans. Susan B. Winnett. *New German Critique* 39 (Autumn 1986): 49–60.
Wittgenstein, Ludwig. *Lectures and Conversations on Aesthetics, Psychology, and Religious Belief*. Ed. Cyril Barrett. Berkeley: University of California Press, 1966.
Wolin, Richard. *Walter Benjamin: An Aesthetic of Redemption*. Rev. ed. Berkeley: University of California Press, 1994.
Wolosky, Shira. *The Negative Way of Language in Eliot, Beckett, and Celan*. Stanford, CA: Stanford University Press, 1995.
Woolf, Virginia. *Between the Acts*. New York: Harcourt Brace Jovanovich, 1969.
---. *The Diary of Virginia Woolf*. 5 vols. Ed. Anne Olivier Bell. London: Hogarth Press, 1977.
---. *Melymbrosia*. Ed. Louise A. DeSalvo. New York: New York Public Library, Astor, Lenox & Tilden Foundations, 1982.
---. *Moments of Being*. Ed. Jeanne Schulkind. San Diego: Harcourt Brace, 1985.
---. "Mr. Bennett and Mrs. Brown." 1924. *Collected Essays*. London: Hogarth Press, 1966, 1:319–37.
---. *Mrs. Dalloway*. New York: Harcourt Brace Jovanovich, 1953.
---. *Night and Day*. San Diego: Harcourt, 1948.
---. *Three Guineas*. San Diego: Harcourt Brace, 1966.
---. *To the Lighthouse*. New York: Harcourt Brace Jovanovich, 1955.
---. *The Voyage Out*. New York: Modern Library, 2001.
---. *The Waves*. New York: Harcourt Brace & World, 1959.
Yates, Frances. *Giordano Bruno and the Hermetic Tradition*. Chicago: University of Chicago Press, 1964.
Yeats, William Butler. "The Celtic Element in Literature." *Ideas of Good and Evil*. London: A. H. Bullen, 1903, 270–95.
Young, Robert J. C. *Colonial Desire: Hybridity in Theory, Culture, and Race*. London: Routledge, 1995.

Index

Abbaye, l': and Unanimism, 117
Abrams, M. H., 26; on "natural supernaturalism," 33, 106, 157
Acéphale: and *Acéphale* (the journal), 124; and Bataille, 119, 120; and Caillois, 120; and Durkheim, 119–20; and Ku Klux Klan, 120; and Society of Jesus, 120; and Unanimism, 120
Action Française, Institute de l,' 110, 122
Adorno, Theodor, 5; and Benjamin, 86; on cultural criticism, 17–20, 196; and "dialectic of enlightenment," 33, 73, 102–3; and Horkheimer, 102–3; and Kracauer, 73, 74, 75, 86
African American churches, 16
Alembert, Jean le Rond d,' 106
Alexander the Great, 106
Ali, Tariq, 14
Almond, Gabriel A., 14, 31
Anderson, Amanda, 196
Anderson, Benedict, 15; on nation as "imagined community," 110
animism, 107
Annan, Noel: on Clapham Sect relationship to Bloomsbury group, 167–68; on Evangelicalism, 163; on intellectual aristocracy, 165; on "spirit of the coterie," 167–68; on utilitarianism of Leslie Stephen compared to Evangelicalism, 172, 177
Apostles (at Cambridge), 165, 175; and immortality of the soul, 187
Appleby, R. Scott, 14, 31
apRoberts, Ruth, 139
Aquinas, 53, 56, 59, 121
Aristotle, 111; and Aquinas, 56, 59, 61; and Arnold, 132, 133, 137; and Blumenberg, 59, 60, 62, 63, 200; on entelechy of nature, 25, 62; and Habermas, 55–57, 94; vs. Judeo-Christian sense of history, 57, 60; MacIntyre on, 54–57, 59, 63, 166; and natural law, 52; and Smith, Adam 55–56
Arnold, Matthew, 18, 55, 63, 131–56, 166; and anti-Christian thought, 135; and anti-Semitism, 135, 136, 153; and Aristotelian entelechy, 132, 133, 137; and Aryans, 154, 156; on Barbarians (modern aristocrats), 146; and Buckle, 140; and Bunsen, 155–56; and Burnouf, 138–39, 154, 156; and Byron, 135, 146; and Calvin, 132, 133; on the Celts, 132, 138–54; and class, 139; and Conrad, 136, 149; on culture, 131, 132, 136–37, 141, 143, 144, 151, 156; and cultural criticism, 197; and cultural studies, 131, 143; and *Culture and Anarchy*, 131,

Arnold, Matthew (*continued*)
136–38, 139, 140–41, 143, 144, 146, 147, 153, 154; and Darwin, 148; and David, 156; and Defoe, 148; on dissenting Protestantism, 132–34, 135, 136, 146, 154–55; and Edwards, 142; and Emerson, 140; on the English, 132, 146–50, 154–56; and ethnology, 132, 138–54; and Forster, 135; on the French, 148, 149, 150; on the Germans, 148, 159; and Gobineau, 141, 154; and Goethe, 135; and Hardy, 135; and Hegel, 135, 141; and Heine, 135, 136; on Hellenism vs. Hebraism, 3, 24, 132, 133, 134, 135–39, 140, 146, 149, 153, 154–56, 195; and Hölderlin, 135; humanism of, 131, 132, 140, 141; and the humanities, 198; and Humboldt brothers, 135; and hybrid vigor, 131, 147, 149, 150, 151–52; on Indo-Europeans, 139, 141, 153, 154–56; and the Irish, 144, 145, 147, 150; and Joshua, 156; and Joyce, 135–36, 144; and Judaism, 134, 154, 155; and Judeo-Christian tradition, 132; on Keats, 146; and Lang, 144, 150; and Lawrence, 136; on letter of Jewish law, 133, 136; and linguistic basis of race, 134; and Lytton, 147; and Macpherson, 144, 145, 146; on Maistre, 144; on Marcus Aurelius, 142; and Martin, Henri, 142; and Mill, 150; on Milton, 146; and modernization, 145; and Monod's alternative accounts of secularization, 132; and nation, 131, 132, 134, 138, 139, 143–44, 147–48, 149, 153; and Nietzsche, 135; on the Normans, 148, 149; and *On the Study of Celtic Literature*, 131, 132, 138–54; and Ossian, 145; and Pater, 135; and philhellenism, 135–36; on Philistines, 135, 137; on Plato, 156; and race, 131, 132, 134, 136, 137, 138, 139, 141, 143, 144–56; and race as substitute for religion, 135, 152, 153; on religious traditions, 131, 132, 136–37, 144, 153; and Renan, 142, 144, 145, 146, 148, 150, 154; on repressed cultural traditions, 131, 145; and Rhys, 144; on Romans, 148, 149, 150; on Saint Paul, 132–35, 155; and Sand, 146; and Schiller, 135; and Schleiermacher, 132, 155–56; and secularization, 133, 134, 135, 137, 143, 153, 206, 207; on Semites, 133–34, 139, 154, 155–56; on Senancour, 145; on Shakespeare, 146; on Shelley, 135; on Socrates, 156; on Spinoza, 142; on spirit of Christian morality, 133, 134; and Strangford, 140; on "sweetness and light," 131, 141, 146, 147; on Teutons/Saxons, 141, 146, 147, 149, 150, 153, 154; and Thierry, 142; and Thomas Arnold, 136, 155; and Tylor, 137, 140; and Wilde, 135; and Winckelmann, 135; and Wolf, 135; on Wordsworth, 135, 146; and Yeats, 144, 150
Arnold, Thomas, 136
Arnot, Robin Page, 169
Aron, Raymond, 89, 115, 116; and *trahison des clercs*, 123
Asad, Talal, 1, 5, 6, 23, 24, 35, 51, 54; on anthropology of secularism, 42, 206, 207; on civil society, 41; and critique of humanism, 198, 199; and discrepant experience, 43; on genital mutilation, 42, 43; on human rights, 42, 53, 64; on Islam, 41; and Nandy, 41, 43; on the nation-state, 41; on recognition of religion vs. tolerance, 41, 43; and Said, 41–43; and secularization, 41–43, 66, 207; and Viswanathan, 41
asceticism, 12, 20
Auerbach, Erich, 33; and Dante, 40, 196; on disintegration of Judeo-Christian and humanist tradition, 189; on T. S. Eliot, 189; on Greek world view vs. Old Testament, 57; and historicism, 157; on Joyce, 189; on Proust, 189; on random moment, 189–91; Said's account of, 40; and secularization, 191; on Virginia Woolf and modernism, 189–91
Augustine, 11, 106

Baader, Franz von, 53, 80, 84; and Benjamin, 80–82; and Böhme, 81, 82; and

Burke, 81; and Durkheim, 81; on historical humanity as sacrificial lamb, 81–82, 99; and Kant, 81; and Maistre, 81; and Molitor, 80–82; and Rousseau, 81; and Schelling, 80, 81

Bacon, Francis, 25, 102, 195
Barker, Eileen, 6
Barrès, Maurice, 110
Bataille, Georges, 96, 111; and Acéphale, 119, 120, 122; and *Acéphale* (the journal), 124; and Caillois, 120; and Durkheim, 119, 122; and T. S. Eliot, 123; on Islam, 119; and Kierkegaard, 124; and nature of society, 120; and Nietzsche, 119; and occultism, 119–20; and Schmitt, 124
Baudelaire, Charles, 79, 96, 157
Bauer, Bruno, 48–49
Bayle, Pierre, 105
Beckett, Samuel, 157
Beckford, James A., 6
Beer, Gillian: on Virginia Woolf, 170, 171
Beethoven, Ludwig van, 184
Bell, Clive, 165, 175; on aesthetic and religious ecstasy, 188
Bell, David, 28
Bell, Quentin, 165
Bellah, Robert, 12–13
Benda, Julien: and *trahison des clercs*, 123
Benhabib, Seyla, 30, 104; and Benjamin's messianism, 94; and Bersani, 95; on Habermas, 94–95; and Kracauer, 94; and Marcuse, 95
Benjamin, Walter, 23–24, 32; and Adorno, 86; and aesthetic aura, 92; and anarchism, 87; and art, 95; on awakening the dead, 78, 88; and Baader, 80–82, 83, 84, 99; on Baudelaire, 79, 86; and Benhabib, 94; and Bloch, 32, 59, 77; and Blumenthal, 80; and Buber, 98; and Catholic philosophy of history, 67, 80–85; on collecting, 86; on communism, 84; and counter-Enlightenment, 87; and cultural criticism, 77; and Derrida, 88, 93; on "dialectics at a standstill," 73, 79; on empty time, 68, 86, 92; and Foucault, 93; and German Youth Culture, 79, 80, 83, 84, 85; and Habermas, 87, 89, 92–95, 96; on the hunchback of religion, 91; on *die Jetztzeit* (now-time), 76, 78, 84, 87, 91, 93, 95, 96, 100; and Judaism, 88, 98; and Kaballah, 67, 78–85, 87, 93, 99, 104; on Kafka's Sancho Panza, 91; and Kierkegaard, 88, 124; and Klee, 87; and Kracauer, 67, 72–76, 85–92, 93, 96, 99–100, 101; on liturgical time, 86, 89, 91; and Loos, 72; on Lotze, 84; and Lukács, 72, 98; and Luria, 78–79, 83, 84, 85; and Luther, 80; and Marburg School, 62; and Marx, 67, 72, 76–78, 84, 85, 86, 87, 93, 99; and messianism, 67, 73, 75–85, 93, 95, 99, 119; and F. J. Molitor, 80, 81, 82–85; and R. Molitor, 81; and Nietzsche, 84, 96, 98; and Novalis, 80; and political theology, 84, 97; on popular culture, 72, 73; on Proust, 86, 89, 91; and Pulver, 80; and Reformation, 80; on rejection of progress, 58, 60, 65, 77, 84, 86, 87, 88, 99, 100; on Robespierre, 87; and Rychner, 84; and Saint-Martin, 81; and Schelling, 80; and Schlegel brothers, 80; and Schmitt, 88; and Scholem, 77, 78, 79, 80, 81, 82, 85, 98; and secularization, 84, 206, 207; and Seligson, 83, 84; and Simmel, 72, 73; on social democracy, 86, 88; and Sorel, 87; on Talmudic interpretation, 84; and "Theses on the Philosophy of History," 75–78, 82, 85–89, 91, 93, 94, 95, 96, 97, 98, 99; and Winstanley, 80; and Wyneken, 79, 83, 84; and Zionism, 98

Berger, Peter L., 5, 11, 12, 13, 50
Bergson, Henri, 104, 118, 189
Berlin, Isaiah, 3, 27, 104; and *trahison des clercs*, 123
Berman, Jessica, 196
Berosus, 106
Bersani, Leo: on Baudelaire, 96; on Bataille, 96; and Benhabib, 95; on Benjamin, 95–96; on deconstructive redemption, 96; on Flaubert, 96; and

Bersani, Leo (*continued*)
    Foucault, 96; and Lawrence, 96; and Marcuse, 96; on self-shattering sexuality, 96
Besant, Annie, 169, 171
Bhabha, Homi, 200–201, 203
Bhutto, 14
Biale, David, 80
bin Laden, Osama, 14
Biruni, al-, 106
Blavatsky, Madame Helena Petrovna, 103
Bloch, Ernst, 32, 59, 77, 119, 159
Bloomsbury group, 116–17, 162; and Apostles (at Cambridge) 165; and Lake Poets, 168; and Pre-Raphaelite Brotherhood, 168; as secularization of Clapham Sect, 165–69, 172, 178, 188, 193; sense of election of, 168
Blumenberg, Hans, 5, 17, 20, 21, 23; and Benjamin, 60, 62; on breakdown of Aristotelian order, 59, 60, 62, 63, 200; and Burkhardt's cosmopolitan individual, 196, 199; on crossing of "epochal threshold," 21, 59–60; and Habermas, 64, 66; and Hegel, 64; and Hobbes, 62, 65; and humanism, 63; and imperialism, 64–65; and intellectual history, 61, 206; and Kracauer, 67; and Krauss, 72; vs. Löwith, 59–62, 64–66, 67, 71; and Luhmann, 66; and MacIntyre, 65; and Marburg School, 62; on "modest self-assertion," 60, 61, 196, 199, 200; on secularization as infinite but non-teleological progress, 59–66, 71–72, 95; on secularization as reoccupation of theological positions, 61, 192, 207; and Schmitt, 61; and Simmel, 72; and Weber, 60, 61, 64
Blumenthal, Herbert, 80
Böhme, Jacob, 53, 81, 82
Bonald, Louis, Vicomte de, 108, 110, 129
Bourdieu, Pierre: on habitus, 151, 160; on the symbolic field, 200
Brecht, Bertoldt, 18
Brennan, Timothy, 196
Brontë, Charlotte, 179
Brooks, Cleanth, 157

Brosses, Charles de, 106
Brown, Callum G., 8
Browne, Sir Thomas, 174
Bruce, Steve, 6, 7
Bruno, Giordano, 59, 60–61
Brunschvig, Léon: on Nuremburg as "religion according to Durkheim," 115
Buber, Martin, 98, 119
Buckle, Henry Thomas, 140
Buddhism, 13, 107
Bunsen, Christian Karl Josias, Baron, 155–56
Burckhardt, Jacob, 58, 89, 90; and Auerbach, 196; and Blumenberg, 196; and cosmopolitan individual, 195–98, 203; and cultural criticism, 197, 203; on Dante, 196–97; on Ghiberti, 197; and imperialism, 197; on Machiavelli, 196; on Malagola, 197; and nation-state, 196; on Renaissance humanism, 195–98; vs. Rousseau, 197; and Said's "secular criticism," 196, 203; on *l'uomo universale*, 198
Burke, Edmund, 81, 166
Burke, Peter, 195
Burnouf, Emile, 138–39, 154, 156
Bury, J. B., 62
Bush, George W., 14, 38
Bush, Ronald, 120
Buxton, Noel, 169
Buzard, James, 153
Byron, George Gordon, Lord, 135, 146

Cadbury family, 165
Caillois, Roger, 120
Calvin, John, 50, 60, 101, 132; and Calvinist doctrines, 162; on "two kingdoms" of spiritual and secular authority, 11, 196
Cambridge Ritualists, 117
capitalism, 1, 7, 9, 15, 17, 20, 26, 28, 49, 51, 73, 75, 98, 111, 198, 203
Casanova, Pascal, 200
Cassirer, Ernst, 27
Catholicism, Roman, 9, 11, 14, 16, 18, 37, 40, 56, 61, 80, 81, 103, 106, 108, 109, 110, 125, 144, 181, 183, 195, 206
Celsus, 106

Celts, the, 131, 138–54; and Celtic Revival, 144; and the English, 146–50; and feminine nature, 141, 146, 147, 148; and the French, 148; and the Germans, 148; vs. Teutons/Saxons, 141, 146, 147
Chadwick, Owen, 6
Chakrabarty, Dipesh, 24, 43; on academic discourse of history, 199–200; vs. Asad, 199; on Bhabha's idea of mimicry, 200–201; and Blumenberg's "self assertion," 200; and Burckhardt's *l'uomo universale*, 200, 201, 203; and Casanova, 200; and Duara, 200; and Habermas, 202, 203, 204–5; on Heidegger, 202; on historicism, 201, 202; and the humanities, 200, 202; on human rights, 199, 202; on individualism, 200; on Marx, 199, 201, 202; vs. Nandy, 199; on non-Western civil society, 201; on "politics of despair," 202; and postcolonial critique, 202–3; on "provincializing Europe," 201; on recovery of past social rituals, 201, 207; on religious culture, 201–2; and secularization, 200, 202; on Subaltern Studies, 199, 201; on Western vs. non-Western modernity, 199–205, 206
Chapman, Malcolm, 145, 149
Chateaubriand, François René, Vicomte de, 108
Chirac, Jacques, 45
Chomsky, Noam, 55; and philosophical nativism, 128
Christianity, 1, 4, 5, 8, 9, 11–16 passim, 26, 31, 35–36, 38–43 passim, 50–52, 54, 58, 59, 61–63, 65, 82, 84, 105, 106, 113, 120, 126, 132–36 passim, 142, 154, 155–56, 163, 167, 175, 176, 177, 202, 203, 204, 206
Church of England, 14, 170, 175, 181
church-state separation, 8, 9–15, 37, 41, 196
Cicero, 12, 106
civic religion, 129; Weber's definition of, 116
civil society, 8, 11, 37, 38, 39, 41–42, 124, 196, 201, 203

Clapham Sect, 24, 161, 162–73, 182, 188; and associated minds, 171, 188, 193; compared to Bloomsbury group, 165–69, 172, 178, 188; and dissociation of emotions, 188; effervescence of, 164, 177, 188; and Fabianism, 169, 188; and inner light, 163, 177, 191, 193; and intellectual aristocracy, 165, 193; translated into Virginia Woolf's literary technique, 161, 172–73, 183, 188; worldly sociality of, 169, 172, 183
Clement of Alexandria, 106
Cohen, Hermann, 62
Cohen, H. Floris, 25
Colley, Linda, 163
Collingwood, R. G., 70
communism/socialism, 9, 13, 15, 18, 26, 28, 57, 68, 84, 102, 103, 118, 119, 129
Comte, Auguste, 57, 108, 170; and Durkheim, 110, 111, 115, 116, 118; Religion of Humanity of, 109, 119; and Schmitt, 124; vision of pan-European order of, 110, 115
Condorcet, Jean Antoine Nicolas Caritat, Marquis de, 68, 102
Confucianism, 13
Conquistadors, 16
Connell, Matt, 20
Conrad, Joseph, 65, 136, 170; and *Heart of Darkness*, 179–80, 189; and *Lord Jim*, 180
Cornford, F. M.: on secularization of religious myth into Greek philosophy, 117
Cortés, Donoso, 11
cosmopolitanism, 195–98
Coulson, John, 157
Coward, Noel, 193
Cowper, William, 184
Crapanzano, Vincent: on proto-fascism of Durkheim's collective consciousness, 115
Creuzer, Friedrich, 106
Croce, Benedetto, 70, 104
Cromwell, Oliver, 11, 16, 78
Crusius, Irene, 6

cultural criticism: Adorno's account of, 17–20, 196; and Arnold, 18, 151–52; and charm, 18; and culture concept, 107; as defined by opposition to all that is "official," 17, 196; and Durkheim, 22–23, 127–28; and the Enlightenment, 19, 68; and globalization, 199, 203; and Habermas, 22; and Hegelian *Aufhebung*, 20–21, 22; and Heideggerian *Verwindung*, 21, 22, 23, 207; and the humanities, 197, 199; and instrumental rationality, 18–20, 102–3; and Kracauer, 73, 96; and magical spell of art, 19–20; and Monod's alternative accounts of secularization, 208; and postcolonial critique, 207; and postmodern thought, 68, 73; and secularization, 1, 6, 17–23, 44, 68, 204, 207, 208; and Weber, 22
cultural defense, 16, 36
cultural relativism, 29–30, 137, 141, 150, 151
cultural studies, 131, 143, 153
culture industry, 103
Curtius, E. R., 89

Daiches, David, 161
Dante Alighieri, 33, 40, 189, 196–97
Darwin, Charles, 107, 148
Darwin family, 165
Davenport, F. M., 117
David, King, 156
Davie, Grace, 6, 7, 28
Defoe, Daniel, 148
deism, 28, 29, 33, 34, 59, 101, 105, 109
DeKoven, Marianne, 179
DeLaura, David J., 135, 138
Delos, Joseph T., 125
Derrida, Jacques, 5, 21, 88, 111, 159; and critique of humanism, 198
DeSalvo, Louise A.: on Virginia Woolf, 174, 176, 181
Descartes, René, 25, 60, 102
D'Estaing, Giscard, 54
dialectic of enlightenment, 29, 33, 73, 102–3; vs. destruction of reason, 103–5
Dickens, Charles: and *Hard Times*, 177; and utilitarianism, 177, 178

Diderot, Denis, 29, 31, 39; and natural religion, 35, 66, 106, 134
Dieckhoff, Reiner, 80, 81
Dilthey, Wilhelm, 70, 89, 104
Diogenes Laertius, 106
Dionysius the Elder, 123
Disraeli, Benjamin, 38, 164
Dobbelaere, Karl, 6, 7, 9
Dreyfus affair, 122, 126
Duara, Prasenjit, 200
Du Bois, W. E. B., 16
Duckworth, George, 174
Dupuis, François, 106
Durkheim, Emile, 5, 17, 21, 23, 26, 30, 55, 104, 206, 207; and Acéphale, 119–20, 122; and ambiguity of religion-society relationship, 112–14, 116, 119, 121–22, 127–30, 159; and Baader, 81; and Bataille, 119, 122; and Benda, 123; and civil society, 124; on collective consciousness, 118, 120–21, 127–28, 162; and communism/socialism, 118, 129; and Comte, 110, 111, 115, 116; corporatism in, 111, 118, 171, 172; and crowd psychology, 115; and cultural criticism, 127–28; definition of religion of, 111; and Delos, 125; and descriptive vs. prescriptive theory, 128; and Dreyfus affair, 122, 126 and ecstatic, proto-fascist community, 115; on effervescence, 108, 113, 114–15, 121, 129; and T. S. Eliot, 120–21, 122; on epistemic primacy of the social, 128; and European Union, 126; and Feuerbach, 113; and Frazer, 111; functionalism of, 129; and Harrison, 117–18, 122; and Hauriou, 125–26; and history of religion, 107; and immanence of sacred sociality, 129; and Institutionalists, 125; internationalism of, 121, 126, 129, 171; on language as collective representations, 112, 114; and Le Bon, 115; and Lévi-Strauss, 114; and Maurras, 122; and Mauss, 114, 115; and McLennan, 111; on mechanical solidarity, 111, 121, 128; and Mill, 128; and Nazism, 128; on organic solidarity, 111, 171;

and pragmatism of James, 112; and political theology, 129; positivism of, 127–28; and Ranulf, 115; and Renard, 125; and Robertson Smith, 111; and Romains, 117, 122; on sacred vs. profane, 112; social theory of religion of, 110–30, 153; as source for Schmitt, 124–26; on the state, 125; on suicide, 163; and Tarde, 115; on the totem of the clan, 111–14, 127; and *trahison des clercs*, 123; on universalizing of religious beliefs, 121, 171; and vitalism, 114

Edwards, William Frédéric, 142
Eliade, Mircea: and history of "history of religion," 105–7
Eliot, Edward, 162
Eliot, George, 170, 179, 182, 187
Eliot, T. S.: and Anglo-Catholicism, 121; and anti-Semitism, 121; and Bataille, 123; on collective consciousness, 120–21; on culture and religion as aspects of the same thing, 120–21, 122, 159, 160; on Durkheim, 115, 120–21, 122; and fragments of religious tradition, 158, 189; and Freud, 121; and Harrison, 119; and Hegel, 121, 122; on Joyce, 157, 176; and Lévy-Bruhl, 120; and Maistre, 123; and Maurras, 119, 122; and modernism, 157, 158; and royalism, 121; and social redemption, 123; and *trahison des clercs*, 123; and *The Waste Land*, 122
Ellmann, Richard, 136, 158
Enlightenment, the, 3, 7, 11, 19, 22, 24, 31, 33, 43, 44, 55, 105, 108, 122, 129, 135; and Aristotelian virtue, 55, 56; and Clapham Sect Evangelicalism, 166, 167; and counter-Enlightenment, 3, 27, 68, 87, 103, 104, 123, 189; and cultural relativism, 29; Foucault on, 27–28; and humanism, 201; and human rights, 54, 198; and imperialism, 65; and Judeo-Christian tradition, 54, 65, 66; moderate, 28; and natural religion, 35, 106; and postmodern cultural criticism, 68; and progress, 23, 57, 61,

65, 67, 68, 70, 87, 90, 92, 102, 203; radical, 26; and scientific revolution, 25–26
Epicurus, 106
Erasmus, Desiderius, 195
Ericson, Edward E., Jr., 157, 158
ethnicity, 15, 31, 37, 129, 152–53, 197
eugenics, 117
Euhemerus, 106
Euphrosyne, Saint, 175
European Union, 54, 207
Eusebius, 106
Evangelicalism, 16, 24, 36, 103, 135, 136, 154; and Clapham Sect, 24, 161, 162–73, 177, 178, 182, 183, 186, 188, 190, 191, 192, 193; and Conrad's *Heart of Darkness*, 164; and English national identity, 163, 193; of Gladstone, 164; and imperialism, 164; and inner light, 163, 177, 191, 193; and intellectual aristocracy, 165, 193; and Virginia Woolf, 24, 161, 162–73, 177, 178, 181, 182, 183, 186, 188, 190, 191, 193
evolutionism, 68

Fabian, Johannes, 207
Fabianism, 116, 169–70; and eugenics, 170; as heir to Clapham Sect, 169, 188, 193; and Nietzschean critique of bourgeois impotence, 170
Fagan, Henry Stuart, 150
Falck, Colin, 159
Faverty, Frederic: on Arnold, 138–39, 142, 144, 149, 154, 156; on Macpherson, 145
Ferry, Luc, 6
Feuerbach, Ludwig, 22, 106, 107, 170
Fichte, Johann Gottlieb, 103, 108
Ficino, Marsilio, 106
Fish, Stanley, 39
Flaubert, Gustave, 96
Fletcher, Richard, 13
Fontenelle, Bernard le Bovier de, 106
Ford, Ford Madox (Ford Madox Hueffer), 158
Forster, Edward Morgan, 135, 158, 165

Foucault, Michel, 1, 27, 29, 55, 96, 159; critique of Hegel of, 71; critique of humanism of, 198; on "effective history," 70; and the Enlightenment, 27–28, 31, 198; on historical ruptures, 90, 206; and progress, 28, 31
Fourier, François Charles, 118
Fox family, 165
Frankfurt School, 55, 85
Frazer, James G., 107, 111, 117
Freeden, Michael, 117
Freemasonry, 103, 105
French Revolution, 13, 44, 46, 48, 49, 52, 77–78, 84, 87, 108, 110
Freud, Sigmund, 22, 27, 101, 104, 107, 121
Frobenius, Leo, 107
Fry, Roger, 165
Frye, Northrop, 32; and mythic criticism, 158–59, 176
Fukuyama, Francis, 204
fundamentalism, 6, 14, 31, 37, 42, 128
Fustel de Coulanges, Numa Denis, 110

Gadamer, Hans Georg, 55, 85, 157
Galileo Galilei, 25
Gallagher, Catherine, 170
Gandhi, Mohandas Karamchand, 16, 38, 169, 198, 199
Gaskell family, 165
Gauchet, Marcel, 44
Geertz, Clifford, 14
Gehlen, Arnold: and *post-histoire*, 58–59
Gellner, Ernest, 15
Ghiberti, Lorenzo, 197
Gibbon, Edward, 105, 175
Giddens, Anthony, 49
Gide, André, 104
Gilman, Sander, 152–53
Gladstone, William Ewart, 164
globalization: and humanism, 24, 195–208; and the humanities, 199, 202–3; and political theology, 159; and sectarianism, 28; and secularization, 1, 6, 7, 9, 14, 15, 16, 23, 44, 53, 65, 153, 197, 203
Gnosticism, 11, 53, 60, 78
Gobineau, Joseph Arthur de, 141, 154

Goethe, Johann Wolfgang von, 33, 135
Gordon, David J., 159
Gossman, Lionel: on Arnold, 135–38, 153, 154
Gottfried, Leon, 135
Graebner, F., 107
Graff, Gerald, 137, 139
Grant, Charles, 162
Grant, Duncan, 165
Gunn, Giles, 32, 157–58

Habermas, Jürgen, 2, 22, 23, 24, 30, 39, 206, 207; and Aquinas, 53; and Aristotelian virtue, 55–57, 94; and Baader, 53; Benhabib on, 94–95; on Benjamin, 49, 87, 89, 92–95, 96, 104; and Blumenberg, 64, 66; on Böhme, 53; on bourgeois public sphere, 196, 203; and Chakrabarty, 202, 204–05; on Christianity, 48, 51–52; on citizenship vs. ethnicity, 44–46, 47; on communicative ethics, 47, 53, 94, 95; on the myth of the fall, 53; on Gnosticism/Kabbalism, 53, 104; and Hegelian history, 53, 57, 94; and human nature, 52; on human rights, 30, 53, 56, 207; on Incarnation of Christ, 52; on individualism, 52; on Judaism, 48, 51–52; on Judeo-Christian tradition, 48, 49, 52, 53, 54, 56, 57, 66, 207; and Kantian morality, 55, 94; and Kracauer, 93, 94; vs. Luhmann, 46–47; and Lukács, 104; on Luria, 53; and MacIntyre, 55, 56, 57; and Marx, 49; on "messianic condition," 92; on modernity as "unfinished project," 30, 57, 64; and modernization, 52; on the nation-state, 45–46, 47; on natural law or right, 47, 52, 55; on "new Paganism," 104; on Piaget, 46, 64; and pluralism, 45, 47; and Rawls, 45, 55; on religion, 45, 47–49, 51–53, 54, 57, 207; on Schelling, 53; on Schwabian Pietism, 53; on "semantic potentials," 49, 53, 64, 92, 93, 94, 96, 204, 207; and Strauss, 47; on universal moral consciousness, 46, 47, 53, 56; and Weber, 46, 49–51, 52

habitus: and class, 151; and secularized religious traditions, 24, 160
Handelman, Susan A., 80, 81
Hanson, Ellis, 157
Hardy, Thomas, 135, 170
Harrington, Austin, 51
Harrison, Jane, 116–19, 122–23; and collective consciousness, 119; on conversion as initiation, 117–18, 122, 127; on Durkheim, 117–18, 122; on Davenport, 117; and T. S. Eliot, 119; on James, 117; on leader as sacrificial victim, 118; on Russell, 117; and secularization, 119; and social redemption, 119, 123; and *trahison des clercs*, 123; on Unanimism, 117–20
Harrison, Thomas, 190
Hartman, Geoffrey, 157
Hauriou, Maurice: and Harrison, 125; interpretation of Durkheim of, 125–26; as source for Schmitt, 126
Hazlitt, William, 172
Hegel, Georg Wilhelm Friedrich, 5, 22, 26, 28, 53, 57, 58, 64, 68, 70, 94, 121, 135, 187; on *Aufhebung* of tradition, 20; and Marx, 78; on master-slave dialectic, 68; on national-racial *Geist*, 142
Heidegger, Martin, 27, 85, 159; critique of humanism of, 198; and Derrida, 21; on language, 21; and Nazism, 21, 123; on postmodern closure of metaphysics, 21, 70; on thinking by means of tradition, 208; and *trahison des clercs*, 123, 128; on *Verwindung* of tradition, 21, 22–23, 99, 105, 122, 126, 190
Heine, Heinrich, 135, 136, 138
Henry VIII, 13
Herbelot de Molainville, Barthélemy d,' 33
Herbert, Christopher: on Wesleyan anxiety over unregulated desire, 110
Herbert, Edward (Lord Herbert of Cherbury), 105
Herder, Johann Gottfried von, 33, 34, 89, 105, 145
Heretics society (Cambridge University), 116–18
Herf, Jeffrey, 104
Hermes Trismegistus, 106
Herodotus, 106
Hess, Moses, 138
Hill, Christopher, 14
Hinduism, 16, 31, 36, 38, 107
Hitler, Adolf, 74, 86, 88, 104, 118
Hobbes, Thomas, 25, 54, 55, 62, 65, 68, 110, 166, 199
Hobhouse, Leonard T., 117
Hobsbawm, Eric, 201
Hobson, Ernest William, 117
Hohendahl, Peter Uwe, 196
Hölderlin, Friedrich, 135
Hollier, Denis, 120, 124
Holyoake, George, 38
Horkheimer, Max: on dialectic of enlightenment, 33, 73, 102–3
Howse, Ernest Marshall, 164
Hughes, Stuart H.: on modern social theory, 104
Huizinga, Johan, 195
humanism, 2, 4, 30, 39, 40; antihumanist critique of, 198–99; and Aristotelian cosmos, 56, 61; of Arnold, 133; Asad's critique of, 198, 199; and Blumenberg, 63, 196, 199; Burckhardt's account of, 195–98, 199; and capitalism, 198; and cosmopolitan individual, 195–98, 199; Derrida's critique of, 198; and the Enlightenment, 201; Gandhi's critique of, 198, 199; and globalization, 24, 195–208; Heidegger's critique of, 198; and Hobbes, 199; and the humanities, 24, 197–200, 203–4; and imperialism, 197, 198; and literary modernism, 159; Nandy's critique of, 198, 199; and the nation-state, 198; Nietzsche's critique of, 198; and non-Western traditions, 35, 43; and paganism, 106; and pluralism, 138; postmodern critique of, 159; and Protestantism, 198; and race, 134–35, 156; of Said's secular criticism, 4, 35, 39, 40, 196, 198, 199; and secularization, 195–96; Tagore's critique of, 198
humanities, the, 197–200, 203–4; and Arnold, 198; and civil society, 203;

humanities, the (*continued*)
  and cultural criticism, 199; and globalization, 199, 203–4; and Habermas's "public sphere," 203; and humanist individual, 197–98, 199, 203; and imperialism, 198–99; and modernization, 204; and secularization, 203
human rights, 30, 42, 53, 54, 64, 199, 202; Universal Declaration of, 42, 55
Humboldt, Friedrich Heinrich Alexander von, 135
Humboldt, Wilhelm von, 135
Hume, David, 28, 105, 106, 107, 178
Huntington, Samuel P., 43; and "clash of civilizations," 30, 51
Husserl, Edmund, 85
Huxley family, 165

Ibn Hazem, 106
Ibn Khaldun, 12
Ibn Rushd (Averroës), 106
immortality of the soul, 187
imperialism, 22, 31, 32, 34–36, 37, 39, 64–65, 66, 164, 169, 186, 197, 198
Incarnation of Christ, 40, 60, 113–14, 189
Indian Home Rule, 169
individualism, 3–5, 7, 8, 17, 26, 38, 39, 40, 52, 112, 126; and cosmopolitan humanism, 195–98; and the humanities, 197–98, 199, 200; in Said's "secular criticism," 196
Islam, 1, 9, 12, 13–16, 31, 35, 40–43, 45, 51, 54, 106, 107, 119; and secularization, 205–7
Israel, Jonathan I., 26, 28

Jacob, Margaret, 28, 105
James, C. L. R., 202
James, Henry, 158
James, William, 107, 112, 116, 117; and religion as inward experience, 161
Jameson, Fredric, 158; on similarity of Marxism to religion, 159
Jellinek, Georg, 51
Joas, Hans, 51
John Paul II, Pope, 15
Jones, William, 34, 105, 149
Joshua, 156

Josipovici, Gabriel, 158
Joyce, James, 40, 135–36, 144, 158, 176; and collapse of Judeo-Christian tradition, 189; and persistence of religious belief, 160; and *Ulysses,* 157, 179
Judaism, 2–3, 4, 12, 13, 35, 40, 48, 51–52, 54, 65, 88, 106, 119, 133–39, 156, 204
Judeo-Christian tradition, 1, 11, 12, 23, 30, 42, 52, 53, 54, 57, 58, 65, 66, 68, 106, 107, 159, 181, 189, 198, 206

Kabbalism, 53, 67, 78–85, 103, 187
Kafka, Franz, 91
Kant, Immanuel, 51, 91; Benhabib on, 94; Benjamin on, 77; and Blumenberg, 63, 64; categories of, 111; critique of proofs of God's existence of, 105, 106; and the Enlightenment, 102, 103; and Habermas's communicative ethics, 47; and Lévi-Strauss, 114; and liberal idea of consensus, 53, 54, 94; and Marburg School, 62, 77; and Moore's aesthetics, 167; rejected by Baader, 81
Keats, John, 146
Keddie, Nikki, 14
Kelleher, John V., 144
Ker, Ian Turnbull, 157
Kermode, Frank, 32
Keynes, John Maynard, 117, 165; on Bloomsbury group as having a religion, 168
Kierkegaard, Søren Aabye, 27, 62, 103, 159; and *Acéphale* (the journal), 124, 126; and Bataille, 124; and Benjamin, 88, 124; and Durkheim, 126; and Schmitt, 124, 126
King, Martin Luther, 42
Klee, Paul, 87
Kojève, Alexandre, 70
Koselleck, Reinhart, 5
Kosmin, Barry, 8
Kracauer, Siegfried, 23, 24, 55, 206; and Adorno, 73, 74, 75, 86; and Aron, 89; and Benjamin, 67, 72–76, 85–92, 93, 96, 99–100, 101; on Blumenberg, 67, 71–72; and Burckhardt, 71, 89, 90; on Collingwood, 70; and capitalism, 73, 75, 98; critique of collectivism of, 74;

critique of conjunction between universal and present interest history of, 69–70, 71, 87, 92; critique of messianism of, 67, 75, 76, 85–92, 93–94, 96, 99–100; on Croce, 70; on Curtius, 89; on differentiated (discontinuous) temporalities, 74, 89–92, 96, 98, 99, 207; on Dilthey, 70, 89; and empty time, 89; epistemological insecurity of, 99–100; and Foucault, 70, 71, 90; and Frankfurt School, 85; and Gadamer, 85; and Habermas, 93; and Hegel, 70, 71, 74; and Heidegger, 70, 85; and Herder, 89; and Husserl, 85; and *die Jetztzeit* (now-time), 86, 88, 100; on Kafka's Sancho Panza, 91; and Kojève, 70; on "last things," 69, 70–71, 92, 95; on Loos, 72; on Löwith, 71; and Lukács, 72; and Lyotard, 90; on Mandelbaum, 89; and Marx, 73, 74, 85, 89, 90; and Nietzsche, 69, 70, 71; and Popper, 70; on popular culture, 72, 73, 74; and postmodern thought, 73; and progress, 67, 69, 70, 71, 72, 91, 99; on Proust, 71, 88, 89, 91; on Ranke, 71, 90; rejection of historical teleology of, 70; and Rorty, 71; on Shapiro, 89; and Simmel, 72, 73; vestiges of utopian thought in, 86, 88, 89, 91, 93; and Weimar culture, 74–75; on White, 90–91
Krauss, Karl, 72
Kristeller, Paul Oscar, 69

LaCapra, Dominick, 89; on Durkheim, 121
Lachman, Seymour P., 8
Lafitau, Jean François, 106
laïcité islamique, 35, 205–7
Lammenais, Felicité Robert de, 108
Lang, Andrew, 107, 144, 150
Laslett, Peter, 8
Lawrence, David Herbert, 96, 136, 158, 166
Le Bon, Gustave: on crowd psychology, 115
Lee, Hermione, 176–77, 187, 192
Lehmann, Hartmut, 6, 36

Leibniz, Gottfried Wilhelm von, 19
Lenzer, Gertrude, 109, 110
Leonard, Philip, 159
Lepenies, Wolf, 109, 110
Le Play, Frédéric, 110
Lessing, Gotthold Ephraim, 106
Levinas, Emmanuel, 159
Lévi-Strauss, Claude, 26, 29, 30, 35, 43, 111; and "floating signifier," 114; on Mauss's theory of magic, 115; and totemism, 114
Levy, Paul, 168, 187
Lévy-Bruhl, Lucien, 107
Lewis, Bernard, 13; on church-state separation in Christianity, 9; and curiosity about the other, 35; on religion as basis of civilization, 30–31, 43, 51; on tolerance of secularized Christianity, 39
Lilla, Mark: and *trahison des clercs*, 123
Lincoln, Bruce, 14
Livy, 12
Lloyd, David, 139, 147
Locke, John, 55, 102
Loos, Adolf, 72
Lotze, Hermann, 84
Löwith, Karl, 26, 41, 110, 159; and Blumenberg, 59–62, 64–66, 67, 71; on circular time, 58, 59, 68; on philosophy of history as secularized eschatology, 57–59, 68, 77
Löwy, Michael, 77, 80
Lübbe, H., 7
Lucian, 106
Lucretius, 106
Luhmann, Niklas: and Schmitt, 47; and Strauss, 66; on "systems theory," 46–47, 66
Lukács, Georg, 119; and Benjamin, 98; on Kierkegaard, 103; and Marxism, 103; on Nietzsche, 103; on resurgence of irrationality in modernity, 103, 116; on Schelling, 103; on Schopenhauer, 103; on Simmel, 72, 103; and Stalin, 103, 123; and *trahison des clercs*, 123, 128
Lukes, Steven, 112
Luria, Isaac, 53, 78–79, 84, 85

Luther, Martin, 39, 50, 54, 60, 77, 80, 101
Lyell, Charles, 106
Lyotard, François: and grand narrative, 65, 68; and *petit récit*, 90
Lytton, Edward George Earle Bulwer-, 147

Macaulay, Selina, 162
Macaulay, Thomas Babington, 36
Macaulay, Zachary, 162
Machiavelli, Niccolo di Bernardo dei, 196
MacIntyre, Alasdair, 23, 39, 61; on Aristotelian virtue, 54–57, 59, 63, 166; on Clapham Sect to Bloomsbury group moral devolution, 165–67; on collapse of moral tradition, 54–57, 64, 165–67; on emotivism, 166, 168; on Hobbes, 166; on human rights, 54–55, 65; on Moore, 166; and secularization, 167
Macpherson, James, 144, 146; and Herder, 145; and Scott, 145
Mailloux, Steven, 42
Maimonides, Moses, 106
Maistre, Joseph de, 27, 68, 81, 103, 104, 109, 110, 129, 144; on government as a true religion, 108
Malagola, Carlo, 197
Malcolm X, 42
Malthus, Thomas Robert, 169
Mandelbaum, Maurice, 89
Manent, Pierre, 59, 63
Manganaro, Marc, 120
Mannhardt, Wilhelm, 107
Marburg School, 62
Marcus Aurelius, 142
Marcuse, Herbert, 95, 96
Mark, Saint, 40
Marquard, Odo, 20
Marrett, R. R., 107
Martí, José, 16
Martin, David, 7, 8
Martin, Henri, 142
Martineau family, 165
Martz, Louis L., 157
Marx, Karl, 3, 8, 30, 50, 57, 58, 73, 84, 89, 93, 99, 158, 199; and Christian eschatology, 61, 68, 76–77, 159; on Cromwell, 78; and Hegelian dialectic, 78; on the "Jewish Question," 48–49; on letting "the dead bury their dead," 78; on Luther, 77; and materialist account of culture, 178; on Oriental despotism, 151; and postcolonial critique, 202–3; on religion as "opium of the people," 107; on Saint Paul, 77; and Subaltern Studies, 199, 201
Massignon, Louis, 32
Maurras, Charles, 110, 119; and Durkheim, 122; and T. S. Eliot, 119, 122
Mauss, Marcel, 111, 114, 115, 118
McCarthy, Desmond, 165
McCole, John, 79, 80
McLennan, John Ferguson, 107, 111
McLeod, Hugh, 6
McMahon, Darrin M., 103
McTaggart, John Ellis, 117; and immortality of the soul, 187
Menand, Louis, 120
Mendieta, Eduardo, 53
Michaels, Walter Benn, 153
Milbank, John, 2, 6, 18
Mill, John Stuart, 150; compared to Durkheim, 128; and Marx, 151; and race, 151
Miller, J. Hillis, 157, 158
Milton, John, 146
modernism: of the Edwardians, 158; and T. S. Eliot, 157; and negative theology, 159; and religious belief, 157–60; and secularization, 157; and the secular writer, 157–60; and Virginia Woolf, 161, 189–90
modernization: in Arnold, 145; in Habermas, 52; and the humanities, 204; and secularization, 7, 8, 9, 15, 16, 17, 26, 28, 30, 35, 51, 145, 189, 191, 197, 200, 203; in Weber, 51, 52, 101, 102;
Molitor, Franz Joseph, 81, 84; and Baader, 80, 82; and Benjamin, 82–85; on Kaballah, 82–85; on Luria, 82–83; and Schelling, 80; and Scholem, 82
Molitor, Raphael, 81

Monod, Jean-Claude, 17, 22; and *laïcité islamique*, 205; on secularization as retreat of religion vs. secularization as transference of religious concepts, 5–6, 67, 205, 208
Montesquieu, Charles Louis de Secondat de, 105
Montesquieu-Fezensac, Count Léon de, 110
Moore, George Edward (G. E.), 117, 166, 167; and immortality of the soul, 187; and *Principia Ethica*, 168; and secularization of Evangelical worldview, 168
More, Hannah, 162
More, Thomas, 195
Mozart, Wolfgang Amadeus, 33
Mülder-Bach, Inka, 73
Müller, Adam, 124
Müller, Max, 106, 107
Münzer, Thomas, 80
Murray, Gilbert, 117

Naipaul, V. S., 201
Nairn, Tom, 193
Najibullah, 14
Nandy, Ashis, 23, 24, 51, 54, 64, 198, 199, 206, 207; on debilitation of religion in relation to modern nation-state, 37–38, 41; on religious tolerance vs. secularization, 37
Nasser, Gamel Abdel, 14
nationalism, 9, 15, 26, 28, 31, 36, 41, 51, 97, 98, 108, 114, 149, 152; French integral, 110; and the populist intellectual, 197
nation-state, 4, 7, 8, 9, 15, 16, 17, 36, 37–38, 41, 43, 45–46, 47, 54, 108, 110; and capitalism, 198; and European narratives of development, 200; and humanism, 196, 198; and the humanities, 200, 203; totalitarian drift of twentieth-century version of, 129
nativism (philosophical), 128
Nazism, 13, 18, 21, 57, 68, 88, 97, 102, 104, 118, 123, 128
Needham, Joseph, 13

neo-Platonism, 103, 109, 187
neo-Pythagoreans, 106
New Liberals, 117
Newman, John Henry, 37, 103
Newton, Isaac, 102
Nicholas of Cusa, 59, 60
Niebuhr, Barthold, 149
Nielsen, Donald A.: on vitalism in Durkheim, 114–15
Nietzsche, Friedrich, 11–12, 27, 28, 29, 39, 95, 99, 124, 135, 170; counter-Enlightenment rejection of progress of, 68–69, 102, 103; critique of Hegel of, 71; critique of humanism of, 159, 198; and German Youth Movement, 69, 84; and history of religion, 107; and Plato, 102; and present interest history, 69, 70, 98; on primitive components of Greek thought, 117; on *ressentiment*, 170, 181; on utilitarianism, 167
Nisbet, Robert A., 110
Novalis (Friedrich Leopold von Hardenberg), 80
Nussbaum, Martha, 42, 55

Occultism, 119, 120
Ogden, C. K., 117
Origen, 106
Orr, John, Archdeacon of Ferns, 105
Ossian, 145
Owen, Robert, 171

pantheism, 28
Parsons, Talcott, 5, 115
Pascal, Blaise, 175
Passerin D'Entrèves, Maurizio, 30, 104
Pater, Walter, 135, 185, 189
Paul, Saint, 24, 77; Arnold's discussion of, 132–35
Pausanius, 106
Pecora, Vincent P., 9, 117
Péguy, Charles, 110
Petronius, 40
Pew Forum on Religion and Public Life, 8, 31
Pew Global Attitudes Project, 9, 10, 31

philosophes, 106
Piaget, Jean, 46, 64
Pickering, W. S. F., 113, 115
Pietism, 53
Pitt, Rosemary, 180
Pitt, William, the Younger, 162
Plato, 59, 102, 123, 156
pluralism, 8, 9, 11, 38, 39, 45, 46, 47, 49
Plutarch, 12, 106
political theology, 15, 24, 116, 129; and globalization, 159; and postmodernism, 159; and secularization, 123
Polybius, 106
Popper, Karl, 70
Porphyry, 106
Porter, Roy, 6
positivism, 68
Pound, Ezra, 158
pre-Socratics, 106
Preuss, Konrad Theodor, 107
primitivism, 159
Prince, Morton, 188
progress, 6, 17, 23, 27, 28, 29, 31, 37, 67, 68, 69, 70, 71, 72, 77, 84, 86, 87, 91, 99, 100, 117, 203; idea of, 57–66
Protestantism, 9, 11–12, 13, 16, 24, 30, 31, 50, 56, 101, 110, 181, 183; and humanism, 198; and nation-state, 196
Proudhon, Pierre Joseph, 1, 118
Proust, Marcel, 19, 40, 88; and Auerbach's "random moment," 189; and collapse of Judeo-Christian tradition, 189; and Virginia Woolf, 176
Prüfer, Sebastian, 6, 15
Pulver, Max, 80
Putnam, Hilary, 39

Quakers, 165

Rabinbach, Anson, 77, 80, 119
race, 13, 15, 24, 31, 32, 98, 103, 110, 115, 117, 128, 129, 143, 154; and culture, 144–53; and ethnicity, 152–53; and family, 152; and humanism, 134–35, 156; and language, 134, 149, 153; and nation, 131, 132, 134, 138, 139, 143–44, 147–48, 149, 151, 153, 155; and religion, 131, 132, 134, 135–39, 149, 151, 153–56;

as substitute for religion in Arnold, 135, 152, 153
Ranke, Leopold von, 71, 90
Ranulf, Svend: on Durkheim's proto-fascism, 115, 116
Rawls, John, 1, 39, 42, 45, 54, 55
Reagan, Ronald, 14
redemption, social and historical, 23, 65, 96–100, 116; and barbarism of paradise, 99; in Benjamin, 67, 75–100; in Bersani, 95–96; in Harrison, 119; Kracauer's critique of, 67, 75, 76, 85–92, 93–94, 96, 99–100; and theory of religion, 122; and Virginia Woolf, 191
Reformation, 9, 11, 50, 54, 80, 101, 195
religious atheism, 103, 118, 122, 123, 129
Renan, Ernest, 3, 32, 142, 144, 145, 146, 154; on chimera of racial nationality, 148, 150
Renard, Georges, 125
Rhys, John, 144
Richman, Michèle H., 120
Rickert, Heinrich, 62
Ricoeur, Paul, 157
Riehl, Alois, 62
Riesterer, Berthold P., 58
Rilke, Rainer Maria, 18
Rivers, W. H. R., 107, 117
Robbe-Grillet, Alain, 158
Robbins, Bruce, 196
Robespierre, Maximilien François Marie Isidore de, 87, 109; and Cult of Reason, 108, 119; and Festival of Supreme Being, 108
Rochester, John, 105
Romains, Jules, 120; and Durkheim, 117; and Unanimism, 117, 122
Rorty, Richard, 71, 99
Rose, Jonathan, 116, 169, 181, 187
Rosenberg, Alfred, 97, 129
Rousseau, Jean-Jacques, 68, 81; on national identity, 197; vs. Burckhardt, 197
Rudolf, R. de M., 162
Rushdie, Salman, 37, 193
Ruskin, John, 166
Russell, Bertrand, 117
Rychner, Max, 84

Saadia, 106
Sade, Donatien Alphonse, Count (Marquis) de, 124
saeculum, 2
Said, Edward W., 23; and Abrams, 33; and Arnold, 35, 132, 144; and Asad, 41–43; on Auerbach, 40, 196; and Benjamin, 32; and Bloch, 32; and Burckhardt, 196; and Christian tradition, 40; on comparative literature, 34; on contrapuntal reading, 28, 34–36, 39, 43; on Dante, 40, 196; debt to Enlightenment of, 34–35, 39, 43; and "dialectic of enlightenment," 33; on discrepant experience, 34–36, 39; and Foucault, 31, 33; on Goethe, 33, 34; on Herder, 33, 34; on heroic, worldly individualism, 3–5, 31, 40, 196; on human rights, 42; on imperialism, 31, 32, 34–36, 39, 64; on Islamic fundamentalism, 35–36; on Jones, 34; on Massignon, 32; on Mozart, 33; on Orientalism, 3, 4, 33; and postcolonial critique, 202–3; on Renan, 32; on secular criticism, 3–5, 31–36, 39–40, 132, 144, 196, 198, 207; and secularization, 31, 33, 36, 39–40, 207; on Vico, 2–4, 33
Saint-Martin, Louis Claude, 81
Sand, George, 146
Sanson, Henri: on *double volunté* in Algerian society, 206; on *laïcité islamique* in Algeria, 35, 205–7; and Weber, 206
Sappho, 175
Sartre, Jean-Paul, 159
Sayre, Robert, 80
Schama, Simon, 6
Schelling, Friedrich Wilhelm Joseph von, 53, 103; and Baader, 80, 81; and F. Molitor, 80
Schiller, Friedrich, 56, 135
Schlegel, August Wilhelm von, 80, 105
Schlegel, Friedrich von, 80, 105
Schleiermacher, Friedrich Ernst, 132
Schmidt, Wilhelm, 107
Schmitt, Carl, 26, 41, 110; and anti-Semitism, 124; and Bataille, 124; and Benjamin, 88; and Blumenberg, 61; and Catholicism, 124; on Comte, 124; on "concrete orders," 125; decisionism of, 125; Durkheim as source for, 124–26; on Hauriou, 126; and Hegel, 124; and Hitler, 124–25; Hobbes as source for, 124; Kierkegaard as source for, 124; Maistre as source for, 124; on Adam Müller, 124; Nazi sympathies of, 123, 124, 126; political theology of, 123–26, 159; on Proudhon, 124; on Friedrich Schlegel, 124; and *trahison des clercs*, 128
Scholem, Gershom G., 77, 78, 79, 80, 81, 82, 83, 85, 98
Schrempp, Gregory, 115
Schwartz, Sanford, 120
science (or theory) of religions, 105–10; Durkheim's contribution to, 110–30; flourishing of, between 1840 and World War I, 110, 116, 129; redemptive social potential of, 116, 122; as response to need for "imagined community" of nation-state, 110; separation from theology of, 106–7, 118
scientific revolution, 25–26
Scott, Nathan A., Jr., 157
secularization, 1–66 passim; and Arnold, 132, 133, 134, 135, 137, 143, 153, 206, 207; and Asad, 41–43, 66, 206, 207; and Auerbach, 191; and Benjamin, 84, 206, 207; and Chakrabarty, 200, 202; of Clapham Sect by Bloomsbury group, 165–69, 172, 178, 188, 193; and cultural criticism, 1, 6, 17–23, 44, 68, 204, 207, 208; and "disenchantment of the world" (in Weber), 11, 18, 25, 107; as eschatological philosophy of history (Löwith), 57–59, 68, 77; of Evangelical worldview (Moore), 168; and globalization, 1, 6, 7, 9, 14, 15, 16, 23, 44, 53, 65, 153, 197, 203; and Harrison, 119; and humanism, 195–96; and the humanities, 203; and idea of progress, 57–66; as infinite but non-teleological progress (in Blumenberg), 59–66, 71–72, 95; and Islam in Algeria, 205–7; and MacIntyre, 167; and modernism, 157–60; and modernization, 7, 8, 9,

secularization (*continued*)
15, 16, 17, 26, 28, 30, 35, 51, 145, 189, 191, 197, 200, 203; and political theology, 123; and race, 135, 152, 153; of religious myth by Greek philosophy (Cornford), 117; as reoccupation of theological positions (Blumenberg), 61, 192, 207; as retreat vs. transference of religious concepts (Monod), 5–6, 67, 205, 208; and Said, 31, 33, 36, 39–40, 207; and science of religions, 106–110; as *Verwindung* of tradition (Heidegger), 21, 22–23, 99, 105, 122, 126, 190; and Virginia Woolf, 160, 161, 162, 169, 172, 178, 181, 183, 186, 191, 192, 193, 206

Seligson, Carla, 83, 84
Senancour, Etienne Pivert de, 145
Shakespeare, William, 146, 185
Shapin, Steven, 25
Shapiro, Meyer, 89
Sharpe, Grenville, 162
Shaw, George Bernard, 117, 158, 170
Shelley, Percy Bysshe, 135
Shore, John, 162
Sieyès, Emanuel-Joseph, Abbé, 30
Silverstein, Brian, 205
Simmel, Georg, 72, 73, 107, 109, 116
Sironneau, Jean-Pierre, 15
Sivan, Emmanuel, 14, 31
Smart, J. S., 145
Smith, Adam: and Aristotelian virtue, 55–56; and Hobbes, 56
Smith, Anthony D., 9, 15
Smith, William, 162
Smith, William Robertson, 107, 111, 182
social (or collective) solidarity, 3, 17, 22, 24, 44; of Clapham Sect, 164, 193; and English national identity, 193; as proto-fascist idea, 115; and religious thought, 105, 108, 113–16, 120, 153; as replacement for religion, 109–10; and society as religious object, 115–16, 118, 119, 129–30, 160
Society for Psychical Research, 187
Socrates, 156
Solidarity (Poland), 15

Sorel, Georges, 87, 104
Spencer, Herbert, 166
Spengler, Oswald, 29, 59
Spinoza, Baruch, 3, 26, 103, 105, 142
Stalin, Joseph, 57, 68, 86, 103, 104
Stark, Rodney, 6
Stephen, James (Virginia Woolf's great-grandfather), 162, 169
Stephen, Sir James (Virginia Woolf's grandfather), 162; on Clapham Sect and reform societies, 171; and Durkheim, 171; on evangelical mission, 163–64, 165
Stephen, James Fitzjames (brother of Leslie Stephen), 165
Stephen, James Kenneth (son of Fitzjames Stephen), 165
Stephen, Leslie, 163; Evangelicalism's relation to utilitarianism of, 167, 172, 177; on imagination, 167, 177, 178; and Virginia Woolf, 170; on Wordsworth, 177–78
Stirner, Max (Kaspar Schmidt), 3, 5,
Stocking, George: on Arnold vs. Tylor, 137, 139–40, 141, 154
Stockton, Kathryn Bond: on religious feeling and lesbian desire, 179
Stoics, 106
Strabo, 106
Strachey, Lytton, 165, 175
Strachey family, 165
Strangford, Percy Clinton Sydney Smythe, Lord, 140
Strauss, David Friedrich, 106, 107, 170
Strauss, Leo, 47, 66
Stravinsky, Igor, 18
Subaltern Studies project, 199, 201
Sukarno, 14
Swift, Jonathan, 32
Synge, John Millington, 158

Tacitus, 40, 106
Tagore, Rabindranath, 198
Taine, Hippolyte, 138, 154
Tan, Kok-chor, 196
Tarde, Gabriel: on crowd psychology, 115
Taylor, Charles, 161

Taylor, Mark C., 159
Tennyson, Alfred, Lord, 169
Tennyson, G. B., 157, 158
Tertullian, 106
Theophrastus, 106
Theresa of Ávila, Saint, 187
Thierry, Amédée, 142
Thornton, Henry, 162, 172, 187
Thornton, John, 162
Thornton, Robert, 162
Tiedemann, Rolf, 77
Tocqueville, Alexis de, 8
tolerance, 13, 29–30, 34, 37–38, 39, 41–43
Tolstoy, Leo, 104
Tönnies, Ferdinand, 115
Toynbee, Arnold, 68
Traverso, Enzo, 77
Trevelyan, G. M., 117
Trilling, Lionel: on Arnold, 137, 138, 140, 154; on Heine, 138; on Hess, 138
Troeltsch, Ernst, 51
Tylor, Edward Burnett, 107, 137, 139, 153

Unanimism, 117–20; and Acéphale, 120; and Durkheim, 118, 122; and guild socialism, 118
Unitarians, 165
Ussher, Archbishop James, 107
utilitarianism, 102, 167, 172, 177

van der Veer, Peter, 6, 36
Varro, 106
Vattimo, Gianni, 21, 59
Vaugeois, Henri, 110
Venn, Henry, 162
Venn, John, 162
Vico, Giambattista, 2–4, 29, 33
Victoria, queen of England, 164
Viswanathan, Gauri, 23, 36–37, 206; and Asad, 41; and Nandy, 37–38; on recognition of religion vs. tolerance, 37–39, 41
vitalism, 109, 114
Voltaire (François Marie Arouet), 26, 68, 101, 106, 109

Waché, Brigitte, 6, 15
Walesa, Lech, 15

Wallace, Robert M., 59
Wallis, Roy, 7
Ward, Graham, 6, 18
Webb, Beatrice, 169
Webb, Sidney, 169
Weber, Max, 2, 5, 7, 9, 12, 13, 27, 28, 46, 61, 64, 104, 107, 153; and charisma, 101–2, 108; on Calvin, 163; on civic religion, 116; on "disenchantment of the world," 11, 18, 25, 107; and globalization, 51–52; on history of religion, 107; on modernization, 51, 52, 101, 102; on Protestant ethic, 49–51, 60, 101, 163; and Sanson, 206; and Schiller, 107; on universal validity of Western civilization, 50–51, 206
Wedgwood family, 165
Wesley, John, 50, 110, 162
White, Hayden, 90–91, 158
Wilberforce, William, 103, 175; and Clapham Sect, 162; on evangelical mission, 164; worldliness of, 163, 164, 172
Wilde, Oscar, 135
Wilder, Amos N., 157
Williams, Raymond: on Arnold, 137
Winckelmann, Johann Joachim, 135
Windelband, Wilhelm, 62
Winstanley, Gerrard, 80
Witte, Bernd, 87
Wittgenstein, Ludwig, 39
Wolf, Friedrich August, 106, 135
Wolin, Richard, 87
Wolosky, Shira, 159
Woolf, Leonard, 165, 175
Woolf, Vanessa: and Bloomsbury, 117
Woolf, Virginia, 40, 157, 160–93; ambivalence toward worldliness of, 172, 173; and "Am I a Snob?" 169; on asceticism, 170, 175, 179, 183, 185; and associated minds, 172, 173, 185, 186, 188, 192, 193; Auerbach's interpretation of, 189–91; and Clive Bell, 188; on Besant, 169, 171; and *Between the Acts*, 183; and Bloomsbury, 24, 117, 165, 168, 178, 188, 193; childhood molestation of, 174, 188; and Clapham Sect Evangelicalism, 24, 161, 162–73,

Woolf, Virginia (*continued*)
177, 178, 182, 183, 186, 188, 190, 191, 192, 193; and Conrad, 170; and Conrad's *Heart of Darkness,* 179–80; and Conrad's *Lord Jim,* 180; on conversion, 185–86; and dissociation of emotions, 188; and Durkheim, 162, 172; and George Eliot, 170; on ecstasy, 187–188, 191, 193; and embodiment vs. disembodiment, 179, 183, 184–88, 193; on Fabianism, 169–70, 171, 188; and gender in relation to religion, 179; and Hardy, 170; and house parties, 169; and imagination, 177, 178–79, 190; and immortality of the soul, 187; on imperialism, 169, 186; on inherited emotional disposition, 188; and inner light, 163, 177, 191, 193; and intellectual aristocracy, 165, 193; and Joyce's *Ulysses,* 179; and lesbian desire, 175, 179; and marriage, 160, 173, 174, 179, 180; and maternity, 174; and *Melymbrosia,* 161; and modernism, 161, 189–90, 193; and Moore's *Principia Ethica,* 168; and "Mr. Bennett and Mrs. Brown," 190; and *Mrs. Dalloway,* 160, 169, 170, 175, 179, 185–87; and neo-Platonism, 187; Nietzschean view of social reformers of, 169, 170; and *Night and Day,* 165, 169; and *Orlando,* 183; personal and cultural narratives intertwined in work of, 168, 185, 188; on proportion, 186; and random moment (Auerbach), 189–91; and religion, 174–88, 193; and *ressentiment,* 170, 175–176, 179, 181, 183, 186; and secularization, 160, 161, 162, 169, 172, 178, 181, 183, 186, 191, 192, 193, 206; and sexuality, 173, 174, 175, 179, 187, 191; and Shaw, 170; social effervescence in, 169, 193; "society of outsiders" of, as secularized religious sect, 172, 193; on Shakespeare, 185; and "A Sketch of the Past," 188; and James Stephen, 188; and Leslie Stephen, 170, 172, 177–79; on Tennyson, 169; and Henry Thornton, 187; and *Three Guineas,* 171; and *To the Lighthouse,* 160, 169, 176, 177, 178, 179, 189–92; on "transcendental theory" of consciousness and sociality, 162, 179, 185–87; transformation of religious habitus into literary technique of, 161, 172–73, 183, 188, 193; and utilitarianism, 177; *Verwindung* of tradition in, 24, 190; and *The Voyage Out,* 160, 168, 173–76, 179–88, 190, 193; wave metaphor in, 160–61, 169, 191; and *The Waves,* 183, 185, 192; and Wilberforce, 172, 175; and women's history, 171, 179; and Wordsworth, 177–78

Wordsworth, William, 135, 146, 177–78
Wundt, Wilhelm, 107
Wyneken, Gustav, 79, 83, 84

Yates, Frances, 106
Yeats, William Butler, 29, 144, 150, 158
Young, Robert J. C., 139, 147, 152

Zinzendorf, Nicholas Ludwig von, 50

www.ingramcontent.com/pod-product-compliance
Lightning Source LLC
Chambersburg PA
CBHW050902300426
44111CB00010B/1344